Take My Word for It

Also by Anatoly Liberman Published by the University of Minnesota Press

An Analytic Dictionary of English Etymology: An Introduction

A Bibliography of English Etymology: Sources and Word List

Take My Word for It

A Dictionary of English Idioms

ANATOLY LIBERMAN

University of Minnesota Press

Minneapolis | London

Published by the University of Minnesota Press
111 Third Avenue South, Suite 290
Minneapolis, MN 55401-2520
http://www.upress.umn.edu

ISBN 978-1-5179-1412-7 (pb)

A Cataloging-in-Publication record for this book is available from the Library of Congress.

Printed in the United States of America on acid-free paper

The University of Minnesota is an equal-opportunity educator and employer.

30 29 28 27 26 25 24 23   10 9 8 7 6 5 4 3 2 1

Nothing is easier than to turn out a popular book on etymologies; you take any respectable dictionary, and weave the words, given there in alphabetical order, into certain arbitrary groups, more or less fanciful in their connexion, and fill up with old jests, and odds and ends of an anecdotic character . . . The essential virtues of a compiler, which is all Dr. Mitchell claims to be, are accuracy and the power of copying correctly; but here, we regret to say, he is signally wanting.

—from an anonymous review of *Significant Etymology*
in *Notes and Queries,* 1908

Contents

Preface

Idioms in Our Life

This book reads like a thriller or a novel, but it is better than a thriller (the genre lauded for unstoppable action and unexpected twists) and better than a novel (called in blurbs *delicious! riveting! gripping!*), because you can open it at any page, go forward or backward, and find yourself neck-deep in a never-ending intrigue. By contrast, who rereads thrillers, even the best-selling ones?

Language is the most mysterious tool we use. No one knows how it originated and at what stage a system of signals becomes language. Do bees speak? Do dolphins? Language allows us to express our thoughts, but, strangely, people do not only say things to make their intentions clear: they use phrases, as though to obfuscate a naïve listener. They leave rooms at sixes and sevens, fly off at a tangent, and "say the darndest things." A rower will be reprimanded for catching a crab (with no crustacean in view) and end up with a flea in his ear (also absent from the picture).

Such phrases are a nightmare for a foreigner, but you may feel like a stranger in your own land if those around you choose to box Harry, put to buck, and stand like a Stoughton bottle. Are they speaking English? Indeed they are. Today, the main forum for satisfying our thirst for knowledge is the Internet. If, out of curiosity, you decide to search for less obscure items featured in this book, with a bit of luck you may find them: someone has perhaps come across the puzzling collocation, sent a query, and received an answer. Collectively we know a lot and hasten to enlighten one another. But when it comes to the origin of such word groups, responsible bloggers exercise great caution and prefer to sit on the fence (figuratively speaking, to be sure).

Thanks to the labors of countless researchers, *The Oxford English Dictionary (OED)* can say when this or that idiom was first recorded in a printed or written text,[1] but as often as not it refrains from suggesting the origin. In the absence of facts, guesswork cannot be intelligent and does more harm than good. Some phrases (like *to sit on the fence*) hardly need an elaborate etymology: the shortest decipherment and reference to the earliest known occurrence will suffice. But why do we learn things *by heart*? And what exactly is *a pretty kettle of fish,* the *nose of wax,* and *spitten image*?

This collection has a special focus. Unlike Robert Allen's monumental work, it does not even begin to lay claim to completeness; it reflects the curiosity of English speakers, who for approximately three hundred years have been asking questions about the meaning but more often about the origin of phrases they have heard or encountered in texts. Many such phrases are local, and the world at large cannot be expected to know them. Others were and still are seemingly transparent, yet even they pose questions. This is especially true when a custom or a historical incident, rather than the wording, has to be explained, as in *hair of the dog that bit you; to hang out the broom; pull Devil, pull baker; like death on a mopstick; a sixty-four dollar question,* and their likes.

Hell is paved with good intentions, while London is paved with gold. Do we know why we say so? Most Americans have probably heard about little old ladies in tennis shoes. Who were they? Conversely, Britishers will be familiar with the phrase *shipshape and Bristol fashion* (even though it does not seem to be in the *OED,* at least in exactly this form). Yet why Bristol fashion? Does this fashion have anything to do with the hotel called Bristol?[2]

The present book is a modest monument to human curiosity and a record of people's interest in language, literature, folklore, history, politics, and many other things. Countless books are mentioned in its text: plays, novels, poetry (old and contemporary), learned treatises, encyclopedias in several languages, historical records, and many more. The indexes at the end of this volume give an idea of the contributors' erudition, and we often stand in awe of it, because most writers were amateurs, simply cultured people. Only a few were professional historians or linguists.

To be sure, erudition and ignorance often meet in the pages of popular journals. Still, reproducing discarded and even silly ideas has its uses, because people tend to make the same conjectures again and again. In most cases, they cannot know anything about their predecessors' mistakes. Those who want to learn how idioms originate, how they are collected, and what sources have been mined for this book will find information in the following essay, "A Historian's View: Idioms as a Late Dessert," and the list of abbreviations after the essay is also instructive.

It now remains for me to acknowledge the contributions of my sponsors and assistants, without whose work the project would not have been begun, let alone completed. The University of Minnesota, Twin Cities, where I have taught since 1975, has a program supporting undergraduate research, and the first student who received a grant to deal with English idioms was Caleb Thilgen. He screened early volumes of *Notes and Queries* and left. Then out of the blue appeared Mr. Frank Bures, a freelance writer who had been aware of my etymological pursuits and decided to write an essay about them. He interviewed me several times and then declared that to understand how dictionaries are put together one should participate in the process. He too was sent to look through the early series of *Notes and Queries,* found a lot, and brought out an excellent article, "Origin Unknown" (published in *Lapham's Quarterly,* January 28, 2016).

Two volunteers, Treffle R. Daniels and William Biermeyer, worked their way through the endless rows of journals at the University library. (Nonspecialists will hardly appreciate that one can spend weeks opening the volumes of seemingly promising *Transactions* and find nothing there.) I contributed to their efforts in that I used annual indexes and bibliographies and did enormous amounts of photocopying, because I discovered rather late that the pages could be printed for free from the Internet. Recently, William Biermeyer joined me in comparing our entries with those in the published dictionaries of idioms to see whether they contained any hypotheses "our" authors had not thought of. For seven years, two paid undergraduate assistants, Lillian Smith and Erika Cornet, sat at the computer, looked for more and more entries, typed my summaries, and shaped up everything. The heavy finishing touches fell to Evan Ward and especially to Ed Caples and Izzy Lundquist.

When long ago I began work on a new dictionary of English etymology, I received multifarious assistance from my university, but the sums did not suffice to defray the many expenses such a venture entails. Only good luck saved my project from bankruptcy, a kind of midlife crisis. More or less by chance, I met two generous donors: David R. Fesler and Richard A. Diebold (both, I am sorry to say, have since died). The grants, from the foundation Salus Mundi, administered by Richard A. Diebold, still last, and I am able to hire undergraduate assistants, none of whom has become rich in my pay. Part of my research was also supported by the Imagine Fund at the University of Minnesota, and I received a semester-long sabbatical to complete this dictionary.

Ever since I became a lexicographer and a bibliographer, I have depended on the help of the Interlibrary Loan Department at the University of Minnesota and its manager, Melissa Eighmy Brown. Innumerable newspaper clippings, unpublished dissertations, and rare books would never have become available to me without her enthusiastic interest in my work. The secretarial staff of my home department has been always ready to assist me, and Cathy Parlin has been especially helpful. Finally, I am grateful to the readers for the University of Minnesota Press, whose suggestions were incorporated into the final version of the dictionary.

I have written the entire text of this book myself and am responsible for the decisions made during the work on it. All praise goes to the people who contributed to the success of the project, but whatever blame there is should be chalked on my door (and I'll cry mapsticks).

Notes

1. The dates given in this book were checked in the online version of the *OED* during summer 2020; an asterisk with the date means that the phrase could not be found there. Idioms that are also featured in Joseph Wright's *The English Dialect Dictionary* are marked at the end of the corresponding entries with the abbreviation *EDD*.
2. Nearly all the quotations here are from British periodicals, and the spelling of the original source has been retained. In my own text and comments, American spelling prevails.

A Historian's View

Idioms turn up naturally in our speech. We beat about the bush, walk an extra mile, and even give quarter to our enemies, with no bush in view, while remaining at home, and without bothering about the meaning of *quarter* in that strange phrase. Some people are fond of embellishing their speech with such collocations; others seldom use them. Yet only language historians know that most idioms appeared in English, as well as in other languages, relatively late.

It takes quite some time to learn Old English well, but, if you know its grammar and have access to a good dictionary, you won't stumble on incomprehensible phrases in it. It never rains cats and dogs in *Beowulf,* and King Alfred's courtiers never pay through the nose for anything: a spade is called a spade in those texts, and there the reference stops. If somebody is said to go woolgathering, rest assured that this person indeed leaves home to gather wool (don't look for a possible figurative sense of that statement). The speech of the people who lived even one millennium ago was, as a general rule, straightforward. Numerous collocations resembling today's *by no means* and *far and wide* occurred, but the likes of *by hook or by crook* was unthinkable. At that time, English writers made wide use of colorful epithets and daring similes. They had not yet discovered the limitless possibilities of the metaphor, though Latin authors, whom they knew, admired, and translated, used it freely.[1]

English is a member of the language group called Germanic. Its closest relatives are Frisian, Dutch, German, Yiddish, all the Scandinavian languages, and many languages that were spoken in the days of the Roman Empire but disappeared in the welter of medieval migrations. Fortunately, part of Gothic has come down to us because the Goths were converted to Christianity in the fourth century and many chapters of the Gothic Bible are extant. A much later monument of that epoch is a poetic retelling of the Gospels in Old Saxon. The Old Saxon poem is splendid, but its language is devoid of idioms as we understand them. Gothic depended on the Greek text.

Truly original narrative Old Germanic prose existed only in Icelandic. The famous sagas were recorded in the thirteenth century. Idioms did occur in them. For example, displaying a white shield signified peace, while a red shield stood for an invitation to battle. The saying *to play with two shields* meant "to indulge in ambiguities" or "to prevaricate." All such expressions resembled the English *to bury the hatchet,* and native speakers had no trouble understanding them. Those were clever circumlocutions rather than metaphors.

Real metaphors, called kennings, also existed, though their use was mainly limited to the type of Icelandic poetry known as skaldic. In it, *an elm of battle* (any other tree name could substitute for *elm*) meant "warrior"; *a field of necklaces* was a kenning for "woman"; and so forth. Those were true metaphors, because a man is not a tree and a woman is not a field. Little is known about the rise of skaldic poetry, and the very word *skald* is of disputable origin. One can only wonder why this genre never existed in Anglo-Saxon England. Regardless of all such considerations, the idioms we use flooded English and other European languages long after heroic songs and eulogies stopped sounding in the halls of medieval kings. Wherever possible, the phrases in this dictionary have been supplied with the dates borrowed from *The Oxford English Dictionary (OED)*. Although the dates only of their first occurrence in texts could be rescued, the gap between the time they were coined and the year they happened to be recorded need not have always been too long. The oldest idioms are translations from Latin or quotations from the Bible. Most others are fairly or even surprisingly recent.

There is a reason for that. In principle, idioms are a feature of postmedieval culture, and the same holds for many other things we usually take for granted. For example, medieval pictures, even the best of them, are flat, like the drawings of children. Medieval narratives, however complicated, are "flat," too. The storyteller did not possess the technique to deal with two actions happening simultaneously in two different places: one strand had to be unraveled for the writer to return to the zero point and pick up the thread of the tale. Languages did not even have the means to connect the strands. The bulky modern words *inasmuch (as), insofar* (or *in so far) as,* and *notwithstanding* reflect the hardships speakers endured while fighting with the new ways of expressing their thoughts. Even *because,* from *bi cause* ("by cause") appeared only in the fourteenth century under the influence of Old French *par cause de* ("by reason of"). To this day, our conjunctions are ambiguous: *as* means "when," "because," and "to that degree." *Since* and *for* do double duty as prepositions and conjunctions. German *wenn* is either "when" or "if."

Perspective in painting was discovered at the dawn of the Renaissance, and some time later storytellers learned to stand away from the picture they described and "look both ways." Those are signs of abstract thinking, like the ability to laugh at verbal jokes and not only at circus tricks and slapstick comedy. Our modern sense of humor is another product of that great mental upheaval. Idioms are phenomena of the same order. Today we can eat crow with our mouths shut; it is also possible to shoot one's bolt without having ever touched that utensil. A medieval speaker would have been thoroughly puzzled by such attacks on common sense, such as walking an extra mile and the rest.[2]

What Is an Idiom?

The term *idiom* is vague, but only one of its senses will interest us here, namely, "a group of words whose meaning has to be learned or explained, even though in separation each of its components is clear." Such groups are probably countless, and they do not form a coherent system. Some resemble long words, except that they are not; *in order to* and *by way of* come to mind. Many words are hard to pry loose from their neighbors. *Goodbye* is a single word only if we spell it without a space, and consider *insofar* and *notwithstanding* and *because,* all products of fusion. In the not too remote past, *today* was hyphenated (*to-day*): perhaps one word, perhaps two, perhaps a word and a half. *For ever* is the British spelling of the American *forever*.

A beginning learner of English will soon encounter the words *give* and *up* but will have no clue to the meaning of *give up*. So far our focus has been on the figurative meaning of phrases, and indeed no one pays directly (literally) through the nose, deals with a man of straw, or sows wild oats. Thousands of idioms are less enigmatic but still puzzling. Do crocodiles really shed tears of remorse? Has anyone ever been sent to Coventry? Why is one mad as a hatter? Again and again, proper names turn up that leave us nonplused. *To rob Peter to pay Paul, as lazy as Lawrence's (Ludlam's, Lumley's) dog, John Johnson's coat, Tamson's mare*—the list goes on and on. Who are (or were) all those people?

Many idioms contain words that occur only in them: we know what *get one's dander up* and *leave somebody in the lurch* mean, but what is *dander* and what is *lurch*? Wolfgang Mieder, a renowned specialist in the area of idioms, once gave an interview on German radio and observed that his American students, when exposed to the phrase *let the cobbler stick to his last,* have trouble not only with *last* but also with *cobbler*. Or we may know the words and still feel lost. A hot dog is not a dog, and one wonders what going the whole hog has to do with swine. Sometimes our etymological dictionaries offer a convincing explanation but more often the user is dismissed with conflicting hypotheses or no answer at all. For example, *lurch* has, with some reservations, been traced to its ancient root, while *dander* remains a puzzle.

In this dictionary, not only phrases but also complete sentences occur every now and then, for instance, *How's your auntie at Tiverton?*; *Good wine needs no bush*; *It always rains Quaker week*; *The Devil overlooks Lincoln*; *Never touch your eye but with your elbow,* and a few more. From a structural point of view, they are as dissimilar as all idioms: these five examples include what looks like a nonsensical question, an unclear maxim, a dubious statement of fact, a piece of urban lore, and facetious advice.

A study of idioms is part of the branch of linguistics known technically as phraseology. Idioms are so many and so different that the compiler of a phraseological dictionary never knows which to include and which to ignore. Only one group, proverbs, is comparatively easy to define, and, predictably, the art of collecting began with them. Proverbs, these nuggets of traditional wisdom, tend to travel from land to land, and it is often hard to decide who borrowed from whom. Human experience suggests the same solutions everywhere (for instance, *look before you leap* or *make hay while the sun shines*), so that it is necessary to count with what historical linguists call parallel development. After several centuries of hard work, we have many splendid collections of proverbs. But very few proverbs made their way into this dictionary. The same holds for so-called familiar quotations, which have also been collected and identified in an exemplary way. This situation brings us to the question about the choice of idioms in the present book: what has been included and what has been left out, and why?

The Makeup of This Dictionary

Here it is necessary to start from afar. More than twenty-five years ago, I began working on a new etymological dictionary of Modern English. Why the idea of such a project occurred to me is told in my books published between 2005 and 2010.[3] This is the story in a nutshell: once, while looking for the origin of the word *heifer,* I saw how inadequate the entries in English etymological dictionaries are and felt deeply disappointed by the tools at my disposal.

To discover how a word was coined, one should be aware of its entire recorded history.

Some words existed long before the introduction of literacy, while others are much later (and new words appear almost every day). Once we have learned all we can about a word's past,[4] we can examine its earliest form and perhaps obtain a clue to the mental process behind its production. After centuries of wandering in the dark, language historians devised a more or less reliable method that allowed them to go beyond guesswork and reconstruct the mechanisms of word creation. But the devices at their disposal are insufficient and imperfect, because language is an astoundingly complex mechanism. In the end, scholars may be confronted with a welter of mutually excluding hypotheses rather than a solution.

This is what also happened in the investigation of the word *heifer,* but no dictionary as much as hinted at the complexity of the problem. A few informed the user about their authors' ideas in a paragraph or two, while most wrote "Of unknown origin." Half a year of research made it clear that numerous useful suggestions about the derivation of *heifer* had existed. Amazingly, no lexicographer had taken the trouble to collect and analyze them. I ended up with my own solution for this particular word, but, more important, decided to remedy the situation in the area of English etymology.

I had excellent models. Etymological, sometimes multivolume, dictionaries containing detailed surveys of the relevant literature (that is, analytic rather than dogmatic dictionaries) have been written for Sanskrit, Classical Greek, Latin, and many Romance, Germanic, and Slavic languages. English is a sad exception. To perform the task I envisioned, I had to read everything ever written in two dozen languages about the origin of English words. This task was accomplished with the help of many volunteers and paid assistants. How the team was assembled, and how I fought for funding, is a special story. What matters here are the sources screened for the bibliography and the database that has grown considerably since publication and keeps growing every day.

I naturally began with scholarly sources. However, my reading alerted me to the fact that many valuable proposals concerning the origin of English words had appeared (and been forgotten or hardly ever noticed) in popular journals. I could rarely keep track of the letters sent to the editors of newspapers unless they appeared later in special volumes, but my volunteers looked through thousands of pages in periodicals, such as *Notes and Queries* (including their rich provincial kin), *The Gentleman's Magazine, The Saturday Review, The Spectator, The Mariner's Mirror,* and so forth. The contributors often discussed not only words but also idioms. While compiling my bibliography of English etymology, I concentrated on words: idioms made their way into the database only when they contained the likes of *lurch* and *dander.* Nine years ago, I decided to return to this material neglected at the beginning of that project.

The periodicals mentioned in the previous paragraph were like our virtual chat rooms: somebody would ask a question about anything (archaeology, numismatics, history, literature, language, and folklore, among other subjects) or share a piece of allegedly valuable information. Questions usually elicited answers. Some subjects could be discussed for months and even years. *Notes and Queries,* as well as several other journals of its type, had excellent annual indexes, but not everyone consulted them before sending a letter to the editor, and the same questions might occasionally resurface years after they had been asked and discussed for the first time. Similar responses would be evoked, and similar conclusions reached and rejected.

Such periodicals are not academic. Even *The Academy,* despite its title, opened its pages to the public, and one notices with amazement how well read and well informed the contributors to those periodicals often were. Many were country squires, the owners of prodigious libraries full of rare books, first editions, and precious artifacts. In England, the tradition of studying the history, geography, and dialect ("popular antiquities") of one's county goes back to at least the sixteenth century. In the nineteenth century, it was at its height.

By the 1850s, etymology had developed a more or less solid method of inquiry. The impulse came from Germany, and here the English-speaking world lagged behind, but a quarter of a century later began to catch up, and among the contributors to *Notes and Queries* we can find first-rate experts: Walter W. Skeat (the author of still the most authoritative English etymological dictionary), Frank Chance (a medical doctor and brilliant philologist), Joseph Wright (the editor of *The English Dialect Dictionary*), Hensleigh Wedgwood (the main etymologist of the pre-Skeat era), James A. H. Murray (the main editor of the *OED*), and several scholars closely associated with Murray and Wright, such as Henry Bradley, A. L. Mayhew, and Frederick J. Furnivall.

Today, the popularity of *Notes and Queries, The Gentleman's Magazine,* and a few other similar periodicals is hard to imagine. Quite often the same people contributed to several of these publications and became well known. With the eclipse of the tradition, represented by this press, their names were often forgotten. This happened to F. C. Birkbeck Terry, Colonel William F. Prideaux, and, most unfortunately, Frank Chance. Many other correspondents also had a good knowledge of Latin, Greek, and two or three modern languages and were in a position to make valuable observations.

The origin of idioms is a particularly fertile field for guesswork. Anyone may suggest why we say *by hook or by crook* and *it rains cats and dogs.* No linguistic algebra is required for the solution. Yet truth in this area is more evasive than it may seem, and fantasies are particularly dangerous because they are hard to counter. One often has solid facts to reject a wrong word etymology (the vowels may not match, or the consonants may be incompatible), but in the study of idioms only historical facts are needed.

Wild hypotheses proliferate. The ghosts of Mr. Hook and Mr. Crook appear in at least three shapes, and the Scandinavian god Odin emerges with two dogs at his heels. Multiple repetition makes those gentlemen and those animals look real. Pretentious rubbish acquires the status of information and becomes common property, like the story of *posh,* allegedly an acronym for "*p*ort (side) *o*ut, *s*tarboard *h*ome," or "*f*or *u*nlawful *c*arnal *k*nowledge" (alternatively, "*f*ornication *u*nder *c*ommand of the *k*ing") as the etymon of our most famous four-letter word. Quite often even respectable manuals perpetuate such legends. In the late nineteenth century, *Dictionary of Phrase and Fable* by Ebenezer Brewer was on almost everyone's desk. Brewer tended to offer solutions without citing evidence, but hundreds of people swallowed them hook, line, and sinker. Though modern authors are more cautious, they face the same difficulties as their predecessors. They, too, tend to have "opinions," anonymous and unsupported by facts. Hence the formulations "Some people think . . . , while other people believe . . ." To exacerbate matters, we are rarely told who those people are.

Yet occasionally it is possible to disprove an explanation on chronological grounds (for example, when the phrase is older than its alleged source), or a mistake can be dismissed (Odin did not own dogs and had nothing to do with rain), or the absence of Messers Hook and Crook in historical records suffices to invalidate the legend. In etymology, as in many other areas of knowledge, it is easier to reject a faulty suggestion than to offer a viable alternative. Yet every now and then, one of the existing conjectures looks attractive. This is what I think happened in the study of the idioms *by hook or by crook, it rains cats and dogs, to pay through the nose,* and quite a few others. But before venturing a conclusion, it is necessary to know all the explanations that exist. In my work on this dictionary, I was inspired by the same idea that years ago made me pursue the etymology of *heifer.*

The Corpus of This Dictionary

Native speakers do not always recognize that a certain word group is idiomatic. Although they may ask questions about *bear the brunt (of),* they have no problems with *bear witness (to).* Yet a speaker new to the language stumbles at both. The idiomaticity of some combinations is indeed weak, but it is there all the same. For example, in English, people *do* an exercise but *make* a mistake. Only a professional language historian will wonder how this distinction came about.

These are the main types of collocations (phrases, idioms) that have been discussed in the pages of popular periodicals:

1. Phrases that contain personal and place names: *Jack Pudding* (who was called this and why?); *before one can say Jack Robinson* (obvious rigmarole, but widely known and interesting because of that); *all my eye and Betty Martin* (an especially famous though now nearly forgotten crux); *it would puzzle a Philadelphia lawyer* (why just a lawyer from Philadelphia?); *all on one side like Takeley Street* (where is this street? why was only one of its sides built up?).

2. Similes. These are numerous, almost countless, and often far from clear: *as jolly as sandboys* (why should sandboys be perennially jolly?); *as sick as a horse* (granted, sandboys tend to be jolly, but horses needn't always be sick); *like an owl in an ivy bush* (what is the nature of the connection?).

3. Phrases whose direct meaning is clear but there may be (and often are) additional overtones: *to lay a ship by the walls; a man of one book; to save face; to take French leave.*

4. Totally puzzling phrases: *to kick the bucket; no great shakes; hue and cry; by and large; once in a blue moon; cock and bull story; sleeveless errand* are among the favorites in popular books on idiomatic sayings.

5. Proverbs and proverbial sayings, like *a rolling stone gathers no moss.*

Several more subgroups could be isolated. A detailed classification of this heterogenous material is not to be expected here, nor is it needed. Three questions dominated the letters to the editor: What does the phrase mean? Is its chronology known? What is its origin?

A note should be added about the treatment of proverbs. Proverbs have been collected (and collected with great success) for centuries. In the periodicals screened for this dictionary, one can find pages of so-called weather sayings (like *April showers bring May flowers*), misogynistic taunts (like *a whistling woman and a crowing hen,* with the implication that both are evil), and local aphorisms about beer making, courtship, and dealing with animals. I included only those that contained remarks on their origin and use.[5]

In principle, the same treatment was accorded the idioms that, though asked about, remained unanswered, but here I allowed myself more leeway. Some phrases were too colorful to leave by the wayside. For example, in Worcestershire, they used to say *to go to Johnson's end* ("to become impoverished"). In 1860, no one, except the letter writer, knew it, and after some consideration I chose not to include it. Yet I spared the equally obscure phrase *that's the chap as married Hannah* ("that's what I need") (Nottinghamshire, 1900), though the world knows as little about Hannah and her husband as about the destitute Mr. Johnson. (See "Unanswered queries" in the theme index at the end of this book.) The dilemma I faced is familiar, and I mentioned it in the Introduction to my *Bibliography of English Etymology*: in the initial stages of collecting, researchers are usually afraid to miss something, then once the work has been completed they recognize the danger of cluttering the finished project with junk.

In sum, I must repeat what I wrote in the Preface: the present dictionary is based on a limited corpus, it reflects the curiosity of many generations of readers from the entire English-speaking world, and it lays no claim to completeness. Yet perhaps it has a certain advantage over its predecessors. Thanks to the multiple references, the study of English idioms will partly lose its anonymity. We can now follow the opinions of real people rather than "some authorities." A look at contemporary phraseological dictionaries shows that today, except in matters of chronology, we rarely know more about the origin of idioms than those who lived a hundred and even a hundred fifty years ago, which makes their pronouncements all the more valuable.

The phrases featured here, unless they are marked with an asterisk, can also be found in the *OED*. Time and again its editors have been able to clarify the date of the first occurrence of the idiom in a written or printed source or refute a wrong derivation, but even the *OED* often cites such phrases without specifying their origin or offers a carefully formulated conjecture. Perhaps the present collection will be of some use to those who work for the *OED* and other great dictionaries.

The Reference Material

A thematic dictionary resembles a haystack: finding a needle in it is hard. Even locating an item may cause trouble. Somebody may remember the phrase *to do one's level best,* search for it, and feel disappointed that it is not included. But it is there, at *level best!* Or what was that law *hanging first, trial afterwards* called? Look up *law.* There it is: *Halifax Law* or *Abrington Law.* More important, the word index in this book allows the user to compare phrases. Most people will have heard the idioms *let the cat out of the bag* and *let sleeping dogs lie,* but do *cat* and *dog* occur elsewhere in this collection? The index will tell them.

The name index would not have needed a comment or an apology, but for one circumstance. Anyone who will, perhaps out of curiosity, read a few consecutive pages of this volume will, like me, be impressed by the correspondents' vast stock of knowledge. They sought information from numerous dictionaries, compendia, and books of encyclopedic character. The same holds for books on art, history, natural history, geography, genealogy, and many other areas of knowledge. Among our contemporaries, very few people outside a narrow circle of specialists ever open these books. Also, we note with amazement and perhaps with envy how well those people remembered the smallest details in Shakespeare, Fielding, Byron, Dickens, Kipling, as well as in Greek and Latin authors.

Most contributors to the periodicals excerpted here were British. Quite naturally, at school they focused on British literature, British history, and British geography, so few would have heard about the Bronx (see *Bronx cheer*), to give an arbitrary example. At present, a book of English idioms will have a good market overseas, and not only in the English-speaking world. Residents of many countries as well as Americans will probably have heard about *The Canterbury Tales* yet not be able to locate Canterbury on a map. We live in a different world and in a different intellectual climate. To millions of people now, the Bronx sounds more familiar than Canterbury. The index will help users to locate towns and counties on the map.

What is true of geography is equally true of history. Even today, with our concentration on modern politics rather than the events of the past, one can hardly finish school in Great Britain and remain ignorant of the fate of Charles I. But the severed head of that monarch, which bothered Mr. Dick, the unforgettable companion of David Copperfield, means nothing to most Americans. The term *Civil War* evokes different associations on both sides of the Atlantic, let alone in the rest of the world. Finally, Fielding, Byron, and the rest are no longer the favorite authors of our contemporaries. Therefore, numerous book titles occurring in the correspondence have been supplied with the date of publication and occasionally expanded, to provide the necessary context—for what does a passing reference like "see Fuller's *Worthies*" say to the modern reader?

The value of the short theme index will probably be taken for granted: it reveals the main themes of the idioms. Reading the indexes is like having a guided tour of an exotic museum or wandering through an old curiosity shop. Queen Anne (still very much alive), Duke Humphrey (a most generous host), and the otherwise evasive Betty Martin are all there, ready to look you straight in the eye.

Notes

1. See "Approaches to Historical Phraseology, with Notes on *Sermo Lupi ad Anglos*" in my book *Word Heath. Wortheide. Orðheiði: Essays on Germanic Literature and Usage,* Episteme dell'Antichità e oltre. Collana diretta da Diego Poli 1 (Rome: Il Calamo, 1994), 356–73.
2. For a detailed discussion of such matters see my books *In Prayer and Laughter: Essays on Medieval Scandinavian and Germanic Mythology, Literature, and Culture* (Moscow: Paleograph Press, 2016), especially chapter 20, "Germanic Laughter and the Development of the Sense of Humor" (406–29) and chapter 21, "In View of the Conclusion: The Limited World of the Medieval Narrator" (430–41), and *The Saga Mind and the Beginnings of Icelandic Prose* (Lewiston, Lampeter: The Edwin Mellen Press, 2018), especially "Space and Time" (89–93).
3. *Etymology for Everyone: Word Origins . . . and How We Know Them* (Oxford: Oxford University Press, 2005; revised edition, 2009); with the assistance of J. Lawrence Mitchell, *An Analytical Dic-*

tionary of English Etymology: An Introduction (Minneapolis: University of Minnesota Press, 2008); and *A Bibliography of English Etymology* (Minneapolis: University of Minnesota Press, 2010).

4. With regard to English, this part of the work has been done in an exemplary way. The main sources are *The Oxford English Dictionary* and *Middle English Dictionary* (University of Michigan, 1956–2001); both are available online.

5. With regards to the main source of this dictionary, see Wolfgang Mieder, *Investigations of Proverbs, Proverbial Expressions, Quotations, and Clichés: A Bibliography of Explanatory Essays Which Appeared in "Notes and Queries" (1849–1983)*. Sprichwörterforschung 4 (Bern and New York: Peter Lang, 1984). We of course consulted this book but still reviewed all the idioms, including those from after 1983, page by page.

Sources and Abbreviations

The Academy

ANQ: *American Notes and Queries*

AOAW: *Anzeiger der österreichischen Akademie der Wissenschaften*

AP: *Anniversary Papers*

AS: *American Speech*

The Athenæum

BM: *Blackwood's Edinburgh Magazine*

BrA: *British Apollo*

Brewer: *Dictionary of [Modern] Phrase and Fable*

The Century Dictionary: An Encyclopedic Lexicon of the English Language, 2d ed. (New York: The Century Co., 1911)

CoE: *Comments on Etymology*

DCNQ: *Devon and Cornwall Notes and Queries*

The Dickensian

EMLR: *European Magazine and London Review*

F&F: Flavell and Flavell, *Dictionary of Idioms and Their Origins*

GM: *Gentleman's Magazine*

GRM: *Germanische-romanische Monatsschrifte*

Holt: *Phrase Origins: A Study of Familiar Expressions*

Hyamson: *A Dictionary of English Phrases*

Johnson-Todd: *A Dictionary of the English Language* (2d ed.)

KZ: (Kuhns) *Zeitschrift für vergleichende Sprachforschung*

LA: *Long Ago*

Literary Digest

LM: *Longman's Magazine*

MarM: *Mariner's Mirror*

MCNNQ: *Manchester Notes and Queries*

MLQ: *Modern Language Quarterly*

MM: Morris and Morris, *Dictionary of Word and Phrase Origins*

NQ: *Notes and Queries*

NY: *New Yorker*

OED: *The Oxford English Dictionary,* 3d edition in progress, www.oed.com

OID: *The Imperial Dictionary of the English Language,* by Charles Annandale, ed. John Ogilivie, 2d ed. (London: Blackie & Sons, 1882–87)

SNQ: *Scottish Notes and Queries*

The Spectator
Time
TPS: *Transactions of the Philologica Society*
Verbatim
WA: *Western Antiquary*; or, *Devon and Cornwall Note-Book*
ZDOW: *Zeitschrift für deutsche Wortforschung*

An Annotated List of Dictionaries and Reference Works

The entries in this dictionary contain references to books on history, geography, jurisprudence, and many other fields of knowledge, as well as to fiction and poems. Most of the titles are featured in the name index at the end of the book. Information is limited to brief references and occasional brief commentary. Almost seventy dictionary titles, encyclopedias, and books of general interest are mentioned, relatively few of them familiar to the modern public. It therefore seems reasonable to add short reviews on their content and value.

Addy, Sydney Oldall. *A Glossary of Words Used in the Neighbourhood of Sheffield* . . . (referred to in this dictionary as *Sheffield Glossary*). London: Trübner & Co., 1888. Addy (1848–1933) was a student of folklore and English dialects. A frequent contributor to *Notes and Queries,* he is often mentioned in this book.

Allen: *[Robert] Allen's Dictionary of English Phrases.* Penguin Books, 2006. This is the most recent and by far the most complete monolingual English idiom dictionary. Every entry contains quotations illustrating the use of the phrase. Allen avoided regional idioms, which occupy a notable place in my book, while I, unlike him, avoided proverbs. Though etymology was not his main interest, he paid constant attention to it and, like me, made wide use of *Notes and Queries.* In discussing conflicting hypotheses of origins, he showed excellent judgment, and very few of the hypotheses he favored have to be modified. Yet he was not intent on giving multiple references to the bibliography. Since the number of idioms is infinite, it won't come as a surprise that numerous phrases featured in *Wild Oats* did not make their way into *Allen's Dictionary.* Like A.V. Kunin (or Kroonin), the author of a monumental English–Russian phraseological dictionary, first published in 1955, Allen mined the riches of the *OED,* while I followed journal publications for four centuries, and the origin of idioms was at the center of my attention.

Apperson, G. L. *English Proverbs and Proverbial Phrases.* London and Toronto: J. M. Dent and Sons Limited, 1929. Apperson was an outstanding specialist in paroemiology, the branch of linguistics devoted to the study of proverbs. His book, based on the *OED* and many other sources, has lost none of its value since 1929.

Bailey, Nathan. *An Universal Etymological English Dictionary.* London: Printed for E. Bell., etc., 1721. Reprinted as *Anglistica and Americana* 52 (Hildesheim, New York: G. Olms, 1969). Innumerable reprints of this dictionary exist, and references to it bear witness to its popularity. Today Bailey's opinions are of only historical interest.

Balch, William Ralston. *Ready Reference: The Universal Cyclopaedia Containing Everything That*

Everybody Wants to Know. London: Griffith & Co., ?1902. One of many books of the type consulted by educated people at that time. Balch was the author of several more compilations.

Barrère, Albert, and Charles G. Leland. *A Dictionary of Slang, Jargon & Cant. . . .* London: The Ballantyne Press, 1889–90. Reprinted 1897 in London by George & Bell & Sons and by Book Tower, Detroit (Gale Research Tower), 1967. This splendid work features numerous "unprintable" words. It has lost none of its value, even though since that time slang has been explored in depth, and the very concept of slang has undergone an important change. One finds both words and phrases there, and the collection is a joy to read.

Bebel, Heinrich. *Proverbia Germanica.* Bebel (1472–1518) put together several volumes of proverbs and popular poems. His complete works (written, naturally, in Latin) were edited and published in Straßburg in 1514. The collection has been reprinted many times since. As an early record, this corpus is of great value.

Bee [Badcock], John. *A Dictionary of Turf, etc.* London: T. Hughes, 1823. The vulgar tongue was of course widely known but could not be used in "good society." Yet even in the more prudish Victorian period, both Grose and Bee (Badcock)'s books made their way into many homes, as evidenced by references to them in *Notes and Queries.*

Bellenden Ker, John. *An Essay on the Archaeology of Our Popular Phrases, and Nursery Rhymes.* London: Longman, etc. and Coupland, Southampton, 1837. Before 1837, little was known in England about the origin of words and idioms, but this book is curious by any standard. Its author reconstructed a "Low-Saxon" dialect close to Modern Dutch and presented numerous words, idioms, and even nursery rhymes as the product of that dialect having been "corrupted" by later usage. His fantasies do not present (and never presented) any interest, but his book is now available online, and some people may rediscover it and take the etymologies given there seriously. Among the contributions to *NQ,* Bellenden Ker's name turned up only once. Most idioms are discussed in the first volume. Volume 2 mainly contains proverbs. But leafing through this book occasionally pays off, for some idioms rarely occur elsewhere. Consider the following: "The man is handsome enough if he does not frighten his horse," "He frets his guts to fiddle strings," "It is all my arse in a band box," "A light heart and a thin pair of breeches," "He put him to his tramps," "A colt's tooth," and so forth. The definitions and notes on usage are excellent, but this entire labor of love was not only a waste but a parody on historical linguistics, though the author quoted Chaucer and Shakespeare and knew some early dictionaries. The volumes have no index, and the entries are not arranged alphabetically. Here is a sample of Bellenden Ker's etymology, the entry titled "On the nail" (I, 116–17): "*Nail* is here, I suspect, our old term. *Nail,* and that as *nael,* q.e. [quod est 'that is'] *after another,* immediately after what had been done (was gone) before; following directly after the other. *Na,* next, close by. *El,* other, one of two. *Nale* was once in general use for the song sung in chorus at merry-makings and festivals, where the tune was set (begun) by one and followed in turn by the others. [Three passages follow.] Probably the French *noel,* the old term for the carol . . . and also for the Christmas festival, is the same word. *Menage's* [= Gille Ménage's] contraction of *natale (dies natalis)* is too scholastic, too artificial [!] to be the source. And the *noel* never meant *nativity song.* Speght's *inn-ale* and so *an ale-house* is in another direction, but equally groundless." (Incidentally,

Thomas Speght, a Chaucer scholar, guessed this etymology almost correctly.) Surprisingly, John Bellenden Ker was a serious botanist and knew what is takes to be a scholar. In addition to *Archaeology,* he published four volumes devoted to the "Low Saxon" origin of nursery rhymes. In *Archaeology,* only a few samples of such rhymes appear.

Bohn. The names of three collectors of proverbs, idioms, etc. come up in this book with special regularity: Bohn, Hazlitt, and Ray. Henry George Bohn (1796–1864) was a renowned editor, bibliographer, and author. The work referred to here has a long title: *A Handbook of Proverbs; comprising an entire Republication of Ray's Collection of English Proverbs, with his additions from Foreign Languages, and a complete Alphabetical Index; as well of Proverbs as of Sayings, Sentences, Maxims, and Phrases.* London: G. Bell and Sons, 1855. The book ran into many editions.

Book of Days. See Chambers, Robert.

Brand, John. *Popular Antiquities.* The title of this book is *Observations on Popular Antiquities. . . .* It is a medley (almost an encyclopedia) of everything pertaining to the customs, superstitions, and quite often words and phrases collected from every part of England. It was first published in 1777 and exists in more than one version. The book is available as a modern reprint.

Brewer, E. Cobham. *Dictionary of [Modern] Phrase and Fable.* This enormous book whose definitive edition appeared in 1894 is a mixed bag of reliable etymologies and bizarre explanations that can still be consulted in a sober modern (severely abridged) edition. The latest one appeared in 2011. The information in even this version should be treated with caution, but the editors had no choice, because the flavor of the original work had to be preserved. For decades this book was the most popular source of information on the origin of words and idioms. Now it is interesting only as a monument to an epoch long gone.

Carew, Bampfylde-Moore (1693–1759) is the author of the once immensely popular book *The Adventures of Bampfylde Moore-Carew, King of the Mendicants,* originally published in 1745. I had access only to *A New and Revised Edition. With an Enlarged Dictionary of the Terms used by that Fraternity, also some account of the Gipsies and of their Language.* London: William Tegg (no date). This book is an example of so-called rogue literature and can even be called a picaresque novel, except that the hero of the picaresque novel (someone like Fielding's Tom Jones) is usually a noble young man prone to making mistakes, while Carew is indeed a mendicant and even a scoundrel. His dictionary of canting terms has been mined by students of slang and attracts word lovers even many years later.

Chambers, Robert. *A Miscellany of Popular Antiquities in Connection with the Calendar, Including Anecdote, Biography, History, Curiosities of Literature and Oddities of Life and Character.* Edinburgh: W & R. Chambers; Philadelphia: Lippincott & Co., 1863–64. Reprinted, Detroit: Gale Research, 1967. Despite its all-encompassing title, this entertaining book, known as *Book of Days,* is reliable. It enjoyed great and deserved popularity.

La Chanson de Roland [The Song of Roland] is an Old French epic poem, composed approximately between 1040 and 1115.

Cleland, John. *The Way to Things by Words. . . .* London: L. Davis and C. Reymers, 1766. Reprinted as *English Linguistics 1500–1800,* vol. 122 (England: The Scolar Press, 1968). Cleland believed in the Irish origin of most English words, but in nineteenth-century England so-called Celtomania was popular, and many people consulted his book.

Cursor Mundi is a Middle English poem, dated to approximately 1300 and originally written in the northern dialect. The Latin title means "The runner of the world." The anonymous narrator "runs" over the main historical events from the Bible, though he also had another source.

Dixon, James Main. *Dictionary of Idiomatic English Phrases.* London: Nelson and Sons, 1891. Numerous reprints (the latest in 2010). This is a collection of words and phrases without discussion of their origin. Dixon taught English in China and wrote his book to help Chinese students understand the words and phrases that puzzled them. There is a Chinese edition of this work.

Domesday Book (in British English, pronounced *Doomsday Book*), from 1086, is a record of England and parts of Wales, put together for tax purposes.

EDD is the acronym for *The English Dialect Dictionary,* edited by Joseph Wright. London, *etc.*: H. Frowde, 1898–1905. Reprinted, London: Oxford University Press, 1970. It is a magnificent monument to British regional speech, and references to it are numerous.

Edwards, Eliezer. *Words, Facts, and Phrases: A Dictionary of Curious, Quaint, and Out-Of-The Way Matters.* London, Chatto and Windus, 1882. Reprinted, Philadelphia: L. B. Lippincott & Co. The title of this book is typical. At that time, many works described "curiosities," discussed "nuggets of knowledge," etc. Edwards concentrated on words and phrases but, according to the fashion of the time, he gave no references, and there is no way of knowing where he got his information and whether it can be trusted. His book was often quoted, and a facsimile edition was printed in 1911 (London: Chatto and Windus). The latest reprint is by Gale Research Co. (2011).

Evans, Arthur B. *Leicestershire Words, Phrases, and Proverbs.* London: William Pickering, 1848. The book was well known and often consulted.

F&F: Flavell, Roger, and Lina Flavell. *Dictionary of Idioms and Their Origins.* Kyle Cathie, 1992. Several later reprints. This dictionary includes many phrases, with illustrations of their usage. The origins are explained without references, so their reliability is hard to ascertain. Sometimes the authors mention several conflicting hypotheses.

Forby, Robert. *The Vocabulary of East Anglia.* . . . London: Printed by and for J. B. Nichols and Son. Reprinted, New York: A. M. Kelly, Newton Abbot: David and Charlese, 1970. Forby, an excellent philologist, wrote several books. His expertise in the dialect of East Anglia and the reliability of his material made this book deservedly popular.

Fuller, Thomas. *Gnomologia*: *Adages and Proverbs, Wise Sentences and Witty Sayings, Ancient and Modern, Foreign and British.* London: Printed for B. Barker, *etc.,* 1732. New edition 1832. Fuller's collection was printed long after his death in 1734.

Funk, Charles Earle. *Curious Word Origins, Sayings & Expressions from* White Elephants *to* Song and Dance. New York: Galahad Books, 1993. This huge volume of 988 pages contains three earlier books by Funk: *A Hog on Ice, Heaven to Betsy!* and *Horsefeathers.* A detailed word index makes the search for all items easy. The second part is only about words, but the first and the third deal with idioms. Some entries are quite detailed.

Green: *(Jonathon) Green's Dictionary of Slang.* Chambers, 2010. The reference is to a three-volume dictionary of slang covering the entire English-speaking world. Etymology plays a very modest role.

Greene, *Menaphon*. This romance (1589) by Robert Greene (first printed in London by T. O. for Sampson Clarke) was once much read.

Grimm, Jacob, 1785–1863. *Teutonic Mythology* (London: G. Bell and Sons, 1882–88) is a translation of the German book *Deutsche Mythologie*, 4th ed. (1878). The translator was James Steven Stallybrass. The book is now available in later reprints.

Grose, Francis. *A Classical Dictionary of the Vulgar Tongue.* The original 1785 edition has been revised and reprinted many times and is now known as *Lexicon Balatronicum. A Dictionary of Buckish Slang, University Wit, and Pickpocket Eloquence.* London: Printed for C. Chapel, 1811.

Halliwell, James Orchard. *A Dictionary of Archaic and Obsolete Words. . . .* London: Thomas and William Boone, 1855 (the most often used third edition). Reprinted, New York: AMS Press, 1973. This was the earliest widely used dictionary of such words, and it is still a good research tool.

Hargrave, Basil. *Origin and Meaning of Popular Phrases and Names, Including Those Which Came into Use during the Great War.* London: T. W. Lauri, 1932. Despite its promising title, this popular book is of little interest and contains many more words than phrases.

Hartshorne, Charles Henry. *Salopia Antique. . . .* London: J. W. Parker, 1841. The full title of this most interesting and useful book is two lines long. Salopia is the old name of Shropshire, and the book deals with the history, customs, and language of this county.

Hazlitt. The names of three collectors of proverbs, idioms, etc., are noted in this book with special regularity: Bohn, Hazlitt, and Ray. Like Bohn, Hazlitt (1834–1913) was an editor and an author (among quite a few other things). The work often referred to in this book is *English Proverbs and Proverbial Phrases. Collected from the most Authentic Sources, Alphabetically Arranged and Annotated* by W[illiam] Carew Hazlitt. London: G. R. Smith, 1869. Published in many reprints and editions, Hazlitt's book competed with Bohn's from the start.

Hearne. The reference is to Thomas Hearne (1678–1735), a celebrated antiquarian and editor. One of his 1715 books bears the title *Memorandum for Mr. Bagford. He Tells Me He Hath a Prospect or View of Oxford, Done by Mr. Wenc. Holler, Which I Am Very Desirous of Seeing. . . .* The place of publication is not indicated.

Herbert, George (1593–1633), was a poet, orator, and priest. In 1652, his posthumous works were published, among them *Jacula prudentum* [Darts of the Wise], a collection of aphorisms and proverbs.

Heywood, John (circa 1497–1580), statesman, playwright, and musician, is mentioned in this dictionary only as the author of *The Proverbs and Epigrams of John Heywood* (1562). This became available as *Publication of the Spenser Society 1* (Manchester: printed for the Spenser Society by C. Simms and Co., 1867). It was reprinted in the original form in New York by B. Franklin, 1967.

Hislop, Alexander (1807–1865) was a Free Church of Scotland minister and a religious scholar. Lexicographers remember only his book *The Proverbs of Scotland.* The edition consulted for this dictionary is the third, "entirely revised and enlarged." Glasgow: Porteus and Hislop, 1862. At more than three hundred pages of text, this is probably the largest collection of such proverbs in existence. No commentary follows the entries, but a comprehensive glossary of Scottish words is appended.

Holt, Alfred H. *Phrase Origins: A Study of Familiar Expressions.* New York: Thomas Y. Cromwell, 1936. Despite its title, the book contains numerous entries not only on "phrases" but also on individual words. The author familiarized himself with important works on word origins and occasionally ventured an opinion of his own. In the Preface, he gave credit to *Notes and Queries*, "this clearing-house of very miscellaneous information" (vi). Holt wrote two more books, on personal and on place names.

Hotten, John C. *The Slang Dictionary.* London: John C. Hotten, fifth ed., 1903; London: Chatto and Windus. The book enjoyed great popularity at a time when slang and cant dictionaries were all but nonexistent, as is also evident from the references in the present dictionary. It is still a valuable source of early slang.

Hulme, F. Edward. *Proverb Law, Many Sayings, Wise or Otherwise, On Many Subjects, Gleaned From Many Sources.* London: Elliot Stock, 1902. Proverbs and idioms are organized in the book by theme. There is no index. Some etymological explanations are reasonable.

Hyamson, Albert M. *A Dictionary of English Phrases: Phraseological Allusions, Catchwords, Stereotyped Modes of Speech and Metaphors, Nicknames, Sobriquets, Derivations from Personal Names, etc., with Explanations and Thousands of Exact References to Their Sources or Early Usage.* New York: E. P. Dutton and Company, 1922. Reprinted, Detroit: Gale Research Company, 1970. The bibliography contains forty-five references to dictionaries of English. Each entry is a few lines short. The subtitle gives a full idea of the content of the work.

Jamieson, John. *Etymological Dictionary of the Scottish Language.* Ed. John Longmuir. Paisley: Alexander Gardner. *Supplement . . .* by David Donaldson, 1887. This is a treasure house of Scottish words and expressions. The contributors to nineteenth-century journals frequently referred to it in their notes.

JBK: *See* Bellenden Ker, John.

Johnson, Samuel. *A Dictionary of the English Language.* London: Printed by W. Strahan for J. and P. Knapton, etc., 1755. The etymologies in this famous dictionary usually depend on Skinner (see the note on him below) and rarely present interest, but compare what is said at the end of the note on Richardson, below. The second edition by H. J. Todd, known as Johnson–Todd (London: Longman, *etc.,* 1827), has more to say on the etymology of both words and idioms.

Johnson, Trench H. *Phrases and Names, Their Origin and Meaning.* London: T. W. Laurie. 1906. Reprinted many times. Very brief definitions as usual in such books; the origins are given without reference to the sources and many are unreliable.

Junius. *Francisci Junii Francisci filii Etymologicum Anglicanum . . .* Ed. Edward Lye. Oxonii: E Theatro Sheldiano, 1743. Reprinted, Los Angeles: Sherwin & Freutel, 1970. This was the third English etymological dictionary (the second was Skinner's), and was still in Latin. Though Junius, a man of great learning and the author of numerous valuable contributions, believed that English words go back to Greek, his etymologies are often ingenious and still worthy of consideration. References to this posthumously published dictionary were not too rare, because in the nineteenth century educated people could read Latin and often knew some Greek.

Knowles, Elizabeth, editor. *What They Didn't Say: A Book of Misquotations.* Oxford University Press, 2006. A useful collection of phrases whose authorship and shape are widely known, but on closer inspection it turns out that "oral transmission" has changed the original wording or that the alleged author never said such a phrase, *etc.*

Larousse. At present, this name is appended to several reference books and has become a synonym for the greatest dictionary of French, but the original reference was to *Grand Dictionnaire Encyclopédique* by Pierre Larousse (1817–1875).

Lighter, Jonathan E. *Random House Historical Dictionary of American Slang,* 1994-. Two volumes (A through G, H through O) were published. The origin of slang phrases is mentioned only in a few cases.

Lily, John (c.1553–1606), an English playwright of the Elizabethan period, now mainly remembered for his plays *Eupheus: The Anatomy of Wit* (1578) and *Eupheus and His England* (1580).

Littré, Émile. *Dictionnaire de la langue française.* . . . 2d ed. Paris: Librarie Hachette. Reprinted, Paris: Gallimard–Hachette, 1959–61. This is a splendid and deservedly famous dictionary. The authors quoted in this book often turned to it for French etymologies and word histories.

Lye. *See* Junius.

Mabinogion is a collection of prose stories in Middle Welsh, put together in the twelfth century from oral tradition. The meaning of the word *Mabinogion* has not been explained to everyone's satisfaction.

Mackay, Charles. *Dictionary of Lowland Scotch.* Edinburgh: privately printed at the Ballantyne Press, 1888. When Mackay did not allow etymological fantasies to carry him away, he produced valuable collections and glossaries. This is one of them.

Mackay, Charles. *The Gaelic Etymology of the Languages of Western Europe and More Especially of the English and Lowland Scotch, and of Their Slang, Cant, and Colloquial Dialects.* London: published for the author by N. Trübner, 1877. A poet and an authority on the language of Shakespeare, obsolete words, and many things Scottish, Mackay had the unfortunate idea that hundreds of English words went back to Irish Gaelic. His dictionary is a sad monument to this illusion, but some people believed him, which explains a few favorable references to the dictionary in *Notes and Queries* and elsewhere.

Markham, Christopher A. *The Proverbs of Northamptonshire.* Northampton: Stanton and Son, 1897. This small, readable book of thirty-nine pages contains not only proverbs but also rhymes and tales related to the county (the East Midlands). For example, it contains a long entry on *It is all along o' Colly Weston,* with reference to E. Baker's valuable *Glossary of Northamptonshire Words and Phrases* (1854).

MM. *See* Morris and Morris.

Montgomery, Hugh [and] Philip G. Cambray. *A Dictionary of Political Phrases and Allusions; with a Short Bibliography.* London: Sonnenschein, 1906. Several modern reprints.

Morris, William, and Mary Morris. *Dictionary of Word and Phrase Origins.* New York: Harper and Row, 3 vols. (1962, 1967, 1971); 2d ed., 1988. This huge work contains many idioms, but the information on their origins should be taken with caution; the explanations are almost never supported by references to reliable sources.

OED is the acronym for the *Oxford English Dictionary,* edited by James A. H. Murray and others, the main and indispensable source of knowledge about the history and origin of English words and phrases. It was published in installments between 1884 and 1928. The second edition was completed in 1992. The third edition is available online by subscription at www.oed.com.

Palmer, Abram Smythe. *Folk-Etymology: A Dictionary of Verbal Corruptions or Words Perverted in Form or Meaning, by false Derivation or Mistaken Analogy.* London: Henry Holt & Co. Reprinted, New York: Greenwood Press Publishers, 1969. Palmer (1844–1917) was not a professional linguist, but his contributions to etymology, as well as to the study of myths and folklore, are still of some value, though he tended to see the products of folk etymology much too often. His main book was occasionally referred to in *Notes and Queries,* and a few of his own short articles are featured in this book.

Palsgrave. The reference is to a book by John Palsgrave, who in 1530 wrote a French grammar in English as a teaching tool. Its title is in French *(L'esclarcissement de la langue fracoyse),* but the language of the work is English. The book is often consulted by those interested in the history of English and French.

Pegge, Samuel. *Anonymiana; or Ten Centuries of Observations on Various Authors and Subjects.* London, 1809. The edition most often used goes under the names of Pegge and John Nichols, 1818. There are several recent reprints. *Anonymiana* is an interesting book of encyclopedic character by an antiquary, poet, and specialist in the English language of his time. It is still excellent reading.

Promptorium Parvulorum (attributed to Geoffrey the Grammarian), that is, "Storehouse of Children," is a sizable Latin–English dictionary put together around 1440. It is often consulted and exists in numerous old and modern editions.

Richardson, Charles. *A New Dictionary of the English Language, Combining Explanation with Etymology.* London: Bell and Daldy, 1837. Numerous reprints by various publishers to at least 1858 are known. The dictionary gives a good history of usage and was often consulted for etymologies, which are unreliable because Richardson was a follower of Horne Tooke (see below). He did mention phrases and sometimes commented on their origin. Those interested in idioms consulted Richardson when those contained obscure words like *brunt* or *lurch.*

Robert Bruce, King of Scotland, 1274–1329. The reference is to *Regiam Maiestatem Scotiae . . . quod acta parliamenti, vulgò vocat.* Londini: Apud J. Billivm, 1613.

SG: Stephen Goranson, Duke University. His publications on the website of the American Dialect Society contain original ideas and antedatings.

Skeat, Walter W. *An Etymological Dictionary of the English Language,* 4th ed. Oxford: Clarendon Press, 1910. Skeat's dictionary is still the most authoritative dictionary of English etymology. It rarely deals with phrases, so references to it in the present book are rare, but Skeat contributed countless notes to *Notes and Queries,* and his name often recurs in the entries here. His opinions, even when refuted, are important.

Skinner, Stephen. *Etymologicon Linguæ Anglicanæ.* . . . Londini: Typis T. Roycroft, 1671. Reprinted, Los Angeles: Sherwin & Freutel, 1970. This is the second etymological dictionary of English ever published (the first was Minsheu's). It is of course only of historical interest, but even in the nineteenth century people consulted it, though the text is in Latin.

Smith, Logan Pearsall. *Words and Idioms: Studies in the English Language.* London: Constable & Co.; Boston and New York: Houghton Mifflin Company, 1925. Multiple editions, including Gryphon Books, 1971. English idioms are the subject of the last chapter (167–92). Logan P. Smith, the author of multiple books, including the once popular *Trivia* and *Autobiography,* discussed the meaning but not the origin of idioms.

Smyth, William Henry. *The Sailor's Word-Book: An Alphabetical Digest of Nautical Terms.* London: Blackie and Son, 1867. Numerous reprints. This inestimable dictionary, known as Admiral Smyth's word-book, has lost none of its value since the time of publication. Smyth often suggests the origin of words and phrases, and his conjectures are useful even when later research has been able to offer better solutions.

Storm, Johan. *Englische Philologie.* . . . Heilbronn: Verlag von Gebr. Henninger, 2d ed., 1892–96. Storm was an outstanding scholar, but in this dictionary books on philology are seldom referred to. His work turns up only once, in the entry on *Oh my and Betty Martin.* It was curious to find what a learned foreigner who did not live in the English-speaking world could say on this English idiom.

Stormonth, James. *A Dictionary of the English Language.* . . . New York: Harper & Brothers, 1885. Despite the existence of several very full dictionaries available at that time, Stormonth is worth consulting and was often used on both sides of the Atlantic.

Svartengren, T. Hilding. *Intensifying Similes in English.* Lund: Gleerupska universitetshandeln, 1918. This is devoted to phrases of the type *as red as a rose* and those with *like* in the middle. The author was a Swedish schoolteacher, and this dissertation was written and published at a time when English books were hard to obtain in Lund, but Svartengren succeeded in bringing out an excellent collection. In 2013, the book was reprinted by HardPress Publishing and exists as a hardcover and a paperback.

Tatian was a second-century theologian, made famous for his "harmony" of four gospels. The reference is to the translation of this work into Old High German, dated to approximately 830.

Thomas à Kempis, a.1380–1471. His *De imitatione Christi* enjoyed tremendous popularity and exists in many early and late print editions.

Tooke, Horne J. *EPEA PTEROENTA. Or, the Diversions of Purley.* 2 volumes. London: Printed for the author at J. Johnson's, 1798–1805. Reprinted as Scholars' Facsimiles & Reprints, 127 (Delmar: New York, 1968). A famous politician, Horne Tooke had rather odd ideas about the origin of English words (he tended to derive them from imperatives). Yet his work was widely read for many years after his death, as follows from the references to him in this dictionary.

Tyndale, William. *The Obedience of a Christen Man, and How Christen Rulers Ought to Govern, Wherein Also (If Thou Mark Diligently) Thou Shalt Find Eyes to Perceive the Crafty Convience of All Iugglers.* Antwerp, 1528.

Vizetelly, Francis Horne, and Julius Leander De Becker. *A Desk-Book of Idioms.* New York and London: Funk and Wagnall, 1926. Vizetelly, the editor of Funk and Wagnall's dictionary, was the author of many reference books. *A Desk-Book* is a huge collection of English idioms, with illustrative examples and notes on usage but without notes on origins.

Walsh, Willian Shepard (1854–1919). *Handy-Book of Literary Curiosities.* A gigantic medley not related to idioms. Philadelphia: J. B. Lippincott, 1892. Numerous later reprints.

Ward, Caroline. *National Proverbs in the Principal Languages of Europe.* London: J. W. Parker, 1842. A multilingual collection of proverbs only.

The Wars of Alexander is a Middle English alliterative poem describing the life of Alexander the Great, a romance, going back to the Greek original. The events are largely fictional. In the Middle Ages, the plot enjoyed tremendous popularity throughout Europe.

Webster, Noah. The first edition of *An American Dictionary of the English Language* was published in 1828. Revised editions appeared in 1864, 1880, and 1890, and the authors quoted here must have seen one of those three. The origin of phrases is not infrequently explained there under the key words.

Wedgwood, Hensleigh. His name occurs in this book with some regularity. Although nearly forgotten, he was the main English etymologist before Walter W. Skeat. His main work, *A Dictionary of English Etymology,* ran into four editions (the latest in 1888). A few of his short articles were published in *Notes and Queries.*

Weekley, Earnest. *An Etymological Dictionary of Modern English.* London: John Murray, 1921. Reprinted, New York: Dover Publications, 1967. This dictionary is much lighter reading than Skeat's. Weekley was a Romance scholar, but this did not prevent him from having interesting ideas about things Germanic. People often referred to this book, because he explained etymologies in a way that did not baffle nonspecialists. His easy style was a reward for profound learning, and he could be quite "technical" when he addressed a professional audience. Weekley is the author of many excellent books about English words, and the origin of phrases always interested him.

Wheeler, William A. *A Dictionary of the Noted Names of Fiction: Including also familiar pseudonyms, surnames bestowed on eminent men, and analogous popular appellations often reflected in literature and conversation.* London, 1870. The title makes annotation unnecessary. However, for an idea of how entries in such nineteenth-century encyclopedic books looked, a sample from Wheeler's book (a new edition, 1870, page 266) is given here. I have consulted this work on various occasions and often found it useful, but, quite obviously, the author's explanations should not be taken for the absolute truth. "**Old Harry.** A vulgar name for the Devil. [Called also *Lord Harry.*] It has been suggested ("Notes and Queries," XII.229) that this appellation comes from Scandinavian *Hari* or *Herra* (equivalent to the German *Herr*), names of Odin, who came in time (like the other deities of the Northern mythology) to be degraded from the rank of a god to that of a fiend or evil spirit. According to Henley, the hirsute honours of the Satan of the ancient religious stage procured him the name 'Old Hairy', corrupted into 'Old Harry'." Odin never had such names, and the Scandinavian words cited do not exist. The reference to Henley is lacking. But when it comes to real characters like

Old Hickory (General Andrew Jackson), *Old Humphrey* (a pseudonym of George Mogridge), or *Old Lady of Threadneedle Street,* he can be trusted."

Whiting, Bartlett Jere, with the collaboration of Helen Wescott Whiting. *Proverbs, Sentences, and Proverbial Phrases from English Writings Mainly before 1500.* Cambridge: The Belknap Press of Harvard University Press, 1968. This is a much-used collection by one of the greatest specialists in the history and theory of proverbs. The idioms in it are listed without comments or etymology.

Worcester, Joseph E. *A Dictionary of the English Language. . . .* Philadelphia: J. B. Lippincott. 1860. Today, Worcester is remembered (if at all) as Noah Webster's rival, but in the nineteenth century his dictionary was often consulted with profit, as follows from the references in popular sources, and it is indeed a good dictionary.

The Idioms, A to Z

A

A1. *Abraham's bosom*

NQ 1897 VIII/11: 67, 214, 494; 1898 IX/1: 516.

The original question sounded so: "Whence came the idea (evidently existing in the days of Christ) that faithful Jews at death were received into the bosom of Abraham?" (p. 67). According to p. 494, "There is a full discussion of this in Lightfoot's 'Horæ Hebraicae et Talmudicæ,' vol. iii., Gaudell's edition, Oxford, at the University Press, 1859, pp. 167–72. A cursory glance leads me to think that it was derived from the Talmud." On the same page, a passage is quoted: ". . . from a note on St. Luke xvi. 22 in 'The Annotated Bible,' by the Rev. J. H. Blunt:—'This was the name by which the Jews designated the intermediate condition of the righteous souls in the state and place of the departed. Thus the Maccabees are represented as saying to each other, 'For when we shall have suffered thus, Abraham and Isaac and Jacob will receive us into their bosoms, and all the fathers will praise us' (4 Macc. xiii. 14, Cotton's ed.). The expression indicates nearness and dearness, as when St. John speaks of the 'Only Begotten Son, which is in the bosom of the Father' (John i. 18); and it may also be associated with rest, from the custom of reclining at meals indicated by St. John when he describes himself as 'leaning on Jesus' bosom' at the Last Supper (John xiii. 23)." OED: 1300.

A2. *Abington Law*

Abington is also spelled *Abingdon*. See *Halifax Law*.

A3. *According to Cocker*

NQ 1871 IV/8: 256; 1881 VI/3: 206; 1891 VII/12: 254; 1912 XI/6: 90, 176, 236, 352.

'Executed with perfection'. William Bates (the author of the note on p. 206) suggested that the original reference was not to Edward Cocker's famous *Vulgar Arithmetick* but to his other book, namely *The Young Clerk's Tutor*. He seems to have been wrong. In VII/12: 254, we read: "The origin, however, of the saying is traced by Professor A. De Morgan to a speech in Murphy's play 'The Apprentice,' viz, 'See Cocker's Arithmetic', which confirms the general belief. De Morgan,

'Bundle of Paradoxes', London, 1872, pp. 454, 455." A list of Cocker's books (a desideratum mentioned in IV/8: 256) is given on p. 176. OED: 1818.

A4. *Act upon the square, to*
NQ 1876 V/5: 305; 10879 V/12: 89, 218.

'To act honestly'. In England, the phrase was believed to be an Americanism, but the quotations showed it to be of British origin (*upon the square* 'honestly'). OED: 1668 *(upon the square)*.

A5. *Adam's ale*
NQ 1864, III/6: 46.

'Water'. The word *ale* has been often used in such phrases, substituting for other beverages. In Newton's day *China ale* seems to have meant 'tea'. *China beer,* with probably the same connotation, has also been recorded. *Adam's ale* is allegedly, "a cant phrase which every Englishman has heard." [It is not obvious that *Adam's ale* is a phrase like *Welsh Rabbit* 'a cheese dish' or *Cape Cod turkey* 'codfish', as suggested by Funk, 841–2] EDD: *Adam's* Ale; OED: 1643.

A6. *Add insult to injury, to*
NQ 1904 X/1: 4.

'To increase the harm done'. Possibly an adaptation of a Latin saying known from a fable by Phaedrus. This origin has been accepted, but the phrase appeared only in the supplement to the original edition of the *OED* (the earliest example, with *injury* in the plural, goes back to 1748). Was Alexander Leeper, the author of the note in *NQ,* the first to trace the English phrase to *iniuriæ qui addideris contumeliam* ['injuries which you would have added to insult']? OED: *a*1743 *(Insult adds to Grief)* and 1748 *(adding Insult to Injuries).*

A7. *Adelphi guest*
NQ 1900 IX/6: 186, 314.

The reference is to The New Adelphi Theatre; hence also the phrase *Adelphi drama.* "Time was when yet another phrase was common, that being 'Adelphi guest,' as typifying the white-cotton-gloved 'super' who vainly tried to pose as a haughty aristocrat while drinking imaginary champagne out of solid gilded goblets; but that kind of thing was reformed out of existence by a more enlightened stage-management so long ago that by now the saying is almost forgotten" (p. 186). (In the OED, only *Adelphi drama* and *Adelphi screamers* are mentioned.)

A8. *After meat—mustard*
NQ 1862, III/1: 428; III/2: 109.

'Something that comes too late'. The phrase is similar to *after death the doctor* and the like. A long disquisition (pp. 109–10) on the use and origin of French *moutarde* sheds no light on the origin of the phrase, unless the anecdote about *moutarde* from Old French *moult me tarde* 'cause one such delay' and the pun on *tarde* 'late' explains its meaning in English. [Is alliteration at play here?] Apperson: 1605. *

A9. *Afternoon farmer*
NQ 1893 VIII/4: 326; 1894, VIII/5: 153, 235.

"Afternoon folks" are the people who begin their work too late. OED: 1742.

A10. *Age of Roden's colt*

NQ 1853 I/8: 340.

This was said ironically about a middle-aged woman ("forty, save one, the age of Roden's colt"). The query about the origin of the phrase was not answered, so that nothing is known about Roden or his colt. (Kidderminster, Worstershire). *

A11. *Ale and history*

NQ 1945, 188: 281.

This old saying was proverbial at one time. The implication seems to be that drinking ale is inseparable from telling a good story. Apperson: before 1635. *

A12. *All holiday at Peckham*

NQ 1854 I/9: 35.

'No appetite' (slang; *Peckham* 'going to dinner'). The note contains only a query about the origin of the phrase. The editor's note refers to Jon Bee's *Lexicon Balatronicum et Macaronicum* (*peckish* 'hungry'). Peckham is a district in South London. OED: 1788.

A13. *All Lombart street to a China orange*

NQ 1874 V/1: 189, 234, 337; 1875 V/4: 17; 1907 X/8: 7, 136; 1910 XI/2: 200; 1912 XI/5: 240.

This is said about a precious thing in comparison to something devoid of value. Numerous variants exist, with words substituted for *orange* (they are listed in Apperson). In the exchange (V/4: 17), *eggshell, Cheyne Row orange, a Brummagen sixpence,* and *ninepence* are mentioned. A China orange was said to symbolize a worthless thing or simply something that came from the East. [*Ninepence* often occurs in idioms: see the word index.] Italian bankers used to meet in Lombard Street, which was known for its riches. OED: 1666 *(China orange)* and 1819 *(Lombard-Street to a China orange).*

A14. *All my eye and Betty Martin*

NQ 1860 II/9: 72, 171, 230, 335, 375, 392; 1867 III/11: 346, 376; 1872, IV/9: 463; 1890 VII/9: 216, 298; 1897 VIII/11: 146, 512; 1897 VIII/12: 298; 1911 XI/4: 207, 254, 294, 313, 377; 1943, 184: 43, 118.

'Nonsense'. Few phrases have been discussed with such vigor and to such little effect. The popular derivation from Latin *Oh, mihi beate Martine* ("O Saint Martin, [grant] me") is almost certainly a product of folk etymology. Although *my eye* (an exclamation of surprise) is known, the origin of the saying remains undiscovered. References to a real woman called Betty Martin are fanciful. In vol. 184, pp. 43–44, several works containing an approximation to this phrase are mentioned. The earliest of them goes back to 1732. On p. 118 (1943), a passage from J. H. Harvey's *The Heritage of Britain* (1943) is reproduced: "Britomartis was the origin of the saying 'All my eye and Betty Martin', which is simply a corruption of the Latin and other versions of 'O mihi Britomarte', as a call upon the goddess for aid". In VII/9: 298, a reference to Francis Grose's *Classical Dictionary of the Vulgar Tongue'* (1785) occurs. Instead of *Betty, Peggy* was known in many parts of England. [Hyamson, p.11, adds: "In all probability the phrase has some kinship with 'to have in one's eye', to have in mind, the suggestion being that not only is it in the mind, but it will remain there and never materialize." It remains unclear where *Betty*

Martin comes in. Was there something particularly attractive in the name Martin? Cf. *Andrew Martin,* below, and *my eye and Tommy.* JBK I, 37–8. OED: 1781.

A15. *All on one side, like Rooden Lane*
NQ 1876 V/6: 86.

No figurative meaning is given in the note, and no explanation is offered, but the phrase functions like a substitution table. See the next three items. Pendleton (Lancashire). *

A16. *All on one side, like Takeley Street*
NQ 1880 VI/2: 307; 1896 VIII/10: 475, 522.

"This would be said of love, justice, right, etc. or of a slanting tower or spire. The village of Takeley, between Dunmow and Bishop's Stortford, has all the cottages on the one side of the road, and the squire's park on the other" (p. 307). Sixteen years later, a correspondent wrote (p. 522): "Takeley is a small village on the road from Bishop's Stortford to Dunmow. I passed through it several times years ago, and my recollection is strong that all, or nearly all, the houses were built on one (the north) side of the high road." The previous and the next two items show that it was common to coin idioms beginning with *all on one side.* Essex. Apperson: 1880. *

A17. *All on one side, like the Bridgnorth election*
NQ 1861 II/11: 150, 219; 1876 V/5: 407, 455; 1876, V/6: 176, 216, 476; 1880 VI/2: 418; 1929, 157: 391, 449.

This is said about anything going awry. In II/11: 219, a man in the town of Stone (Staffordshire) explained that "there had once been an election in Bridgnorth, when all the votes had been on one side." "The origin of this Shropshire saying has been discussed by Mr. Hartshorne in his valuable *Salopia Antiqua,* London, 1841, 8vo., see p. 336, without a successful derivation being traced. I believe, however, that the phrase arises from the really one-sided nature of an electioneering contest at Bridgnorth. Influence in the borough was supposed to be a possession of the owner of the neighbouring Apley estate, which includes nearly all the town. The member was thus always the nominee of Apley; the opposition candidate never had any chance: hence the proverb" (V/5: 455). In V/6: 176, the author explains that "when the saying came into vogue, there were *two* members (one having been lost by the Reform Bill of 1868), and these two were not *always* the nominees of Apley." He also goes into detail about the history of the election. A still more precise description of the election is given in V/6: 216. [The idiom is known in many places, which complicates the search for its origin]. In Exeter (Devonshire) they say: "All on one side like Kingswear boys." The comment from 1929: 449 may be worth quoting: "This saying is largely quoted from traditional history, and though Bridgnorth is connected with it, it might very easily apply elsewhere. It refers to the days of 'tied' Boroughs, when at a certain election a Whig dared to oppose the two Tory members, with the result, it is said, that only one vote was recorded for the opposition candidate, and that one was his own. Hence the election was all one side. This occurred before the Ballot Act, in the days of open voting, and could not very well occur to-day." Cf. the previous two phrases and the next one. Apperson: 1841. EDD: *Bridgnorth election.* *

A18. *All on one side, like the lock of a gun*
NQ 1861 II/11: 219.

The lock, as the note confirms (!), is indeed on one side. Devonshire. Cf. the previous three phrases. *

A19. *All over, like the fair of Athy*
NQ 1858 II/6: 458.

The phrase refers to a matter ending almost as soon as it has begun. Nothing in the note is said about the fair and its disastrous fate. Ireland. *

A20. *All right*
NQ 1909 X/12: 228, 314, 433, 497; 1916 XII/2: 207, 298.

The citations confirm the idea that the phrase *all right* originated in the language of the guards of mail-coaches. In the 1820s, the phrase was current in the form *all's right.* Even in 1916, *quite all right* sounded to at least one British speaker as a vulgar Americanism. OED: a1413.

A21. *All round Robin Hood's barn*
NQ 1878, V/9: 486; V/10: 15; 1896 VIII/10: 391; 1897 VIII/11: 130, 177.

'All over the place'. No comments on the origin of the phrase or its historical connection with Robin Hood, let alone his barn, have been offered. [Funk, pp. 197–8, suggested that, since Robin Hood's house was Sherwood Forest, he had no house or barn. To go around his barn was to make a circuitous route around the neighboring fields.] EDD: *Robin* Hood; OED: 1797 *(Going round Robin Hood's barn).*

A22. *All Sir Garnet*
NQ 1913 XI/8: 70, 117; 1927, 153: 28, 69, 141, 196, 231, 287.

'All right'. The reference is to Sir Garnet Wolseley's winning the battles in Egypt in the 1880s. *All serene* 'all's well' was a catchword at that time. OED: 1894.

A23. *All talk and no cider*
NQ 1858 II/5: 233.

"This expression is applied to persons whose performances fall far short of their promises. It is said to have originated in Bucks county, Pennsylvania, at a party assembled to drink cider, at which one of the guests thought that too much time was wasted in preliminary conversation." *

A24. *All the go*
NQ 1855, I/12: 426.

'The height of fashion'. A French source of this phrase has been suggested *(tout de go).* OED: 1784.

A25. *All the world and Bingham will be there*
NQ 1863, III/3: 233; 1909 X/11: 490; 1909 X/12: 13, 93, 177.

'Everybody'. The implication is that the company will be more numerous than select. "Bingham is in Notts; and being what the provincial papers delight to call 'a rising town', receives of course a fair share of snubs from those who do not enter into the spirit of its petty ambitions" (p. 233). "A variant of this saying is 'All the world and Little Billing!' Little Billing is a parish in Northamptonshire with (in 1841) a population of only a hundred and one, while Great Billing had four hundred. 'All the world and Little Billing' therefore means, like 'All the world and his wife', every one, and do not forget Little Billing, small part of the world though it be. There is a similar phrase, but with a somewhat dissimilar meaning, 'All the world and Bingham', which is accounted for by a notice-board once posted on an ancient hostelry at Newark, bearing the words 'Passengers and parcels conveyed to all parts of the world, and Bingham'" (p. 13). Several correspondents pointed to the obvious fact that the phrase is a variant of *all the world and his wife*. Nottingham. Apperson: 1863. *

A26. *Almighty dollar*
ANQ 6, 1891: 268; NQ 1911 XI/3: 109, 179, 211.
In the correspondence, the phrase was ascribed to Washington Irving (with reference to Wheeler's *Dictionary of the Noted Names in Fiction*). The model for the phrase could be *almighty gold* (p. 211). OED: 1836.

A27. *Always a feast or a fast in Scilly*
NQ 1864 III/5: 275.
The explanation given is: "The prodigality of the Scillonians in old times was proverbial." The Isle of Cornwall. Apperson: 1750. *

A28. *American way, the*
ANQ 1, 1941: 23.
'The unique life style, real or imagined, of the people in the United States'. The correspondent found a 1928 citation of *The American way,* but *An American way of life* occurred in 1936, and, as the *OED* shows, much earlier. OED: 1883.

A29. *Andrew Martin*
NQ 1892 VIII/2: 127.
'Any departure from the established rule by a clergyman'. The question about the origin of this phrase remained unanswered, and nobody knew anything about that unconventional gentleman. Leister, Ireland. *

A30. *Andrew Millar's [= Miller's] lugger*
NQ 1886 VII/1: 327, 435.
'Slang for a man of war and for government and government authorities'. Sometimes *Andrew* occurs without *Millar,* as in *The Merchant of Venice* I, 1:27 ("My wealthy Andrew docked in sand"). According to one conjecture, a large ship was called by the name of the famous Genoese admiral Andrea Doria. Also on p. 435, other (rather unconvincing) conjectures are given. OED: *Andrew*, as in Shakespeare, and the full phrase: 1819.

A31. *Angels on horseback*
NQ 1898 IX/2: 145, 250; 1899 IX/3: 360.
'Oysters rolled in bacon and served on toast'. The phrase also occurred (rarely) "as a species of mock-heroic commendation." In Winchester, it denoted excellence. The dish is still well-known. OED: 1888.

A32. *Anna Matilda*
NQ 1886 VII/2: 267.

The phrase characterizes "a certain class of ultra-sentimental novels. Mrs. Hannah Cowley used this name in her poetical responses in the *World* to Della Crusca (R. Merry); see Gifford's 'Baviad'." This is indeed how the phrase may have originated. OED: 1788.

A33. *Annie Oakley*
NQ 1933, 165: 206; M&M III:13.

'A pass to circus and other performances after it is punctured'. So called after Annie Oakley, famous for sharp-shooting achievement. "One of her tricks was to cut out the pips on a playing card." She was the star of a once popular show. M&M III:13 quote a letter from a correspondent, according to which a large manila envelope having two columns for listing senders and recipients was also called *Annie Oakley.* By crossing out the last entry, the envolopes could be used multiple times. The point is that two sets of holes are punched in the envelope, so that one can see if it is empty and so available for use and also to insure that it is not thrown away while there is still something in it. US. *

A34. *Another story*
NQ 1898 IX/1: 349, 417; IX/2: 133; 1909 X/11: 107.

'A different matter'. *Another story* is "a familiar quotation," made popular by Kipling, but its originator was said to have been Sterne. The collocation *another story* is so easy to coin that earlier cases of its use were suggested, including a vague reference to Lucian. OED: 1688.

A35. *Answer by milestones, to*
NQ 1884 VII/9: 186.

'To flee'. A defendant, when served a summons, replied that he would serve it by milestones (synonymous with *leg bail*). North Yorkshire. *

A36. *Anthony pig, an*
NQ 1894, VIII/5: 486; *Brewer* (p. 38, 1062).

The phrase refers to a worthless object, but the reference, as usual in such idioms, remains unexplained. Brewer (at *Tantony Pig*): "The smallest pig of a litter, which, according to the old proverb [not quoted] will follow its owner anywhere. So called in honour of St. Anthony, who was the patron saint of swineherds, and is frequently represented with a little pig at his side." OED: 1425.

A37. *Apple-pie order*
NQ 1851 I/3: 330, 468, 485; 1852 I/6: 109; 1865, III/7: 133, 209, 265; 1866, III/9: 255; 1894 VIII/6: 6.

'Perfect order'. It has been suggested (p. 468) that alternative layers of sliced pippins and mutton are a picture of perfect order. On p. 485, the idiom was traced to *cap-à-pied,* which could have been understood as *cap à pie,* but the *OED* points out that *cap-a-pie order* has not been recorded. On p. 109, a children's story is quoted. It begins so: "A was an apple-pie; B bit it; C cut it; D divided it; F fought for it; G got it; H had it," etc., to the end of the alphabet. Hence the suggestion that *apple-pie order* refers to the order in which the letters follow each other. Some other correspondents referred to "a corruption of alpha-beta" and the orderly way an apple pie is made. [M&M I:13–4 derive the idiom from French *nappe plié* 'folded lines', which is probably wrong; see the next item. They also cite "a widely held theory" of early New England house-wives "baking seven pies ahead for the new week just starting." They cite no sources and state that "there isn't a shred of truth in it." Hyamson, p. 19, after citing the traditional explanations, quotes Barrère and Leland: "Order is an old word for a row, and a properly made apple-pie had, of old, always an order or row of regularly cut turrets, or an exactly divided border." They also include, without comment, the idiom *to give a child apple-pie* 'when correcting a child for sit-ting with one or both elbows on the table, the parent raises the arm and knocks it on the table'.] JBK I 44–5. OED: 1870.

A38. *Applepie bed*
NQ 1866: III/4

F&F (p. 9): "A practical joke in which a bed is made using only one sheet, folded over part way down the bed, thus preventing the would-be occupant from stretching out." [An adaptation of the definition in the *OED*.] The phrase may be a folk corruption from the French *nappe philée* (folded cloth). Alternatively, the expression may well refer to an apple turnover, which is a folded piece of pastry (just as the sheet is folded over in the bed), with an apple filling in the middle." The *OED* points out that this suggestion is unnecessary and that it overlooks the fact that French *nappe* ordinarily denotes a tablecloth [cf. Engl. *napkin*] but not a bedsheet. It ig-nores the apple turnover idea. EDD: *Apple-pie* bed; OED: 1781.

A39. *April fool*
GM 36, 1766: 186.

Not the wording, but the custom has to be explained here. The author pointed out that at one time, the year began on the 25th of March. The festivities celebrating the event "were attended with an octave," continuing for eight days. Thus, April 1 was both the festival of the annihila-tion and the beginning of a new year, "a day of extraordinary mirth and festivity." [Edwards, p. 30, says: "There is a tradition among the Jews, that the custom of making fools on the first of April arose from the fact that Noah sent out the dove on the first of the month corresponding to our April, before the water had abated. To perpetuate the memory of the great deliverance of Noah and his family, it was customary on this anniversary to punish persons who had for-gotten the remarkable circumstance connected with the date, by sending them on some boot-less errand, similar to that on which the patriarch sent the luckless bird from the windows of the ark." He does not refer to any sources and does not cite the authority for this explanation.] EDD: *April*-fool; OED: 1629.

A40. *Arch never sleeps*
NQ 1888 VII/5: 198.

This proverb has been ascribed to the Hindus, who argued that "if one abutment settles it is not alone the arch itself which is affected, but all parts of the building with which it is connected." *

A41. *Are you from Seaford?*
NQ 1884 VI/9: 401 no. 64.

An obscure Sussex phrase addressed to a person who leaves doors open. [A pun on *Seaford*? Judging by C43, not necessarily so.] *

A42. *Are you there with your bears?*
NQ 1872, IV/9: 310; 1898 IX/1: 387, 496.

'Again the same story!' The first note tells an anecdote about a parishioner who was exposed to what he thought had been the same sermon by the same preacher, though he went to a different church. Allegedly, this is indeed the background of the phrase. In 1642, the idiom seems to have been known in France (p. 496). [Is the English phrase of French origin?] OED: 1741 (*Are you thereabouts with your Bears?*).

A43. *As big as a bee's knee*
NQ 1896 VIII/10: 92, 199, 260, 521.

'Very small'. Correspondents from several parts of England confirmed their knowledge of this simile. One of them cited a 1797 example. The modern phrase *bee's knees* is a later coinage. Svartengren: 291. EDD: *Bee*; OED: 1797 (slang, originally *U.S.*).

A44. *As big as a Dunstable lark*
NQ 1913 XI/8: 469, 515.

The simile occurs in *Gulliver's Travels*. The following is said on p. 515: "In Dean Swift's days, and long before his time, Dunstable larks were highly esteemed by epicures by reason of their plumpness and savour, and Dunstable and its neighbourhood are still noted, though not to the same extent as formerly, for the number of larks that congregate there." *

A45. *As bitter as soot*
NQ 1891 VII/12: 304, 392, 455; 1892 VIII/1: 212.

This is (or was) a living phrase in many parts of England. The simile is old, and an Old English phrase with the same reference is given. There is an analog in French. On p. 455, the correspondent testifies to the bitterness of soot. One of the discussants was Skeat (p. 455). A correspondent from Worksop (Nottinghamshire) noted that the expression there "and in Derbyshire . . . has probably been in use since the time when coals began to be burnt generally instead of wood and peat." Apperson: 1305. Svartengren: 303. *

A46. *As black as Itchul*
NQ 1930, 158: 242, 286, 337.

Two conjectures were offered. 1) People used to say *as black as hell,* which they disguised by pronouncing *h-l*; *itchul* is allegedly what has become of *aitchel* [this explanation sounds like a good example of folk etymology]; 2) *Itchul* goes back to *ysel,* from Old Engl. *ysel* 'ember, spark'. *

A47. *As black as Newgate knocker*
NQ 1881 VI/3: 248, 298; 1940, 179: 293, 335, 355, 341, 412.

Reference to Hotten purports to explain the origin of the saying in thieves' cant. The phrase never lost its popularity and underwent several alterations, with *as nook's knocker* and *as newker's knocker* substituted for *Newgate knocker*. According to vol. 179: 355, the reference is probably not to Newgate prison, where felons were incarcerated after conviction, but to the turreted Newgate, part of the City Wall that spanned Newgate Street, slightly east of Giltspur Street and the Old Bailey. Svartengren: 244. OED: 1851 *(Newgate knocker)*.

A48. *As black as the Devil's nutting bag*
NQ 1854 I/10: 263; 1872 IV/9: 57, 167, 225, 267; 1879 V/11: 327, 437; 1879 V/12: 457; 1899 IX/4: 478; 1900 IX/5: 38, 95, 197; 1909 X/12: 388; 1910 XI/1: 33; 1940, 179: 187.

The saying may have roots in one of the old harvest festivals that was held when hazel nuts are ripe. The festival of nutting day was celebrated with a great disturbance of peace (I/10: 263). On the other hand, on St. Matthew's day (September 14), "no one would go out nutting, or indeed, if possible, pass along the lanes of the village [in East Sussex], fearing to meet his satanic majesty" (IV/9: 57). The simile is known in many parts of England. In XI/1: 33, the custom is described in some detail. An old play shows that on Holy-Rood Day people did go nutting. Apperson: 1866. Svartengren: 239. EDD: *Nutting.* *

A49. *As blind as a beetle*
NQ 1902 IX/ 9: 12. ANQ 5, 1890: 116.

Although some beetles are indeed blind (p.116), the origin of the saying remains controversial. See the comment at *As deaf as a beetle*. Svartengren: 172. EDD: *Beetle*; OED: 1420 *(As bleynde as a betulle)*.

A50. *As bright as a bullhus*
NQ 1879, V/11: 247; 1879, V/12: 193.

Bullhus appears to be *bullace* 'a variety of the common sloe or of the wild plum'. The reference to a dialectal (Sussex) name of a dog fish *(bull huss)* is fanciful. *

A51. *As bug as a lop*
NQ 1893 VIII/3: 418.

This is a synonym of several phrases beginning with *as proud as*. *Bug* means 'pert, overbearing, fear-inspiring, *etc.*' The pun (*bug* 'pert' and *bug* 'insect' is obvious). *Lop* is 'flea'. The correspondent quotes a less-known version of the nursery rhyme: "What are boys made of?/ Lops and lice,/ Rats and mice./ That's what boys are made of. " *

A52. *As busy as Batty*
NQ 1850 I/1: 475; I/2: 43; 1911 XI/4: 250, 314.

'Fully and entirely occupied in the duties performed'. No one knew who Batty was. A related phrase is *beat as Batty* 'exhausted'. In Eastern Cornwall the phrase had "a satirical suggestion, it being applied to those who made a parade of their energy—who, in fact, were bustling rather than truly busy" (p. 314). Devonshire. [Is Batty a mere product of alliteration or a pun on *batty* 'resembling a bat'? See the next two items.] Apperson: 1850. Svartengren: 123. EDD: *Busy.* *

A53. *As busy as Beck's wife*
NQ 1889 VII/8: 368.

No information is given about Beck's wife. Compare the previous and the next item: Beck alternates with Batty, and alliteration is again at work, but the model is provided by *Throp's* wife. Svartengren: 123. *

A54. *As busy as Throp's wife*
NQ 1876 V/6: 449; 1877 V/7: 35; 1900 IX/5: 414, 526; 1914 XI/9: 12, 175.

This saying has a variant with *throng* or *thrang* for *busy*. Throp's wife was reported to have hanged herself. This saying is (or was) widely known in northern England. Svartengren: 123. EDD: *Throp*; OED: 1762.

A55. *As clean as a clock*
NQ 1874 V/1: 327, 454.

Quoted from *An Antidote Against Idolatry* by Henry More (1669): "But you will meet with the holy Society of the Wipers everywhere, who will be ready to wipe you *as clean as a clock* before you come to the castle" (p. 327). "A common phrase in Yorkshire, referring to the shining and clean-looking black beetles (always called *clocks* in the North), which are to be found under every piece of cow-dung which has been dropped a few hours" (p. 454). Svartengren reproduces the same passage and wonders whether clean can have an adverbial sense (as in *to wipe clean*). Cf. *As cool as a clock*. Svartengren: 322. *

A56. *As clean as a pink*
NQ 1882 VI/6: 409; VI/7: 72, 495.

Pink 'flower'? 'Minnow'? 'Hunters' apparel?', or with reference to the pink of perfection? In VI/7: 72, some discussion occurred about the meaning of the verb *pink*. If it means 'to pierce eyelet holes' (rather than 'to stamp the edge of a stuff with a zigzag pattern'), it will be seen that such holes are perfectly round (hence, allegedly, the idiom). On the same page, *pink,* a fencing term, is cited. A clean thrust through the body "might . . . give rise to the proverbial phrase." Svartengren: 322 (lengthy discussion). OED: 1847.

A57. *As clean as a whistle*
NQ 1867 III/11: 360, 361, 466, 469, 511; 1868 IV/1: 256; 1925, 149: 263, 303.

The simile has been explained with reference to the manufacturing of whistles or to *clean* meaning 'empty' (an interpretation refuted by another correspondent), or to *whistle* standing for *whittel (wittel)*. Skeat (III/11: 361) suggested that *clean* in this phrase means 'clear'. Others referred to the fact that the mouthpiece should be clean of extraneous matter, or to the analogy of the expression *to cut clean*. Svartengren: 321. JBK I: 48–9. EDD: *Clean*; OED: 1828.

A58. *As coarse as bean-straw*
NQ 1876 V/5: 477.

The simile can be applied to both people and things. Lincolnshire. Svartengren: 107. Cf. the next two idioms. *

A59. *As coarse as Garasse*

NQ 1876 V/5: 94, 216, 477.

The suggestion was made that this is the source of the saying *as coarse as gorse* (p. 94). In Kariant, in the vicinity of Nottingham, *as coarse as Hickling gorse* occurs. In the Lowlands of Scotland, they say *as coarse as heather* (or *hemp*) about people with rude manners. Craven, North Yorkshire. Cf. the previous and next two items. Apperson: 1876. *

A60. *As coarse as heather*

NQ 1876 V/5: 216.

Said about people "of rude, boorish manners." Cf. the previous two items and the next one. The Lowlands of Scotland. Svartengren: 107. *

A61. *As coarse as hemp*

NQ 1876 V/5: 216.

The reference is the same as in the phrase above. The Lowlands of Scotland. Cf. the previous three items. Svartengren: 107. *

A62. *As cold as a maid's knee*

NQ 1870, IV/6: 495; 1871 IV/7: 43.

An old man from Huntingdonshire cited the full text of the saying: "A maid's knee and a dog's nose are the two coldest things in creation." West of Scotland. Svartengren: 312. Cf. *Dog's nose cold*. *

A63. *As cold as charity*

NQ 1869 IV/3: 217; LA 1, 1873: 148; 2, 1874; 80-1; NQ 1878, V/10: 136, 358; 1942, 182: 122, 180, 195.

According to Svartengren, the phrase is biblical in origin, but some people thought that the source of the simile is *as cold as charity in the heart* (or *pocket*) *of a lawyer*. Svartengren: 312. OED: 1382 *(The charite of manye schal wexe coold)* and 1864 *(cold as charity)*.

A64. *As contrairy as Wood's dog*

NQ 1880 VI/2: 166.

This is said about someone who would neither go out nor stay at home. As usual, the identity of the person involved remains unknown. Selmeston, Sussex. Svartengren: 101. *

A65. *As cool as a clock*

NQ 1914 XI/10: 247.

This is a 1592 quotation: "A little kindness maks him who was as hote as a tost, as coole as a clock." Apparently, *as cool as a clock* means the same as the phrase *as clean as a clock*. *

A66. *As cool as a cucumber*

ANQ 5, 1890: 176.

The note contains a reference to Drayton's *Poly-Olbion*, song 20, but there the phrase is "the cucumber is cold". Svartengren: 61. OED: *a*1732.

A67. *As cool as Dilworth's*

NQ 1886 VII/2: 230, 297.

"Dilworth was the author of a treatise on arithmetic, which was for a long time extensively used in schools" (p. 297). *

A68. *As crooked as Crawley*

NQ 1879, V/11: 54.

The simile probably goes back to a winding stream at Hail Weston, near St. Neots, Bedfordshire. Brewer (p. 273, at *Crawley*) also mentions Crawley brook, arising near Woburn in Bedfordshire. *

A69. *As cunning as crowder*

GM 24, 1754: 211, 256.

The first author (p. 211) explains [quite correctly, as it seems] that *crowder* in this alliterating simile means 'fiddler', while *cunning* has its old meaning 'skillful'. On p. 256, a story is told about a certain Samuel Crowder, a typical folklore fool, who separated salt and tobacco by putting them in a pail of water. [The story must have been invented in retrospect to explain an incomprehensible simile without *a* before *crowder*. The earliest occurrence of *crowder* is dated in the *OED* to *a*1450. Svartengren: 31. EDD: *Cunning*.

A70. *As dark as a swep's sut bag*

NQ 1909 X/12: 318.

The reference is to the bag the little chimney sweeps put over their heads before they began their climb. *Sut* is a variant of *soot*. *

A71. *As dead as a doornail*

NQ 1892, VIII/2: 66, 153; 1893 VIII/4: 275, 316, 354; 1894 VIII/5: 335, 392, 418; KZ 34, 1897: 376; NQ 1919, XII/5: 266, 303; 1921 XII/6: 134; 1936, 171: 370.

The contributions to the eighth series concerned themselves only with the dating of the simile. Among others, Skeat took part in the discussion. By the middle of the 14th century, the idiom had established itself in poetry; its use in Shakespeare was also noted. The contribution to XII/5: 303 suggests that a nail constantly beaten on the head is indeed dead (a suggestion seemingly going back to Johnson-Todd), but this reference has been countered by the (now universally accepted) explanation that the phrase appeared when doornails became immovable. The conjecture in vol. 171 looks fanciful (reference to the ancient practice of nailing the skin of malefactors to church and barn doors). In 1893 (p. 316), F. Adams, a frequent contributor to *NQ*, cited *dom [dumb] as a dorenayle* from *The Wars of Alexander* (line 4747), a late fifteenth-century northern poem. A dramatically different interpretation was offered by W. Bruinier (*KZ* 34, 1897: 376), who referred to *Naglfar,* the ship of the dead in Scandinavian mythology. He understood the idiom as meaning 'corpse'. [Imaginative, but not trustworthy: such an idiom did not exist in either Old Icelandic or Old English. Holt, p. 94: "In the absence of any other theory, I incline to the one that the nail may once have been the specific name for the one whose head the knocker kept banging until life (if any) surely must have departed. Ordinary nails are, in fact, not used in the building of doors. It is possible that in its original use the phrase may have implied being as dead as something that never existed.The same was said in XII 15/5:303; see above.] JBK I, 24. Svartengren: 142–5. OED 1362 (And ded as a dore-nayl).

A72. *As dead as a herring*

NQ 1854 I/9: 347; 1919, XII/5: 303.

Two references are given to the behavior of the herring. "This fish dies immediately upon its removal from the native element from want of air; for swimming near the surface it requires much air, and the gills, when dry, cannot perform their function" (p. 347) and "a herring's gills are so delicate that it dies the instant it is taken out of the water." To this the second correspondent adds: "Is not the real explanation that in the early days Dutch salted herrings were largely used on days of fast and that the herring was known to most people solely as a dead fish—as dead as mutton?" Svartengren: 146–7. EDD: *Herring*; OED: 1664 (to be dead as Herring).

A73. *As dead as Chelsey*

NQ 1879, V/12: 29, 75, 118.

Allegedly, 'as dead to the service as a pensioner in Chelsea Hospital'. Grose identified the phrase with slang. [The simile bears a curious similarity to *as deep as Chelsea*. Are the existing explanations the product of folk etymology?] Svartengren: 145. * Apperson: 1823.

A74. *As dead as mutton*

NQ 1919 XII/5: 303.

No explanation is offered in the note. One finds only the rhetorical question: "What can be deader than mutton?" The phrase is well-known, but the query has not elicited a single response. Svartengren: 142. EDD: *Mutton*; OED: 1792.

A75. *As dead as Queen Anne*

NQ 1910 XI/1: 347, 430; 1916 XII/1: 289, 357; 1916 XII/2: 57; 1930, 158: 98–9, 160, 196, 231.

The note on p. 357 quotes a 1740 source of the saying. In his book (pp. 140–1), Svartengren devoted a whole page to this phrase, known to most from the idiom "Queen Anne is dead." Here is a passage from the note on p. 430 (1910): "Queen Anne died 1 Aug., 1714, and there was much mystery at the time as to her successor. . . . It seems it was the aim of the Jacobite party to keep the fact of the death of the Queen a secret till their plans for the proclamation of the Pretender were matured . . . . Not only was there uncertainty as to the death of the Queen, but there was uncertainty as to the fate of whoever should make a wrong move. There would be the question, 'Is the Queen really dead?' which, when afterwards the Whigs were triumphant, would be sarcastically asked, 'Is Queen Anne dead?' which became a proverbial saying for trite well-known news." Despite Swift's quip "Queen Elizabeth's dead" in his *Polite Conversations,* Queen Anne's death did "occasion a political crisis of the first magnitude . . . and there was every reason to fear a fresh outbreak of civil war over succession" (1930: 98–9). The author stressed the tentative nature of his explanation. Svartengren: 141. OED: 1770 (Queen Anne is dead).

A76. *As dead as a rat*

NQ 1868 IV/1: 434.

The note contains only a query (which has not been answered) about the origin of this simile and its near-synonym *as weak as a rat*. The writer asked: "Have they any connection with the rat-hunting propensities of some of our greatest nobility in the days of George III?" [Also, can there be some connection with rhyming rats to death? (See **R13**.)] Svartengren: 145. *

A77. *As deaf as a beetle*

NQ 1867 III/11: 34, 106, 167, 328, 410; III/12: 299, 398; 1902 IX/ 9: 12.

As blind as a beetle also exists (see it above). The author of the note in IX/9: 12 suggests that *beetle* refers to a wooden instrument called this. Other than that, a seemingly improbable explanation has been offered: allegedly, not *beetle*, but *beadle* is meant, "God and beadle save you." More to the point seems to be the fact that "a large sledge-like implement for driving wedges was known as *beetle*, and there is a curious tavern-sign survival of that usage, namely 'Beetle and Wedge'." See also 'to cleave a tree with a beetle without a wedge' (Fuller, 'Holy War', iii. xxiv, 1840: 162). Cf. *Between the beetle and the block*. Svartengren: 176/2. EDD: *Deaf/Beetle*; OED: 1520 *(be made dull as a betle)*.

A78. *As deaf as the adder*

NQ 1886 VII/2: 9, 115, 152, 314.

The notes are devoted to a discussion of the adder in the Authorized Version of the Bible and of whether some snakes are really deaf. [According to Funk, pp. 545–6, the allusion is to the ancient Oriental belief that certain serpents were able to protect themselves against being lured by the music of charmers by stopping up one ear with the tip of the tail and pressing the other firmly to the ground. He does not give references to his source.] Svartengren: 174–5. OED: 1597 *(Adder-deafe eares)*.

A79. *As deep as Chelsea (Reach)*

NQ 1857 II/3: 258.

An old lady who said (in 1857) that her cat was as deep as Chelsea could not explain the reference. Norfolk. Cf. *As dead as Chelsey*. Svartengren: 33. *

A80. *As deep as Garrick*

NQ 1856 II/2: 307; 1867, III/11: 469; 1881 VI/4: 386, 540; 1907 X/8: 251, 376; 1912 XI/ 5: 326, 496; *NC* 1910, 68: 550.

In X/8: 376, Carrick, a small rocky island off the north coast of Antrim, is mentioned, and Garrick has often been explained as a folk etymological alteration of *carrick* 'a submarine rock' (a word current on the coast of Cornwall), but the phrase is also known outside Cornwall. Reference to the famous actor's name seems unlikely, though, according to some, its influence cannot be ruled out. In Wiltshire, *deep* is used in the sense of 'artful', but this fact does not shed light on *Garrick*. A. Smythe Palmer, in his book on folk etymology, suggests that *Garrick* goes back to Gerarde, one of the Devil's many names, whose origin may be sought in Norse mythology. [Unlikely.] The West Cornwall variant *as deep as garlick* is a clear case of folk etymology. Svartengren: 28–30. EDD: *Deep*. OED: 1819.

A81. *As different as chalk from cheese*

NQ 1924, 147: 219.

'Looking somewhat alike but being quite different'. It has been observed that skim milk cheese resembles chalk. [The origin of such seemingly nonsensical alliterating phrases is always hard to trace.] Svartengren *(As analogous as chalk and cheese)*: 333. OED: 1393 *(Lo, how they feignen chalk for chese).*

A82. *As drunk as Blaizers*

NQ 1880 VI/1: 434; VI/2: 92.

The phrase is usually referred to St. Blaizers, with the reference being to "Blaizers," the participants in the procession honoring St. Blaize, who, according to legend, used to get more than ordinarily drunk. The connection of the idiom with the phrase *as drunk as blazes* remains unclear. The sign on a pub in Nottingham read (1880): 'Old Bishop Blaize'. Svartengren: 194. *

A83. *As drunk as Chloe*

NQ 1851, I/3: 507; 1860 II/9: 462.

The simile is said to refer to the lady often mentioned in Prior's *Poems,* a notorious drunkard. *Chloe* alternates with *Floe.* Svartengren: 196. *

A84. *As drunk as Davy's sow*

NQ 1865 III/7: 243; 1881 VI/3: 188, 394; 1894 VIII/6: 88, 118, 438; MM 2, 1912: 25 (112).

Grose is quoted as the author of a fanciful story explaining the origin of the phrase, but in such phrases, the names of the owners of various animals are usually beyond reconstruction. Svartengren: 204. Apperson: 1671. JBK I, 24. *

A85. *As drunk as mice*

NQ 1876 V/5: 228, 314, 358, 394, 458; 1876 V/6: 78.

The phrase *dronke as a mous* occurs in Chaucer (*Knight's Tale,* 403), but the explanations offered in the exchange carry little conviction: "It takes little alcohol to make a mouse drunk" (Skeat V/5: 315); or that *mice* is really Irish Gaelic *miosa* 'worse; worst' (the improbable Celtic conjecture is by Charles Mackay: V/5, 394). Reference to a folktale about a mouse drowning in a brewing vessel, saved by the cat and escaping, seems to be irrelevant. Svartengren's material (pp. 207–8) is excellent, but his explanation (the mouse is often used as a symbol of what is valueless, *etc.*) does not go far. JBK I: 77. Apperson: 1307. EDD: *Drunk.* *

A86. *As dull as a fro*

NQ 1887 VII/3: 368, 503; 1887 VII/4: 177..

Fro: possibly 'an instrument for splitting wood'. There is also the word *frower* (the same meaning), recorded in 1573. *

A87. *As false as Louth Clock*

LNQ 2, 1891: 217.

This idiom is interesting in that is shows that references to proper and place names sometimes have recoverable foundations: "There is now no clock on Louth Church, and has not been for nearly 50 years, so that the saying may have become obsolete through the absence of the cause. The clock which used to be thereon is now at Patrington in Holderness, and as one face is always an hour and five minutes before the other, the proverb still lives there, and is repeated to any stranger who remarks on the difference of time recorded by the two faces." *

A88. *As fess as Cox's pig*

NQ 1912 XI/5: 326.

Fess is an alteration of *fierce*. The word means 'eager; ill-tempered; lively; conceited'. As usual in such cases, the identity of Cox and the story behind the idiom remain a mystery. Svartengren: 122. *

A89. *As fierce as a dig*

NQ 1861 II/12: 309, 511.

"A dig is a duck in Lancashire," but the sense of the saying is obscure. The query about *dig* has not been answered. Cf. *As fierce as a tick* (*NQ* 1909 X/12: 218) recorded in Leicestershire, and *as full as a tick,* below. Svartengren: 93. Apperson: 1877. *

A90. *As fierce as a maggot*

NQ 1881 VI/4: 309, 355; 1909 X/12: 148, 218.

In VI/4: 355, the following comment appears: "[The simile] is not local, but general in England, and is short for *fierce as a maggot with its tail cut off*—a metaphor which commends itself to apple-eaters." *

A91. *As fit as a fiddle*

NQ 1908 X/10: 188; 1947 192: 159.

Perhaps the reference is to the fact that a fiddle is strung up to the adequate pitch before it is used (p. 188). The note in vol. 192 offers a detailed discussion of the semantic development of both *fit* and *fiddle*. When the idiom was coined, *fit* meant 'excellent' and the fiddle was a model of beauty. The variant *fine as a fiddle* is also known. Both phrases depend on alliteration. Svartengren: 152. OED: *a*1605.

A92. *As full as a tick*

NQ 1896 VIII/9: 20, 65-6, 294.

The comparison is said to be widely known. "We have been told, and believe, that it refers not to a bed-tick, which is seldom so full of feathers that it would not hold more, but to the mite known as the dog-tick, which frequently charges itself with blood almost to the bursting point." This explanation was supported by Skeat (p. 66). On the same page, the synonymous phrase *as full as a louse* is given. And on p. 294, two correspondents cite *as full as vetch* (or *fitch*). *Vetch/ fitch* is a seedpod, so that the simile refers to a pod ready to burst. Cf. *As fierce as a tick* (and *As fierce as a dig*). EDD: *Full*; OED: 1678 ("full to repletion, especially with alcoholic drink", *as full as a piper's bag; as a tick*).

A93. *As funny as a crutch*

NQ 1945, 189: 61; ANQ 5, 1945: 9; ANQ 6, 1947: 158.

An odd, seemingly unexplained idiom. Perhaps the source of the idiom is Alonzo F. Hill's book *John Smith's Funny Adventures on a Crutch,* first published in Philadelphia in 1869 (p. 158). Lighter adds the definition: 'decidedly funny' (1919); with the ironic sense 'not funny' (1916). *

A94. *As good as a play*

NQ 1853 I/8: 363.

This is said to have been a remark of King Charles II when he revived a practice of his predecessors and attended the sittings of the House of Lords. Svartengren: 316. OED: 1638 *(It was as good as a Comedy)*.

A95. *As good as George of Green*

NQ 1861 II/11: 310.

George of (a) Green, "the famous Pinder (or pound-keeper) of Wakefield, and subsequently one of the followers of Robin Hood. The saying applies to his courageous conduct and impartiality in the discharge of his public duties; and more particularly when he resisted, single-handed, Robin Hood, Will Scarlett, and Little John, in their joint attempt to commit a trespass in Wakefield." Svartengren: 417. Apperson: 1670. *

A96. *As hot as Mary Palmer*

NQ 1876 V/5: 329.

The simile allegedly derived from some occurrence during the Commonwealth and used by Cavaliers to tease the puritans. The circumstances and the identity of Mary Palmer are unknown. Svartengren: 310. *

A97. *As independent as a hog on ice*

NQ 1946, 191: 18; ANQ 6, 1946: 92.

The *CD* connects *hog* with *hog* in the game of curling, but the author of the note (p. 18) questions this explanation. The phrase was popular around 1900 in the American Middle West. It was used ironically about people who paraded nonexistent independence. [Funk spent years trying to discover the origin of this saying and called his first (1948) book *A Hog on Ice*. See the story in Funk, 8–14. While preparing the book for publication, he may not have seen the notes referred to above. Yet Funk came to the conclusion, similar to the one given in the *CD*, though he did not think that the stone used in this game was neccesarily connected with curling, as we today know it. He also considered the possibility of the idiom's origin in northern England, though no evidence presented itself.] OED: 1857.

A98. *As innocent as a bird*

ANQ 10, 1971: 40.

The query contains only a question about the origin of the simile, but the questioner was the distinguished scholar Archer Taylor, which lends it status. He received no answer. *

A99. *As jealous as a couple of hairdressers*

NQ 1869, IV/4: 196, 266-7.

This simile has been recorded in the south of England. In the north of France, especially in the neighborhood of Boulogne, they say: "Jaloux comme un coiffeur ['jealous as a hairdresser']." On p. 267, a quotation from an 18ᵗʰ-century French poem (C. Langlois, 1721) is given; two hairdressers are mentioned in it, [so that the simile may have originated in France]. Svartengren: 86. *

A100. *As jolly as sandboys*

NQ 1866 III/9: 331; 1867 III/11: 443; 1870 IV/5: 257; 1905 X/3: 260; 1919 XII/5: 180, 279.

The sign "The Jolly Sandboys" in Dickens's novel *Old Curiosity Shop* (1841), may have contributed to the popularity of the simile. An association between sandboys and merriment is old, but its source remains unclear. Definition of *sandboy*: "a boy who hawks sand for sale." John Bee characterized sandboys as "all rags and all happiness," [probably an attempt to rationalize in retrospect a popular phrase] Svartengren: 76. OED: 1821.

A101. *Ask near, sell dear*

NQ 1881 VI/3: 326.

'Don't overprice the things you sell'. (In the text, *ask* is given as *ax*.) *

A102. *As lazy as a dog*

ANQ 5, 1890: 76.

The note lists several (often contradictory) similes: *drunk as a dog, work like a dog, hot as a dog, cold as a dog, sweat like a dog, dank (= damp) as a dog, he swore like a dog,* and *sweat like a dog,* but none of them explains the reference to laziness. Cf. the next three items. [Is it possible that this simile is an abbreviated version of such phrases?] *

A103. *As lazy as Laurence's dog*

NQ 1882 VI/6: 177; 1900 IX/5: 503.

Lazy Laurence (apparently a fictitious character) personified indolence. The phrase may depend on alliteration. Brewer cited the long form: "'Lazy as David Lawrence's dog that leaned his head against a wall to bark'. This is not given by Bohn, but seems to bear out the suggestion that the *saint* named Lawrence is not intended" (p. 177). On p. 503, Brewer's idea is called suspect. Since, for whatever reason, *Lawrence* personifies laziness *(OED)*, it could be expected that his dog should also be lazy. [Hyamson, p. 218, also cites *as lazy as David Launce's dog,* with the explanation: "From Laurence, the Scot[tish] folk patron of the lazy."] Svartengren: 121. Apperson: 1886. See the next two items and *Lazy Lawrence. *

A104. *As lazy as Ludlum's dog* (as laid him down to bark, *and other variants*)

NQ 1850 I/1: 382, 475; 1850 I/2: 42; 1851 I/4: 165; 1873, IV/12: 239, 482.

The phrase, which both Ray and Bohn knew, was common in South Yorkshire, especially in Sheffield. Like the previous item, this one may own something to alliteration. Brewer, in the first edition of his book, tells a story about a real dog [such stories are always suspicious]. In IV/12: 239, a synonym of this phrase is quoted: "As lazy as Joe the Marine, who laid down his musket to sneeze." Robert Southey is known to have asked: "Who was Ludlam, whose dog was so lazy that he leant against a wall to bark?" See the next and the previous two items. Svartengren: 121. Apperson: 1670. *

A105. *As lazy as Lumley's dog*

NQ 1890 VII/9: 328, 397.

The full version again seems to be "as lazy as Lumley's dog that leant up against a wall when he wanted to bark." (Suffolk.) With regard to the image, cf. *As poor as Job's turkey.* See the previous three items. Svartengren: 121. EDD: *Lumley. *

A106. *As lean as MacFarlan's geese*
NQ 1914 XI/9: 270, 314.

The following story is given on p. 314: "It is said that King James VI once visited the chief of the MacFarlans in his residence on one of the islands in Loch Lomond. He was much taken with the appearance of the geese that disported themselves in large numbers about the place, and he was pleased to express his royal approbation of their activity. When, however, one of the lively fowl was served up for dinner, his Majesty found it but a tough morsel, and caustically observed, 'MacFarlan's geese like their play better than their meat'." "Spoken to children when their earnestness keeps them from dinner." *

A107. *As like as two patterns*
NQ 1880 VI/ 1: 191.

'As like as two peas'. The idea probably is *to be joined* (or *joint*) *pattern with someone* 'to be exactly like someone'. *

A108. *As long as the eleventh of June*
NQ 1875 V/4: 127.

This is said about a tall man, but it is not explained what happened or happens on the eleventh of June. [Is the difference between two calendars meant, with reference to the longest day of the year?] Irish. *

A109. *As mad as a coot*
NQ 1856 II/2: 307.

Judging by a mention in John Skelton's *The Book of Philip Sparowe,* the image is at least five hundred years old. In 1856, the simile was still current in the west of Cornwall, applied to someone "excessively angry." Svartengren: 42. *

A110. *As mad as a hatter*
NQ 1869 IV/3: 64; 1871, IV/8: 395, 489; 1879, V/12: 178; 1888 VII/6: 107, 176, 218; 1897 VIII/12: 47, 213; 1900 IX/6: 448; 1901 IX/7: 251, 396; 1905 X/3: 20; 1913 XI/7: 149, 238; 1929, 157: 415; ANQ 4, 1889: 67.

'Rabid'. The notes offer an inconclusive explanation of the idiom's origin. For example, we are told about solitary people (shepherds in Canada) who make cabbage tree hats and are "a bit" mad. Another note refers to miners who refuse to have partners and thus work "under their own hat." Those hatters also tend to be eccentric. Two other explanations are not much better: from French *il raisonne comme une huître* 'he reasons like an oyster' (= 'he is a fool') and from a story about the father of the poet William Collins (the man spent some time in a lunatic asylum, and the other lunatics, on discovering that he was a hatter, are credited with having coined the saying). Several correspondents believed that the original form of the saying was *mad as a natter (a natter = an adder),* which degenerated into *mad as a 'atter (hatter).* According to the note in VIII/12: 213, the full text of the proverb should run "as mad drunk as a hatter" or "as mad through drunkenness as a hatter." A story is told about the events that occurred around 1826. If the story can be taken seriously, the odd simile gets a plausible explanation. Reference to a real hatter who was a drunk need not be dismissed, but it is not improbable that the simile had existed earlier and was made to fit the situation described on p. 57 of *Life of P. T.*

Barnum. As could be expected, another prototype has been suggested. In VII/6: 107 (1888), we find the following excerpt from *The Daily Chronicle*: "The proverbial madness of hatters is said to be derived from 'the candidature of Mr. Harris, elected at the head of the poll for Southwark nearly sixty years ago, and to the surprise of everybody. He was a hatter in the Borough, and proved to be out of his mind'." In 1929 (p. 415), the same explanation is offered and called ingenious by an anonymous correspondent, with reference to Sir Austen Chamberlain in the *Times Literary Supplement* (no date is given). Still another mad hatter is mentioned in XI/7: 238 (but he died in 1680). The puzzling thing is the late date of the idiom's emergence in texts and its immediate acceptance by English speakers. Of some interest is the observation that *mad* also means 'very angry' and that Scots *to hatter* has been glossed by Jamieson as 'to be confused, etc., anything violent' (IX/7: 251). On the other hand, it has been suggested that "the hatter's madness was dipsomania, induced by working with hot irons in a heated atmosphere and in a standing position. The tailor works under similar conditions, but seated; his condition is therefore less aggravated, and he accordingly gets credited only with pusillanimity and lubricity" (IX/7: 396). [Cf. the idioms containing the word *tailor* in this book!] A curious question appears in XI/7: 149 ("Does a mad hatter make madcaps?"). Could the phrase's origin be as simple as that? No explanation accounts for the late emergence of the simile. Charles Mackay had the unfortunate idea that hundreds of English words are derived from Irish Gaelic and wrote a (totally unreliable) etymological dictionary (1877). He could not explain the idiom but noted that "there is no reason to accuse hatters of madness in a greater degree than any other artificers or trades" and referred to Gaelic *at* 'to swell, puff, to bluster' and its derivatives. The *OED* also favors a medical explanation but ascribes "madness" to mercury poisoning. [This guess needs more evidence to solve the riddle.] Lewis Carroll's book postdates the earliest occurrence of the simile. Cf. *Blue devils*. Svartengren: 36. OED: 1829.

A111. *As mad as a March hare*
NQ 1851 I/4: 208; 1857 II/8: 514; 1917 XII/3: 297, 522; MCNNQ 5, 1884: 47; ANQ 1, 1888: 104.

In his *Glossary,* Nares offers an explanation of the simile ("hares are said to be unusually wild in the month of March, which is their rutting time" (p. 104), and the *OED* shares this view. But an old sportsman, also quoted in Nares, had another explanation. XII/3: 297 cites *as strong as a March hare,* yet there was some doubt about the implication of that epithet (p. 522). Svartengren: 40–2. JBK I, 83. EDD: *Mad*; OED: 1529 *(As mad not as marche hare)*.

A112. *As mad as a tup*
NQ 1884 VI/9: 266; 1901 IX/8: 501; 1902 IX/ 9: 98, 237.

Tup 'ram'. This is said of a young woman who constantly seeks the society of men. North of England and Scotland. Svartengren: 383. EDD: *Mad*; OED: 1901.

A113. *As mad as the baiting bull of Stamford*
NQ 1902 IX/9: 98.

Allegedly, the phrase has its origin in a custom that took place annually in that town, derived from a traditional incident recorded in histories of Lincolnshire. Svartengren: 39. *

A114. *As mean as tongs*

NQ 1899 IX/4: 206.

Perhaps the association is with pincers, an instrument that "pinches" and may go back to the old practice of clipping money. Svartengren: 127. Apperson: 1899. *

A115. *As merry as a grig*

NQ 1866 III/10: 516; 1867 III/11: 443; 1904 X/1: 36, 94.

Grig 'cricket'. Skeat (1866) understood *grig* in this simile as meaning 'cricket' and cited many dialectal homonyms (*grig* 'eel; cricket; way', *etc.*) Also, *merry* in this phrase is either 'lively, full of motion' or 'joyous, cheery'. In 1867 (p. 11), he cited *merry as a pismire* [see the next item], with reference to *merry* meaning 'lively' (here: 'nimble', that is, 'nimble as an ant, eel, *etc.*'). In some parts of England, *grig* means 'bantam', 'eel', or 'tadpole' (p. 36). Skeat mentioned those senses, as well as 'to pinch' and a slang term for 'farthing'. Many people's belief that *grig* means 'Greek' cannot be supported. Svartengren: 72. EDD: *Grig*; OED: 1566.

A116. *As merry as a pismire*

NQ 1867 III/11: 443.

Prismire 'ant'. Allegedly, the saying refers to the rapid movement of an ant in the sand. Cf. the previous item. OED: *a*1643.

A117. *As narrow in the nose as a pig at ninepence*

NQ 1862 II/2: 304.

This is said of a stingy person. The image has not been explained. Only the alliteration is conspicuous. Cf. *ninepence* in the index. Curiously, in Russian, *piatachók* means 'a tiny piece of land' and 'pig's snout.' The word is a diminutive form of *piaták* 'a five-kopek coin.' Is the association between a pig's snout and a round coin of the same nature in both languages? Irish. Svartengren: 128. *

A118. *As nice as a nun's hen*

NQ 1866, III/10: 169, 215.

Skeat (p. 215) explained *nice* as 'fastidious'. There was a northern proverb implying that a nun's hen was "something peculiarly delicate and pure." Svartengren: 85. OED: *a*1500.

A119. *As pert as a louse*

NQ 1893 VIII/3: 418.

This is a synonym of *as proud as a louse* (see it below). Cf. also *As bug as a lop.* *

A120. *As pert as a pearmonger*

NQ 1855 I/11: 114, 232, 392.

Bohn cites a longer version: "As peart as a pearmonger's mare" (*pert* 'nimble'). Svartengren: 157. The alliteration is obvious, but the image remains unexplained. OED: 1565.

A121. *As plain as a pikestaff*

NQ 1896 VIII/9: 346; 1896 VIII/10: 141; 1897 VIII/11:32; 1928, 154: 406, 444, 464; 1928, 155: 49.

Vol. 154 provides references and discussion. In the variant *as plain as the packstaff,* the noun designated the object on which the pedlar carried his pack. Whether *pikestaff* was at one time substituted for *packstaff* is not certain. The word was sometimes hyphenated. Svartengren: 365–6. OED: 1542 *(plain as a pack-staff)*. [F&F (p. 147) offer a detailed discussion: "Some authorities believe that the phrase refers to the pike, a weapon used by the infantry. The pike was rather like a spear, but its shaft was so very long that it was easily visible to all around. This explanation fits in very neatly with the modern meaning of 'extremely obvious.'" Then they turn to the earlier *packstaff* theory: "Constant use wore the word plain." Hyamson, p. 274: "In allusion to the pikestaff which clearly [!] denoted the status of the pilgrim who carried it."]

A122. *As poor as Crowborough*
NQ 1873 IV/11: 238, 350.

The reference in this local phrase is to Crowborough Commons, whose soil is of the iron sand formation. Sussex. *

A123. *As poor as Job's turkey*
NQ 1853 I/7: 180; 1860 II/10: 229; 1879, V/12: 175.

In the US, the simile sometimes has "specifications," as in "As poor as Job's turkey that had but one feather in his tail" and "As poor as Job's turkey that had to lean against a fence to gobble." In V/12, the American Indian saying is cited: "I am as poor as a turkey in summer." In summer, the birds in the wild have trouble finding food. Whether this fact has any relation to Job's turkey remains unexplained. With regard to the image, cf. *As lazy as Lawrence's* [or *Lumley's*] *dog*. Svartengren: 342. OED: 1817.

A124. *As proud as a dog with side-pockets*
NQ 1869 IV/3: 529.

Apparently, this simile is more common in northern England. Cf. also *as proud as a toad with side-pockets* and *to have no more use (for something) than a dog (or monkey) has for side-pockets*. [It should be remembered that pockets, as we know them, were a comparatively late invention.] Svartengren: 83. OED: *(to have as much use for something as a dog has for a side pocket)* 1788.

A125. *As proud as a louse*
NQ 1893 VIII/3: 388, 418.

The simile was said to be common in some part of Yorkshire. In Lincolnshire, *as pert as a louse* occurred (see it above). Svartengren: 84. *

A126. *As proud as a toad with a side-pocket*
NQ 1874 V/1: 18.

Cf. *No more use than a side pocket to a toad* and *As proud as a dog with side-pockets* (above). Apperson: 1785. See also *Old Cole's Dog*. *

A127. *As proud as old Cole's (or the cobbler's) dog*
NQ 1850 I/1: 475; I/2: 43.

The longer variant is: "As proud as old Cole's dog which took the wall of a dung-cart, and got crushed by the wheel." This is one of the many seemingly nonsensical phrases agout dogs' erratic behavior. Svartengren: 82. *

A128. *As queer as Dick's hatband, that went nine times round his hat and was fastened by a rush at last*
NQ 1850 I/1: 475; 1856 II/2: 189, 259; 1870, IV/6: 211, 308, 478; 1897 VIII/11: 467; 1897 VIII/12: 37, 96, 171.
"A personage resident in the village, and known as 'Silly Dick', was thought to have originated this proverbial phrase, but a similar honour has been claimed for one 'Dick Wheelbant' of Bury" (IV/6: 211). Likewise, in II/2: 259, it is suggested that *Dick* refers to a man from Cornwall, where a certain Tumbledown Dick "might be said to have found the pressure of his father's hat too heavy for him, and his hatband too tight." This saying has been recorded in various parts of England, which makes its attribution to a certain individual suspect. The shorter version is *that's like Dick's hatband* (with reference to something improbable or annoying). This is James A. H. Murray's note on p. 467 (1897): "The phrases, 'as tight,' 'as queer,' and 'as fine as Dick's hatband,' are generally explained in modern dictionaries, &c., as referring to the dignity of Lord Protector of England conferred upon Richard Cromwell. The originator of the phrase is assumed to have supposed that Cromwell's authority was typified by some sort of fillet or crown. But no evidence of this origin is offered, and it may easily be one of the noxious guesses with which the soil of English etymology is cumbered. I shall be glad to have any instances of the use of these phrases, and any reliable information as to their origin." The responses to Murray's note are of interest only in so far as they cite minor variants of the idiom: *queer, curst, fine,* and *odd* for *tight,* along with . . . *went half way round and tied in the middle* or . . . *and would not tie.* Svartengren: 97–8. OED: 1742 *(as queer as Dick's Hat-Band).*

A129. *As queer as Tim's wife looked when she hanged herself*
NQ 1870 IV/6: 487.
Sometimes *pale* is used for *queer.* The writer had nothing to say about Tim's wife but noted that in his area there is a saying about careful Abigail, which is "not quotable," so that the original reference must have been opprobrious. See also *As throng as Throp's wife.* Craven. Svartengren: 339–40. *

A130. *As right as a ninepence*
NQ 1901 IX/7: 335.
'Quite right'. The image is not explained, but see *ninepence* in the index. Svartengren: 368. EDD: *Right/Ninepence;* OED: 1890.

A131. *As right as a trivet*
NQ 1867 III/11: 360, 361; 1901 IX/7: 227, 335; 1909 X/12: 227, 273, 313, 376, 435.
The phrase appears to refer to the fact that a trivet or any other utensil with three legs or points of support will invariably stand firm. According to a different explanation, "the trivet, to be a good one, must be *right* angled" (see the first two references, above). Svartengren: 369–70. OED: 1835.

A132. *As right as rain*
NQ 1901 IX/7: 335; 1903 IX/11: 148.

'Quite right'. Allegedly, this saying "implies a sense of comfort," [but its main support seems to be the *r-r* alliteration]. In 1903—see p. 148—the simile was felt to be recent, and with good reason. Svartengren: 371, OED: 1891.

A133. *As round as a Pontypool waiter*
NQ 1855 I/11: 472.

In Pontypool, Monmouthshire (Wales), japanned tinware was produced. The reference may be to round waiter trays of this ware. Svartengren: 279–80.

A134. *As salt as fire*
NQ 1852 I/5: 112.

"Probably from the Roman custom of throwing meal and salt (the *mola* ['grain mixed with salt sprinkled on sacrificial animals']) into the fire at sacrifices." Svartengren: 305–6. *

A135. *Asses' bridge*
NQ 1884 VI/9: 389.

The same as Pons Asinorum. 'A humorous name now given to the fifth proposition of the first book of Euclid's Elements'; hence 'an ignorant fellow'. The author of the note writes: "What is the earliest mention of this? I have seen it stated that the application of the appellation to *Euclid,* i. 5, is a modern error, and that the original asses' bridge was the proposition, 'Any two sides of a triangle are together greater than the third side', the demonstration being that an ass at A will walk along the third side AB to his provender at B, rather then climb the bridge ACB formed by the other two. Can anyone confirm this?" No answer followed. OED: 1607.

A136. *As sick as a cat*
NQ 1868 IV/2: 530.

It is seemingly the beginning of the phrase whose second half is *with eating rats.* Cats, according to the note, do become sick if they eat the rat they succeed in killing. Svartengren: 162–3. OED: 1915.

A137. *As sick as a horse*
NQ 1885 VI/12: 109, 134.

A horse, the writer explains, is unable to vomit. Therefore, its nausea is more noticeable and enduring. Svartengren: 163. EDD: *Sick*; OED: 1765.

A138. *As silent as a fish*
NQ 1924, 146: 8, 52, 272; 1924, 147: 452.

The entertaining correspondence on this simile shows that many fishes make various, sometimes loud sounds. *

A139. *As slow as old Jon Walker's chimes*
NQ 1889 VII/8: 368, 473.

John Walker was known as a character whose chimes went slowly. The writer quotes a short poem to this effect: "Old John Walker's chimes,/ They went so very slow,/ That old John Walker could scarcely tell/ Whether they went or no" (p. 368). [The joke is apparently based on the fact that the character's name is Walker, but his chimes do not move.] Svartengren: 373. *

A140. *As sore as a pup*
ANQ 9, 1970: 41; 1971: 135.

Both the query (by Archer Taylor, a great folklorist) and the comment present interest. In his reply, B. Hunter Smeaton indicated that the noun after *as* need not make sense, for the prosody of the formula carries the bulk of the message and diminishes or even eliminates its sense; hence *drunk as a lord, mad as a wet hen,* and the like. Alliteration also comes in useful *(pleased as punch)*. In any case, pups are not more prone to anger than any other pets. *

A141. *As sound as a dollar*
ANQ 6, 1946: 56; ANQ 6, 1947: 158.

According to one suggestion (p. 56), "in the auricular test given to coins, the coin is dropped on a hard surface and its quality gauged by the nature of the resulting ring." But the correspondent on p. 158 believes that *sound* here means simply 'of high quality'. *

A142. *As sound as a roach*
NQ 1874 V/2: 274, 314, 458, 525; 1875 V/3: 37, 98, 197; 1914 XI/10: 468; 1915 XI/11: 18, 96.

A French analog has been pointed out: "Mr. Walcott asserts very positively that St. Roche, and not the fish called a roach, is alluded to in this saying; but is he aware that the same saying exists in French? 'Sain comme un gardon' is literally 'as sound as a roach.' How are we to account for this coincidence, except by some supposed quality in the fish?" (p. 458). According to the suggestion on p. 314, St. Roche was invoked against pestilence. Ray translated German *gesund wie ein Fisch* 'sound as a fish' using *trout* (see the next item). One of the discussants was Hensleigh Wedgwood (p. 525). Svartengren: 154. EDD: *Sound/Roach*; OED: 1655.

A143. *As sound as a trout*
NQ 1874 V/2: 224, 274.

This simile is old and common on both sides of the Atlantic. Furnivall (p. 224) quoted it from *Cursor Mundi*. EDD: *Trout*; OED: 1599.

A144. *As sour as a crab*
NQ 1912 XI/6: 36.

In this simile, *crab* means 'crab apple'. Somerset, Wiltshire. *

A145. *As sour as a grig*
NQ 1912 XI/6: 36.

Here a grig is the bullace (wild plum); thus, no connection with *grig* 'cricket' (see *Merry as a grig*). Svartengren: 155. Somerset, Wiltshire. EDD: *Grig.**

A146. *As sour as a wig*
NQ 1912 XI/5: 326, 434.

In this simile, *wig* = *whig* = *whey*. Apperson: 1854. *

A147. *As straight as a die*
NQ 1872 IV/9: 119, 185, 249, 345, 448, 520; 1872 IV/10: 51, 138.

"This old phrase is usually applied to a very distinct, clear, and inevitable course of action, and is derived of a 'straight', true, and regulated descent of a 'die' by the old method of stamping metal before the screw-press came into such general use" (IV/9: 185). The variants *as clean as a die* and *as clear as a die* exist too. *As straight as a candle* has also been recorded (and see the next item). C. Chattock (p. 51) insisted that the phrase should have been *as level as a die*. However, on p. 249, the correspondent pointed out that "if not shaped with the utmost exactness, the dice would be false and worse than useless." To this remark it was objected (p. 345) that in such a case the saying should have been "as square as the dice." In the remaining part of the exchange, the same arguments were repeated: should a die be straight, square, or level? Svartengren: 273–4. OED: 1857.

A148. *As straight as a loitch*
NQ 1882 VI/5: 28, 177, 337.

The suggested explanations include *loitch = loach* (a straight fish), *larch, leech,* and 'a wooden spindle'; the phrase is synonymous with *as straight as a roach.* (Yorkshire.) Svartengren: 276. *

A149. *As stupid as an owl*
NQ 1938, 174: 394.

[All the demeaning phrases about owls probably refer to the bird's blindness by day. In proverbs, the bat shares the same fortune.] Svartengren: 51. OED: 1882.

A150. *As sure as a gun*
NQ 1854, I/10: 264.

The correspondent asks: "Does the above saying take its origin from the circumstance of a gun being regularly fired at sunrise and sunset from all castles and other fortified places, as well as from ships at sea?" Svartengren: 357. OED: a1640 *(right as a gun)* and 1655 *(as sure as a gun).*

A151. *As sure as eggs is eggs*
NQ 1864 III/6: 203; Athenæum 1861, 2: 883.

The article in *The Athenæum* by A. de Morgan suggests that this is an alteration of *x is x.* Allegedly, *eggs* is a "corruption" (hence *is* instead of *are*). The same author gives a summary of the article in *NQ.* Svartengren: 356. OED: 1857.

A152. *As sure as God's in Gloucestershire*
NQ 1861 II/11: 310.

"Such was the former fruitfulness of Glocestershire, that it is (by William of Malmesbury, in his *Book of Bishops*) said to return the seed with an increase of an hundred-fold. Others find a superstitious sense therin, supposing God by his gracious presence more peculiarly fixed in this county, where there were more and richer mitred abbeys than in any two shires of England besides." Svartengren: 354. OED: 1721.

A153. *As sure as there is a hip on a goat*
NQ 1899 IX/4: 187, 461.

Only a question on p. 187 (which remained unanswered) appeared about the meaning of the simile. Butler wrote in *Hudibras* "So shepherds use/ To set the same mark on the hip,/ Both of their sound and rotten sheep" (p. 461). These lines may contain an allusion to the phrase. [In trying to explain the meaning of obscure English idioms, interpreters rather often refer to Old Scandinavian myths. Most such references should be discarded, but see *Sow one's wild oats, to*! In one of the better-known myths, the god Thor slaughtered his goats, and his companions were invited to eat the meat; he only warned them not to touch the bones. Yet the host's son sucked the marrow from a bone. When Thor resuscitated the animals, one of the goats was lame. This is a typical case of ritual mutilation in Scandinavian mythology. Could **A153** be an echo of Thor's adventure, assuming that the tale had currency in the Middle period, for example in the North?] Svartengren: 359. *

A154. *As tall as the Devil's nutting bag*
NQ 1899 IX/4: 478.

See *As black as the Devil's nutting bag.*

A155. *As the crow flies*
NQ 1904 X/1: 204, 296, 372, 432.

'In a straight line'. The correspondents cited Brewer; and allegedly, "[e]very one has seen the crow flying home at the end of the day, going, as Dr. Brewer says, straight to its point of destination" (p. 372). OED: 1803 *(the crow's road)* and 1810 *(as the crow flies).*

A156. *As the Devil walking through Athlone*
NQ 1900 IX/5: 336, 425, 464; 1900 IX/6: 14.

'Furiously'. The reference is to the devastating march of Cromwell's army in Ireland. *

A157. *As the sow fills, the draff sours*
NQ 1865 III/8: 57.

The phrase refers sarcastically to someone who eats something and disparages the food. The proverb *It's the still (quiet) sow that eats up the draff* is known in Scotland. Apperson: 1639. Hislop (44). *

A158. *As thick as inkle-makers*
NQ 1908 X/10: 186, 235; 1891 VII/12: 206, 394.

This is said about very close friends with reference to the narrowness of the loom. The phrase was "obviously derived from the woolen manufacture, which gave employment in the district." It "is explained by the fact that when the tape *(inkle)* was woven by hand, one tape to a loom, the weavers had to work very close together." P. 235 contains an antedating to the *OED*'s *inkle* (1532). (West Country.) [The reference is to the first edition, but the Supplement missed this note. Hyamson, p. 197–8: "An alternative derivation is from the secrecy with which the Flemish weavers who introduced the industry into England in the 16th cent[ury] geared their craft. These weavers were few in number, and forming a close corporation amid alien surroundings, became proverbial for their mutual friendship." He does not indicate his source, but, if the phrase has Flemish roots, Skeat's suggestion begins to look probable. He notes that the origin of the word is unknown and adds: "Perhaps from Middle Dutch *enckel,* Dutch *enkel,* single, as opposed to double; but there is no obvious connexion." Weekley copied this explanation. In any case, *inkle* is not related to *inkling,* whose origin, contrary to what is often said, is known.] Svartengren: 327. EDD: *Thick/Inkle.*

A159. *As throng as Throp's wife*
NQ 1850 I/1: 485; 1923 XII/12: 70.

Throng means 'busy'. It is not improbable that the reference is opprobrious. See also *As queer as Tim's wife looked when she hanged herself.* Svartengren: 123–4. OED: 1828 *(as thrang as Throop wife).* EDD: *Throng.*

A160. *As true as the Devil's in Dublin city*
NQ 1880 VI/2: 309; 1881 VI/3: 296, 418.

Some people referred to a neighborhood in Dublin once called Hell, others to Devilina, Dublin's name in Higden's *Polychronicon.* * [One wonders whether alliterating phrases like *God in Gloucestershire* (A152) and *Devil in Dublin* ever had any foundation in fact.]

A161. *As true steel as Ripon rowels*
LA I, 1873: 283, 306–7.

"I take the following . . . from Nichols' 'Fuller's Worthies,' ii., 494:'As true Steel as *Rippon Rowels.* It is said of trusty persons, *men of metall,* faithfull in their imployments. . . . Indeed, the best *Spurs* of England are made at Ripon, a famous Town in this County, whose *Rowels* may be inforced to strike through a *Shilling,* and will *break* sooner than *bow*" (pp. 306–7). *

A162. *As warm as a bat*
NQ 1873 IV/12: 168, 215, 376; 1901 IX/8: 142, 293.

Bat means 'coal' (regional; two other names for it are *bath* and *bass*). It can also mean 'turf cut for burning; a slaty piece of coal that will not burn, but retains the heat for a long time'. A correspondent from Scotland (p. 215) heard *as warm as a bap,* that is, the flat breakfast roll peculiar to the 'land 'o cakes'. A hot brick could also be called a bat (p. 293). *

A163. *As weak as a rat*
NQ 1868 IV/1: 434.

See *As dead as a rat.* Svartengren: 393. OED: 1840.

A164. *As wet as thack*
NQ 1857 II/3: 383, 439.

Thack means 'thatch'. As explained in II/3: 439: "Thatch is always thoroughly soaked before it is applied to a building or rick. Hence the phrase." Svartengren: 301. Apperson: 1889. EDD: *Wet.* *

A165. *As wick as a scopril*
NQ 1926, 150: 370, 428, 447; 1926, 151: 33.

'Very quick and lively'. The usual spelling of *scopril* is *scopperill,* a word known in many northern British dialects and noted in the *EDD.* Its meanings vary: 'spinning top, teetotum; squirrel; bone foundation for a button; a term of reproach'. Also, *maggot* has been recorded in place of *scopperill. Wick = quick* 'living', as in *quicksilver, the quick and the dead,* and *touch to the quick.* *

A166. *As wise as the women of Mungret*
NQ 1858, II/6: 208, 253.

Ferrar's anecdote told in his *History of Limerick* is quoted (II/6: 208). It runs as follows: "A deputation was sent from the college at Cashel to this famous seminary at Mungret in order to try their skill in the languages. The heads of the house of Mungret were somewhat alarmed lest their scholars should receive a defeat, and their reputation be lessened. They, therefore, thought of a most humorous expedient to prevent the contest, which succeeded to their wishes. They habited some of their young students like women, and some of the monks like peasants, in which dresses they walked a few miles to meet the strangers at some distance from each other. When the Cashel professors approached, and asked any question about the distance of Mungret, or the time of the day, they were constantly answered in Greek or Latin; which occasioned them to hold a conference, and determined them not to expose themselves at a place where even the women and peasants could speak Greek and Latin." Similar trickster tales have been recorded elsewhere, but the eloquent rustic described on p. 253 is a male (no less a person than Roger Bacon). *

A167. *As wise as Waltham's calf*
NQ 1882 VI/5: 7, 136; 1929, 157: 227, 247.

In vol. 157, two long versions are cited, both illustrating the calf's stupidity. This is the note by William Platt: 'As wise as Waltham's calf', is a proverb which belongs exclusively to Essex, but is frequently applied to other places of the name of Waltham, in Berkshire and elsewhere, and varies in form. In the *Brainles Blessing of the Bull,* c. 1571 (Mr . Huth's vol. 335), it runs thus: 'For Waltham's calves to Tiburne needs must go To sucke a bull and meete a butcher's axe' (p. 136). On p. 7, the same phrase dated to 1647 is given. Svartengren: 48–9. Apperson: 1570. *

A168. *At bay*
NQ 1873 IV/12: 14, 116; 1881 VI/3: 149; 1881 VI/4: 353, 412; 1882 VI/5: 89.

To keep somebody or something at bay 'to hold off a disaster by keeping a dangerous opponent at a distance'. The phrase is an ossified hunting metaphor. *Bay* here means 'bark'. A cornered animal is too tired to keep running, faces its pursuers, and dares them attack it. The dogs stay away and wait for the hunter to shoot it. In the meantime, they bark and are kept literally at bay. The source of the phrase is French. In the fifteenth century, people said *to bring (turn,* etc.) *at a bay,* but the correct reading may be *at abay,* for Old French had *abay* and *aboy* (Modern French *aboi*). The origin of *bay* in *at bay* has often been discussed, but the history of the word's source can be separated from the meaning of the phrase and the reference to hunting. Wedgwood initially traced *at bay* to Italian *stare at bada* 'to stand at gaze', and his etymology was often repeated, but he let Frank Chance convince him that the source was French (VI/4: 353 and VI/5: 89–90). However, he had some suggestions on the development of the French idiom. [F&F (p.115) discuss at length the idea that the ancients attached great significance to the bay tree. They refer to "one source". This source is Brewer, who wrote about the bay, the tree of Apollo. This hypothesis seems to be without merit, like many others deriving English idioms from old myths.] OED: *a*1314.

A169. *At Dulcarnon*
NQ 1852, I/5: 180, 252, 254, 325.

'In a difficult situation'. This very old phrase is included here because as late as the middle of the 19th century some people still used it. OED: *a*1374.

A170. *At gaze*
NQ 1855 I/12: 106, 194.

This "is a term used in stag-hunting. When the stag first hears the hounds, he looks around in all directions, and is said to be 'at gaze', that is, in doubt or apprehension of an unseen danger. In heraldry, the hart, stag, buck, or hind, when borne in coat armour full-faced, is said to be 'at gaze'." EDD: *At*; OED: 1578.

A171. *At outs*
NQ 1912 XI/6: 447.

'At variance'. "It occurs in the congressional debates of 1884, and is probably an Americanism." EDD: *At*; OED: 1824.

A172. *At sixes and sevens*
NQ 1851 I/3: 425; 1874 V/2: 20; 1902 IX/9: 427; 1902 IX/10: 55, 95; 1903 IX/11: 266; 1913 XI/8: 190, 238.

'In a state of confusion'. The note in I/3: 425 suggests a connection with a verse from the book of Job. The author of the note in IX: 55 seeks the origin of the idiom in the process of teaching arithmetic. Skeat (IX/10: 95) rejects this explanation and refers to gambling or dice. The idiom first turned up in Chaucer's *Troylus and Criseyde* in the form *set on sex and seven,* an alteration of the French dicing idiom *set on cinque and sice* 'to risk everything', *six and seven* being the highest numbers (its original sense was also 'to do something in reckless disregard of the consequences'). The change from *five and six* to *six and sevens* remains unexplained, unless (as suggested in XI/8: 238) the reason is that six and seven make the unlucky number thirteen. [Could alliteration prompt the change? Funk, p. 179, cites one more unlikely hypothesis, but, unfortunately, does not cite his source. It seeks an explanation in the Arabic numerals 6 and 7, which he points out, extend higher and lower respectively in a line of figures than do the others, hence, that these two are irregular." Allen (p. 667) cites two more improbable explanations.] JBK I, 132. OED: 1374.

A173. *Ax(e) to grind*
ANQ 1, 1888: 55.

'To have private interests to serve'. The authorship of the phrase has been claimed for several people, including Benjamin Franklin. The note also mentions Charles Miner, editor and proprietor of the *West Chester Village Record,* as someone who coined the idiom, but no chronology is given. [Holt, p. 10: "OED's first reference is to Miner's 1811 use of the phrase, when Franklin was already twenty-one years old." Funk (p. 71) retells the story and gives the same explanation for the confusion as Holt: Miner's story "was reprinted later in a collection, *Essays from the Desk of Poor Robert the Scribe,* confused by many people with *Poor Richard's Almanac* and for that reason associated with Franklin."] OED: 1815.

B

B1. *Babies in the eyes*
NQ 1893 VIII/3: 181; 1902 IX/9: 405, 516; 1902 IX/10: 56, 195, 299.
This was a favorite phrase in seventeenth-century English poetry. The "Babies" in the eyes of the amorous man were probably Cupids. OED: 1607 *(Mine eyes lookt babies in).*

B2. *Back and fill, to*
MM 1, 1911: 56.
'To hesitate'. The idiom is said to be nautical in origin. OED: 1777.

B3. *Bad form*
NQ 1890 VII/10: 308, 458.
The phrase and its opposite were considered Oxford slang. But, according to a former student, at Cambridge, they "generally imagined that the expression 'good form' and 'bad form' were metaphors borrowed from the cricket-ground, the cinder-path, and the river" (p. 458). OED: *good form* (1868), *bad form* (1883).

B4. *Bad money drives out good*
ANQ 7, 1969: 89.
This is "the great fundamental law of the currency," rather than an a proverb. It is usually but wrongly believed that the law was first formulated by Elizabeth I's counselor Gresham. However, he was indeed familiar with the principle (Knowles, p. 10). *

B5. *Bag and baggage*
NQ 1879, V/12: 229, 293, 457; 1880 VI/1: 125; 1912 XI/6: 108; MCNNQ 6, 1885: 124.
'With all belongings saved, *etc*'. The notes are interesting only in that they contain several sixteenth-century examples. [The attraction of the phrase seems to depend on its alliterative tautology. Hyamson, p. 30: "Originally all the property of an army. 'Bag' was an allusion to the soldier's receptacle for his portable property; 'baggage' was the term used for the female followers of an army, either from the baggage wagons in which they rode or from Ital. *bagascia,* harlot." The *OED* sees no no need to invoke the influence from French *bagasse* on Engl. *baggage* 'rubbish', which is found in Spanish *bagage*.] EDD: *Bag*; OED: 1525.

B6. *Bags I*
NQ 1870, IV/6: 415, 517; 1871, IV/7: 44.
The phrase "asserts a claim to some article or privilege" (p. 415). Allegedly, "it expresses a resolve on the part of the speaker to bag or pocket (American, *trowser*) anything" (p. 517). It "evidently carries with it the idea of getting into one's possession or into one's bag the object in question" (p. 44). [Yet the syntax of this phrase remains puzzling and is reminiscent of *Fains I.*] OED: 1866.

B7. *Baker's dozen*

NQ 1862 III/1: 111; 1868 IV/2: 464; ANQ 2, 1889: 223; M&M I: 23.

'Thirteen'. Walter W. Skeat wrote (1868): "I do not know if the following passage in the *Liber Albus* has been noticed. It occurs at p. 232 of the translation by Mr. Riley: 'And that no baker of the town shall give unto the regratresses the six pence on Monday morning by way of Hansel-money, or the three pence on Friday for curtesy-money; but, *after the ancient manner,* let him give thirteen articles of bread for twelve'. That is, the retailers of bread from house to house were allowed a thirteenth loaf by the baker, as a payment for their trouble." (See *Thirteen to the Dozen,* below.) The author of the note on p. 223 refers to a 1588 passage in Arber's reprint of *Martins Mar-Prelate*: "I will owe you a better turne, and pay it you with advantage, at the least thirteen to the dozen," but no baker is mentioned there. [M&M I:23, refer to "many theories," without citing their sources. They mention three such theories: 1) "The practice developed of giving thirteen loaves on every order for twelve, thereby guaranteeing that there would be no penalty for shortages"; 2) "It [the phrase] developed by analogy from *printer's* dozen, for in the early days of publishing it was the custom of printers to supply the retailer with thirteen cop-ies of a book on each order of twelve," and 3) "It seems that the bakers of the medieval period had such a bad name that the word *baker* and *devil* were sometimes used interchangeably." All three "theories" look risky, but in connection with the third see *Pull devil, pull baker.* It may perhaps be worth noticing that the Russian for *baker's dozen* is *the Devil's dozen (chertova diu-zhina).* The Russian phrase is hardly native, because in other languages, including English, the same phrase has been recorded. But *baker's* seems to be uniquely English. Is it possible that the original, unattested variant in English was also *the Devil's dozen,* replaced later by *baker's dozen,* under the influence of the popular puppet show?] OED: 1599.

B8. *Banbury saint*

NQ 1887 VII/3: 128, 158, 252.

'A particularly rigid Puritan'. "A 'Banbury saint' was a Puritan, or rather a particularly rigid, or silly, or even hypocritical Puritan. The expression is explained in several of the usual books of reference, as Nares's 'Glossary,' Halliwell's 'Dictionary of Archaic Words,' which give refer-ences to passages in which a parallel phrase occurs, under 'Banbury'. Mr. S. R. Gardiner, in his 'History of England,' vol. viii. p. 93, in speaking of the resistance to ship-money, under the year 1635, says: 'Banbury, that most Puritan of all Puritan towns, in which, according to a jest which obtained some circulation, men were in the habit of hanging their cats on Monday for catching mice on Sunday,' with a reference to Braithwait's 'Drunken Barnaby.' The name or epithet 'Banbury' was applied in a depreciatory sense before the Puritan times, as may be seen by the quotation 'before 1535', given by Dr. Murray in 'A New English Dictionary' from Latimer."*

B9. *Banbury story*

NQ 1887 VII/3: 403.

Despite the existence of the phrase *Banbury saint* (see it above), the correspondent suggested that *Banbury story* meant 'horsey slang' and might go back to the rhyme "Ride a cock-horse to Banbury Cross/ To see a fine lady ride on a white horse." He also suggested why and how

Nicholas Cox, the author of the book *Gentleman's Recreations,* could have coined this phrase. It remains unclear whether *Banbury story* is a collocation at all known to English speakers. *

B10. *Barnard castle*
NQ 1863, III/3: 232.
Barnard Castle is said "of a person who is guilty of a circumlocutory act." This saying was (still is?) known in some parts of the county of Durham, where the town called Barnard Castle is situated. It has been suggested that the numerous negative references to Barnard Castle go back to the uprising of the north, later quelled by Elizabeth I. Sir George Bowes referred to fight with the rebels, but "poor Barnard Castle has always been the butt of the Bishoprics." *

B11. *Bear away the bell bastard, to*
NQ 1856 II/2: 487; GM 50, 1780: 515.
'To win; to have success'. The saying was known to Ray: "A bell was a common prize. For example, a little golden bell was the reward to victory in 1607 at the races near York" *(GM).* "The saying signifies the greatest ignominy imaginable." Perhaps *(NQ)* the phrase *bell bastard,* used about an illegitimate child of a woman who is herself illegitimate, goes back to that saying. See the next item. *

B12. *Bear off the bell, to*
SNQ 3, 1889: 62.
'To get the prize'. The phrase seems to have originated in the game of racing for a bell. See the previous item. [Edwards, at *bell,* p. 55, gives the following explanation: "To 'bear the bell' is a proverbial expression to denote one who has achieved some distinction. By some it is thought to allude to the practice of attaching a bell to the neck of the most courageous sheep in a flock; but a more probable origin is in the custom which formerly prevailed of giving silver bells as prizes in horse-racing; the winner of a race being said to 'bear away the bell'"]. *

B13. *Bearskin jobber*
NQ 1884 VI/6: 9, 53, 73.
'A speculator for a fall'. The discusants agreed that the phrase goes back to the proverb *sell not the bear's skin before you have caught him,* with exact anologues in several other West European languages. Shakespeare in *Henry V,* IV:3 alluded to *the man that once did sell the lion's skin / While the beast lived* (he "was killed with hunting the animal"). OED: 1728. The reference is to the passage in Defoe that initiated the correspondence.

B14. *Beat a (the) dog before the lion, to*
NQ 1874 5/II: 144; 1894, VIII/5: 407–8, 457; 1894 VIII/6: 76, 377.
'To punish a small offender, in order to frighten a more serious one'. Walter W. Skeat (1874) referred to Chaucer and Shakespeare and wondered whether the saying has its source in Greek or Latin. Cotgrave gives a French version of it and a gloss (quoted by Skeat). In 1894 (VIII/5: 407–8), in response to the same query, he reprinted his old note. Apperson: 1368. *

B15. *Beaten to a mummy*

NQ 1853 I/7: 206.

The writer of the note wondered why one is beaten "to a mummy" if a mummy is supposed to preserve the corpse intact. Is *mummy* an alteration of *mammock* 'a broken piece'? The *OED* lists 'pulp' among other senses of *mummy* without comment. OED: 1693 *(I'll beat thee into Mummy)*.

B16. *Beat the hoof, to*

NQ 1867 III/11: 443.

'To walk'. "One of the minor punishments in our cavalry regiments is still called 'pad drill', where the culprit for a certain time walks back and forwards on a limited portion of the barrack yard, carrying not only his own but also his horse's accouterments." Cf. *Pad the hoof, to.* OED: 1687.

B17. *Beauty sleep*

NQ 1871, IV/7: 143, 419; 1889 VII/8: 429; 1890 VII/9: 33; 1932, 163: 119.

'The sleep before midnight'. The queries about the origin of the phrase were not answered. Northern England and Scotland. OED: 1828.

B18. *Bed of roses*

NQ 1911 XI/4: 126, 176, 216.

To lie on a bed of roses 'to occupy a position of complete comfort'. In *Ossian*, the phrase *the bed of roes* occurs, but despite the confusion *the bed of roses* has an independent existence. OED: 1576.

B19. *Bee in one's bonnet, a*

NQ 1866 III/9: 325; 1897 VIII/11: 260.

'A whim'. From the editor's note: "There is a bee in your bonnet, equivalent to the English proverb 'There's a maggot in your head'" (p. 325). The Scotch variant is: "There is a maggot in your bonnet-case" (p. 260). OED: 1553 *(hede full of beis)* and 1845 *(bee in his bonnet)*.

B20. *Before one can say Jack Robinson*

NQ 1852 I/6: 415; 1876, V/6: 287; 1909 X/11: 232, 317, 357; 1915 XI/12: 279, 387.

'In a very short time'. Grose's explanation is quoted in I/6 [a fanciful allusion to the "very volatile gentleman of that name"]. For *Jack Robinson* "an old play" has *Jackie robys on* (p. 279). The following conjectures (all on p. 232) may be worth quoting: 1) "John Robinson, at one time chaplain to the British Embassy in Sweden, became Bishop of London in 1714, and d. 1723. He was a fierce debater in the House of Lords." 2) "An umbrella was called a Robinson at Paris in the time of Marie Antoinette, when 'Robinson parties' were given by her at Versailles and at St. Cloud; and the name thus became a part of French argot. There was a "village Robinson" between Sceaux and Plessis, where rude huts, either on the ground or in the forks of great trees, served as refreshment rooms; and another on an island in the Seine. The suggestion is that visitors, overtaken by rain, would call out "Jacques! Robinson," and the rain sometimes came down before they could call for the umbrellas. 3) "Jack Robinson, who became the mark for Cobbett's satire, was the first Earl of Ripon. He boasted of the prosperity of the country, and, when a financial crash came, Cobbett called him prosperity Robinson; and it was said that the crisis arrived 'before one could say Jack Robinson'". The statement that Sheridan coined the phrase is inconsistent with chronology. An earlier form *before ye could cry Jack Robinson* appears on p. 387. [Holt, p. 23, dismissed Grose's conjectures that Jack Robinson used to make flying visits of extraordinary brevity and that a 19th-century song by Hudson first used the phrase (it is found in Fanny Burney *Evelina,* 1778). He does not name his sources, but he may have found the reference to the volatile gentleman not in Grose but in Hyamson, p. 201. Holt believed that *Jack Robinson* was nothing more than a "name familiar to all, and easy to say," for it "is in the very forefront of common names in England."] OED: 1763.

B21. *Be good to yourself*
NQ 1905 X/3: 116.

According to the note, this is what in 1905 Americans said at parting. [Is this what has become *have a good one?*] *

B22. *Benefit of clergy*
GM 89, 1819: 305.

"The art of reading made a very slow progress. To encourage it in England, the capital punishment of death was remitted if the criminal could read, which is termed Benefit of Clergy." OED: 1500.

B23. *Berm woman*
MCNNQ 5, 1884: 328, 329.

"This means a woman who sells berm, or barm. Such women used to be well-known on the streets of old Lancashire towns; where they went from door to door, crying 'Dun yo want ony berm?' and they carried a great can-full of berm with them; and a kind of ladle-measure, to serve it out in penny-worths." *

B24. *Beside the cushion*
NQ 1891 VII/12: 368, 513.

'Beside the point'. Apparently, obsolete. Numerous examples are cited in the notes. OED: 1576.

B25. *Better the day, the better the deed, the*
NQ 1870 IV/5: 147, 249, 285, 548.

Perhaps this proverb means "on a great day great deeds should be performed," but other interpretations have also been offered. The saying may be a rendering of the French proverb *bon jour, bonne œuvre.* Apperson: 1607. *

B26. *Between a rock and a hard place*
ANQ 17, 1978: 61.

This familiar phrase was recorded in the 1920s mainly in Arizona with the sense 'to be bankrupt'. The old idiom refers to the difficulty of navigating between Scylla and Charybdis *(hard place = difficult place).* OED: 1921.

B27. *Between the beetle and the block*
NQ 1902 IX/9: 12.

Beetle was the name of a sledge-like instrument, and such could be the word's meaning here. Cf. the explanation at *As deaf as a beadle.* OED: 1590.

B28. *Between the Devil and the deep sea*
NQ 1901 IX/7: 449; 1901 IX/8: 48; 1902 IX/9: 360; 1903 IX/12: 128, 272; 1921 XII/9: 371; ANQ 2, 1889: 119; MM 1, 1911: 32 (17).

'Exposed to danger on both sides'. "The expression is made use of by Colonel Munro in his *Expedition with Mackay's Regiment,* published in London, 1637. In the engagement between the forces of Gustavus Adolphus and the Austrians, the Swedish gunners, for a time, had not given their pieces proper elevation, and their shots came down among Lord Reay's men, who were in the service of the King of Sweden. Munroe did not like this sort of play, which kept him and his men, as he expressed it, *between the devil and the deep sea.* So an officer was sent to the batteries with the request that the guns should be raised, but several of Lord Reay's soldiers were killed before the mistake was rectified. Monroe's meaning seems to be that he was in a fix, exposed to danger from friends as well as foes—and that there was no means of escape" *(MM).* See also the comment at *Devil to pay and no pitch hot.* The explanation quoted above may be true, but for curiosity's sake compare the following: "It has been suggested to me that this phrase was adopted, if not originated, by the Royalists in allusion to Cromwell, 'the deep C.', the relationship of the devil to the deep 'C.' being implied in a book or pamphlet of the time entitled 'A True and Faithful Narrative of Oliver Cromwell's Compact with the Devil for Seven Years on the day on which he gained the Battle of Worcester. Printed and Sold by W. Boreham at the Angel in Paternoster Row, 6d." (IX/8: 48). The phrase, the English equivalent of Latin *inter sacrum et saxum* ['between the altar and the stone' (in Plautus, *inter sacrum saxumque*)], is also found as *between the Devil and the dead sea.* [It has been suggested that here too *devil* means 'the seam on the ship's deck nearest the side, hence a most dangerous one to walk or file with pitch'. Anyone between the devil and the deep (blue) sea had a very narrow footing, a narrower margin for choice. Funk (p. 538) heard and quoted this explanation from a correspondent but did not mention the story told in the entry above.] OED: 1621 (with *dead* for *deep*).

B29. *Between the dog and the wolf*
NQ 1928, 155: 100.

'At dusk'. This is the editorial note: "'Entre le chien et le loup', as an expression for the dusk, is explained as signifying the hour when dog and wolf are indistinguishable; or, again, as the hour when the dog goes home and the wolf comes out." *

B30. *Binsey, God help me!*
NQ 1851 I/3: 44.

A phrase of the same type as *Crawley, God help us* and *Tickhill, God help me* (see them below). Binsey is a village between Oxford and Godstow. Cf. *From Lincoln heath, God help me; Melverley, God help me,* and *Saffron Walden, God help me.* *

B31. *Biscuit's throw*

NQ 1909 X/12: 326, 376.

'A very short distance'. Synonymous with *within a stone's throw*. This is a nautical phrase. Apparently, hard ship's biscuits are meant. OED: 1834.

B32. *Bishop's had his foot in it, the*

NQ 1849, I/1: 87; 1876 V/5: 49, 333; 1884 VI/10: 226; BrA November 24–6, #83: 2.

The phrase is (or was) traditionally said by women when some food in the process of cooking burns. Edward Solly (NQ V/5: 333) gave Tyndale's *Obedyence of a Chrysten Man* (p. 109), 1528, as the source. The saying has also been derived from French. Other derivations are mere conjectures. The basis of the saying is that *bishop's foot* means 'something causing harm'. *The British Apollo* could suggest only the following explanation: "We presume 'tis a proverb that took its origin from the unhappy times when every thing that went wrong, was thought to have been spoil'd by the Bishops." See also the next item. Apperson: 1528. EDD: *Bishop*. *

B33. *Bishop that burneth, the*

NQ 1849 I/1: 87.

In Suffock, ladybirds (ladybugs) were (still are?) called Bishop Barnaby. Whether the phrase alludes to those insects as unwelcome guests in a dairy or to the "bishop who had his foot in it" (see it above) remains unclear. The connection between the ladybird and "Bishop Barnaby" is equally obscure. *

B34. *Black Maria*

NQ 1883 VI/7: 355; 1893 VIII/4: 272; 1901 IX/8: 263.

'A prison van'. The following story appeared on p. 272: "The origin of this name is thus given in a late number of the *Million*:—"During old colonial days, Maria Lee, a negress, kept a sailors' boarding house in Boston. She was a woman of gigantic size and prodigious strength, and was a great assistance to the authorities in keeping the peace, as the entire lawless element of that locality stood in awe of her. Whenever an unusually troublesome person was to be taken to the station-house, the services of Black Maria, as she was called, were likely to be required. It is said that she took at one time, and without assistance, three riotous sailors to the lock-up. So frequently was her help required, that the expression 'Send for Black Maria' came to mean 'Take the disorderly person to gaol.' It is easy to see how the name became fixed to the prison van." [A product of folk etymology? Hyamson, p. 49, also adds somebody's derivation from *black* 'marinated' (transported to a convict-settlement abroad) or 'married' (chained to another prisoner).] OED: 1835.

B35. *Blindman's holiday*

NQ 1852 I/5: 587; 1857 II/3: 137, 218.

This is said about the time at dusk when it is too dark to work without candles and so explained in 1857 II/3: 218. EDD: *Blindman*; OED: 1599.

B36. *Blood is thicker than water*

NQ 1867, III/11: 34, 103, 163; 1888 VII/6: 50-1; 1891 VII/11: 487 1891 VII/12: 53, 78, 114; 1901 IX/8: 238, 428; 1917 XII/3: 356.

'A relative is closer than a stranger'. The meaning of the saying caused little discussion. However, on p. 163, it was suggested that the reference is to the water of baptism, which cannot replace or exceed in value the affinity by blood. It was also pointed out that *thick* here means "closer," as in *thickset* and *thick as thieves.* On p. 51 (1888), exact or very close analogs of this saying are given. The often repeated statement that the proverb appears in Ray's collection is wrong. [Edwards, p. 65, says the following: "Many think that this saying originated with Commodore Tatnall, of the United States Navy, who assisted the English in the Chinese waters, and, in his dispatch to his Government, justified his interference by quoting the words." It is most unfortunate that we are not told who those many are. However, he does not support this derivation, because, in his opinion, the proverb occurs in Ray's 1672 collection.] OED: 1737.

B37. *Blue devils*

NQ 1886 VII/2: 167, 235, 334.

'Deep melancoly'. A few examples dated to the end of the eighteenth century were given in the notes. The quotation from Brewer's *Dictionary of Phrase and Fable* does not go too far: "Indigo dyers are especially subject to melancholy; and those who dye scarlet are choleric. Paracelsus also asserts that blue is injurious to the health and spirits." His reference to German ("the German *blie* (lead), which gives rise to our slang *blue* or *bluey* (lead), seems to bear upon the 'leaden, downcast eyes' of melancholy") is irrelevant. Also, the German for *lead* (the metal) is *Blei.* With regard to an alleged connection between idioms and professions see also *As mad as a hatter.* JBK I, 22. OED: *a*1616.

B38. *Blue nose*

ANQ 7, 1891: 8.

'A nickname of the Nova Scotians'. The note offers the following explanation: "It is the name of a potato which they produce in great perfection and boast to be the best in the world. The Americans have, in consequence, given them the nickname 'Blue Noses'." OED: 1785.

B39. *Blue pencil*

NQ 1916 XII/2: 126, 174, 299.

'Proofreader'. The verb *to blue-pencil* also exists. "In editorial and printing rooms alike the blue pencil has for many years past been a serviceable tool, and for a considerable time the common phrase in which the term is used, either as substantive or verb, invariably signifies condensation or deletion. The use of the blue pencil is chiefly the prerogative of the sub-editor, but the foreman printer finds it handy in numbering the folios and regularizing the style of his 'copy'" (p. 174). OED: 1845.

B40. *Blue pigeon*

NQ 1890 VII/9: 249, 316.

'Fraud' (slang). References to *pigeon* 'dupe'and 'fraud' are common, e.g. *to pluck a pigeon* 'to dupe somebody'. *Blue* may be associated with metal, especially lead, for stripping and stealing lead from a building was a well-known criminal act. OED: 1676.

B41. *Blue plate luncheon*

ANQ 2, 1942: 103; ANQ 5, 1945: 92.

Blue plate special was said to refer to a low-priced meal that usually changes daily. The name "may well have come from the over-popular 'willow pattern' of the chinaware." This explanation poses the question about "when designers introduced the theoretically excellent, but actually disturbing, practice of dividing a large luncheon plate into compartments." Additionally, the correspondent to ANQ 5, 1945 wrote: "There is a possible clue to the source of this expression on page 43 of Dixon Wecter's *The Hero in America* (1941), in the course of a description of Forefathers' Day, a New England tradition first observed in December, 1798. He cites the 1820 celebration—the bicentenary of the landing—as one of particular significance. Daniel Webster, on that occasion, gave one of his finest orations, and the banquet, Wecter reports, was 'eaten from huge blue dinnerplates specially made by Enoch Wood & Sons of Staffordshire'." *

B42. *Bobby dazzler*

MCNNQ 7, 1888: 210, 213.

'A showy man'. *Dazzler* seems to have been a well-known term for a showy woman. It is the addition of *bobby* that makes it applicable to a man, though, according to p. 213, in north Westmoreland, *bobby* is used only for emphasis. Contrary to some statements, *dazzler* is not an Americanism. OED: 1866.

B43. *Bob's a-dying*

MM 51, 1965: 368 (25); MM 53, 1967: 77 (25).

'Great racket; boisterous merriment'. This phrase, cited in the *EDD,* has several variants. It is said about someone making a lot of fuss and has the variant *Bobsy-die.* The derivation is unknown (nautical?). Cf. *Kick up Bob's a-dying.* OED: 1829.

B44. *Body and sleeves*

NQ 1862, III/2: 427.

The phrase "was primarily applicable to the Scots Body Guard in France: for it would seem that the first twenty-four guards, to whom the first Gendarme of France being added, made up the number of twenty-five, were commonly called 'Gards de Manche'—*sleeve* Guards; and were all Scots by nation. Thus, in the time of James VI, 1599, it appeared in answer to his and the Queen-mother (Mary's) remonstrances against the admission of any but Scottish gentlemen, sprung of good families, that 'three-fourths of the Yeomen, as well of the body as of the sleeve, were still Scots.' *

B45. *Bolt from the blue, a*

NQ 1887 VII/3: 388, 522; 1887 VII/4: 212, 333; 1893 VIII/3: 345, 457; 1893 VIII/4: 175, 290, 455; 1894 VIII/5: 56, 236; 1900 IX/6: 29; 1914 XI/10: 448.

'Something utterly unexpected' (like lightning out of a clear sky). The variant *bolt out of the blue* also exists (or existed). In the late 1880s, the idiom sounded new or strange to some, and the association between *bolt* and *thunderbolt* was not obvious. German and French have identical idioms (VIII/3: 345), though in those languages, *thunder* and *lightning* occur in place of *bolt* (VIII/3: 457). After that publication, the discussion moved towards meteorology: Can thunder occur under a clear sky? Another argument centered on the use of metaphors in language. In a trenchant answer to his opponent, whose rejoinder he calls partly finical and partly incorrect, Frank Chance wrote (among many other things): "It seems to me that the expression 'bolt from the blue' may well have had its origin, in part at least, in that form of summer lightning which is usually seen on the horizon of a clear and starlit sky, but which really indicates a storm at such a distance that the clouds are not visible and the thunder is not heard" (VIII/4: 176). The ensuing controversy is instructive and amusing, but it concerns natural phenomena and the figurative use of language and has nothing to do with the origin of the phrase. OED: 1837 *(bolt out of the blue)*.

B46. *Bolton quarter*

NQ 1888 VII/5: 406.

'Present death without mercy'. The phrase "is recorded and explained by Isaac Ambrose in his *Media; or Middle Things,* London, 1650, quarto, p. 72: '1644, May 2. Bolton was taken. Colonel R. Forces Routed, and many a sweet saint slain: no Quarter would be given, so that it grew into a Proverb. 'Bolton-quarter,' that is, present death without mercy'." *

B47. *Boot and saddle*

NQ 1881 VI/3: 86; 1892, VIII/1: 209, 318; 1892, VIII/2: 15, 78.

'A call sounded upon the trumpet before it possessed valves and keys'. Quite probably, an alteration of French *botte selle* 'boot [and] saddle'. So Wedgwood in *TPS* 1855, p. 70. OED: 1697.

B48. *Born and bred*

NQ 1881 VI/4: 68, 275; 1882 VI/5: 77, 112, 152, 213, 318, 375, 416; 1882 VI/6: 17, 259, 496.

See *Bred and born.*

B49. *Born with a silver spoon in one's mouth*

NQ 1928, 154: 367; 1931, 164: 371; 1934, 167: 412.

'Born into a wealthy family of high social standing'. According to S. O. Addy, an active student of antiquities (Vol. 154), the reference is to giving silver spoons to children at their baptism. OED: 1801.

B50. *Box Harry, to*

NQ 1866 III/9: 155; 1893 VIII/3: 128, 237, 275; 1902 IX/9: 449; IX/10: 13, 98; 1916 XII/1: 453.

'To do without food' or occasionally 'to do it on the cheap'. According to John Bee's *Sportsman's Slang,* "Confined truants, without fire, fought or boxed an old figure, nicknamed Harry, which hung up in their prison, to keep heat" (III/9: 155). The phrase was common in northern

England. This is the note by James Hooper in VIII/3: 128 (he was unaware of the earlier discussion): "When George Borrow in the summer of 1854 reached the village of Pentraeth Cock, in Anglesey, Mrs. Pritchard, the hostess, could offer her hungry guest no fresh meat, and, of course, suggested bacon and eggs, where upon the Romany Rye exclaimed, 'I will have the bacon and eggs with tea and bread-and-butter, not forgetting a pint of ale—in a word, I will box Harry'. Later on he explained that a great many years ago, when he was much amongst 'commercial gents', those whose employers were in a small way of business, or allowed them insufficient salaries, frequently used 'box Harry', that is, have a beefsteak or mutton-chop, or perhaps bacon and eggs, with tea and ale, instead of the regulation dinner of a commercial gentleman, namely, fish, hot joint and fowl, pint of sherry, tart, ale and cheese, and bottle of port at the end of all ('Wild Wales,' chap. xxxiii.)." [Can the phrase mean 'to beat the Devil'?] EDD: *Box Harry*; OED: 1823.

B51. *Box the compass, to*
NQ 1916 XII/1: 226.
'To blow in different directions' (said about the wind); 'to come full circle'. According to the note, the phrase goes back to Spanish *boxear el mundo,* etc. with *boxear* meaning 'to go around'. OED: 1753.

B52. *Box the fox, to*
NQ 1916 XII/1: 307, 453.
'To rob an orchard'. *Box* means 'trap'. The note was written by J. H. Murray from Edinburgh, not by James A. H. Murray! Dublin. *

B53. *Braid St. Catharine's tresses, to*
NQ 1878 V/10: 495; 1916 XII/1: 447, 498; 1916 XII/2: 18.
This is a translation of a French saying meaning 'to remain a virgin until marriage'. A long passage from Larousse explaining the custom is quoted. St. Catherine of Alexandria is meant. The editorial note contains the following explanation: "The expression is said to come from the sixteenth or seventeenth century. According to the received French tradition, it became the custom, in certain churches in France in which there was a statue of St. Catherine, to dress the head of the statue afresh for the saint's feast-day, and this service was rendered by young women between the ages of 25 and 35 who were unmarried. There is a modern saying that at 25 a maid puts a first pin into St. Catherine's head-dress; at 30 a second; at 35 the *coiffure* is finished" (p. 498). *

B54. *Brass knockers*
NQ 1878, V/10: 34, 77.
'The next day remains of a dinner party'. Two correspondents on p. 77 suggest that the phrase originated in Anglo-Indian from Hindustani *basi* 'cold' and *khana* 'food; dinner'. *

B55. *Break Priscian's head, to*
NQ 1908 X/9: 268, 375, 414; BrA January 26-8 #101: 2.
'To speak false Latin'. This is probably a transformation of the Renaissance or medieval phrase *diminui Prisciani caput* ['cracked P's head']. "The *locus classicus* for the idea that 'speaking false

Latin' is equivalent to inflicting violent personal injury on Priscian is Nicodemus Frischlin's comedy 'Priscian Vapulans' ['P. Beaten'] (the preface to which is dated 1 Jan., 1584). Here the luckless grammarian is unmercifully beaten with the bad Latin of philosophers, physicians, lawyers, and theologians" (p. 376). OED: *a*1529.

B56. *Break the flag, to*
NQ 1906 X/6: 69, 136, 196.
'To unfurl the flag when the king sets out to sea'. "In the days of Trafalgar flags were shot away, and thus very literally broken from the mast" (p. 69). *

B57. *Break the square(s), to*
NQ 1855, I/12: 273; 1885 VI/12: 198.
'To break the regular order'. Usually the phrase is *it breaks no squares* 'it does not matter'. The note contains only a query about the origin of the phrase. EDD: *Break*; OED: 1860.

B58. *Bred and born*
NQ 1881 VI/4: 68, 275; 1882 VI/5: 77, 112, 152, 213, 318, 375, 416; 1882 VI/6: 17, 259, 496; 1894 VIII/5: 33.
The question was about the word order in this alliterating phrase: why *bred and born,* if one is born first and bred ('educated') later. Many contributors showed that *born and bred* was an equally common variant, but the others defended the place of *bred* before *born.* "The position of these two words is quite correct. Any progeny must be bred before it is born. *Bred* is the passive participle of the verb 'to breed', which has no other meaning than 'to generate'. The objection to the position in question arises from a confounding of the participle *bred* with the entirely separate word *breeding.* This means 'education' or 'bringing up', no doubt. But the substantive *breed* (whence the verb 'to breed') means 'race'. The common phrase 'ill bred', though conventionally used as meaning 'badly brought up', really means much more" (VI/5: 152). "Surely *bred* must be the correct word to take precedence in the above proverb or phrase. We frequently speak of some peculiarity in an individual as being 'bred in the bone'. When we speak of cattle, horses, etc., as also we sometimes do of the human race, as being 'well bred', we undoubtedly do not refer to their education, but to their antecedent breeding; neither does the latter word convey to my mind any analogy to education, which is, I suppose, what is meant when we say of any one that he or she has been well brought up" (VI/5: 318). OED: *a*1340 *(be born and bredde).* Cf. *Born and bred.*

B59. *Bring a noble to nine-pence and nine-pence to nothing, to*
NQ 1865 III/7: 291.
This is said about persons living beyond their means. Cf. *His noble has come down to nine-pence* and see *ninepence* in the index. OED: 1568 *(hath increased a noble iust vnto nine pence).*

B60. *Bring another mayor and another bottle*
NQ 1897 VIII/11: 273.
"Legend has it that a bygone Mayor of Wigan attended some meeting in London, accompanied by various other mayors from provincial centres. After the usual banquet, the mayors one by one succumbed and were carried off to bed. The Mayor of Wigan, alone remaining,

cried out: 'Bring another mayor and another bottle'. This story has long been current in West Lancashire." Cf. *Here's to the mayor of Wigan.* *

B61. *Broach the admiral, to*

NQ 1898 IX/1: 128, 271, 350; 1898 IX/2: 154, 230; 1934, 167: 208, 247.

'To get liquor and become drunk'. *Tap* occurs as a synonym of *broach* in this slangy phrase. There is an apocryphal story that was widely known and is curious as an example of folk etymology: "It is said, I know not on what authority, that when the body of Lord Nelson was brought to this country for burial, it was preserved in a cask of rum, but that the sailors, who at that time would 'stick' at no opportunity which presented itself for 'sucking the monkey', had, before the arrival of the gallant admiral's corpse, drained the cask completely dry by means of the usual straw. Hence the phrase 'tapping the admiral'" (p. 271). In 1934, the same story was alluded to. *

B62. *Bronx cheer*

ANQ 2, 1942: 106-7; ANQ 2, 1943: 156.

'A sound of derision made by blowing through closed lips with the tongue between them'. The same as British *blowing a raspberry.* "Some say the 'cheer' originated at the old Fairmount Athletic Club in The Bronx; others associate it with the Yankee Stadium, also in The Bronx." "Mr. Clarence Edward Heller, in *Our Sunday Visitor,* a Catholic publication, once traced the origin back to the thirteenth century, in the south of Italy. His point was later confirmed by an editor of an Italian paper (published here in the United States) who said that the mouth salute has long been somewhat common in that region." "Damon Runyon says that the cheer (that is, the vulgar form) was 'discovered and titled by 'Tad' [Thomas A. Dorgan (1877-1929)], the great cartoonist, a matter of thirty years ago'. It came about, he states, when 'Tad' made a trip of exploration to the old Fairmount Boxing Club in The Bronx." The explanation came from James J. Lyons, the then President of the Borough of the Bronx (pp. 106-7). Lighter gives a 1927 citation. OED: 1929.

B63. *Broth of a boy*

NQ 1875, V/4: 169.

This is the query by A. L. Mayhew: "Would any Irish scholar tell me whether I am right in supposing that the expression, 'He's a broth of a boy', may originate from the Irish *Broth,* passion, *Brotha,* passionate, spirited, its meaning being, 'He is a lad of spirit'?" No answer followed the query. EDD: *Broth;* OED: 1823.

B64. *Brown and Thompson's penny hotels*

NQ 1904 X/2: 297.

'A popular nickname for two Roman Catholic chapels in Moorfields at the time of the Gordon Riots'. [Lord George Gordon was an agitator. The protestant demonstration against the removal of civil restrictions from Catholics (June 2-7, 1780) became an orgy of mayhem.]*

B65. *Brown study*

NQ 1850 I/1: 352, 418; 1862, III/1: 190; 1880 VI/2: 408; 1881 VI/3: 54; 1882 VI/5: 53; *Nation* 48, 1889: 288.

'A state of intense reverie'. Johnson emphasized the idea of gloomy meditation. Comparison with the imagined *brow study* or *barren study* is useless. But the editor's note in III/1: 190 seems to make sense. French *avoir l'humeur brune* 'to be of a somber, melancholy temperament' suggests the French origin of the English idiom. Engl. *brown* 'gloomy, serious' did not exist, as pointed out in *Nation*'s review of the original *OED*. Apperson: 1300; but his early citations contain only *in a study*. "This form," he says, "persisted for centuries after the inexplicable 'brown' had been introduced." His first example with *brown* (*lead a man into a brown study* is dated 1530, but the *OED* begins its list with 1555 and does not mention the French derivation.) OED: *a*1555.

B66. *Bubble and squeak*

GM 60/2, 1790: 801, 1075.

'Fried beef and cabbages'. The correspondent writing in 1790 (p. 801) believed that the phrase was recent but could not explain it. According to a cook, who was asked about the phrase, the dish "ought to be made of *boiled* beef and cabbage *fried,* and that she supposes it acquired that name from the ingredients in the first instance *bubbling* in the pot, and afterwards *squeaking* in the pan." Wikipedia gives a somewhat different explanation, but, whatever the origin of the phrase, the dish is still popular. OED: 1762.

B67. *Buck fever*

ANQ 2, 1964: 71; ANQ 4, 1966: 121.

'A kind of fever one experiences in the presence of a strong opponent'. This Americanism had its heyday on the sport pages of the 1920–1930s. The variant *buck ague* also exists. OED: 1841.

B68. *Burying has gone by, and the child's called Anthony*

NQ 1874 V/1: 468; V/2: 13, 178; 1891 VII/11: 148, 235; 1917 XII/3: 478.

This is said when a person arrives too late for the occasion. *Berrin'* is the local pronunciation of *burying*. Lancashire. In Craven, it is chiefly schoolboys' slang. Apperson: 1791. *

B69. *Butter out of a dog's mouth*

NQ 1908 X/10: 387.

The phrase is used in two senses: "you can't retrieve what you have lost" and synonymous with "you can't make a silken purse out of a sow's ear," but the reference to the second sense is dubious. Apperson: 1732. *

B70. *Button your lip*

NQ 1868, IV/1: 603; IV/2: 114.

'Shut up!' This was a popular slang expression in the 1860s. Not improbably, it has a Biblical origin. OED: 1601 *(buttoned vp their lips).*

B71. *Buy a pig in a poke, to*
NQ 1854 I/10: 187; 1873 IV/11: 198; ANQ 2, 1889: 247.

'To make a blind bargain'. *Poke* means 'pouch' (Skeat IV/11: 198). The French buy a cat in a poke *(acheter chat en poche)* or are advised not to do so. ANQ 2 gives the French and the Welsh analogs. The note on p. 198 does not comment on the role of alliteration but cites the proverb with the opposite meaning ("When the pig's offered, hold up the poke," that is, never refuse a good offer), so that the connection between *pig* and *poke* is traditional. EDD: *Pig*; OED: *?a*1325 *(Wan man ʒevit þe a pig, opin þe powch).*

B72. *Buy something for a song*
See *Not worth an old song.*

B73. *By-and-by*
NQ 1851 I/3: 73, 109, 193, 229, 433; 1865 III/8: 459; 1883 VI/7: 486, 518; 1883 VI/8: 96, 273, 527; 1884 VI/9: 34, 138; 1889 VII/8: 409.

'Later on'. *By and by* is an evasive collocation, and those who wrote about it in 1851 and 1865 were aware of the difficulty. Except for a few unfortunate guesses ('by the way' and 'goodby'), the suggested glosses are acceptable. It seems that when, much later, the correspondents to *NQ* returned to *by-and-by,* they were unaware of the contributions of their predecessors. The discussion in the early eighties again dealt with the older senses of the phrase, which in the past had reference to space ('side by side'). It could also mean 'in a parallel direction; in due order, successively, gradually, separately, singly'. 'In course of time', a later sense, yielded 'immediately' (so in the Authorized Version of the Bible) and 'after a while', as in Present-Day English. See especially VI/9: 34, Skeat. The latest exchange in *NQ* took place in 1883 and 1884, shortly before the appearance of the first volume of the *OED*. In the dictionary, the material is richer, but Skeat's conclusions are confirmed. Special attention is called to a similar development of *anon* and *presently*. The reference to *presently* is instructive in that it shows how firm Murray's grip on the entire vocabulary of English was at the time the first letters went into print. OED: 1526.

B74. *By and large*
NQ 1926, 150: 209, 249; MM 1, 1911: 56; MM 50, 1964: 70, 326, 329.

'On the whole, comprehensively'. Considering the nautical meaning of *by* and *large,* the phrase must have meant 'to the wind and off it within six points', that is, 'at any point of sailing'. OED: 1627.

B75. *By hook or by crook*
NQ 1850, I/1: 168, 205, 222, 237, 281, 405; I/2: 78, 204; 1851, I/3: 116, 212; 1856 II/1: 522; 1871, IV/8: 133, 196, 464; 1872 IV/9: 77; 1892 VIII/1: 185; 1905 X/3: 409; 1915 XI/11: 66, 215; 1923 XII/12: 473; 1923 XIII/1: 15; MCNNQ 1, 1878: 23; MCNNQ 3, 1881: 95, 98, 106; MCNNQ 4, 1882: 200, 204; ANQ 1, 1888: 68; 1889 VII/8: 306; ANQ 7, 1891: 195, 270.

'By any means available'. In IV/8: 133, Skeat quoted Wyclif; no antedating appears in the *OED*. Thus, the phrase was already known in the second half of the 14th century. Attempts to explain the idiom's origin are numerous. For instance, in IV/8: 196 we read: "This proverb is said to be as old as the English invasion of Ireland. Hook and Crook are well known historic places in the port of Waterford; and the pilots of the invading fleet are said to have declared that they would safely land the invading forces 'by hook or by crook'. It is what may be called a traditional proverb, thus explained, in Waterford and Wexford." The same was said in I/1:222. Especially popular is the following story: "In the great fire of London many boundary marks were destroyed. This, in consequence of many disputes as to the sites of different properties, had a tendency to hinder the rebuilding of the city. In order to escape from the delay, it was decided to appoint two arbitrators, whose decision should be final in all cases. The surveyors appointed were a *Mr. Hook* and a *Mr. Crook,* who gave so much satisfaction in their decisions that the rebuilding proceeded rapidly. From this circumstance comes the saying 'by Hook or by Crook'" (IV/8: 464). This derivation is, to quote the *OED,* at odds with chronology. One may also wonder at the innocence of those who believed in the existence of Mr. Hook and Mr. Crook. According to still another version, there were two judges who in their day decided "most unconscientiously" whenever the interests of the crown were affected, and "it used to be said that the king could get anything by Hooke or by Crooke." Or such judges were famous for the perpetual diversity of opinion, so that every suitor was sure to have either Hook or Crook (allegedly spelled as Croke: see an amusing note in VII/8: 306) on his side. By contrast, the note by E. Smirke deserves to be quoted almost in full: "The use of the expression, *by hook or by crook,* is founded on the old practice of mediæval conveyancers, when they had to frame grants intended to convey or reserve a limited *easement* or grant of dead wood for fuel or other like purposes, over a tract of woodland, which might be available without materially interfering with the more substantial use and profits of the timber for the general purposes of the landowner. On such occasions it was often well worth the while of an adjacent tenant or neighbour to have or reserve a precarious authority to carry away any refuse, dead, or damaged portions of the trees, provided they could be readily removed without material detriment to the owner of the wood, by simple means, falling far short of the more effective axe, bill, or saws incidental to the felling of timber for general purposes. Among these simple modes of removal are the hooked poles, or crooks, by which dry or dead bits of wood can be detached and pulled down from the upper branches of a tree. The ordinary local glossaries supply instances of this kind, such as Halliwell's, Nares', and Grose's; in the latter of which the '*crook-lug,* for pulling down dead branches', is mentioned as a familiar term in Gloucestershire. So we have, in the old French custumals, a right to take 'brancas siccas cum crocco ligneo sive ferreo' ['dry branches with dead wood, without the use of iron'] in royal forests (Ducange, tit. *Branca*), with other authorities in Michelet's *Origines du Droit français*, edition Bruxelles, 1838, pp. 111, 112" (IV/9: 77). [*Hook* and *crook* were interchangeable synonyms; see the *OED,* where *a shepherd's hook* means the same as *a shepherd's crook.* Thus, *by hook or by crook* would be a tautological binomial like *safe and sound,* only based on rhyme instead of alliteration.] ANQ 7, 1891: 68 lists four explanations of the idiom, two of which seem to be little-known: 1) "Wilson's 'Origin of Familiar Words and Phrases' [no bibliography in the world lists this book!] says that it probably means 'foully like a thief or holily like a bishop,' the hook being used by burglars, the crook being the bishop's crozier." 2) "An old London legend tells us that the numerous families of Hook and Crook formerly did the ferry business for the whole of the British metropolis. No odds on what boat you crossed the Thames, you were sure to ride with Hook or Crook." [Again Mr. Hook and

Mr. Crook!] In MCNNQ 4, 1882: 200, still another explanation is offered: "In olden times a man living beyond reach of the few cart-roads of the country could take home his merchandise in but one of two ways—on his own back or on that of a beast of burden. Packmen still carry their bundles at the end of a hooked stick. The simplest pannier was formed of bent poles, and was called a crook, a name still familiar in Devonshire. So, then a man's goods had to be conveyed from place to place, from stow to stead, either on his own shoulder or by means of a pack-horse, and all he wanted had to be 'got either by hook or by crook'." This explanation was partly endorsed on p. 204. But there the reference is to reaping and wool gathering: "Lands may be made to yield a living by growing corn [that is, grain] or breeding sheep (arable land and grazing land) 'by hook or by crook'" (Winscombe, Somerset) (See *Go wool gathering, to* below.) The survey in MCNNQ is also useful in that it supports the most reasonable suggestion. A correspondent to MCNNQ 1878 gives the explanation coinciding with Smirke's. [By way of postscript, something should be said about the letters in Series XI. Correspondents often wrote to *NQ* without bothering to consult the indexes, and thus rehashing the idea abandoned or agreed on long before. This is a perennial problem of etymology: poorly informed people keep reinventing the wheel and making it roll. In *The Oxford Dictionary of English Proverbs,* 3rd ed., 1970, p. 421, the reference to the block of wood is given as the explanation of the idiom. Holt, p. 198, only remarked: "There are possibilities here," and Hyamson, p. 208, mentions this etymology as probable. JBK I, 21–22.] OED: *c*1380 *(wiþ hook or wiþ crok).*

B76. *By jingo*

NQ 1861 II/12: 272-3, 336; 1878 V/10: 7, 96, 456; 1880 VI/1: 284; 1880 VI/2: 95, 157, 176, 335; 1881 VI/3: 78; 1881 VI/4: 114, 179; 1892 VIII/2: 50; 1893 VIII/3: 228, 334; 1894 VIII/6: 51, 74, 149-50, 312-3, 373; 1895 VIII/7: 10-2, 232; 1898 IX/ 1: 227, 276, 350, 411; 1901 IX/8: 63, 386.

The origin of this exclamation depends on the etymology of *jingo*. From early on, the candidates for *jingo* have been St. Gingoulph (Gengo) 'victorious wolf' or Jove ~ Jupiter; a character in Oliver Goldsmith swears by the living Jingo. Several more hypotheses have been offered: *Jingo* as "a corruption from *je reive Dieu,* a watchword of the rebels as in the wars of the Jacquerie"; perhaps from *Jove Domingo* (so Ferdinand Holthausen in his *Englisches etymologisches Wörterbuch*), and as Basque *Jenco* 'devil' or *God* (!), that is, "*Jaungoicoa,* abridged *Jainkoa,* meaning 'the Lord on high' or 'the Lord of the moon' *(gocko)*" (a comment by A. L. Mayhew, a distinguished language historian in V/10, 1878: 7). High Jingo turned up too (VI/3 1881: 78). The origin from Jingo in India has also been suggested: allegedly, *by Jingo* came to England from Anglo-Indian slang. Even Arabic *jihad* and Persian *jung* or *jang* 'war' figured as etymons (VIII/6, 1894: 51); this hypothesis was rejected on very good rounds by Colonel Prideaux (VIII/6, 1894: 315), a frequent and extremely knowledgeable contributor to *NQ*. In 1894 (VIII/6, 1894: 149–50), Skeat joined the discussion. He rejected the Basque etymology (tentatively supported in the first edition of *The Century Dictionary*) as undocumented and improbable. He also found reference to St. Gingoulf, martyred in the eighth century (so already in Halliwell and Webster) plausible. If so, the oath originated in France. Skeat's derivation was challenged by Frank Chance, another active and astute etymologist of that time (VIII/6, 1894: 312-3). He contested the possibility of *Gingoulf* becoming *Jingo* and pointed out that this saint was unknown in England; moreover, no one ever swore by *St. Jingo* (but only by *Jingo*). He suggested St. Gingues as a more likely candidate. According to him, *Jingo* was a euphemism for *God* (VIII/2, 1892: 50). E. Cobham Brewer advanced the improbable derivation of *Jingo* from *Je'-n-Go'*, that is, *Jesus-son-of God* (VIII/6, 1894: 373; in his dictionary he vouched for Basque *Jainko*). In 1898, a 1661 use of the phrase was cited, and St. Gigron, possibly identified as St. Guignolet, invoked by barren women in Brittany, appeared as the etymon of *Jingo* (IX/1: 350). George Jacob Hoyoake wrote in IX/8, 1901: 63 "The term was first used as a political designation in a letter which I addressed to the Daily News, and which appeared 13 March, 1878, entitled 'Jingoes in the Park,' under circumstances mentioned in 'N. & Q.'" If the phrase *by Jingo* had not been popularized by the music hall and if *jingoism* had not become a synonym for aggressive chauvinism, few people would have been interested in the word *jingo*. The origin of the word remains unknown. Later in life, Skeat did not insist on his old derivation. *The Century Dictionary* quoted the *OED* but retained reference to the Gypsies. St. Gengulphus has been dismissed by the *OED* online as a joke by the author of the *Ingoldsby Legends* (references to this book are numerous in the notes cited above). Burns used the phrase *by jing,* but the correspondent in VI/2, 1880: 95 disagreed that it had anything to do with *jingo* and took *jing* for an onomatopoeia, as in *jing-bany! OED*: 1694.

B77. *By the elevens*
NQ 1860 II/10: 326; 1873, IV/12: 47; 1885 VI/6: 437; 1887 VII/3: 307, 335; 1888 VII/5: 236.

This obscure oath occurs in Goldsmith's play *The Good-Natured Man*. The queries about its origin remained unanswered, but the author of the note in VII/5: 236 believed that in both cases Goldsmith uses the oath "it is laid in the mouth of badly educated persons," so that perhaps *elevens,* stressed on the first syllable, is a "corruption of *elements (by the elements* occurs three times in Shakespeare)." The editor (p. 47) suggests: "Perhaps it refers to the legends of Undecimilla," while the contributor on p. 437 refers to the saying "Possession is *eleven* points of the law" and adds: "The oath being in one instance put into the mouth of a bailiff suggests reference to this saying." [The *OED* has no other citations of the phrase and offers no etymology.] OED: 1773.

C

C1. *Call a spade a spade, to*
NQ 1851 I/4: 274, 456; 1852, I/4: 274, 456; 1856, II/2: 26, 120; 1857. II/3: 474 1860, II/10: 58; 1880 VI/2: 310; 1881 VI/3: 16, 476; 1884 VI/9: 260; 1886 VII/1: 366, 496; 1905 X/3: 169, 217.

'To call a thing by its real name, without mincing words'. The phrase was known in Classical Greek and has an analog in Latin. The notes contain quotations from many authors who used this idiom, though the meaning of the key word in Greek has been questioned (VII/1: 366). Allen, p. 685, has more to say about this subject. Skeat (X/3: 217) trashed the idea that *spade* refers to the suit of playing cards. OED: 1542 *(had not the witte to calle a spade by any other name then a spade).*

C2. *Call cousin with, to*

NQ 1939, 177: 479.

'To claim kinship'. The note contains only a query about the origin of the saying (why just *cousin*?). No reply followed. EDD: *Cousin*; OED: *a*1632 *(So neer I am to him, we must call Cousins)*.

C3. *Call(ing) of the sea, the*

NQ 1890 VII/9: 149, 213; 1891 VII/11: 151, 372; 1898 IX/2: 11, 533 1917 XII/3: 69, 216.

The call(ing) of the sea is explained on p. 149 as a non-metaphorical moaning or roaring sound heard from the ocean. Some people believe that this noise, usually in calm weather, "is not from the waves that break, but a kind of prophetic voice from the body of the sea itself announcing great gales" (p. 372). However, the phrase has to be understood in a broader context. The first to write *the call of* seems to have been Kipling, though he used it more as a phrase than as a title. He referred to the call of the red gods, and so forth. Such is also the source of Jack London's title *The Call of the Wild*. An 1896 quotation in the *OED* shows that the call of the sea could be understood as "a longing that may not rest or tire." OED: 1843.

C4. *Canterbury gallop*

NQ 1862, III/2: 352.

'The gallop of an ambling horse'. The note gives an explanation confirmed in the *OED*: the verb *canter* is a back formation on *Canterbury,* and *Canterbury horse* refers to pilgrims' horses (as, for instance, described in Chaucer). OED: 1636 *(Canterbury paces)*.

C5. *Carling Sunday*

MCNNQ 5, 1884: 212.

"Carling Sunday falls this year on the 30th of March, but to many country people it is obsolete; even the name itself is passing out of recollection. Mothering Sunday is, however, still kept up to some extent, and this is but another name for the same Sabbath Day. About this period it was customary for farm servants to have a holiday on purpose to visit their parents, or go a-mothering; hence the name Mothering Sunday." The author explains that *carling* "is derived from the grey shop peas" (not from 'an old woman'), known in the North as carling peas. OED: 1681 *(Carlinsunday)*.

C6. *Carry coals to Newcastle, to*

NQ 1855 I/11: 281; 1865 III/8: 12; 1870 IV/6: 321; 1892, VIII/2: 484; 1893 VIII/3: 17; 1898 VIII/3: 136; 1903 IX/11: 495; 1907 X/7: 105; 1916 XII/2: 250, 299; ANQ 3, 1889: 245, 253; ANQ 4, 1890: 227.

'To give alms to the rich'; figuratively, 'to do a stupid and useless thing'. Similar phrases from Greek, Latin, French, Italian, and German have been cited. ANQ 3: 245 offers analogs in six languages, and more examples are given on p. 253 (1889). On p. 227 of ANQ 4, the author tells a story about the influence on the public of the discovery of coal in Newcastle. There was an earlier idiom, namely *to carry coals* 'to stand anything, to do dirty work, submit to insult' (VIII/3: 17), while *to carry no coles* (spelled so in the 1602 quotation, VIII/3: 17) meant 'to be furious'. With regard to Newcastle, people used to say *as common as coals in Newcastle* (VIII/3: 136). A curious ad, published on October 6, 1709 is reproduced in XII/2: 250: "Labour in Vain; or coals to Newcastle. . . ." OED: *a*1614 *(colles to Newcastell)*.

C7. *Carry meat in one's mouth, to*
NQ 1888 VII/5: 108.

The note contains only a query about the meaning: 'to carry nourishment' or 'to couple performance with promise'? The *OED* defines the idiom so: 'to be a source of profit, to pay one's way', occasionally 'to be a source of entertainment or instruction (1580; the latest example: 1668). It suggests that the phrase was originally said of a hawk. OED: 1580.

C8. *Carry one's office in one's hat, to*
ANQ 6, 1891: 156.

'To do one's work honestly'. The phrase is said to go back to the Australian word *hatter,* glossed here as 'a poorly equipped but legitimate miner (one who is not a *fossicker*)'. With regard to hatters see also *As mad as a hatter.* *

C9. *Cash on the nail*
NQ 1854 I/9: 196, 384; 1890 VII/9: 366; 1890 VII/10: 31, 214; 1897 VIII/12: 83 1906 X/6: 365, 416-7; 1912 XI/6: 47, 212; MCNNQ 5, 1884: 33.

'Ready money'. The origin of the phrase is debatable. Several hypotheses have been offered. 1) In the 1870s in Yorkshire, "almost every tradesman had affixed to his counter, by a round-headed brass nail, a counterfeit coin—usually a half-crown. Payment 'on the nail' meant prompt cash, but also a challenge to test the genuineness of cash" (X/6 365); 2) At the same time, in the main street at Newport, Monmouthshire (Wales), a little round table stood. It was supported by one leg and looked exactly like a large flat-headed nail. Market people were said to put money on this nail after completing their bargains (p. 417). Limerick and Bristol have been cited in the same contex. The *OED* states that such explanations are wrong for chronological reasons. It cites almost identical sayings in other languages. [In both cases, the situation seems to depend on the existence of the populat idiom]; 3) Perhaps the idiom goes back to the phrase *to strike the nail of the head* (the same page). An ingenious explanation of how this phrase could have originated is given in VII/10: 31: "to pay down the coins in such a way as they can be tested with the nail, to ascertain that they are sterling and true" [scratching and biting a coin are indeed well-known methods of discarding counterfeit money]. Part of the following long note merits attention because its author was the distinguished word historian A. L. Mayhew: "I think we may refer it to the thumbnail. The origin of the phrase may probably be traced to an old drinking custom, called in Latin *supernaculum,* and in German *Nagelprobe,* that is, the pouring of the last drop of beer or wine 'on the nail' to prove that the cup was empty. . . . Compare the French phrase in Cotgrave (*s.v.* 'Ongle'): '*Boire la goutte sur l'ongle,* To drink all but a drop to cover the nail with'; and the German '*Nagelprobe trinken* (or *machen*), to leave no heeltaps, to drink supernaculum'. . . . It is quite easy to see how the phrase 'on the nail' was transferred from the drinking custom to the making of prompt money payments, the link of association being the notion of promptness combined with freedom from deception" (p. 47). On p. 212, it is mentioned that "an act of parliament of King Robert the Bruce (Thomson's 'Acta Parl. Scot.,' i. 123) contains the phrase 'super unguem' for 'on the nail', in the sense of 'cash down'." See also *Paid down upon the nail.* Latin *ad unguem ~ in unguem* means 'with utmost care, perfectly'. "*Paid down on the nail* is a well known half-slang phrase used for a cash payment" (VII/9: 366); *on the nail* 'ready money'. OED: 1569 *(payed on the nayle)* and 1720 *(money on the nail)*. See also *In a merry pin*. [Allen, p. 500: "The relevance of *nail* here is uncertain, but it seems likely to be in the same sense area as in *hit the nail on the head* and *right on the nail,* in which the image is one of accuracy and concentration of effort." The American version of this idiom is *cash on the barrel(head)*. Its origin is obscure. The barrel also figures in Russian *(den'gi na bochku)*. None of the three historical dictionaries of Russian phraseology say anything about the idiom. German and French have no analogs. Borrowing from American English into Russian is most unlikely.]

C10. *Castles in Spain*
ANQ 4, 1889: 73; NQ 1911 XI/4: 66, 113, 178, 259.

'Splendid structures of the imagination'. More common is the phrase *castles in the air* occurring in several languages. The English idiom is a borrowing from French, but its origin there remains unclear. [Hyamson, p. 76, points out that originally the phrase was French and went back to the eleventh century. It "may have arisen out of the wonderful rewards that fell to Henry of Burgundy and his followers on their invasion of Spain and Portugal. . . . At that time the castles of Spain were very few in number and every French baron who settled in the country had to build one for his occupation." Allen, p. 135: "The reference is thought to be to the time of Moorish rule in Spain, when any scheme to build a (Christian) castle would have been highly unrealistic."] OED: *a*1400 *(make castels thanne in Spayne)*.

C11. *Cast the cat in the kirn, to*
NQ 1868 IV/2: 297.

Kirn, the northern variant of *churn,* is a vessel or machine for making butter. Apparently, the reference is to a desired situation: once there, there will be no possibility to extricate the cat from the kirn. But compare **C15**! A 1691 example is cited. *

C12. *Catch a crab, to*
NQ 1876, V/6: 203-4, 272, 524; 1877, V/7: 18, 38, 136.

"To fall backwards by missing a stroke in rowing." In V/6: 203-4, Frank Chance examined the similar Italian idiom *pigliare un granchio a secco* 'to catch a crab on the dry ground', which means 'to make a mistake' and 'to pinch one's finger, so that it bleeds'. The phrase can also be applied to an accident at rowing. Frank Chance believed that the English idiom, like the Italian one, goes back to the experience of those who walked on the beach after the tide is out, found crabs stranded, picked them up, and got pinched. However, he was derided for his hypothesis. On p. 272, he wrote in response: "Among oarsman, the 'catch' and 'to catch' refer to the 'hold' obtained on water by the power of the rower, especially when, at the instant of dipping the blade of the oar or scull, the strength of the rower is brought to bear on the implement and act on the boat. The rower is said to 'catch' the water at this moment, and the word is an admirably expressive one. If he misses the water, and falls on his back, he is then said to catch a crab—a body with wavering legs and arms—when the crustacean, supine and angry, lies on the bottom of a boat." Another correspondent (V/6: 272) said the following: "The expression is commonly used when the oar is turned in the water at the end of a stroke which has been made *too deep,* and cannot be got out without some difficulty. Now it is easy to see how *this* came to mean 'catch a crab', for when the oar is in this position, it appears as though something were holding the end of it under water, and preventing its being drawn out, as you might imagine a crab to do if it had the strength." A third explanation is similar (V/6: 272): "I believe the phrase originated from the opposite of which Webster describes as the meaning of 'catching a crab'. When an inexperienced rower does not feather his oar properly, in pulling the blade through the water it sometimes strikes obliquely downwards, and remains fixed as if in a vice. He has 'caught a crab'. The loom of the oar generally pushes him backwards into the bottom of the boat, where he remains till he frees his oar, by turning it in the rowlock, or till the boat stops, when the oar floats. Missing a stroke also throws the oarsman off balance, and, the results being similar, the same name has been given to both causes." The notes that follow deal with the different meanings of the idiom in Cambridge and on the Thames, but, as Chance stated, 'to make a mistake' is the basis of both. OED: 1785.

C13. *Catch a weasel asleep, to*
NQ 1879, V/12: 146, 258.
'To catch a dangerous person, allegedly unaware of the attack'. The story quoted was obviously invented in retrospect, to explain the idiom. OED: 1825.

C14. *Catch the speaker's eye, to*
NQ 1896 VIII/9: 208, 338; 1899 IX/3: 211; 1910 XI/2: 285.
According to *Words, Facts, and Phrases* by Eliezer Edwards, as quoted on p. 338, "The custom of leaving the Speaker to call on the members originated on November 26, 1640, when, a number of members rising together, 'the confusion became intolerable'. At last 'the House determined for Mr. White, and the Speaker's eye was adjusted to be evermore the rule'." OED: 1834.

C15. *Cat is in the cream pot*
ANQ 4, 1889: 77.
'A row in the house'. The phrase, which has some interest because its meaning is unexpected, was listed without comment among many other local idioms about animals. Compare *Cast the cat in the kirn,* whose meaning seems to be obscure. Isn't it a synonym of *Cat in the cream pot*? Northern England. Apperson: 1678. *

C16. *Cat may look at a king*
NQ 1891 VII/12: 245; 1897 VIII/11: 387, 452; VIII/12: 33.
'The humblest have their rights, even in the presence of the mightiest.' Especially informative is the note in VIII/12: 33, for it was written by G. L. Apperson, a great specialist in the history of English idioms. It deals with the dating of the phrase in dictionaries (no antedating to Heywood). The model for the phrase may have been a Greek adage. OED: 1546.

C17. *Caught napping*
NQ 1868 IV/2: 325, 460, 471, 570; 1869 IV/3: 95.
To be caught napping means 'to be caught off one's guard, to be taken unawares'. There is the verb *nap* 'to cheat at dice', and some discussion ensued about whether *napping* should be understood as 'slumbering' or 'cheating'. The early examples point unambiguously to the first sense. OED: *a*1576 *(take thee napping)* and 1793 *(caught napping).*

C18. *Caw me, caw thee*

NQ 1884 VI/10: 266, 315, 472; 1885 VI/11: 33, 58; 1885 VI/12: 358; 1887 VII/4: 293.

'Scratch my back and I'll scratch yours'. The discussion was provoked by the use of this Scots proverb in Byron's *Don Juan* and centered on the variant *claw me, claw thee*. Skeat wrote: "The old form of the proverb was certainly *ka mee, ka thee*. . . . It is explained to mean 'Swear for me, and I'll do as much for you', that is, 'Call me as a witness, and I'll call you'. Thus *ca* would appear to be, as usual, the Scottish form of *call*. I have little doubt that there was a parallel form, 'Claw me, claw thee,' but I suspect it to be a later substitution. I have also somewhere met with it in the plain English form, 'You scratch my back, and I'll scratch your back'" (p. 315). [Curiously, *scratch my back* . . . was almost unknown in England at the end of the 19th century (VI/12: 358).] Even though *caw* or *ca'* stands for *call* (VI/10: 315), *ca'* also meant 'wash up the linen, put on a horseshoe, *etc.*'" (VI/11: 33)*

C19. *Chalk on the door*

NQ 1898 IX/1: 408; 1898 IX/2: 37.

Discussion of the numerous uses of the custom did not result in discovering the origin of the phrase. In Scotland, "a chalk on the door" warned the tenant of eviction. The same sign is said to have been used on doors when the plague raged. *To chalk up a grudge* and other similar phrases also refer to warnings. Accounts were likewise chalked up in alehouses, but there is no certainty that this custom gave rise to the idiom. *Chalk,* with reference to alehouse: *a*1529 (OED); to chalk (it): 1597 (OED). [Cf. the German analog *ankreiden* 'to chalk up, to hold something against somebody'.]

C20. *Champagne to the masthead*

NQ 1862 III/1: 112.

'Plentiful supply of the wine at table'. The editor's note: "We have heard the expression 'Swimming in champagne', and 'We drank champagne enough to float a ship'. But we suspect that like champagne itself, the phrase 'Champagne to the mast head' has not come into common use. It may probably be regarded as an extension or exaggeration of the expressions which we have cited."*

C21. *Chap as married Hannah, that's the*

NQ 1900 IX/6: 346, 434.

'That's what I need'. No comments on the origin of this odd saying have been provided. Not unexpectedly, the story behind that marriage, if it ever existed, is lost. [SG suggested that the reference is to the Biblical Hanna.] Nottinghamshire. Apperson: 1900. *

C22. *Chapter and verse*

NQ 1882 VI/5: 206, 277.

'An exact reference'. William Platt explained: "This proverbial expression originated, just before the Civil Wars under Charles I., with the Puritans, who were described by South as 'those mighty men of *chapter and verse*', from their frequently appealing to the Bible on the most frivolous occasions. These sanctimonious enthusiasts were perpetually opening their gilt pocket Bibles, and with such self-sufficiency and imperfect knowledge of the original, that the learned

Selden attended their 'assembly of divines' for the purpose of exposing their ignorance" (p. 206). There is a short correction on p. 277: "John Selden cannot be said to have attended the Assembly of Divines for the purpose of exposing the ignorance of its members. He was a member thereof himself." But correct the divines he did. OED: 1628.

C23. *Charity begins at home*
NQ 1854, I/10: 403; 1943, 185: 108.

'One's first responsibility is for the needs of one's own family and friends'.1/Tim, V:4 is given as a possible source of the familiar quotation. OED: *a*1625 *(charity and beating begins at home).*

C24. *Charley horse*
ANQ 18, 1980: 111; SR 7, 1980: 78; CoE 22/8, 1993: 3-5; 23/5, 1994: 6-8.

'A cramp in an arm or leg'. This definition has been contested. Thomas H. Middleton *(SR)* argued that a charley horse is 'a muscular pain in the leg—specifically in the thigh. A muscular pain in the arm is called a sore arm. A pain in the calf or hamstring is a cramp." Numerous tales have been told about the evasive Charley. Here is one of them: "It was none other than Billy Sunday who coined the term in 1886. Sunday bet on a horse named Charley which went lame and finished last. Next day during a baseball game, a gentleman named George Gore hit what looked to be a home run, but strained a muscle rounding second, so pulled up at third, whereupon Sunday yelled, 'Here comes that Charley horse'" *(ANQ)*. Two notes on Charley Horse appeared in *CoE*. The first version confirms the story that one day Charley, the favorite of the race, pulled up lame. The following day a player pulled a tendon in his leg and was nicknamed as Charley horse. Other versions are similar and date the phrase to the early 1880s. Joe Quest figures prominently as the person with whom the phrase originated. By contrast, "Charles F. Funk mentions a reference to a lame horse used by the grounds keepers of the Chicago White Sox baseball park in the 1890s." OED: 1888.

C25. *Cheap and nasty*
NQ 1890 VII/9: 424.

'Inexpensive'. The correspondent asked whether the phrase was first used by "Prince Louis, the heir presumptive to the Bavarian crown, in the First Chamber of the Diet, with reference to the promotion of art in Munich" or by "the Rev. Charles Kingsley, who, in 1850, under the pseudonym of 'Parson Lot', wrote a tract entitled 'Cheap Clothes and Nasty,' to expose the slop-selling system." No answer followed the query. OED: 1822 (as early as 1823, already known as slang).

C26. *Cheese it*
NQ 1881 VI/3: 188, 373; 1881 VI/3: 475; VI/4: 38.

'An exclamation of warning: Stop it.' Its synonyms, mentioned in the correspondence, were *hek, nix,* and the near-universal *barley.* The expression was well-known in New York. One [fanciful?] idea about the origin of this slangy phrase was "suggested by the readiness and cleanness with which cheese may be cut with the knife" (p. 188). Or "has this expression any connection with the fact that many school dinners wind up with cheese?" (p. 475). The *OED* suggests tentatively an alteration of *cease.* OED: 1811.

C27. *Chew the rag, to*

NQ 1888 VII/5: 469; VII/6: 38.

'To abuse or to be angry with one'. The phrase is (or was?) especially common in the military; e.g. "He was chewing the rag at me the whole evening." Connection with *rag* 'to tease' has been suggested (the verb can also mean 'to torment'). In Lincolnshire, to get a boy into a rage was called "getting his rag out" (p. 38). [Holt, pp. 66–7: "As for the sense of this 'rag', there may be some connection with the *rag* signifying 'razz', or criticize. Someone has also noted with interest that a sulky child often chews the handkerchief, or failing that, its shirt, collar of apron."] OED: 1885.

C28. *Chip in porridge*

NQ 1850 I/1: 382; 1853 I/8: 208; 1854 I/9: 45.

'A nonentity, a thing of no importance'. EDD: *Chip*; OED: 1688 (many variants are cited).

C29. *Cleanliness next to godliness*

NQ 1863, III/4: 419; 1864, III/6: 259, 337; 1865, III/7: 367; 1885 VI/11: 400; 1897 VIII/12: 260; 1940, 179: 151, 232; MCNNQ 1, 1878: 318, 323.

'If your body is clean, your soul will be pure'. The correspondents discussed the examples illustrating the phrase and its relevance. Only the note in III/7: 367 is curious. An old woman used this saying to explain why the Saturday night's tub-washing should precede the Sunday morning's appearance at church. [Edwards, p. 119, wrote the following: "The author of this phrase, quoted by John Wesley, is not known. Something similar to it is found in the 'Talmud,' and Plutarch tells us that amongst the ancient Egyptians 'health was no less respected than devotion.' A Jewish lecturer, on December 3, 1878, reported in 'The Jewish World,' said, 'This well-known English phrase had been taught by the Rabbins of the "Talmud" many centuries ago, both as a religious principle and a sanitary law.'"] OED: *a* 1791.

C30. *Clean sword and a dirty Bible*

NQ 1952, 197: 106, 196.

"At farmers' dinners at the White Lion posting-inn at Hadleigh, Suffolk, at the beginning of the 19th century, it was the custom to drink to 'rusty swords and dirty Bibles,' otherwise 'peace and piety'" (p. 196). The idea is that a sword should not be used, but the Bible should be sullied from constant reading. *

C31. *Clear out for Guam, to*

NQ 1881 VI/4: 447; VI/11: 314.

'To be bound for an indefinite location'. The reference is to the fraud to which passengers sailing to Australia were exposed in connection with the gold fever. *Quam* was a typo for *Guam*. OED: 1881.

C32. *Clever devils*

NQ 1891 VII/12: 9, 77, 158, 254.

'Children educated without religion'. The phrase was attributed to the great Duke of Wellington (p. 77), but it already occurred in 1696 (p. 254). *

C33. *Cloud nine*

ANQ 18, 1980: 78.

'The height of happiness'. Cf. *cloud seven* and the biblical 'the third heaven', "later raised to 'seventh heaven', that is, the highest in the Ptolemaic system. William and Mary Morris (*Dictionary of Word and Phrase Origins,* II, 279–80) date 'cloud nine' to the early 1950s, but their meteorological explanation [like so many others] should be considered cautiously." OED: 1959.

C34. *Club the battalion, to*

NQ 1901 IX/7: 110, 171, 314.

"To invert or alter the order of companies in field evolutions, in days when the consecutive numbers of companies were fixed" (p. 171). The note on p. 314 contains numerous examples of the use of the verb *club* in the army. The most common object of *club* was some weapon, but perukes and the hair could also be clubbed. "The military use of the word *club* with reference to wigs and natural hair is probably the origin of the phrase 'to club men on parade'—to get them into a knot, the result of ignorance or forgetfulness or defiance of the rules of drill" (p. 314). OED: 1806.

C35. *Cock and bull story*

NQ 1851 I/4: 312; 1852 I/5: 414, 447; 1852 I/6: 146; 1854 I/9: 209; 1857 II/4: 79; 1859 II/8: 215; 1863 III/3: 169; 1884 VI/10: 260; 1889 VII/8: 447; 1890 VII/9: 270, 452, 494; 1905 X/3: 268, 334.

The initial discussion was unenlightening, because the idea prevailed that the phrase had an ecclesiastical origin (*bull* from the pontifical bullas, with *cock* referring to Peter and the crowing of the cock). But the editorial conclusion (III/3: 169), quite reasonably, sided with II/8: 215 and suggested the origin in an old fable. James A. H. Murray (VII/8: 1889) pointed out that he needed the phrase rather than stories of a cock and a bull (see below). He received an antedating from *Tristram Shandy* (VII/9: 452), though not in the form the *OED* needed. Grose used an article before *bull*: *a cock and a bull story.* The long note appended here will be interesting to anyone who wants to know more about the history of the *OED* and of James A. H. Murray's inimitably pugnacious style. "If Mr. Case and D. S. will excuse me from turning to 'Tristram Shandy' for a quotation which was before me when I wrote my query, and will themselves turn to the said query in 'N. & Q.' of December 7, 1889, they will find that I anticipated them by 150 years with examples of the phrases 'story of a cock and bull', 'to talk of a cock and a bull', and the like. What I asked for was an example of the modern phrase 'cock-and-bull story' prior to 1828. I have noticed that people who offer us what we have already, and therefore do not ask for, generally accompany their superfluous gifts with an unnecessary expression of innocent surprise that what they offer 'should have escaped the notice of Dr. Murray'. It sounds critical, and it is not worth while to find out whether it is true, as that might spoil the rhetoric. What surprises Dr. Murray is that people should rush into print with replies (save the mark!) to his queries without having read them. I wish people *would* read them, for, as I have said often before, my object in asking questions in 'N. & Q.' is the practical one of speedily getting needed information, and I usually want to know *just what I ask,* and not something else rather unlike it. Answers intended to be of use to the 'Dictionary' ought also to be sent *to me* direct, addressed 'Dr. Murray, Oxford'. 'Cock-and-bull' went to press several months ago, and the answers now in 'N. & Q.', if they had been ever so intelligent and ever so relevant, would have been of no use to me. Fortunately, intelligent and relevant answers were sent direct, one of which carried 'cock-and-bull' back to 1796. Mr. Terry's reference, of the same date, for 'cock and a bull story' would have been useful as leading up to the modern phrase if it had been sent in time; but the 'Dictionary' cannot stop four months for any word." Allen, p. 159, quotes the same letter. JBK I, 26. OED: 1795.

C36. *Cock of the walk*
NQ 1873, IV/11: 211, 291.

'The person who dominates others'. IV/11: 291 gives the following explanation: "The place in which game cocks were trained, used to be called the walk, and the term 'cock of the walk' was applied to the stoutest and most successful combatant." EDD: *Cock*; OED: 1823.

C37. *Cock one's fud, to*
NQ 1857 II/3: 519.

'To be in good spirits'. *Fud* is a rabbit's tail. Scotland. EDD: *Cock*. *

C38. *Cock's span*
NQ 1878, V/10: 257, 412, 521; 1879, V/11: 296.

The phrase describes the lengthening of the day after Yuletide. Its synonym (variant) is *a cock's stride* and *a cock's footstep. Skip* for *span* also occurs. *

C39. *Cockshut time*
NQ 1904 X/1: 121, 195, 232

'Twilight'. Skeat (p. 121) explains "a little consideration of all the quotations will, I think, show that *cockshot* and *cuckshut* are both mere shortenings of *cockshoot*; indeed, the latter is the nearer of the two. Surely it is clear that *cockshoot time* was simply the time when the *cockshoots* were utilized; and that is the whole of it. The *cockshoots* were not nets, but glades. The glades were left to set nets in. And, when it grew dusk, the nets (called *cockshoot-nets*) were set. Not even a woodcock would have been caught in a net at midday, when the danger was visible." *Cockshut* (*OED*: 1353) is explained as a broad woodland glade, *etc.,* but the phrase (which occurs in Shakespeare) does not seem to be featured in the *OED*.

C40. *Coggeshall job*
NQ 1851 I/3: 167; 1880 VI/2: 307, 418.

'Any blundering or awkward contrivance.' "The local tradition reports that when the Coggeshall or Coxall men went out fishing, many years ago, they took with them tubs of water to put the fish in." Essex. Apperson: 1880. *

C41. *Cold pig*
NQ 1873 IV/11: 211, 288; 1931, 161: 335.

'A suit of clothes returned to a tailor if it does not fit'. No explanation about the origin of the phrase followed the 1931 query. In some part of East Anglia, *to give one some cold pig* means 'to souse the person with cold water' (p. 211). A learned etymology of *cold pig* was given on p. 288 (an adaptation of Latin *colaphus* 'a blow with the fist', [but did a broader sense of the idiom exist?]. *

C42. *Cold pudding settles one's love*
NQ 1852 I/5: 30, 189.

"In some parts of the principality (Hoxton, London) it is customary on the morning of the wedding-day for the bridegroom, with a party of his friends, to proceed to the lady's residence; where he and his companions are regaled with ale, bread and butter, and cold custard pudding" (p. 189). OED: 1866.

C43. *Come from Topsham, to*
NQ 1907 X/8: 127, 418; 1913 XI/7: 229.

"Do you come from Topsham?" This is said to those who leave the door open. Topsham is in Devonshire, but the phrase was recorded in Yorkshire. [Apparently, a migratory formula is at play, and the place name is more or less arbitrary.] In X/8: 127 and 418, the "door-shutting proverb" from Nottinghamshire "I see you come from Warsop way; you don't know how to shut doors behind you" is discussed (said when people don't shut doors properly). No explanation followed this "proverb". Cf. **A41** *

C44. *Come in if you're fat*
NQ 1879, V/11: 187; 1884 VI/9: 80.

A "fatuous expression, addressed to a person knocking for admittance at the door of a room." Apperson: 1738. *

C45. *Come Lord Audley, to*
NQ 1879, V/11: 267, 419.

'To deceive'. *John Audley* (a cant term) is synonymous with *cut it short* 'dupe gullible people'. On p. 419, it is suggested that "perhaps this phrase, especially around Devizes, may perpetuate the memory of a Wiltshire nobleman, Mervin, Lord Audley, and also Earl of Castlehaven in Ireland, who was executed in 1631 for certain deeds of violence." *

C46. *Come to grief, to*
NQ 1871, IV/7: 429, 526; IV/8: 57.

'To meet with disaster'. The correspondents were right calling the phrase recent. In the early 1870s, it was considered to be slang. The *OED*'s verdict is less severe: "Chiefly colloquial; somewhat rare in dignified use." [Twentieth-century dictionaries find it stylistically neutral.] OED: 1850.

C47. *Come out the little end of the horn, to*
NQ 1887 VII/4: 323; 1889 VII/7: 257, 376; 1899 IX/4: 114, 156; 1900 IX/6: 98.

'To get the worst of a bargain; to come to grief'. When the idiom was recorded, it had local currency (perhaps only in the Midlands), but the reference was to the once popular graphic image of a torture: an unfortunate man is being squeezed through a narrowing horn and comes out mutilated. The torture warned of the act of suretyship. Many pictures of it are extant. The phrase *to put to the horn* has a different meaning: it referred to the proclamation of outlawry against offenders made, according to Scottish custom, after the horn had been sounded at the city cross. OED: 1805.

C48. *Common or garden*
NQ 1890 VII/9: 68, 132; 1891 VII/12: 293; 1899 IX/4: 89, 155; 1921 XII/8: 392, 459.

This collocation, when used attributively, is said in the note on p. 68 to be one of the novelties of colloquial English. Its humor consists in adding *or garden* to *common (common or garden influenza, common or garden rats)*. But *common or garden lettuce* (thus, without any attempt at humor) occurs in Johnson's dictionary (p. 293), and the *OED* gives a 1657 source. As a jocular substitute for "common, ordinary" the earliest example in the *OED* is also dated to 1657. However, see the 1890 and 1891 notes.

C49. *Conspicuous by one's absence*
NQ 1880 VI/1: 495, 524; 1882 VI/5: 409, 438; 1882 VI/6: 18-9, 419; 1885 VI/12: 360; 1897 VIII/12: 68.

'Calling attention by not being where expected.' This proverbial phrase has been traced to Tacitus. The letter on pp. 18-9 (1882) gives the reference to the first use of the phrase in English: allegedly, by Lord John Russell in 1859, not antedated by later research, and the correspondent's indignant letter to the *Times* (April 7, 1859: J. J. Aubertin). OED: 1859 *(one provision was conspicuous by its presence, and one by its absence)*.

C50. *Constable of Oppenshaw sets beggars in the stocks at Manchester*
NQ 1873, IV/12: 388, 524.

This is a Cheshire proverb. It is explained so on p. 524: "Openshaw is a township in the parish of Manchester, and about three-and-a-half miles from the Cathedral, where the stocks were formerly placed, and the beggars might obviously have been impounded nearer home at a very much smaller cost of time and labour. The proverb hits the *un-wisdom* of the Openshaw people." Apperson: 1678. *

C51. *Constable with a back on his bill*
NQ 1867 III/11: 443.

The reference is allegedly to an "endorsement on his warrant. If this has been granted by the authorities of one county, a constable cannot execute it in an adjoining one until it has been backed by a magistrate thereof." *

C52. *Copy of your countenance*
NQ 1865 III/8: 30, 114.

'That is not spoken sincerely, it is a deception'. Examples of *copy* meaning 'disguise' are given. "The allusion may be to the copy . . . of an engraved plate, which . . . reverses the plate" (p. 30). However, the meaning of *copy* remains obscure. EDD: *Copy*; OED: 1579.

C53. *Correct to a T*
NQ 1909 X/12: 227, 273, 313, 376.

'Absolutely correct'. In X/12: 227, the following note by James A. H. Murray appeared: "Our earliest quotation for this, or for the kindred phrases 'to suit one to a *t*', 'to fit to a *t*', 'to know one to a *t*', is of 1693. Can any one help us to an earlier example? No one of our many instances throws any light upon its origin. A current obvious conjecture would explain 'a T' as meaning 'a T-square'; but to this there are various objections: we have no evidence as yet that the name 'T-square' goes back to the seventeenth century, and no example of its being called simply 'a T'; and in few, if any, of our instances would the substitution of 'a T-square' for 'a T' make any tolerable sense. The notion seems rather to be that of minute exactness, as it were 'to the minutest point'. But the evidence is mainly negative: if examples can be found of 'T-square' before 1700, or of its reduction simply to 'T', or of earlier examples of 'to a *t*', they may help to settle the actual origin." According to several correspondents, T may stand for *title,* and one contributor to the discussion noted that *tāw* is the last letter of the Hebrew alphabet. *Right as a trivet* was mentions as a synonym (p. 273; see this phrase below). Two more suggestions appeared on p. 313 1) "I venture to suggest that in this expression T stands for the (Scotch) dialect word *tee* so well known to golfers as denoting the small cone of earth from which the ball is driven. *Tee* in a wider sense means 'a mark', 'a (fixed) point'; see 'Dial. Dict.' [= *EDD*] *s.v.* ['at this word'] 'Correct to a point (= *tee*)' would be equivalent to the German phrase *genau bis aufs Tüttelchen (auf dem i),* 'correct to a tittle', thus expressing the notion of minute exactness which, according to Sir James Murray, is implied in it." 2) "May I suggest that possibly the original form of this saying was "to the crossing of a *t,*" and that the shade of that meaning still hangs about it? For many generations over-close attention to the minutiæ of accurate writing was held to be the index of a 'clerk' as distinguished from a 'gentleman', or of a man too much immersed in larger affairs to waste time or care on such pettinesses; and of these the dotting of the *i*'s and the crossing of the *t*'s were singled out as the most frivolous, and most significant of petty pedantry." See also *Fit to a T, to* and *It suits to a T.* OED: *

C54. *Counsels of perfection*
NQ 1895 VIII/8: 288, 328.

"This phrase owes its origin to the ecclesiastical 'counsels of perfection', a term used by the schoolmen of the Middle Ages to express certain voluntary habits of life which opened the way to a perfection of holiness not attainable by all. They consisted of three vows—the vow of voluntary poverty, the vow of perpetual chastity, and the vow of obedience. These vows were only to be taken by those who were able and willing to fulfill them. They were never more than 'counsels', and hence their name, 'counsels of perfection'" (p. 329). OED: *a*1678 for the singular *counsel* and 1886 for the plural.

C55. *Coup the creels, to*
NQ 1876 V/6: 64.

In Northern England, this is said of a person who in bargaining makes 100 per cent or doubles the purchase price. *Coup* 'to overturn', *creel* 'basket'. *The Century Dictionary* glosses the phrase as 'to tumble head over heels; to die'. EDD: *Coup/Creels*; OED: 1718 (to tumble head over heels).

C56. *Cowardly, cowardly, custard*
NQ 1872, IV/9: 292.

This alliterative taunt was used by boys (reported by a correspondent from Philadelphia). "It is supposed to have its origin in the shaking, quivering motion of the confection called 'custard'. In *Microcosmos* (1687) [by Johann Martini], Act III., Tasting says 'I have a sort of cowardly custards, born in the city, but bred up at court, that quake for fear." OED: 1833.

C57. *Crab harvest*
NQ 1889 VII/8: 248.

'The end of a project after which the worker has to look for another employment'. Worstershire. *

C58. *Crack a bottle, to*
NQ 1863 III/3: 493; III/4: 18.

'Open a bottle so as to drink up its contents'. On p. 18, the idiom is traced to "the ready and apparently soldierly habit of deftly knocking off its head." [German *eine Flasche zerdrücken*.] OED: 1800 (cf. the date of *Crush the bottle*).

C59. *Crawley, God help us*
NQ 1854, I/9: 446; I/10: 223; NQ 1878, V/9: 345.

A phrase of the same type as *Tickhill, God help me,* below. If not in reference to a winding river (see *As crooked as Crawley*), then perhaps to "Judge Crawley, 1632–1645." Bedfordshire. Cf. *Binsey, God help me; From Lincoln heath, God help me; Melverley, God help me,* and *Saffron Walden, God help me.* Apperson: 1878. *

C60. *Cried by the cock and cryer, to be*
NQ 1902 IX/9: 248, 313.

This is the exchange concerning the phrase: "I read recently that some silver plate had been lost in February, 1718/9, from the royal household, and that it was 'ordered to be cried by the Cock and Cryer' with a view to its recovery. What is the full meaning of this phrase?" (p. 248). "For an explanation of this phrase see Chambers's 'Book of Days,' i. 240, from which it appears that there was an official so named in the Lord Steward's Department of the Royal Household so lately as 1822" (p. 313). *

C61. *Crocodile's tears*
NQ 1882 VI/6: 92, 296, 496.

'A show of false regret'. The discussion concerned the source of the idiom. No earlier mention of a weeping crocodile than the end of the 15th century (in Latin) was found. OED: 1563.

C62. *Cross and pile*
NQ 1852 I/6: 513; 1858 II/6: 177, 220; 1861 II/7: 255, 332, 404; 1869 IV/3.

'Heads or tail' and rarely 'money'. Some coins had the cross and the wedge-like shape of the shield on them. The discussion continued for years, with the main difficulty being the meaning and derivation of *pile,* which was glossed as 'ball', 'ship', 'head', 'shield', 'arrow', and 'cap'. Consequently, the etymologies of *pile* went in many directions. Nor did it become clear whether the pile appeared on the front or the reverse side of the coin. The French origin of the phrase seemed probable to some. The *OED* confirms the statement by several correspondents that pile was the reverse side and the derivation of *pile* from French. Known as early as the end of the fourteenth century, the phrase occurred in this form in a written text in 1460.

C63. *Crow's age*
NQ 1887 VII/4: 386, 532.

'A very long time'. ("It's a crow's age sin' I seen you.") Yet an analogous phrase turns up in Horace (p. 532). Nottinghamshire. EDD: *Crow.* *

C64. *Croydon sanguine*
NQ 1886 VII/2: 446; 1887 VII/3: 96, 171, 395, 416, 523.

This obsolete phrase was used with reference to Croydon, well-known "for the number of charcoal-burners who plied their trade there. Any one who has seen the ruddy colour mantling in the cheek of a person of southern or quasi-Oriental race will quite understand what this compound means" (p. 446). Or was it a polite form of *smutty-face*? (p. 523). OED: *a*1566.

C65. *Crush a bottle, to*
NQ 1863 III/3: 493.

The same as *Crack a bottle.* A 1599 example is cited. *

C66. *Crutches for lame ducks*
NQ 1920 XII/7: 209, 254-5.

Cf. *Layovers for meddlers,* to which *and crutches for lame ducks* is sometimes added. The saying has several variants. On p. 255, a medieval play is quoted in which this phrase occurs. *

C67. *Cry bee to a battledore, to*
NQ 1870 IV/6: 221.

See *Cry bo to a goose, to.* See more at *Say bee to a battledove.* OED: 1599 *(Euery man can say Bee to a Battledore).*

C68. *Cry bo to a goose, to*
NQ 1870 IV/6: 94, 164, 221, 372, 513.

The phrase is usually applied to those so shy or inactive that they can't say 'bo' to a goose. On p. 94, Samuel Johnson's amusing explanation is cited, according to which there once lived Captain Bo, a man so terrible that his name became proverbial. On p. 164, Nash's *say bee to a battledore* is given *(Lenten Staffe).* However, Skeat (p. 221) explained that the two sayings have nothing in common. A hornbook was originally shaped like a battledore, and *bee* stands for the letter *b*. *To say B to a battledore* meant to recognize this letter and thus have a little knowledge, while *to say boo to a goose* means to show little courage. OED: 1588 *(to say bo to a goose).*

C69. *Cry down credit, to*
NQ 1894 VIII/5: 506; 1894 VIII/6: 76; 1895 VIII/7: 331; 1903 IX/12: 29, 138, 213, 257, 352; 1929, 156: 298.

"This is but a variant of the phrase 'crying notchil', that is, advertising as if by the crier that a man will not be responsible for his wife's debts. But in connexion with a regiment which is temporarily quartered in any town, it is to warn the townsfolk against contracting debts with private soldiers, a custom said to date—though I do not know on what authority—from the time of the Commonwealth" (IX/12: 138). The discussion seems to have confirmed this explanation. But compare the curious opposite custom: "'Going down the hill again, he met two drummers, a sergeant, and several soldiers and marines, who were, by beat of drum, proclaiming that the tavern and shopkeepers might safely credit the soldiers and marines to a certain value.' This was in Boston. 'Adventures of B. M. Carew,' p. 122. So it appears it was not always the custom to proclaim to shopkeepers not to give credit to soldiers, as is stated at the first reference" (VIII/7: 331). See *Cry one's wife notchel.* EDD: *Cry.* *

C70. *Cry mapsticks, to*
NQ 1856 II/2: 269, 315.

The phrase was used by Swift. It apparently means 'to apologize'. "In Tempest's *Cryes of the City of London, Drawn after the Life,* fol., 1711, is depicted a damsel with a bundle of common domestic mops, sticks and all, on her head, with her cry in English, French, and Italian" (p. 315). Cf. *Like death on a map-stick* and *Cry matches, to.* *

C71. *Cry matches, to*
NQ 1877 V/8: 491; 1878 V/9: 55, 318-9.

'To apologize'. The exclamation might be an Americanism (p. 491). It has been derived from *crime hutches* (given without reference on p. 491) and to *cré matin* (possibly introduced to America by the French Canadians; p. 55). *Cry* has also been called an equivalent of *Christ* (p. 491). The synonymous phrase with *crimes* and believed to be an alteration of *Gra'mercy,* was well-known in England. According to still another hypothesis, the etymon of the phrase is *cry aim,* an exclamation, once used to encourage archers (pp. 318-9). [The phrase bears a curious resemblance to *Cry mapsticks.* Both look like folk etymological variants of a third long-forgotten phrase.]*

C72. *Cry of the morning*
NQ 1877 V/8: 129, 275, 378, 396.

'A light shower'. Cf. *Pride of the morning.* *

C73. *Cry one's wife notchel, to*
MCNNQ 5, 1884: 325.

'To advertise that a man will no more be responsible for any debts his wife may contract'. The correspondent asked about the derivation of *notchel*. The *OED* cites dialectal texts from 1681, 1839, 1882, and 1902. The phrase is not limited to the wife. The idiom is *to cry (a person) notchel* and has been recorded from Cheshire, Lancashire, and West Yorkshire. The origin of *notchel* is said to be unkown. See also *Cry down credit to.* Apperson: *(To cry notch)* 1681. *

C74. *Cry out death before you are past Durham, to*
NQ 1876 V/6: 64, 117.

This is said to a person who predicts disaster too soon. The saying becomes clear in light of *Durham and death.* *

C75. *Cry roast meat, to*
NQ 1867 III/11: 378, 463; 1923 XII/12: 176.

'To be foolish enough to proclaim one's success'. In the exchange that followed the first note, no one offered the source of the idiom. [Roast meat as a metaphor for a piece of luck?] OED: 1600.

C76. *Curate's egg, the*
NQ 1926, 150: 207.

'Something good and bad at the same time'. Definitive evidence is given here that the joke did not originate in *Punch* (1895, p. 222). The author was Tom Wilkinson, a contributor to *Judy* (by 1926, already defunct). The correspondent to *NQ* (E. W.) expressed the hope that the *OED* would incorporate the correction into the supplement, but the note has so far not been taken into account. OED: 1905.

C77. *Curry favor, to*
The Academy 45, 1894, pp. 228–9; NQ 1921 XII/8: 512; 1921 XII/9: 77, 92.

'To try to ingratiate oneself'. The exchange is worth including, because it is typical of the progress of etymological research. By 1921, the origin of the phrase had been explained many times, but people kept writing letters to popular journals instead of opening a dictionary. Reference to Brewer, instead of Skeat and the *OED* (finally quoted on p. 92), is also characteristic. *To curry favor* goes back to the obsolete phrase *curry favel,* which is a partial translation of Old French *estriller (torcher) fauvel* 'to rub down the fallow horse'. It remains unclear why this action became a metaphor for duplicity in the *Roman de Fauvel* (1310), whose protagonist is a counterpart of the perfidious villain Reynard the Fox (Reineke Fuchs of the Dutch-German tradition). Henry Bradley (in *The Academy*) suggested the following explanation: "Fauvel represents the 'pale horse' *(equus pallidus)* which in the Apocalypse (vi. 8) is ridden by one 'whose name is Death.' According to patristic exegesis, the rider was Antichrist (so in St. Ambrose); and in the twelfth century his 'pallid' steed was explained as representing the hypocrites who gain a reputation for sanctity by the ascetic pallor of their countenances" (p. 229). JBK I 68–9. OED: 1557.

C78. *Curtain lecture*
ANQ 11, 1972: 24.

"A curtain lecture is a scolding given a husband by his wife and is so called from the curtained bed in which such a lecture might take place . . . . In 1637 Thomas Heywood published *A Curtaine Lecture,* composed of several short tales about shrewish wives' mistreatment of their husbands. . . . The use of the term and depictions of curtain lecturers [sic] continued up through the 19th century in plays, novels, and essays." OED: 1633.

C79. *Cut and run, to*
NQ 1882 VI/6: 246; MM 1, 1911: 56.

'To make a speedy departure from a hazardous situation rather than deal with it'. The nautical origin of the phrase was pointed out but without comment, probably because it is non-controversial: to escape imminent danger, the ship would depart, cut at the rigging and anchor, and sail with the wind; hence the metaphorical sense. OED: 1704.

C80. *Cut away, to*
NQ 1885 VI/11: 264, 454.

'To depart in a hurry'. Now the phrase is conversational or slang. Skeat (p. 264) suggested its origin from the phrase *cut a way* 'cut or force one's way through a wood'. He also suggested that *cut a stick* and *cut one's sticks* (which see) had a similar origin. His note was followed by a long discussion of *cut over,* but it shed no light on *cut away,* and it is not referenced here. *

C81. *Cut off one's nose to spite one's face, to*

NQ 1889 VII/8: 487.

'To do something stupid out of spite'. There is an exact French analog. The question about which came first has not been answered. OED: 1788 *(He cut off his nose to be revenged of his face).*

C82. *Cut of one's jib*

NQ 1854 I/10: 482; MM 2, 1912: 95 (31).

'One's appearance'. The reference is to the impression one makes on a stranger. Originally, 'a striking peculiarity of one's appearance'. Halliwell cites *to hang the jib* 'to look cross'. The correspondent to *MM* explained the nautical origin of the phrase: in time of war an enemy's ship is recognized by the cut of her jib (the foremost sail of a vessel). He quoted a 1740 text in which it is said that the natives of Central America recognized Europeans by their jib, staysails, and steering sails, the latter of which they seldom or never set. He wondered whether this could be the origin of the idiom. The editor added the following note: "The origin of the expression cannot have been much earlier than the date referred to (1740), for jibs had then but recently come into general use in full-rigged ships. The phrase seems to have become common during the Great French Wars, there being a decided difference between French and English cut jibs. The English jib was, I think, cut fairly high in the clue, while the French jib had its clue close down to the bowsprit." OED: 1823.

C83. *Cut one off with a shilling, to*

NQ 1854, I/9: 198; I/10: 75; 1875 V/3: 444, 513; V/4: 276, 333; 1880 VI/2: 324, 389 1881 VI/3: 89; 1928, 154: 244, 300, 337, 374, 429.

'To be disinherited from a will by being bequeathed a single shilling rather than nothing at all'. In I/10: 75, it is suggested that for a testator to prove that he was mentally alert, he had to leave the child at least something. The note in V/3: 444 discusses the early use of the law that allowed fathers and husbands to disinherit their children and wives by leaving them only a sixpence. In the note in VI/3: 89, the same circumstances are mentioned. In vol. 154, p. 374, a 1754 citation of the phrase is given. In a comment on the blog "The Oxford Etymologist" for August 18, 2021, SG gives a 1733 citation from *GM* (1733), p. 215. OED: 1762.

C84. *Cut one's stick, to*

NQ 1859 II/8: 413, 478–9; II/9: 53; 1860 II/9: 53, 207; 1874 V/1: 386, 493; 1943, 184: 286; 1898 IX/2: 326, 417; 1899 IX/3: 272, 434; 1907 X/8: 348; 1908 X/9: 132.

'To flee in a hurry'. In the note in II/8: 413, it is suggested that the phrase *to mo(u)lt one's stick,* once common in high life, was the predecessor of the "vulgarism" *to cut one's stick.* In II/8: 479, reference is given to Zechariah IV: 4–14, in which the cutting of a stick is described as the symbol of abruptly breaking off the brotherhood between two parties. In II/9: 53, the correspondent suggested the origin in the printing office (a compositor about to leave "cuts his composing stick"). All three hypotheses are rejected in II/9: 207. There, the idiom is traced to the song sung about 1820: "In the Saltmarket, Glasgow, beginning: 'Oh I creished my brogues and I cut my stick', being the adventures of an Irishman, in which of course the cutting of the stick referred to the common practice in Ireland of procuring a sapling before going off. It afterwards came to be the practice, when any one ran off or absconded, to say, that chap has cut his stick too, and thus the phrase originated and spread over the country." The same reference is given in IX/3: 272 and IX/3: 434 (the latter by James A. H. Murray). In X/8: 348, the custom is described that is of a similar kind: a hired worker on a farm would cut a new stick from the hedge and place it in the chimney corner if he meant to leave at Michaelmas. See also *Cut away* and *Hook it!* The references to dying Vikings (V/1: 386) and runaway American slaves (V/1: 493) can probably be discounted as irrelevant. OED: 1825.

C85. *Cut the cackle and get to the 'osses [horses], to*
Spectator 1929 142: 862; 1930, 158: 10, 51.

'To stop talking and come to the point'. The saying allegedly goes back to Andrew Ducrow, a horseman and actor, who believed that in a play action rather than dialogue [the text has *dialect* here] was important. OED: 1889 *(cut your cackle, and come to the 'osses)*.

C86. *Cut the loss, to*
NQ 1905 X/3: 69, 156.

'To diminish the loss'. The phrase (with *loss* in the singular) was known so little in 1905 that an explanation followed, though on p. 156 David Ricardo's (1772–1823) advice to this effect was quoted. OED: 1912.

C87. *Cut the mustard, to*
ANQ 10, 1971: 53.

'To achieve the standard of performance necessary for success'. The author of the note derives the idiom from *cut the muster* (*muster* 'sample'). But *cut the mustard* also means (or meant) 'to escape', and SG suggested that the idiom might once have meant cutting a path through overgrown mustard weeds. [Allen, p. 193, refers to *mustard* as meaning 'something outstanding, hot stuff.'] OED: 1891.

C88. *Cut the painter, to*
NQ 1903 IX/12: 307.

'To make off with oneself'. Of nautical origin. In the note, James A. H. Murray asked for early examples. (*Painter* 'a rope attached to the bow of a boat'.) OED: 1699.

D

D1. *Damned literary fellows*
NQ 1918 XII/4: 154.

The phrase was current in the form *d-d littery fellers* and became widely known in the 1870s; the "fellows" were the men of letters vilified by politicians. It seems to be certain that the phrase originated in the United States in connection with the nomination of Richard Henry Dana, the author of *Two Years Before the Mast,* as minister to England in 1876. *

D2. *Dam up Niagara with a pitchfork, to*

NQ 1880 VI/2: 164.

'To attempt the impossible'. A parallel to *Mop up the Atlantic.* *

D3. *Dance in a pig-trough, to*

NQ 1871 IV/8: 203, 291.

'To marry before one's older sibling'. Allegedly, on the wedding day, the unmarried elder siblings were expected to dance barefooted over furze brushes on the floor. The *pig trough* may have a similar origin. Dorsetshire. *

D4. *Dance the Phibbie, to*

NQ 1891 VII/12: 206, 394.

'Horse whipping'. The phrase has reference to an old dance called the Phœbe. West-country. EDD: *Phibbie.* *

D5. *Dance the ropes, to*

NQ 1904 X/2: 533.

This obsolete phrase probably referred to the items "of expenditure devoted to the pleasures of the time." *

D6. *Darnall for dim sight*

CS 1 1878, 22, 35.

The saying refers to a plant that hurts vision. It is known in various parts of England and was mentioned as early as 1597. Darnall "is not the estate in Cheshire of the name, but the hurtful weed which the farmers of every county would like to see banished from their fields."*

D7. *Davy Jones*

NQ 1851, I/3: 478, 509; MM 1, 1911: 358 (112); MM 2, 1912: 25 (112).

'The sailors' devil'. "There was in 1606 one David Jones, mate of the *Roebuck,* a vessel that plundered two Indian junks." This pirate "had a pet phrase about the place to which it was prudent to consign plundered ships and persons who knew too much" (p. 358). However, the phrase got into print more than a century later. There also is the idiom *Davy Jones's locker.* In NQ 1851, I/3: 509, the author derived Davy Jones from the prophet Jonah. [Holt, p. 93: "OED declines to guess, but does accent *duppy* as a West Indian word for ghost. Webster and others give 'dubby' as a variant of this, and 'dubby Jonah' as the origin of Davy Jones.] OED: 1726 *(David Jones's Locker)* and 1751 *(Davy Jones).*

D8. *Dead man's chest, the*

NQ 1934, 166: 98, 212.

The phrase was made famous by Robert L. Stevenson in *Treasure Island.* He borrowed it from Charles Kingsley's *At Last.* But, as the correspondent explains on p. 212: "I have always understood that a 'chest' in the West Indies means a small uninhabited island, so that 'The Dead Man's Chest' = Treasure Island." OED: 1883.

D9. *Dead Season*

NQ 1916 XII/2: 147.

'The period when 'society' has departed from a place of resort'. The author of the note points to the 1655 advertisement of the book mentioning the phrase but does not quote from it. OED: 1789.

D10. *Dear knows*

NQ 1897 VIII/11: 5, 57, 175, 253.

An adjunction. It was (or still is?) known in Scotland and among "the descendants of Scotch-Irish families settled in the United States." Some suggested that *dear* stands for "God," others that it is a euphemism for "Devil." [Compare *dear knows* 'God knows', *dear keep us* 'Lord save us', and *dear be here* 'good gracious' in Modern Scots.] There was some discussion of whether *dear* in the phrase is the same as in *dear me,* in *dear heart alive,* and especially in *deary-me-to-day.* See also *O dear me.* EDD: *Dear*; OED: 1876.

D11. *Defects of his qualities*

NQ 1898 IX/1: 367, 435.

This is A. L. Mayhew's comment (p. 435): "In the dictionary of Larousse, 1875, *s.v.* 'Defaut,' the phrase is quoted from the writings of Bishop Dupanloup: 'Heureux l'homme quand il n'a pas les défauts de ses qualités!'['Happy is the man who does not have the defects of his qualities']. I have always understood the phrase 'the defects of one's qualities' to mean the defects usually found in company with certain qualities—for instance, a man having the quality of thrift is liable to a corresponding defect in generosity." OED: 1845.

D12. *Derby ram*

NQ 1917 XII/3: 70, 154, 309.

"This legendary animal of gigantic proportions has been regarded as a quasi patron saint of Derbyshire for hard upon two hundred years" (p. 154). "The ram has been immortalized in a ballad of fifteen doggerel verses, originally published in a miscellany entitled 'Gimcrackiana', by one Richardson at Derby in 1833." "*The Derby Ram* was also the title of an intermittent illustrated periodical which appeared at election times in the sixth and seventh decades of the last century; and the phrase had such a vogue generally that a ram was adopted as the mascot of the 95th (Derbyshire) Regiment" (p. 155). ". . . the ballad was popular with the freshmen at Harvard College in the early sixties of the last [19th] century. It was sung with much enthusiasm, with a chorus or refrain of:—O! hunkey, dunkey Derby Ram, /A hunkey, dunkey day./ O! a hunkey, dunkey Derby Ram,/ A hunkey, dunkey day. The words of the song, I grieve to say, were decidedly coarse" (p. 309). OED: 1867.

D13. *Derry Down*

NQ 1910 XI/1: 228-9, 394.

'A meaningless refrain of popular songs.' This is neither an idiom nor a familiar quotation, but questions about its origin keep turning up in word columns, and it is clear that modern commentators do not know the answers once given in *NQ*. Perhaps *derry down* deserves an entry as a special word group. Allegedly, the refrain is of ancient Welsh origin, with *hai down ir deri danno* meaning 'come, let us run to the oak grove'. It is believed to be part of an old Druidic song, a call to the people to their religious assemblies in the groves but, as pointed out, "the talk about old religious rites is rubbish" (pp. 228-9). EDD: *Derry Down*; OED: *a*1556 (perhaps the 1910 exchange in *NQ* deserves an honorary mention).

D14. *Devil among the tailors*
NQ 1880 VI/1: 215, 402.

The phrase, which initially meant 'a disturbance', is said to derive from a well-known Scottish reel tune, but it seems to go back to tailors' riot in 1805. It was caused by the performance of the play *The Tailors*. A crowd of tailors felt that the play was offensive and rebelled. Today it is a table game, a country dance, fiddle music, etc. EDD: *Devil*; OED: 1756.

D15. *Devil overlooks Lincoln*
NQ 1857 II/3: 308-9; II/4: 197; 1876 V/5: 510 1876 V/6: 77, 275, 415, 459; 1877 V/7: 216, 257; 1891 VII/12: 340; 1892, VIII/2: 128, 210.

In NQ II/3: 308-9, a long passage from Fuller's *Worthies,* containing an explanation of the phrase, is given. The author of the note in II/4: 197 quotes a passage from John Pointer's *Oxoniensis Academia*: 1749, p. 53: "The image of the devil, that stood many years on the top of this college (or else that over Lincoln Cathedral), gave occasion for that proverb, to look on one as the devil looks over Lincoln." In VIII/2: 210, two Lincoln towers are again discussed. More probable, according to the author, is the reference to Lincoln College, Oxford. Edwards's *Words, Facts, and Phrases* and *The Gentleman's Magazine* for September 15, 1731 are quoted to support this conclusion. The phrase occurs in *Fortunes of Nigel* (Chapter 21). OED: 1546 *(Lyke as the deuill lookt ouer Lyncolne).*

D16. *Devil to pay (and no pitch hot)*
NQ 1861 II/12: 380; 1900 IX/6: 327; MM 1, 1911: 32 (17), 59 (17).

'Service expected, and no one ready to perform it'. The phrase becomes less obscure if *the devil* means the seam between the covering board and the deck planking, but no authority for such a suggestion is given; Cf. *Between the Devil and the deep sea.* One of the authors (II/12: 380) sees the full form as proof of nautical origin, [but Allen, p. 211, rejects it and refers to a contract with the Devil]. JBK I, 107. OED: *a*1500.

D17. *Dicky o' t' Linkins*
LNQ 1, 1889: 87.

'A person who is too idle to keep to any one calling, but lives by getting occasional jobs'. Only a query about this idiom appeared; no response followed. *

D18. *Die in beauty, to*
NQ 1911 XI/3: 7, 74, 112, 234.

'To die gracefully'. The phrase became popular in several languages from Ibsen's *Hedda Gabler,* but it was coined by Charles Doyne Sillery (1807-1836), a Scottish poet, in whose eight-line poem "Eldred of Erin" every line began with "she died in beauty." The song enjoyed great popularity in the United States. *

D19. *Dine with Duke Humphrey, to*

NQ 1869, IV/4: 313, 397; 1873, IV/12: 439; 1881 VI/4: 166, 337, 475; 1882 VI/5: 58, 175; 1909 X/11: 158.

'To stay without dinner'. Allegedly, the reference is to the Duke Humphrey of Gloucester. Two explanations have been offered. The first must have been written tongue in cheek: 1) "Surely, to dine with this excellent duke is to take your crust to the Bodleian when you have got nothing better to eat, and there consume it contentedly in a corner of his library over some of the stores of mental pabulum provided—erstwhile at least—by his bounty" (IV/4: 397). 2) "The Beauchamp tomb in Old St. Paul's, erroneously called Duke Humphrey's (the 'good' Duke was entombed at St. Alban's), was near the walk to which men resorted, while others dined. The Exchange was said to be the trysting place of the supperless" (IV/2: 439). [In an ironic panegyric of the Chuzzlewits, Dickens refers to the nobility with whom one of them hobnobbed: he constantly dined with Duke Humphrey. Hyamson, p. 193, adds: "The phrase, however, orig[inally] meant 'to accept hospitality,' after the proverbial hospitality extended to all comers by Humphrey, Duke of Gloucester (1391-1447)".] JBK I: 54. OED: 1592 *(To seek his dinner in Poules with duke Humphrey).*

D20. *Dirty work at the crossroads*

NQ 1917 XII/3: 509; 1918 XII/4: 25; 1933, 165: 141.

Vol. 165, p. 141, offers the suggestion that the phrase is connected with the custom of burying suicides at crossroads with stakes through their hearts, but cites no evidence. *There has been dirty work at the crossroads* is a quotation from one of Walter Melville's melodramas popular in the 1900s, *A Girl's Cross Roads.* OED: 1914.

D21. *Dish of tea*

NQ 1909 X/12: 287, 377, 436; 1912 XI/6: 370, 433, 494.

"The expression 'dish of tea' arose from the practice of drinking tea from the saucer, and not, as usual now, from the cup. . . . There used to be engravings on the backs of old copybooks, and one represented 'Taking a Dish of Tea'" (p. 377). It "arose from the fact that the earliest teacups were made without handles, and were very wide and shallow" (p. 436). However, on the same page, we read: "It cannot be conceded that the expression 'dish of tea' originated in the practice of drinking tea from the saucer, because in Shakespeare's time, and later, a 'dish of milk', a 'dish of aqua vitæ', a 'dish of coffee', and a 'dish of tea' were common locutions for a quantity more or less indefinite; and saucers, which were specially used for sauce (hence their name), had not come into general use, nor had teacups. . . . If the term 'dish' has any particular reference to the shallow vessel, it is to the bowl." The notes published in 1912 are interesting only in so far as they trace the progress of the word *dish* in early Modern English. EDD: *Dish/Tea;* OED: 1694.

D22. *Distance no object*

NQ 1954, 199: 497.

In *Society for Pure English, Tract 36* (1931), Charles T. Onions traced the origin of several kindred phrases. *

D23. *Do as the cow o' Forfar did, take a stannin' drink, to*
The Athenæum 1862/1: 112.

'To take a drink without paying for it'. An anecdote from *Waverly* is given, to illustrate the saying. Scotland. Hislop (81). *

D24. *Dog in the morning*
MM 60, 1974: 438 (19); 61, 1975: 90 (19); 61, 1975: 199 (19); 61, 1975: 297 (19).

The exchange offers a detailed discussion of the mock sun and related weather phenomena. The entire saying is "A dog in the morning, sailor take warning;/ A dog in the night is sailor's delight." *

D25. *Do gooseberry, to*
NQ 1860 II/10: 307, 377; 1861 II/12: 336; 1898 IX/1: 147, 293, 452; Englische Studien 24, 1898: 151; The Spectator 111, 1913: 564.

'To act as a chaperone'. *Gooseberry* enters into at least three idioms that may be relevant to this phrase: *old gooseberry* 'Devil', *play old gooseberry* 'play the devil', and *gooseberry fool* 'a dish of stewed, etc. fruit'. Sometimes a young girl went on a date and asked a friend to accompany her for propriety's sake; the accompanying person was known as *gooseberry fool*. To this *kick up old gooseberry* 'to create commotion in the room by romping, etc.' can be added . Many correspondents suggested that this shrub had been associated with the Devil because the berries are prickly (the Devil it reputed to have horns, his tail stings, and he is said to carry a fork and the darts to throw). The "botanical" explanation (IX/1: 293) that "to play gooseberry with anything means to invert it, as is done with old gooseberry bushes when their roots become branches and their branches roots" sounds too clever. Still another idea, shared by Johan Storm (*Englishe Philologie,* 2nd ed., p. 103), who quoted Theodore Hook's *Parson's Daughter,* is that "one who picks gooseberries for you, saves you the thorns, the petty troubles and worries of life." Several correspondents to *NQ* offered a similar conjecture. In II/2: 336, it is said that "gooseberry picking" has the provincial synonym *daisy picking*. That *gooseberry picker* means 'chaperon' is obvious. The original connection with the Devil is less so, though it does not look improbable (on *Gooseberry* 'Devil', especially in Lancashire, see *Germania* 21, 1876: 76). OED: 1837 *(play gooseberry).*

D26. *Dog's interest*
NQ 1887 VII/4: 505.

'Kindly sympathy'. The reference is to a dog appreciating its master's kindness ('He didn't take a dog's interest in what I did for him'). Apparently, local usage, but the place where the phrase occurred was not specified. *

D27. *Dog's nose cold*
NQ 1870, IV/6: 495; 1871, IV/7: 43, 114.

This is part of the longer saying *A maid's knee and a dog's nose are the two coldest things in creation.* In 1870, the phrase about the dog's nose was still common in the west of Scotland. Cf. *As cold as a maid's knee.* *

D28. *Donkey's years*

NQ 1916 XII/2: 506; 1917 XII/3: 39, 74.

'A very long time'. This piece of slang, a pun on *donkey's ears,* was new in London in 1916 but familiar to a correspondent from Wiltshire in the 1870s. OED: 1916.

D29. *Don't cross the bridge until you come to it*

AS 1921: 344; ANQ 1, 1941: 105; ANQ 2, 1942: 79.

'Don't worry about the problem until it appears'. On p. 79, Apperson is cited, who dates the proverb to 1921 (Apperson depended on the first edition of the *OED*). The discussion started in connection with Longfellow's use of the saying, and this is still the earliest quotation known. OED: 1850 *(Do not cross the bridge till you come to it).*

D30. *Don't give up the ship!*

NQ 1929, 156: 453.

'Fight to the end'. The situation is described in which this proverbial phrase was allegedly used for the first time [1813]. OED: 1816 *(Not to give up the ship).*

D31. *Do one's darg, to*

NQ 1879, V/12: 128, 239.

Darg is a syncopated form of *daywerk* or *daywark* 'daywork' *(OED).* P. 239 offers a fanciful reference to Scandinavian mythology, but the association with *day* is correct. Thus, "a love-darg is a day's free help given to a farmer by his neighbors; and a Scotch newspaper of today reports a short darg movement among the coal miners of Wishaw in Lancarshire." Scotland and northern England. *

D32. *Do the dancers, to*

NQ 1900 IX/6: 288, 418.

'Trick one' (slang). This is the situation in which "doing the dancers" was played on the landlord of an inn: "Two men, it appears, entered the taproom, and, calling for drinks, tendered a coin which necessitated the attendant going upstairs to the cashbox for change. The position of the latter was thus discovered, and a short time only had passed before the box and the money it contained were stolen" (p. 288). A synonymous phrase was *to ring the changes.* The following explanation appeared on p. 418: "'Dancers' was criminals' slang for the steps of the treadmill, the 'stepper', the 'wheel of life', the 'everlasting staircase', or 'Colonel Chesterton's everlasting staircase', after the inventor. Hence the word's application to the domestic staircase. The term probably came in vogue with the invention of the treadmill, which was often the first act in the drama which culminated in the 'dance upon nothing', that is, hanging." *

D33. *Down chests, up hammocks*

MM 35, 1949: 251 (15).

'Prepare for action'. Nautical use. *

D34. *Down corn, down hops*

NQ 1885 VI/12: 467; 1886 VII/1: 192.

Usually *up corn, down horn,* which see. *Corn* of course means 'grain'. East Suffolk. *

D35. *Down to the ground, to*

NQ 1898 IX/1: 145, 291-2; 1898 IX/II: 73.

'To satisfy completely'. The phrase had a slangy tinge, and the discussion turned round the use of *down to the ground* in the Old Testament, but there it had a direct meaning (with references to bodies on the ground and with *suit*; see the Authorized Version, The Book of Judges XX: 21, 25; the Hebrew text is unambiguious here). Apperson (p. 292) noted that for 'completely' English once had the phrase *up and down*. *

D36. *Downright dunstable*

NQ 1882 VI/6: 228, 377; 1883 VI/7: 276.

'Plain-spoken'. The allusion is to the phrase *as plain as Dunstable Highway*. Fuller, Nares, and Halliwell cite it. OED: 1546 *(As playne as Dunstable hye waie)*. Svartengren: 266 *(plain as Dunstable Highway)*.

D37. *Drag the Devil by the tail, to*

NQ 1913 XI/8: 467; 1914 XI/9: 14.

The proverb alludes to the daily struggle of the poor and is often used as a warning against early or improvident marriages. Ireland. OED: 1788 *(To pull the devil by the tail)*.

D38. *Draw a bead, to*

NQ 1926, 150: 100, 178.

'To take aim'. Apparently, the phrase is an Americanism. The bead is the foresight of a rifle. EDD: *Draw*; OED: 1831.

D39. *Draw the long bow, to*

NQ 1861 II/11: 349, 513; 1867, III/12: 185.

'To lie, tell falsehoods'. In II/11: 513, numerous sayings derived from archery are cited: *to out-shoot a man in his own bow, always have two strings to your bow, get the shaft-hand of your adversaries, draw not thy bow before thy arrow be fixed, to kill two birds with one shaft, to shoot wide of the mark, the fool's bolt is soon shot; he had a famous bow, but it was up at the castle,* and *an archer is known by his aim, and not by his arrows.* OED: 1667 *(Drawing the long Bow)*.

D40. *Draw the nail, to*

NQ 1884 VI/ 9: 46.

'To break a vow'. "This is a curious Cheshire metaphorical expression, which is occasionally heard, and which signifies the breaking of a vow. It originates in an equally curious custom, not, perhaps, very common, but practised now and then in the neighbourhood of Mobberley and Wilmslow. Two or more men would bind themselves by a vow—say, not to drink beer. They would set off together to a wood at some considerable distance, and drive a nail into a tree, swearing at the same time that they would drink no beer while that nail remained in that tree. If they got tired of abstinence they would meet together and set off 'to draw the nail', literally pulling it out from the tree; after which they could resume their customary drinking habits without doing violence to their conscientious feelings." [This custom might be a distant echo of the folklore motif known from the tales in which two brothers part but drive an object into a tree. Rust on it will mean that one of the characters is in danger or dead.] Cheshire. EDD: *Draw.* *

D41. *Dressed up to the nines*
NQ 1897 VIII/12: 469; 1898 IX/1: 57, 211, 338; 1902 IX/10: 387, 456; 1903 IX/11: 34, 90.

'Dressed up elaborately'. The discussion was about whether *to the nines* goes back to *up to the eyne* 'up to the eyes' or to *nines,* meaning Muses. In 1898 (IX/1: 57), Skeat defended the first of those interpretations. He had two allies: A. Smythe Palmer and Charles P. G. Scott, the etymology editor for *The Century Dictionary* (IX/11: 90). OED: 1719 *(To the nines).* [Allen, p. 511, mentions and rejects another nonsensical explanation.]

D42. *Dresser of plays*
NQ 1883 VI/7: 209, 455, 479.

'Someone who "alters and amends" old plays'. The phrase was traced to Ben Jonson's *Poetaster,* and seems to have enjoyed some popularity at that time. *

D43. *Drimble-pin to wind the sun down*
NQ 1874 V/1: 189.

The phrase was used with reference to an unprofitable enterprise. No indication is given of the locality where it was once used or the circumstances that brought forth the allusion. *

D44. *Drink by word of mouth, to*
NQ 1919 XII/ 5: 98, 136, 330.

'To drink from the bottle by turns'. "Often a bottle of beer came into a hayfield unexpectedly. A search would be made under every coat and shawl lying on the ground for a glass or mug to drink from. Should this search prove unsuccessful, and no small receptacle be found to pour the beverage into, then it was said, 'We must *drink by word of mouth*'. This meant to drink from the bottle by turns, which naturally gave a great advantage to the old toper accustomed to absorb his liquor from the bottle. The origin of the saying was probably the Fleet prison, about 9 miles west of our town; thus this notorious locality would make it of Cockney derivation" (p. 136). But the phrase was not limited to the hayfield, as follows from its use in Swift's *Polite Conversations* (p. 330). OED: 1688.

D45. *Drink like a fish, to*
ANQ 5, 1890: 49.

The note points out that fish hardly ever drink. Therefore, "the simile has no meaning, except so far as the *appearance* is concerned." Svartengren: 212. OED: 1744.

D46. *Drown the miller, to*
NQ 1859 II/7: 70, 137, 384.

This was said about someone who happened to make toddy (whisky punch) too weak by mixing too much water with the spirit. An explanation from Jamieson was quoted: "The primary meaning of this phrase is used in regard to baking, when too much water is put in, and there is not meal enough to bring the dough to a proper consistence; and also to the operation of making punch or toddy, when more water is poured in than corresponds to the quantity of spirituous liquor. In short, the saying is applied to anything which, however acceptable in itself, defeats the end for which it is desired, by its excess or exuberance. It is used sometimes to denote bankruptcy" (p. 70). The reference to the miller appears on p. 137: "*Drown the miller* means too much water at the mill. If the mill-stream below the mill is dammed or stopped, the water is ponded back and the mill becomes what the millers call 'tailed'; and there being too much water, the mill cannot work, and so the miller is said to be 'drowned'." The note on p. 384 develops the same theme. Scotland. EDD: *Drown*; OED: 1805.

D47. *Drug in the market*

NQ 1904 X/1: 149, 235, 316; 1921 XII/9: 529.

Drug 'a commodity no longer in demand (and thus unsaleable)'. The *OED* has an early citation for the phrase in which *in* alternates with *on*, but it is unclear whether we are dealing with *drug* having several meanings or homonyms. OED: 1622 *(Drug)*, 1804 *(Drug in the market)*.

D48. *Ducks and drakes*

NQ 1920 XII/7: 229.

The phrase *to make ducks and drakes with one's money* is based on a well-known game. The note suggests that not only flat pebbles but also real coins were also thrown over the surface of water. EDD: *Ducks*; OED: 1585 *(Ducke and a drake)*.

D49. *Duck's news*

NQ 1915 XI/11: 110, 174.

'Stale or dead news'. The phrase was known at least as early as 1875–1885. No explanation is offered in the notes. Cf. the next item and *Roper's news.* *

D50. *Duck's storm*

NQ 1915 XI/11: 174, 188, 254, 370.

'Old news'. Also *goose's storm* and several other similar sayings are known in different parts of England and Scotland (see especially p. 370). Perhaps, it was suggested, duck's storm brings rain, while goose's storm brings snow.

D51. *Durham and death*

NQ 1876 V/6: 117.

"In the days of Border warfare travellers of extra nervous temperament going from England to Scotland, dreading the terrible running of the gauntlet between the two kingdoms, doubtless bothered their friends by their evil prognostications at an unnecessarily early period of the journey and thereby received the appropriate rebuke, 'Ye aye cry death or ye're by Durham', Durham being at that time a day's journey at least from the Border." Cf. *Cry out death before you are past Durham.* *

D52. *Dusty melder*

SNQ 1901 II/2: 142; 1901 III/2: 16.

'The last of a group or a batch'. *Melder* is 'a quantity of meal ground at one time'. Jamieson explains a dusty melder as meaning the last melder of a crop. But why *dusty*? This is the suggested explanation: "An old Act of the Scotch Parliament enjoined upon all farmers to thresh out the whole crop remaining in sheaf at May 1, whether in stack or barn, no doubt to prevent keeping up grain for a high price. When harvest drew near, all grain not sold had to be dressed and sent to the mill, and after lying in a barn all summer the last part of the crop must have been a very dusty melder" (p. 16). Scotland. EDD: *Melder.* *

D53. *Dutch courage*
NQ 1859 II/7: 277; 1881, VI/3: 289, 458, 498; 1892, VIII/2: 304; 1895 VIII/7: 88, 314, 375; 1903 IX/11: 47, 97, 237.

'Bravery induced by drinking'. According to William Platt (VI/3: 458), "this is an ironical expression, dating its origin as far back as 1745, and conveys a sneering allusion to the conduct of the Dutch at the battle of Fontenoy. At the commencement of the engagement the onslaught of the English allied army promised victory, but the Dutch betook themselves to an ignominious flight." The explanation is refuted by the chronology. A less serious interpretation is offered on p. 498: "I thought everybody knew that 'Dutch courage' was a jocular term for a glass of hollands, when resorted to as a fillip for a faint heart." A still more ingenious tale is told on p. 304. The source is *The Streets of London* by J. T. Smith, who refers to a 1738 story: "Very merry, and very mad, and very drunken the people were; and grew more and more so every day. As to the materials, beer and ale were considerable articles; they went a great way in the work at first, but were far from being sufficient, and then strong waters, which had not been long in use, came into play. The occasion was this: In the Dutch wars, it had been observed that the captain of the Hollander's men-of-war, when they were about to engage with our ships, usually set a hogshead of brandy abroach afore the mast, and bid the men drink *sustick* that they might fight *lustick* ['merry']; and our poor seamen felt the force of the brandy to their cost. We were not long behind them; but suddenly after the war we began to abound in strong-water shops." Cf. the following suggestion for what it is worth: "May not this expression have arisen out of the practice, stated to have existed, of making Dutch criminals sentenced to death drunk before hanging or beheading?" (p. 237). OED: 1826.

D54. *Dutch month*
NA 1881 VI/3: 187.

The note contains only the following question: "What is the origin of this duration of time when it takes the meaning of a long time, as in the following sentence?—'why, you will be as long as a Dutch month'." *

E

E1. *Eat crow*
ANQ 1, 1888: 161; CoE 48/2-3: 44-7

'To suffer humiliation'. The phrase was coined in the US. Two stories are told about some offenders made to eat crow (a dish they did not like), allegedly explaining the origin of the phrase. CoE provides numerous quotations. All the versions agree that a cantankerous farmer was outwitted by his boarders and wound up eating crow (in the direct sense of the word). The punch line was "I kin eat a crow, but I'll be damned if I hanker after (arter) it." "The phrase *eating crow* was widely used and explained in the presidential election of 1880, which evidently played a role in its popularization." OED: 1851 *(eat a crow).*

E2. *Eat humble pie, to*

NQ 1850, I/1: 54, 92, 168; 1898 IX/2: 286.

'To suffer humiliation'. The notes explain the phrase as it is done in all dictionaries (*humble* = *umble*) and give references to some older sources. [Does *eat the leek* 'to suffer humiliation' have anything to do with it? JBK I, 59.] OED: 1830.

E3. *Eat one's hat, to*

NQ 1887 VII/3: 94, 197, 352, 433.

'A threat meaning that the speaker will do such an improbable thing as eating his hat if something happens'. The discussion turned around the suggestion that *hat* was a substitution for *heart*. But this is unlikely, because *boots* and *head* (the latter in *Oliver Twist*) appear as synonyms for *hat* in the phrase. The origin of the "threat" with *hat* in it was not ascertained. OED: 1767 *(I'll eat my hat)*.

E4. *Egg and the halfpenny*

NQ 1874 V/1: 326, 432; 1874 V/2: 57.

The phrase is synonymous with *you cannot eat the cake and have it too,* that is, if you spent some money for an egg, you will have only the egg, not the money. Judging by the discussion, the phrase goes back to E *le œuf et le maille* [*maille* is the smallest coin]. *

E5. *Either make a spoon or spoil a horn*

NQ 1909 X/12: 509; 1910 XI/1: 57.

The meaning of the idiom was obscure to the author of the note (p. 509), but the *OED* gives the phrase with the explanation 'to make a determined effort to achieve something, whether ending in success or failure' (originally Scottish), and explains that the making of spoons out of the horns of cattle or sheep was common in Scotland till late in the 19th century. Interesting details are given on p. 57; they match the information in the *OED*. EDD: *Spoon*; OED: 1817.

E6. *Ember Days*

NQ 1852 I/6: 194; 1878 V/9: 308, 453.

'The name of the four periods of fasting and prayer'. The correspondent writing to 1852 cited several valueless explanations but knew the promising conjecture that *ember* goes back to Old Engl. *ymbren* 'run about' (*Ember days* 'fasts in course'). However, he derived the phrase from Latin *Quattuor tempora* 'four periods' (Dutch *Quatertemperdag*, German *Quatember Woche*). On p. 308, an ingenious comparison is made between *ember days* and *Ash Wednesday*. However, *ember* turned up only in Middle English (the Old English for *ember* was *æmerge*), while *ymbērne* 'ember days' in texts is as old as 1000 *(OED)*. Most correspondents favored the Latin source. ("If we consider that the ember days are institutions of the Roman Catholic Church, and has no special name in Anglo-Saxon [which is wrong], it is clear that we must look to the language of the Romish ritual for an explanation," p. 453). The *OED* finds it not improbable that *ember days* is a folk etymological alteration of the Latin phrase. OED: *a*1000 *(ymbren-wican)*.

E7. *Emerald Isle*
NQ 1889 VII/8: 245, 333; 1892 VIII/2: 245, 397.

'Ireland'. There is good evidence that the phrase was coined by Dr. William Drennan. The conclusion was called into question on p. 245 but for no valid reason. OED: 1795.

E8. *Enough to make a man strike his own father*
NQ 1881 VI/3: 430; 1881 VI/4: 54, 78.

This phrase reported on p. 430 from Warwickshire has several variants (*grandmother* and *daddy* instead of *father*) and is said about a sight, a deed, *etc.* It was known on both sides of the Atlantic. *

E9. *Every bullet has its billet*
NQ 1877 V/8: 68; 1891 VII/11: 18, 117, 275, 478; 1891 VII/12: 94; 1920 XII/7: 109, 138.

Literally, 'every soldier is assigned his destination'. On p. 138, the phrases *every bullet hath a lighting place* and *every ball had its billet* are given. OED: 1765.

E10. *Every cock is proud on his own dunghill*
NQ 1894 VIII/6: 286, 457; 1895 III/7: 54.

This is a mocking reference to local patriotism. In VIII/6: 286, the variant *every cock crows on his dunghill* is cited. [Analogous phrases exist in many languages.]*

E11. *Every man has his price*
NQ 1878, V/9: 328, 371; 1907 X/7: 367, 470, 492; 1907 X/8: 313; 1908 X/9: 378; 1914 XI/10: 66.

'No one is incorruptible'. The notes offer an instructive discussion of the context of the phrase. OED: 1734.

E12. *Every man is a fool or a physician at forty (thirty)*
NQ 1850 I/2: 349; 1943, 185: 77; 1879 V/11: 425; 1879 V/12: 215, 516; 1889 VII/7: 68, 270; 1890 VII/9: 38; 1928, 154: 27.

The phrase has several variants. On pp. 425 and 516, it is shown that the proverb goes back to Tacitus and eventually to Tiberius. The discussion is series VII sheds no additional light on the proverb's source, except for pointing out that at forty a man can be "both." OED: 1606 *(A foole or a physition).*

E13. *Every pea hath its vease*
NQ 1858 II/6: 397, 423.

Vease (= *feeze*), now regional US, is explained in the *OED* as 'rush, impetus'. But the sense of the proverb remains obscure (p. 397). Ray, as quoted in Bohn, gave an ungrounded derivation of the word from Italian (p. 423) and the unacceptable gloss 'flatulence' for *vease*. OE *besam,* according to the *OED (pace CD),* has nothing to do with *fȳsan.* *

E14. *Exception proves the rule*
NQ 1873 IV/11: 197; 1936, 170: 407, 443.

Prove means 'to test' in this saying (Skeat). OED: 1664.

E15. *Eye of the master (is worth both his hands), the*
NQ 1861 II/12: 380.
Often only *the eye of the master* is said. This is general advice to be careful, but the full form had a different implication, namely, that a good master should oversee the work of others rather than do everything himself (p. 381). *

F

F1. *Face the music, to*
NQ 1896 VIII/9: 168, 272, 477; 1896 VIII/10: 226, 306, 403; 1898 IX/2: 135; ANQ 1888 vol. 1: 203.
"According to J. Fenimore Cooper, the phrase is derived from the stage, and used by actors in the green-room when preparing to go on the boards to literally *face the music.* Another explanation traces it to militia-muster, where every man is expected to appear fully equipped and armed, when in rank and file, *facing the music*" *(ANQ).* A similar explanation, but referring to military riding, is as follows: "When a horse is young to his work, it is one of the difficulties of his rider to get him to 'face' the regimental band" (VIII/9: 272). In VIII/9: 477, Barrère's *Dictionary of Slang . . .* is quoted: "Originally army slang (American) applied to men when drummed out to the tune of the 'Rogue's March'." The note in VIII/10: 306 says: "The correct or usual rendering of the above American slang ejaculation is, 'Wake up, hoss, and face the music'. . . . it was commonly addressed by drivers, overseers, and employers generally, to men as well as horses, by way of an incentive or spur of activity." [Funk, pp. 192–3, repeats the explanation referring to army slang.] OED: 1834.

F2. *Fains* or *fain it*
NQ 1856, II/2: 388; NQ 1871, IV/7: 44; XIII/3: 377.
'A request for a truce in a game'. The correspondents suggested that *feign* is meant. *NQ* XIII/3: 377 contains several letters on this word under the rubric *faintits,* and II/2: 388 has a letter entitled "Fain play": the author wondered whether the etymology *faineanter* 'to do nothing' sheds any light on *fain(s),* and also suggested the equation of *fain* with *feign.* Cf. *Bags I.* OED: 1870.

F3. *Fair field and no favor*
NQ 1855, I/12: 167; 1944, 186: 116.
'Equity in the conditions, fair play'. The note suggests a classical source (Livy XXV. 9). OED: 1470 *(fayre fylde)* but 1703 for *A fair field and no favor.*

F4. *Fair play is a jewel*
NQ 1865 III/8: 317.
This saying is or was to be found in Kent as part of a longer formula: 'Fair play is a jewel! Lucy, let go of my hair'. 'Here the young audacious' is supposed to be in conflict with his *sister.* Against his *mother* however, according to the vernacular of the same parts, he managed differently: 'A brave boy, and a bold un! cut off his hair to fight his mother.'" OED: 1799.

F5. *Familiarity breeds contempt*

NQ 1878, V/9: 467, 497; NQ 1878, V/10: 39, 239; 1883 VI/7: 117; 1888 VII/5: 247; 1888 VII/6: 216, 332; 1889 VII/7: 75; 1908 X/9: 407; ANQ 4, 1889: 41.

The phrase may be a rendering of a Latin proverb (X/9: 407). The same note contains a brief discussion of the precise meaning of the phrase. In series VII, several old authors are quoted, but the quotations show that the idea, rather than its exact formulation in English, is very old. OED: 1539 *(familiartitie might breade him contempte).*

F6. *Far-fetched and little worth*

MCNNQ 1, 1878: 18.

There was an early proverb, known to Ben Jonson, *far-fetched and dear-bought.* The question was whether William Cowper's *far-fetched and little worth* used in *The Task* (1785) had been proverbial or his coinage. OED: 1748 *(Far-fetch'd, and dear-bought is fittest for the Ladies).*

F7. *Fear no colors, to*

NQ 1966, 211: 54.

'To have no fear'. The note gives a few early occurrences of this idiom. The *OED* quotes Nashe, 1592 and marks the phrase as obsolete (no examples after 1882). OED: 1592.

F8. *Feather in one's cap*

NQ 1854 I/9: 220, 378; I/10: 315; 1935, 166: 409; 1934, 167: 69.

'A matter of pride'. The prevailing opinion was that among warlike people, every feather stood for a killed enemy. On p. 315, a more peaceful origin is suggested: "Among the ancient warriors it was customary to honour such of their followers as distinguished themselves in battle by presenting them with a feather for their caps, which, when not in armour, was the covering for their heads." However, no one provided references to their sources. P. 409 cites analogs in French and Dutch. JBK I, 239–40. OED: 1655 *(A feather in his cap).*

F9. *Feathers off a frog*

NQ 1872 IV/10: 521; 1873 IV/11: 63.

'A thing impossible to obtain'. There is a French analog *être chargé d'argent comme un crapaud de plumes* [literally, 'to be as full of money as a frog of feathers'], that is, to be as poor as a church mouse. [Thus, the senses do not match too well]. *

F10. *Feed a cold and starve a fever*

NQ 1881 VI/3: 429; 1887 VI/4: 54.

A query was asked about the meaning of this proverbial saying, occurring, among others, in Mark Twain. There is a variant with *stuff* for *feed.* The implication seems to be that, if you cure yourself of a cold, a fever will not develop. The *OED* has only the phrase *to starve a fever* 'to treat (a disease) by withholding or limiting the patient's food' (several variants from 1617 onward).

F11. *Feed the Armenians, to*

NQ 1939, 177: 443.

This may be part of the phrase *enough to feed the Armenians,* that is, much more than enough. Probably an American coinage, even if an echo of the policies in Gladstone's days. *

F12. *Feed the brute, to*
NQ 1904 X/1: 416; 1904 X/2: 257, 298.

A humorous recommendation to a married woman for making her husband happy. No source of the phrase was indicated. *

F13. *Fegges after peace*
NQ 1898 IX/2: 387, 430, 536.

Fegges = *fecks* 'faith'? or 'fair'?, or an Anglicised version of Latin "Ficus post pisces"? [literally, *a fig tree after fishes.*] EDD: *Fegges.* *

F14. *Fetch a compass, to*
NQ 1872, IV/9: 390, 454; IV/10: 37.

'To turn around'. *Fetch a compass* means the same as *fetch a windlass* (the two words were at one time synonyms). On p. 37, *fetch a walk* is cited, a phrase common in the West of England. OED: 1535 *(fetcheth his compase)*.

F15. *Fiddler's money*
NQ 1876 V/6: 536; 1877 V/7: 138.

'Small silver coins'. The phrase perhaps "originated in the fact that a sixpence was the time-honoured coin and amount for a party of dancers to give a fiddler for playing a 'three-handed' or 'four-handed reel' at village fairs" (p. 138). OED: 1597 *(fidler's wages)*.

F16. *Fight dog, fight bear (the Devil part you)*
NQ 1861 II/12: 381.

The idiom "seems to be merely a recommendation to go stoutly to work. But the old ending is, 'the devil part you'; and it seems to mean that when two quarrelsome persons fall foul of each other, no one but a lover of mischief would set them free to annoy their peaceable neighbours." The short variant probably means: "Go and do your work well." OED: 1583.

F17. *Fill the bill, to*
NQ 1913 XI/8: 390.

'To suit the case'. The editorial note explains with reference to the *OED*: "The phrase would seem to be theatrical slang, and the bill a playbill—'filled' in the sense that a playbill is filled by a 'star' actor's name, to the exclusion of the names of minor actors." OED: 1861.

F18. *Find a pin for every bore, to*
NQ 1879 V/11: 89.

'To be able to find a fit for every situation' (*bore* 'hole'). The phrase is said to go back to an old allegory. The question was about that allegory, but it received no answer. *

F19. *Fine words butter no parsnips*
NQ 1885 VI/11: 228, 358; 1893 VIII/4: 480; 1894 VIII/5: 174.

"'Mere words are not enough as sustenance', 'do not talk: act!' In this proverb, *fine* alternates with *fair* and *soft*. The saying's natural complement is *hard words break no bones*" (p. 228). *Good words fill not a sack* (p. 358) means the same. *Parsnips* must have been chosen more or less arbitrarily, because *cabbage* also occurred in its place (p. 174). The stupid idea of buttering vegetables informs Fool's taunt in *King Lear* (II. 4): "Twas her brother that, in pure kindness to his horse, buttered his hay" (p. 358). OED: 1638 (*Faire words butter no parsnips*).

F20. *First catch your hare*
NQ 1885 VI/11: 90, 197; 1886 VII/2: 398, 492; 1891 VII/12: 404, 453; 1892 VIII/1: 33; 1895 VIII/7: 106, 233; 1903 IX/12: 125, 518; 1904 X/1: 175, 254, 338.

According to the note in VII/2: 398, this is probably a garbled version (because of a misprint) of *first case* [that is, skin] *your hare* in Mrs. Glasse's famous cook(ery) book, but the author's suggestion is at odds with chronology. In VI/11: 197, Brewer refers to his book, the entry "Glasse," and in VIII/1: 33, Mrs. Rundle's cook(ery) book is mentioned as a possible source. A most unexpected explanation appeared in VIII/7: 106: "Hitherto the expression had been universally attributed to Mrs. Glasse, but Mr. G. A. Sala stated that he had examined no fewer than twelve editions of her celebrated cookery book, and had failed to find it. It really originated in the following way. 'Tis sixty years since', or something like it, that Frederick Yates, the comedian, father of the lamented Edmund, took the town by storm with his clever impersonations in the entertainment entitled 'Mr. Yates at Home'. Amongst other characters represented was that of Mrs. Glasse. In this he appeared as a frumpish old lady, ostensibly reading out of a well-thumbed cookery book the following words, written expressly for him by Thomas Hood: 'Ahem! Hare. First catch your hare! Then do him till he's done!' For the above interesting elucidation of the phrase that might have remained permanently obscure, I am indebted to the octogenarian Raymond Yates, a nephew of the actor." In 1840, an exact French version of this saying was known (IX/ 12: 125), and the exchange in Series X deals mainly with it. Knowles (2006, p. 38), confirms Sala's conclusion. OED: 1855.

F21. *First in the wood and last in the bog*
NQ 1872, IV/10: 79, 525.

One interpretation of this proverb is: "The first to get into danger, and the last to get out of it" (p. 79); so in Scotland. The other (p. 525) is "wholly different." "The person who goes first through a wood, where the underwood is thick, escapes the numerous and severe slaps in the face from the twigs, which spring back as he moves forward, and which his immediate follower receives, as I know right well from experience. In a bog the first person runs the risk of sinking in a quagmire, or falling into a boghole full of water, but wherever he can find a safe footing his follower is pretty certain of being able to stand." So in Ireland. (*Wood* was quoted in the form *wid*.) *

F22. *Fit to a T, to*
NQ 1857 II/4: 71; 1904 X/1: 478.

'To fit perfectly'. The editorial note gives the universally accepted explanation: "The phrase has reference to the T, or Tee square, an instrument used in drawing and mechanics, and so named from its resemblance to a capital T" (p.71). But see also *Correct to a T* and *It suits to a T*. OED: 1896 (*Fits him to a T*).

F23. *Flea in one's ear*

NQ 1854, I/9: 322; 1886 VII/2: 265, 332; 1903 IX/12: 67, 138, 196; 1904 X/1: 34.

'A severe rebuke'. The first note suggests [most unconvincingly] that *flea* stands here for *flee*. It is much to the credit of James Robert Brown (p. 265) that his dating (1577) still stands. Note the following remark by Skeat: "In the supplement to Godefroy's 'Old French Dictionary', *s.v.* 'Puce,' it is shown that the phrases 'avoir la puce en l'oreille', to be uneasy, and 'mettre à quelqu'un la puce en l'oreille', to make one uneasy, were both current in Old French" (p. 67). On p. 138, two relevant passages from Rabelais are quoted. The German idiom *einem einen Floh ins Ohr setzen* is a remote analog, for it means 'to say something that discomposes the hearer' (p. 196). JBK I, 94. OED: 1577.

F24. *Fly a kite, to*

NQ 1884 VI/9: 326, 394.

'To put one's name to an accommodation bill'. An accommodation bill, known as *wind-bill* in Scotland and *kite* in England, is drawn by one person to enable another to obtain credit or raise money on it, rather than in payment of a debt. When a child flies a kite, the wind raises it, while here the kite raises the wind. Brewer offered a similar explanation. The note on p. 326 cites an episode in which the phrase was explained. OED: 1739 *(if you were to fly your kite)*.

F25. *Fly on the corporal*

NQ 1892, VIII/2: 147; 1893 VIII/3: 298, 416, 478.

The meaning and the origin of the phrase are obscure, unless, as suggested on p. 478, the allusion is "to the 'corporale'," which Bailey thus explains 'A communion Cloth used in the Church of Rome, being a square Piece of Linen on which the Chalice and Host are placed by the Priest who officiates at Mass'. The presence of a fly thereon would be regarded as desecration."*

F26. *Foggy bottom*

ANQ 1, 1962: 8, 56; ANQ 1, 1963: 155.

"As an area term Foggy Bottom applies only to a relatively small section of Northwest Washington between the White House and Georgetown." "As a political term Foggy Bottom refers to the State Department only and not to government in general. It was presumably coined on analogy with Whitehall and the Quai d'Orsay." "My personal recollection associates the term as well with the gas works and its emanations, which until recently were distinguishing qualities of Foggy Bottom." The term became common after World War II. But on p. 56 another conjecture is given: "A friend who lived in Washington, D.C., mentioned FB as an area/ district name. This would take it to 1915 and earlier. I assume that *bottom* is a reduction of *bottomland,* and that *foggy* refers to the morning miasma of the Potomac or its eastern branch, the Anacostia. *Time,* 25 June 1951, p. 18/2, reporting on Louis Johnson's testimony at the MacArthur Hearings: 'Johnson had noted in Foggy Bottom a seeming hostility to Chiang's government. . . .' And on 23 July 1961, the *San Francisco Chronicle*, p. 22/1–2, 'Reston Reports', in a column on Chester Bowles, 'The Fall Guy of Foggy Bottom', by the *New York Times*' feature writer: 'This, however, is not his fault. Like most undersecretaries from Sumner Welles to Herbert Hoover, Jr., he is merely the fall guy of Foggy Bottom'. OED: 1947.

F27. *Fool in the middle, the*
NQ 1887 VII/4: 386, 412.

The phrase allegedly comes "from the game of the King and Queen of Siberia," but nothing is said about the rules (p. 412). The editorial comment to p. 386 runs as following: "In the West Riding the rhyme was current: 'Heigh, didle diddle,/ on the fool in the middle'. Had it a reference to a piece of looking-glass placed between two objects, in which the gazer sees his own face?"*

F28. *Fool's paradise*
NQ 1871 IV/8: 64; 1982 VI/5: 7, 139; 1882 VI/6: 318; 1896 VIII/9: 414, 496; VIII/10: 32; 1923 XII/12: 14.

'A state of illusory happiness'. The long exchange was devoted only to the dating of the phrase. On p. 318 (VI/6, 1882), Brewer's opinion is quoted. Brewer states "with reference to the Paradise of Fools, that the Hindus, Mahometans, Scandinavians, and Roman Catholics have devised a place between Paradise and 'Purgatory' to get rid of a theological difficulty. If there is no sin without intention, then infants and idiots cannot commit sin, and if they die cannot be consigned to the purgatory of evil-doers; but not being believers or good-doers, they cannot be placed with the saints. The Roman Catholics place them in the Paradise of the Infants and the Paradise of Fools." OED: 1462.

F29. *Forbes-Mackenzie hour of eleven*
NQ 1910 XI/1: 268, 353.

"The Act for the Better Regulation of Public-Houses in Scotland (16 and 17 Vict. c. 67), popularly known as the 'Forbes Mackenzie Act', was passed in 1853. It derived its popular designation from its introducer, Mr. William Forbes Mackenzie, M. P. for Peebles-shire. Among other provisions it enacted that no liquor should be sold by hotel-keepers, publicans, or grocers after elven o'clock at night" (p. 353). *

F30. *For the million*
NQ 1881 VI/4: 449, 472; 1884 VI/9: 245, 315.

'For the multitude'. No examples predating the early 1800s were quoted, but Hamlet's "The play pleased the million; twas caviare to the general" (II. 2: 466) is a possible source, according to the note on p. 315. OED: 1850 (R. W. Emerson).

F31. *Forty days of wet weather*
GM 87, 1817: 512.

"St. Swithin, at his own previous solicitation, was buried in the church-yard, instead of the chancel of his cathedral, and when an order was obtained to remove his relicks into the choir, a most violent shower of rain fell on the destined day, and continued for the 39 successive days without intermission, in consequence of which, the idea of removal was abandoned as displeasing to St. Swithin, though the Saint afterwards relented, and suffered his bones to be taken from the cemetery and lodged among the remains of the other Bishops in the year 1093.—The vulgar adage, that we shall have 40 days continuance of wet weather, whenever rain falls on St. Swithin's festival (July 15), doubtless arose from this presumed supernatural circumstance." *

F32. *Found in the vocative*

NQ 1860 II/9: 445.

'To be found wanting'. Perhaps from Latin grammars specifying nouns without vocatives with the formula *vocative wanting*. *

F33. *Fourth estate*

NQ 1855 I/11: 384, 452; 1878 V/9: 167, 213, 277, 378; 1881 VI/4: 428; 1882 VI/5: 16; 1895 VIII/7: 148, 290, 390; 1909 X/12: 184.

'The press, the journalists'. The phrase has been attributed to Lord Brougham (I/11: 452 and V/9: 213 and V/9: 378), Edmund Burke (VI/5: 16), and Hazlitt in an essay on Cobbett (VI/4: 428). In VIII/7: 390, it is shown that Carlyle was not the originator of the phrase and a quotation dated to August 20, 1826, is given. The expression *The Fourth Estate* is early. It was known as early as 1703, but not applied to the press (X/12: 184). OED: 1752.

F34. *Fox's Wedding*

DCNQ 2004 39: 183–6.

The reference is to the phenomenon of simultaneous rain and sunshine. Sayings of this type have been collected and analyzed from a historical point of view by Matti Kuusi (*Regen bei Sonnenschein: zur Weltgeschichte einer Redensart* ['Rain while the Sun Shines: On the World History of a Saying']. FFC Communications 171. Helsinki: Academia Scientiarum Fenica, 1957. In the article published in *DCNQ*, J. B. Smith comments on Kuusi's material and adds a few notes. All kinds of improbable events are described in such sayings, which feature animals, the devil, and human beings. Among the latter, cuckolds and tailors predominate, the traditional figures of fun. "In a nutshell, Kuusi's conclusion is that the idea of the fox's wedding is primary. It will have arisen in India and spread from there to diverse points of the globe, adapting on its long journey to different cultural backgrounds, linguistic environments and patterns of thought" (p. 184). Easily available to English speakers is No. 38 in the Grimms' collection of tales ("Die Hochzeit der Frau Füchsin" [The Wedding of Mrs. Fox]). *

F35. *Friday's hair and Sunday's horn goes to the dule on Monday morn*

Spectator 140, 1928: 790.

Two explanations have been offered: (1) "It certainly seems to have an Ecclesiastes flavor, and to suggest that fasting and feasting come to all the same thing in the end, are all vanity and vexation of spirit." (2) "I imagine that the proverb refers to the superstition that it is unlucky to cut one's hair on Friday or one's nails on Sunday. The latter half of the Scots proverb is repeated in the English proverb 'Better had he ne'er been born, than on a Sunday cut his horn'. *Dule = dool = dole* 'grief'. *

F36. *From bloom till bloom*

NQ 1885 VI/12: 143; 1886 VII/1: 135.

The question was "whether there is any law in existence called and dating 'from bloom till bloom,' giving a landlord power to terminate any lease in July, notwithstanding any agreement in writing to the contrary." "It is well known that farming tenancies, in the vast majority of cases, expire in March, the reason being that the tenant is thereby enabled to gather in all the fruits of the year. The question seemed to be founded upon some ancient phrase *from bloom till bloom*. . . . Palsgrave has "blome a flour, *fleur.*" The *Promptorium Parvulorum* has *blome flowre Flos.* "The supposed termination of the lease in July instead of in March or April appears to be an error in the tradition" (p. 143). The correspondent on p. 135 adds: "This appears to refer to floral rents, which were far from uncommon in respect of copyhold lands, and particularly what are known as 'customary freeholds'. The lord of the manor received 'a red rose' or 'a gilly-flower on the Feast of Saint John the Baptist, yearly'. This feast, according to the old calendar, would fall on our July 5, and this would explain the date. . . . Grimm ('Teutonic Mythology', trans. Sallybrass, i. 58) refers to lands in Hessian townships paying a bunch of May-flowers (lilies of the valley) every year for rent, and he considers this kind of rents to be relics of the ancient floral sacrifices." *

F37. *From Lincoln Heath, God help me*
NQ 1850, I/1: 422.

See the notes on *Binsey, God help me*; *Crawley, God help us*; *Melverley, God help me*; *Saffron Walden God help me,* and *Tickhell, God help me.* *

F38. *From pillar to post*
NQ 1875 V/4: 169, 358; 1882 VI/6: 337; 1883 VI/7: 38, 477; 1905 X/4: 528; 1906 X/5: 11.

To send somebody from pillar to post means 'to send one from place to place without providing help'. The note on p. 169 suggests a "corruption" of the German saying *von Pilatus zu Pontius* ['From Pilate to Pontius']. The note on p. 358 quotes Brewer, with reference to pillars and posts of a riding ground. The *OED* says: "Apparently originally alluding to the rapid movement of a ball around the court in real tennis." It indicates that the earliest form of the saying was *from post to pillar,* but there is no evidence for the statement that that form was *to go from post* (that is, whipping-post) *to pillary,* as in Edwards's book *Words, Facts, and Phrases* (see his note on p. 477). The publication of the entry in the *OED* was preceded by James A. H. Murray's note in X/4: 528 containing numerous variants of the verb, a mild criticism of Brewer's suggestion, and the hypothesis, formulated most cautiously, that the idiom originated in tennis. In X/5: 11, this hypothesis is endorsed. The correspondents succeeded in unearthing some very early citations. [See more details in Allen, p. 557. Funk, p. 199, mentions another explanation, which he calls groundless. Allegedly, the origin of the idiom should be sought in the old style riding academy, the pillar being the center of the ring and the posts being upright columns placed two and two around the circumference of the ring.] JBK I, 18. OED: 1550.

F39. *From the teeth outwards*
NQ 1924, 146: 84, 141, 198, 294.

'In profession, but not in reality'. The phrase may have the Italian source *fuor' de denti*, which, however, means 'to speak sincerely, openly; without unconvincing words'. OED: 1561 (*from the teeth forward*).

F40. *Funny bone*

NQ 1886 VII/1: 249, 331. AS 26, 1951: 306.

'The nerve at the back of the elbow where it rests against a prominence of the humerus.' Striking this place produces a tingling sensation, which is not in the least funny. The odd name of the nerve may be due to a pun on its Latin name *humerus* (so already in Hotten). *Os humeri* ['the bone of the upper arm'] is thus not a bone, and the origin of the name is unknown. Suggestions that *funny* is somehow related to *funk* or Gothic *fon* 'fire' do not merit discussion, because the English phrase is very late. The American synonym *crazy bone* looks like a secondary formation on *funny bone,* but in regional German, the nerve is also called 'crazy, giddy', so that *funny* may have some such sense. OED: 1826.

F41. *Furry day*

GM 1790 60: 520, 875; The Academy 1884, 25: 132; The Literary Digest 1935, 119: 29.

'A festival observed at Helston, Cornwall, on May 8'. The festival is also called simply *Furry.* Folk etymology refers it to Flora, the Roman goddess of vegetation, or to a tune and dance (a morris-dance) called Faddy, or to Latin *feriae* 'holiday' (so in the 1790 notes), or to Latin *ferire* 'to kill a sacrificial animal'. The local legend connects the name Helston with the victory of St. Michael, the patron of the town, over Satan but does not concern the origin of *Furry* (1935). During the dance, the song is sung: "Robin Hood and Little John, / They both are gone to the fair, O, *etc.*" Allegedly, *Furry* goes back *to fair, O* (1935). In 1884, Skeat wrote: "The word 'furry' is merely the Western pronunciation of the M[iddle]-E[nglish] *ferie,* O[ld] *ferie,* Latin *feria,* so that 'furry-day' is simply 'fair-day'." The *OED* gives cautious support to this explanation. OED: 1790.

G

G1. *Gas and gaiters*

NQ 1906 X/6: 348; 1932, 163: 154.

A nonsensical alliterative phrase coined by Dickens in *Nicholas Nickleby* (1839). It means approximately 'all is well'. OED: 1856.

G2. *Gay deceiver*

NQ 1894 VIII/5: 157, 254, 297.

'A rake, seducer'. The phrase enjoyed some popularity in the past. It first appeared in a song in George Colman's play *Love Laughs at Locksmiths. Gay* here means 'vicious, evil'. OED: 1710.

G3. *Get a wiggle on!*

NQ 1904 X/2: 28, 153, 274.

'Be quick, look alive'. "[This phrase] is used by motor-men and conductors (guards) on American street-cars (tramway-cars) when they wish to accelerate the speed of a person who is dilatory or too deliberate in boarding a car. The phrase is used more frequently in addressing women than in addressing men, because men are quicker in their gait and occasion less delay. The phrase, as used by motor-men and conductors, is vulgar and in every way offensive" (p. 274). OED: 1896.

G4. *Get down the banks, to*
NQ 1862 III/1: 189.

'To go all lengths', e.g. "I got down the banks for my pains" or "If he dares to do it, he'll get down the banks, I promise him." In the South of Ireland, the phrase is often heard in a threatening sense. The origin in India has been proposed [but the connection is weak]. *

G5. *Get down to brass tacks, to*
NQ 1931, 160: 296, 393, 447, 463; 161: 17, 105, 123, 139, 232, 304; 1932, 163: 461; 1953, 198: 270; *CoE* 2015 44/8: 21–66.

'To come to business'. The notes contain an inconclusive discussion of the phrase. The idea that it emerged as military slang has been refuted on chronological grounds. Some attention has been devoted to the variant *to get down to brass tin-tacks.* In vol. 198, three suggestions are given: (1) that 'brass tacks' is rhyming slang for 'hard facts,' (2) that they are the tacks which hold fast the inner foundation of a shoe-sole, which make themselves felt when the sole is worn thin, (3) that brass tacks were placed on drapers' counters to measure cloth. In the 2015 publication, Peter Reitan on the strength of an 1875 newspaper article makes a case for *brass tacks* being connected with the preparation of a coffin. Although the *OED* has no pre-1897 citations, *brass tacks* circulated much earlier. There is a consensus that the saying originated in the U.S. Consider the following: "In a programme of Fox and Sharpley's Minstrels at the Stuyvesant Institute, 659, Broadway, New York (unfortunately without date, but procured with a number of other broadsides dated 1861) I find that the performance was 'To conclude with the Plantation Song and Dance, Come down with the Brass Tacks!!' This is an interesting variation of the phrase, and suggests that a humorous story is at the bottom of it" (1932: 461). [So many phrases originated in music-hall performance and street songs that this hypothesis does not sound unreasonable. However, it fails to explain what kind of brass tacks was meant. Funk, p. 102: "Because tacks, other than ornamental, are made of copper rather than brass, I surmise that 'brass' was a figurative use. I think, therefore, that the phrase was originally nautical, that the reference was to the cleaning of the hull bolts which held its bottom together. Those bolts were, of course, of copper, but 'brass tacks' would be a typical American substitution for 'copper bolts'. The recently advanced supposition that the saying originated from the brass upholstery tacks placed upon counters in drapers' shops for use in measuring lengths of cloth seems fanciful to me, for that practice is not old and tacks of that description are of comparatively modern manufacture".] Cf. *Hungry enough to eat brass tacks.* OED: 1897 *(Come down to brass tacks).*

G6. *Get into a scrape, to*
NQ 1853, I/8: 292, 422, 601; 1879, V/12: 174; 1880 VI/1: 101, 145, 284.

'To get into an unpleasant situation'. The following explanation is given on p. 174 : "I have somewhere read that deer, at certain seasons, dig up the ground with their fore feet, in holes to the depth of a foot or more. These are called 'scrapes'. To tumble into one of these is sometimes done at the cost of a broken leg. Hence a man who finds himself in one of them is said to have 'got into a scrape'." [*Scrape* (dial.) means 'a trap for catching birds' = *shrape,* with the amplification of the meaning: 'snare'.] Of interest is the passage quoted on p. 284: "A writer in *The Book of Days* (vol. i. p. 78), thinks that we must look northwards for the origin of this phrase, which 'involving the use of an English word in a sense quite different from the proper one, appears to be a mystery to English lexicographers." He continues the quotation:— ["indeed, in his additions to Johnson, he points to *skrap*, Swedish, and quotes from Lye:] 'Draga en in i *scraepert*—to draw any one into difficulties' [*skräp* means 'rubbish, offal']. But it may be asked, what is the derivation of the Swedish phrase? "There is a game called golf [!], almost peculiar to Scotland, though also frequently played upon Blackheath, involving the use of a very small and hard elastic ball, which is driven from point to point with a variety of wooden and iron clubs. In the north it is played for the most part upon downs (or links) near the sea, where there is usually abundance of rabbits. One of the troubles of the golf player is the little hole which the rabbit makes in the sward in its first efforts at a burrow; this is commonly called a *rabbit's scrape,* or simply a *scrape.* When the ball gets into a scrape it can scarcely be played. The rules of the most golfing fraternities, accordingly, include one indicating what is allowable to the player *when he gets into a scrape.* Here, and here alone, as far as is known to the writer [that is, Robert Chambers], has the phrase a direct and intelligible meaning." Perhaps the most important observation appears on p. 422. The correspondent compares *scrape* and *rub,* as in Hamlet's *there's the rub. Rub,* in games on the green, is an exact synonym of *scrape,* so that there is every reason to believe that *getting into a scrape* is a sporting term. *Rub* occurs in Shakespeare multiple times. The *OED* suggests tentatively: "Probably from the notion of being 'scraped' in going through a narrow passage." OED: 1709 *(in a scrape).* Cf. *Get into the hat, to.*

G7. *Get (St.) Lawrence on the shoulder, to*
NQ 1882 VI/5: 266, 474; 1882 VI/6: 78, 299.

The phrase is used about idle or sluggish people. No legend of this saint explains the image. Perhaps *Lawrence* by alliteration suggested *lazy.* [Hyamson, p. 217: "Possibly an allusion to the hot season during which St. Laurence's Day (Aug. 10th) falls. From the Germ[an] *Der faule Leny,* current in the 16th cent."] Kent. Cf. *Lawrence bids* and *Lazy Lawrence.* *

G8. *Get into the hat, to*
SNQ 1904 II/6: 29, 47.

'To get a wigging, to get a severe scolding'. According to the first suggestion (p. 29), the currency of the phrase "is probably due to the popularity of some stage catch phrase or song, but the first application is not very evident." On p. 47, a tentative connection is made with "getting into a hole" in cricket. EDD: *Hat.* * Cf. *Get into a scrape, to.*

G9. *Get one's dander up, to*
NQ 1912 XI/6: 468; 1913 XI/7: 15, 52, 153.

'To become angry'. To understand the origin of this phrase, one has to know what *dander* means. The least promising approach to this word is through dissecting it into two parts. Charles Mackay believed *dander* to be the sum of two Irish Gaelic components, while E. Cobham Brewer stated with absolute conviction that *dander* is *d(amned) anger.* The correspondents to *NQ* compared *dander* with various similar-sounding provincialisms and nouns in the Standard: *tinder, tander* 'a rotten phosphorescent stick', *dander* 'ferment', "now commonly called *dunder,*" *danders* 'smithy cinders' (Scotland), *dandy* 'distracted', and *dunderhead* 'blockhead, fool'. The prevalent train of thought seems to have been that *dander* has something to do with fire (or, if the word is a borrowing, perhaps with thunder). [However, other paths of enquiry may be more profitable. In dialects, a few more nouns begin with *dunder,* for instance, *dunderchunk* 'a big, stupid person'. *Tantrum* resembles *dander* in sound and meaning and co-exists with the enigmatic dialectal triad *antrims ~ antrums ~ antherums* 'airs, whims, caprices (with an implication of temper)'. Especially suggestive is the name of the devil Tantarabobus (this name has several variants). The word was applied in some British dialects and in the US to a noisy child, occasionally as a term of endearment. Close by are Engl. *dander* 'to walk around; to talk incoherently' and Old High German *tantaron* 'to be out of one's mind'. Carew (1847), cites in his dictionary of cant language, appended to *The Adventures of B.M. Carew,* "peg *tandrums,* as *gone to peg tandrums,* dead" (p. 407). More probably, *dander* does not refer to fire but is a sound-imitative word denoting "noise"; however, the details remain undiscovered. The often-repeated statement that *dander* 'anger' is an Americanism is wrong. *Tantarabobus* may be a formation like *Flibbertigibbet* and his kin. Perhaps getting a person's dander up suggests arousing his or her devil.] Cf. *We shall live till we die, like Tantrabobus.* EDD: *Dander*; OED: 1831 *(His dander was raised).*

G10. *Get Rorke's drift, to*
NQ 1927, 153: 404, 447.

'To be brought to a sudden stop'. Apparently, this odd phrase, has nothing to do with the ford in South Africa, the place of the once well-remembered battle. It has been suggested that the phrase is rhyming slang for *short shrift.* *

G11. *Get (a person's) shirt out*
NQ 1902 IX/10: 156.

'To provoke a person's anger'. *Rag* occurs in this slangy phrase as a synonym of *shirt.* "Probably the expression 'to have (or get) one's shirt out' has arisen, says Dr. Lentzner in his 'Dict. of Australian Slang,' from the shirt working out between the breeches and waistcoat during a struggle. In Surrey 'shirty' means short-tempered, irritable." The earliest citation of *shirty* 'ill-tempered' in the *OED* (not dialectal!) is dated to 1846. The word is still relatively well-known. OED: 1859.

G12. *Get the sack, to*
NQ 1852 I/6: 19, 88; 1874 V/1: 169; WA 3, 1883: 113; NQ 1888 VII/5: 116, 398.

'To be discharged'. *Bag* and *canvas* sometimes occurred in place of *sack.* According to the author in *WA, to sack,* along with *give ~ get the sack,* "is supposed to have reference to the custom among Eastern potentates" of ordering those whom they disliked "to be sewn in a sack and thrown into the sea." He did not say who offered this hypothesis. [Funk, pp. 91–2, alludes to the ancient Roman punishment of putting a condemned person into a sack and drowning him in the Tiber. Allen, p. 628, states that the phrase is derived from French *donner le sac* (= bag).] See also *Give the sack, to* and *Receive the canvas, to.* OED: 1825.

G13. *Get the wind up, to*

NQ 1922 XII/10: 415; 1923 XII/12: 334.

'To get frightened'. Like *go west,* the phrase became popular slang during the First World War. "'Getting the wind up' did not at first imply cowardice or fear, but apprehension or a fluttering emotion. When the phrase became common, it lost its fine signification and meant frightened" (p. 334). OED: 1916.

G14. *Get upon one's high horse, to*

NQ 1854, I/10: 242; 1911 XI/4: 490; 1912 XI/5: 15, 54, 114.

'To have questionable high pretensions'. The first note deals with the origin of the French saying *monter sur ses grands chevaux* [literally, 'to mount one's big horses']. In 1911–2, no one remembered that note. The French analog was again cited on p. 54. The exact origin of the phrase has, however, not been discovered. EDD: *Horse*; OED: 1782.

G15. *Gilt off the gingerbread*

NQ 1926, 150: 134, 178, 230.

'Glamour gone'. On p. 178, the custom of exhibiting gilded figures in the market square is described. Pieces of goldleaf were used for the purpose. When the gilt was off, the figure "lost the great part of the charm for the children." Hence *to take the gilt off the gingerbread.* OED: 1837.

G16. *Gin work*

ANQ 9, 1971: 120.

'Little daily chores that must be done close around the farm house as opposed to the harder, all-day work of the farm'. "In Salem, a central West Virginia town, there are older persons who were told as children that the expression was brought in by people from the Valley of Virginia. In that region before the Civil War, male slaves who became too old or feeble to work in the fields were known generically as the 'Jims'. They were brought into the plantation house and given lighter work, 'Jim Work', in the house, yards, and outbuildings. Other farmers, whether slave holders or not, picked up the term to designate work of lesser importance." It is suggested that *gin work* (the same meaning) may be an alteration of *Jim work.* *

G17. *Give a Roland for an Oliver, to*

NQ 1850 I/1: 234; I/2: 132; 1854 I/9: 457.

'Tit for tat'. The now universally accepted reference to the Old French epic was suggested very early. Sometimes *Roland* is changed to *Rowland.* Then Oliver Cromwel is meant. JBK I, 12–3. OED: 1548.

G18. *Give a sop to Cerberus, to*

NQ 1888 VII/5: 427; 1888 VII/6: 333, 493.

'To bribe or propitiate a dangerous opponent'. The correspondence was in answer to James A. H. Murray's quest for quotations. In the exchange, no example predating 1666 turned up. The allusion to the helldog of Greek mythology needs no comment. OED: 1695 (in exactly this form).

G19. *Give it best*
MCNNQ 2, 1879: 184.

Apparently, the phrase originated in Australia. "The idea seems to be that the person who is hard pressed will acknowledge evil fate or ill fortune to be the better man. But whence this form of speech? It is new to me." EDD: *Best*; OED: 1851 *(I give him best)*.

G20. *Give one a breakfast, to*
NQ 1879 V/11: 227.

'Give one a bellyful'. This was said by Cromwell about the lords. In the note, the phrase is called proverbial, but it remains unclear whether it was Cromwell who coined it. *

G21. *Give one a cold shoulder, to*
NQ 1890 VII/9: 228.

'To display intentional coldness'. The note is only of historical interest. It was one of many similar notes written by James A. H. Murray who dealt with extremely late examples of phrases that looked old. In 1890, the first citation he had of *to give somebody a cold shoulder* came from Walter Scott. Murray's request for earlier examples remained unanswered in the pages of *NQ*. OED: 1816 *(just shewing o' the cauld shouther)*.

G22. *Give one goss, to*
NQ 1930, 158: 406.

'To punish'. The expression seems to have been popularized by Mayne Reid. The whole saying, as quoted, is "I'll give him goss, I reckon." [No etymology of *goss* is known. Can it go back to *God's (damn)?*] *

G23. *Give one hell and Tommy, to*
NQ 1861 II/7: 167; 1862 III/2: 169; 1930, 158: 406, 428, 445.

'To cause pain'. According to one suggestion (1861), the phrase should be Hal and Tommy, in allusion to Henry VIII and Thomas Lord Cromwell, "the tyrant's congenial agent in seizing and rifling the religious houses." "Walsh's *Handybook of Literary Curiosities* suggests as a more prosaic origin, namely, that it is a corruption of *Hell and Damn Me*" (p. 428). More to the point is the following "The supplement to Wright's 'English Dialect Dictionary,' *s.v.* 'Hell,' gives the phrase 'to play hell and Tommy with' as meaning 'to set utterly at variance'. One quotation, for Northumberland, is given: 'She played fair hell-an'-Tommy wi' Geordie an' Charlie', from Howard Pease's 'The Mark o' the Deil, and other Northumbrian Tales,' London, 1894, p. 21" (1930, 158: 445). Northern England. OED: 1825 *(play hell and tommy)*.

G24. *Give one monkey's allowance, to*
NQ 1896 VIII/9: 429.

See *Pay in monkey's coin, to*. OED: 1785 *(Monkey's allowance)*.

G25. *Give one sneck posset, to*

NQ 1888 VII/6: 487; 1889 VII/7: 116.

'To lock a person out'. *Sneck* 'the latch of a door'; *sneck posset* is thus the entertainment one receives when not admitted to the place where something is happening. Northern England, Scotland. OED: 1876 *(A sneck posset I gat)*. See also *Put a sneck in the kettle crook, to*.

G26. *Give one the seal of the morning, to*

NQ 1899 IX/4: 129, 175.

'To say hello, to pass the time of day'. *Seal* here goes back to Old Engl. *sæl* 'time, season'. *Day* for *morning* occurs too. On pp. 175–6, many examples are given. (Norfolk?) *

G27. *Give quarter, to*

NQ 1856 II/1: 321.

'To show mercy'. The note repeats the old explanation that this "phrase originates from an agreement between the Dutch and the Spaniards, that the ransom of an officer or soldier should be a quarter of his pay. Hence to beg quarter was to offer a quarter of their pay for their safety, and to refuse quarter was not to accept that composition as a ransom." This explanation, as stated in the *OED*, is wrong, but the origin of the phrase remains partly unclear. OED: 1611 *(quarter, or faire war)*.

G28. *Give somebody the ticket for soup*

NQ 1862 III/2: 169.

'To beat an electioneering opponent'. The phrase is cited in the editorial note without comments. [In David Crystal's book *That's the Ticket for Soup! Victorian Views on Vocabulary as Told in the Pages of* Punch. Bodleian Library, 2020, p. 1, the following is said: "As it was a card given to beggars to go to a soup kitchen, it seems to have initially carried the meaning 'You've got what you came for, so now off with you'. But it gradually softened, influenced by the wider use of *ticket* to mean 'the needed, correct, or fashionable thing to do' (as in the expression, still heard, 'That's the ticket'). 'That's the way you'll get what you want' and 'That's the way you'll get rich'." As can be seen, this explanation fits the one quoted in *NQ* only in an ironic sense: "You wanted to oppose me: enjoy the result!"] EDD: *Ticket*. *

G29. *Give the mitten, to*

NQ 1888 VII/6: 126; 1916 XII/2: 351, 454.

'To turn down a suitor' (who was allegedly offered a mittened hand, while the successful rival was allowed to kiss the girl's hand). According to Farmer, this is a translation of a French idiom. On p. 126, E. Cobham Brewer wrote: "[w]ithout doubt, the Latin *mitto*, to send (about your business), dismisses, is the *fons et origo* of the word." Of Brewer's many fanciful ideas this was probably the worst, and there is hardly a more dangerous locution in etymological studies than *no doubt*. Mainly or only US. Cf. *Give turnips, to*. OED: 1873 *(For me she mittened a lawyer)*.

G30. *Give the old woman her ninepence, to*

MCNNQ 3, 1882: 321; MCNNQ 4, 1882: 327.

The meaning of this saying puzzled people. The first suggestion (p. 321) was: "[w]hen labourers got a shilling a day the wife got ninepence of it, and the husband retained threepence for his own expenses." But the correspondent who wrote a week later quoted a note from the 1818 edition of *Hudibras*: "Until the year 1696, when all money not milled was called in, a ninepenny piece of silver was as common as sixpences and shillings, and these ninepences were usually bent, as sixpences commonly are now, which bending was called 'To my love', and 'From my love'; and such ninepences the ordinary fellows gave or sent to their sweethearts as tokens of love." See *ninepence* in the index. *

G31. *Give the sack, to*
NQ 1852 I/6: 19, 88; 1874 V/1: 169; ANQ 4, 1889: 75.

'To discharge'. The most interesting part of the note in ANQ is a short list of synonymous phrases and their equivalents in other languages. "'To give the sack' to a person in one's employ is to dismiss him; the meaning being, that as workmen usually bring their tools in a sack or bag, the presentation of that article to its owner, if made before his day's work were completed, would clearly intimate a desire to get rid of him." The *OED* (*sack*, sb. ¹, 4) notes that the French equivalent has been known in that language since the 17th century. H. Wedgwood (p. 19) also cited the French phrase *donner son sac et ses quilles* 'give the sack and crumbs', but it is unclear whether he looked upon it as the source of the English idiom. W. Pinkerton (ibidem) referred to the beggar's bag in Ireland and Scotland. On p. 88, the same French phrase is given without *et son quilles,* and an improbable explanation from Gropius is cited (the near-identical form of the word for *sack* is referred to the Tower of Babel, *etc.*). Cf. *Get the sack, to* and *Receive the canvas, to.* OED: 1841.

G32. *Give the straight tip, to*
NQ 1878 V/9: 386, 498.

'To speak plainly and decisively'. The phrase seems to have been more often used in rural districts. It was suggested that this had been a turf phrase, but this suggestion may be at odds with chronology. The correspondent on p. 498 says: "I can remember it [the phrase] nearly fifty years," that is, before "tips were spoken of in connexion with the turf." The expression was new at that time. *

G33. *Give turnips, to*
NQ 1855 I/11: 501.

When a girl rejects her wooer, she is said to have given him turnips. Cf. *Give the mitten, to.* EDD: *Turnips.* *

G34. *Glorious uncertainty of the game*
GM 1830 148: 77, 98; NQ 1899 IX/3: 247; 1901 IX/8: 164, 231.

This is the letter by Henry Bradley: "A writer in the *Gentleman's Magazine* for August, 1830 [p. 80], says that this phrase originated at a dinner of the judges and counsel at Serjeants' Hall not long after Mansfield's elevation to the position of Lord Chief Justice in 1756. The toast of 'the glorious memory of King William' having been honoured according to the then prevailing custom, a Mr. Wilbraham proposed, amid great laughter, 'The glorious uncertainty of the law', in sarcastic allusion to Lord Mansfield's frequent reversal of former decisions. The story (which has already been quoted in 'N. & Q.') seems plausible enough, but I should be glad to know whether there is any authority for it older than 1830" (p. 247). [In fact, the author of the obituary of King George IV in *GM* only wonders: "Was this the first employment of that now proverbial expression?"] Two years later, the following comments were printed: "It is no doubt the suspense and uncertainty as to what will be the result of a game of skill like cricket that render it to the sporting mind 'glorious'—an uncertainty especially characteristic of the national summer pastime. The expression 'glorious uncertainty' is said to be originally from a play of Macklin's in the eighteenth century, but I have no means at hand of verifying this" (p. 231). The explanation may be right, but one should beware of all etymologies containing the phrase *no doubt*. In any case, on pp. 231–2, we can read a related explanation: "The 'glorious uncertainty of the law' is an ironical expression of long standing to encourage a litigant to hope, however desperate his case may be, and I suppose sporting reporters have borrowed the phrase because the results in cricket matches and lawsuits are equally uncertain." OED *(glorious uncertainty of the law)*: 1803.

G35. *Go ashore with the sheet anchor, to*
MM 3, 1913: 57.

'The ultimate expression of attention to duty'. "The story ran of a British captain, a devoted ship keeper, who, to a lieutenant remonstrating on the little privilege of leave enjoyed by the junior officers, replied: 'Sir, when I and the sheet anchor go ashore, you may go with us'." Cf. *With the hook.* *

G36. *Go bung*
NQ 1896 VIII/9: 224.

Part of the note runs as follows: "There is a slang phrase in very common use in Australia, to 'go bung.' It implies failure. . . . In the aboriginal language 'bong' means 'dead.' *Billabong,* for an *anabranch* . . . means properly a dead river. *Milbung* is pigeon-English for 'blind.' Humpy Bong, near Brisbane, was originally Oompie Bong, 'deserted houses.'. . . . I have, therefore, been in the habit of believing that the phrase is of Australian origin. In Barrère and Leland (1889) this occurs: 'A pickpocket, sharper, a purse. This very old English cant word is still in use among American thieves in the phrase 'to go *bung*,' which is the same as 'to go *bang*,' derived from the popping of a cork, or the bung of a barrel; lost, gone.' To my mind, this does not seem satisfactory. I cannot but hold that the greater frequency of the use in Australia is due to the influence of the aboriginal word." OED: 1882.

G37. *Go by the beggar's bush or the game of trey trip [tray-trip], to*
NQ 1861 II/11: 299.

"*Beggar's bush* (says Halliwell), according to Miege, is a rendezvous for beggars. To go by the beggar's bush is to go on the road to ruin. Beggar's bush was also the name of a tree near London. Tray-trip is a game at dice." OED: 1592 *(beggar's bush)*; *(trey trip)* 1564.

G38. *Go snips*
NQ 1891 VII/11: 73.

'To go shares'. The *OED* marks the phrase as obsolete or dialectal. At the end of the nineteenth centery, the variant with a negation *(go no snips)* was remembered. The etymology of *snip* 'a small piece' (from Low German or Dutch) was discovered long ago. EDD: *Go*; OED: 1671.

G39. *God's baby*
NQ 1871, IV/7: 235.

'A deranged person'. Apparently, in use at that time "among the lower orders" in London. *

G40. *God's acre*
NQ 1880, VI/2: 173.

'Cemetery'. The phrase became familiar thanks to Longfellow's poem "God's Acre." The poem's opening lines are: "I like that ancient Saxon phrase, which calls/ The burial ground God's Acre." However, there is no such Saxon or Old English phrase. Longfellow says, quite aptly, in his *Hyperion* (II:9): "A green terrace or platform on which the church stands, and which in ancient times was the churchyard, or, as the Germans devoutly say, God's acre." The German phrase reached England at the beginning of the 17th century, and at the end of that century it gained some currency in Massachusetts. Longfellow did not come to Cambridge, MA before 1836. At that time, *god's acre* was well-known, and he must have assumed that the phrase had been coined in antiquity. German *Acker* means 'field'; the word is related to Engl. *acre*, but *acre* has always designated only a measure of length. Before Longfellow, *God's acre* occurred almost only in descriptions of Germany and with reference to the German idiom. However, as noted above, it was not unknown in seventeenth-century Cambridge; the "calque" probably owes its existence to the earliest German colonists. The most detailed description of the history of the idiom will be found in J. A. Walz's essay in *Anniversary Papers by Colleagues and Pupils of George Lyman Kittredge . . .* New York: Russel and Russell, 1913, 217–26. OED: 1605.

G41. *God save the king*
NQ 1896 VIII/10: 295, 417; 1897 VIII/11: 111.

'A prayer for the monarch's well-being'. The phrase originated in the Bible, and, as noted on p. 417, "it had become customary by the time of Edward I [who became king in 1272] to conclude letters addressed to the king with a phrase of prayer for his well-being and long life." OED: 1300 (and 1367 in exactly this form).

G42. *God speed you and the beadle*
NQ 1902 IX/9: 12, 111.

The note suggests that *beadle* stands for *beetle* 'mallet' ("God speed the plough"). An improbable explanation explains *beadle* as an afterthought: "God and the beadle speed you." Cf. *As deaf as a beetle*. *

G43. *God tempers the wind*

NQ 1850, I/1: 325, 357, 418; 1853 I/2: 193; 1870, IV/6: 90, 163, 256, 357; 1872, IV/10: 430, 514; 1885 VI/11: 240, 336, 395, 512; 1898 IX/1: 400, 491; 1898 IX/2: 136; 1924, 147: 83, 125, 162; The Academy 64, 1903: 149; 67, 1903: 150.

The proverb is French *(À brebis tondue Dieu mesure le vent)*. The *OED* offers an antedating for the quotation in Sterne, mentioned in *NQ*. Several books of French proverbs, beginning with 1594, have been cited. IV/10: 514 contains discussion of the proverb's source with the conclusion that it goes back to Languedoc. Note the following from IX/1: 491: "Sterne quotes almost word for word from the 'Prémices' of Henri Estienne, 1594. The saying is closely followed in Herbert's 'Jacula Prudentum,' 1652. Sterne seems to have frequently placed in italics sayings of which he disclaimed the authorship." With regard to *Jacula Prudentum,* see IX/2: 136. Cf. the curious remark on this proverb in *The Academy* 67, 1903, p. 150 "'God tempers the wind to the shorn lamb' is another instance of proverbial perversity. It is untrue; it is simply a bad kind of poetry, the art to which we owe perhaps more falsifications of life than even to the novel." OED: 1768.

G44. *Go it [or out] baldheaded*

ANQ 7, 1969: 88, 136, 121.

'To be impetuous'. On p. 121, Ernest Weekley's suggestion is cited that *baldheaded* is an alteration of Dutch *baldadig* 'audacious'. One of the authors wondered whether the phrase originated when the wearing of wigs was the custom (*baldheaded* = without a wig?). [*Urban Dictionary* gives some modern developments of the phrase.] OED: 1848.

G45. *Go North about, to*

NQ 1869, IV/3: 145, 228.

'To die'. This is said by sailors about a shipmate who died other than by drowning. But other people used the idiom as meaning "that the sailor to whom it referred had gone no one knew whither, and, as was supposed, was not likely to return; being perhaps unwilling to maintain his family, or to trouble with his presence the district regarded as his home. It was always understood to have jocular reference to the 'north-west passage'." *

G46. *Good wine needs no bush*

NQ 1854 I/9: 113; 1855 I/11: 294; 1873 IV/11: 198; LA 1, 1873: 375–6; NQ 1884 VI/10: 246; *The Athenæum* 1881, 2: 260; ANQ 1, 1888: 195, 260.

Bush means that which was tied to the end of an ale stake (Skeat in IV/11:198). The earlier notes do not explain the origin of the saying. A study of the records in the days of Edward III [1327–77] suggests (so R. R. Sharpe in *The Athenæum*) "that it was customary to place a bunch or bush of rosemary or other herb in a drinking vessel (much in the same way as we put borage in 'cups' of the present day), either to give a particular flavor to the beverage, or, as was probably more often the case, in order to disguise the inferior quality of the wine." He commented: "Of bush in this sense it is clear that good wine stands in no need, and this seems in my opinion to offer a better explanation of the proverb than that generally accepted; for if good wine need no advertisement to recommend it, and no sign of a bush to show where it may be bought, would it not *à fortiori* be true to say that 'bad wine needs no bush'?" *ANQ* 1, 1888: 195

traces the phrase to Latin. However, for *bush* we find *hedera* 'ivy' there. The author does not comment on the word *bush* but suggests that *bosky* 'drunk' (slang) goes back to it. The *OED* also derives *bosky* from *bosk* 'bush', though it offers a less direct path from "bush" to "tipsy." *ANQ* 1, 1888: 260 discusses the proverb with reference to a publication in *The Athenæum*. There is great "antipathy" between ivy and wine. "It may fairly be argued, therefore, that the ivy bush not only signified that wine was to be had within, but was meant also as a hint that 'good wine hurts nobody'. Probably the same notion had something to do with the dedication of the ivy to Bacchus." In mythologizing the plot, it should be remembered that in France, laurel or any evergreen could be used for the purpose (VI/10: 246). OED: 1611 *(Good wine draws customers without any help of an iuy-bush)*.

G47. *Goody two-shoes*
ANQ 5, 1890: 3.
Contrary to the opinion of many people, this nickname was not coined by Goldsmith (1728–1774), who wrote a popular comedy with this title. As early as 1670, it signified "one of contempt, bestowed by the husband upon his wife." The author quotes Charles Cotton's *A Voyage to Ireland in Burlesque*. OED: *a*1687.

G48. *Go out with the tide, to*
NQ 1876, V/6: 186, 305, 356.
'To die'. It is noted that "death takes place rather in the ebb than the flow of the tide." OED: 1891.

G49. *Go the round(s), to*
NQ 1904 X/1: 9, 158.
'To go from one (person or place) to another in succession'. The phrase seems to have originated in the watchman's rounds. Close analogs exist in German and French (German *die Runde gehen*). "This was borrowed from the French *faire la ronde* about the time of the Thirty Years' War, and first had reference to the watchman's *going his rounds.* In the United States a *rounds-man* is a policeman who inspects other policemen on the beats" (p. 158). EDD: *Go/ Rounds*; OED: 1669.

G50. *Go the way of all flesh, to*
NQ 1884 VI/10: 188; 1922 XII/11: 530; 1958, 203: 257; 1923 XII/12: 34.
'To die'. The biblical phrase *the way of all the earth (terrae)* yielded the variant *the way of all flesh (carnis).* The source seems to be 1 Kings II: 2. Many Latin quotations are given on p. 34. OED: 1564 *(entred the way of all fleshe)*.

G51. *Go the whole hog, to*
NQ 1851, I/3: 224, 250; 1852, I/4: 240; 1858 II/5: 49, 113. Time (NS), 1888, VIII: 581–2.
'To go all the way, to do something completely.' In I/3: 224, an uncertain guess traces the idiom to William Cowper's fable "The Love of the World Reproved," and the *OED* tentatively shares this derivation, for no pre-1782 citation is given. On p. 250, it is said that *going the whole hog* "is the American popular phrase for radical reform, or democratical principle, and that it is derived from the phrase used by butchers in Virginia, who ask their customer whether he will go

the whole hog, or deal only for joints or portions of it." But the correspondent on p. 240 traces the idiom to Irish *hog* 'shilling': *to go the whole hog* allegedly meant 'to spend the entire shilling'. The Irish are reputed to have taken the phrase to America. Fowke in *Time* heard "that 'going the whole hog' was a gambler's term for staking an entire coin—hog here being a corruption of the Jewish-German 'hoger,' derived in its turn from Hagar, she having been banished from Abraham's family, as the golden ducat was excluded until 1559 from the German currency". The ungrounded suggestion that the phrase traces to the line from *Faerie Queene* about two boars fighting until they are exhausted appears in II/5: 49. [The often repeated Scandinavian origin of this expression, with *hog* going back to the word for "a blow," is not mentioned in the works cited here.] On p. 113, it is added that the value of the Irish hog varied. OED: 1782 *(From the whole hog to be debarr'd)*.

G52. *Go to Ballyhack, to*
NQ 1889 VII/8: 69.

'To go to hell'. The author wonders whether the phrase is an Americanism. *Ballyhack* has the variant *Ballywhack*. The origin of Ballyhack is uncertain. The *OED* offers a detailed discussion and admits the possibility of the American origin of the phrase. Cf. the other synonymous phrases beginning with *go to* (see them below). OED: 1843 *(to Ballyhack)*.

G53. *Go to Bath, to*
NQ 1854 I/9: 577.

'To make oneself scarce'. Like many writers on etymology, the author of this note seemed fully confident that his explanation was correct. He wrote: "I have little doubt but that this phrase is connected with the fact of Bath's being proverbially the resort of beggars; and what more natural, to one acquainted with this fact, than to bid an importunate applicant betake himself thither to join his fellows? See also Fuller's *Worthies*" (Somerset). OED: 1840.

G54. *Go to Freuchie*
SNQ 1900 II/1: 142.

The phrase "is usually employed to signify that, in the speaker's opinion, the observations of his friend are nonsense, and require no answer. How is it related to 'Go to Banff?' Freuchie is the name of a village in Fifeshire, near Falkland, and of a burn near Bankfoot, Perthshire. The phrase is used in Caithness in the north, and Perthshire in the centre." *

G55. *Go to Halifax, to*
NQ 1875 V/4: 66, 154.

'To go to hell'. A connection to the Tories leaving the United States after the revolution for Halifax, N.S. has been suggested. The notes on p. 154 point to the alliteration in *hell* and *Halifax*. An association with the Halifax Gibbet Law may also be relevant. The saying was popular in East Cornwall in the 1820s. Edward Peacock (p. 154) quotes the lines: "From hull, hell, and Halifax/ Good Lord, deliver us." Hull "on a memorable occasion refused to admit its King within its walls." Cf. *Go to Ballyhack* and *Halifax Law*. EDD: *Halifax*; OED: 1630 *(To any place, Hull, Halifax or Hell)*.

G56. *Go to Hexham, to*

NQ 1863 III/3: 232.

'To go to hell'. This is a northern variant of *Go to Jericho* and *Go to Ballyhack*. EDD: *Hexham.* *

G57. *Go to Jericho, to*

NQ 1856 II/2: 330; 1876 V/5: 415, 474; 1876, V/6: 37, 119; 1890 VII/9: 343, 394; 1900 IX/6: 405; 1901 IX/7: 55, 472.

'To go to hell'. To wish one at Jericho would wish one out of the way. The notes in Series V merit special attention because their authors are Frank Chance and J. A. Picton, distinguished philologists. There is a legend that a house at Blackmore was one of Kind Henry VIII's houses of pleasure disguised by the name of Jericho. His courtiers used to call his "excursions" going to Jericho. The story seems to be based on fact. But of greater importance is Skeat's note (VII/9: 343): "I have never seen a really satisfactory explanation of this phrase, though Nares seems to have understood it rightly, judging from his 'Glossary', *s.v.* 'Jericho'. The allusion is, as might be expected, scriptural. The particular story intended will be found twice over, viz, in 2 Sam. x. 5 and 1 Chron. x. 5. When David's servants had half their beards cut off, and were not presentable at court, the king advised them to 'tarry at Jericho till their beards were grown'. Hence it will be seen that to 'tarry at Jerricho' meant, jocularly, to live in retirement, as being not presentable. The phrase could be used, with particular sarcasm, with reference to such young men as had not yet been endowed naturally with such ornaments; and, in their case, they would have to wait some time before their beards could suggest their wisdom. . . . Thus the original saying insinuated a charge of inexperience; and a sending to Jericho was equivalent to making such a charge. The person sent was deemed not good enough for the rest of the company. And this explains the whole matter." Residences called Jericho were known before the days of Henry VIII. The name is of course of biblical origin and must always have had "playful" connotations (IX/7: 55 and 472). Cf. *Go to Ballyhack*. OED: 1648.

G58. *Go to Old Weston, to*

1851, I/3: 449; 1853, I/8: 232.

The full version is: "You must go to Old Weston before you die." The saying is known in Huntingdonshire and Northamptonshire. Old Weston, an out of the way village, exists. It was almost unapproachable in winter, but the meaning of the saying remains obscure. Cf. *It's all along o'Colly Weston*, which poses similar questions. *

G59. *Go to pot, to*

NQ 1869 IV/3: 33, 70, 1907 X/7: 106; ANQ 3, 1889: 284.

'To perish' (also recorded with the sense 'to go to prison'). The note in IV/3: 70 suggests that the saying is traceable to the punishment of poisoners, who were boiled to death. According to the *OED,* "originally, to be cooked or eaten, to be cut in pieces like meat for the pot." The correspondent to ANQ 3 found the following tale in "an interesting article 'Odd Phases in Some Popular Phrases'": "A tailor, who lived near a cemetery in Samarcand, the birthplace and royal city of Timurleng or Timur the Great, had by his counter an earthen vessel into which he was accustomed to cast a pebble whenever a corpse was carried past, and by this means ascertained the number of daily interments." Allegedly, when he died, his neighbors replied that "he had gone to pot." [Nonsense of this type is rarely met with in print, but it is instructive as a sample of folk etymology. Funk, p. 165, mentions and discards two more conjectures. According to one, borrowed from a 1860 dictionary of slang, the phrase comes down from the classic custom of putting the ashes of the dead in an urn. Brewer wrote that the allusion is to the pot into which refuse metal is cast to be remelted, or to be discarded as waste.] OED: 1531 (*goeth a parte of little flocke to potte*).

G60. *Go to Skellig, to*
NQ 1852 I/6: 552.

Skelling was a place in the South of Ireland, where on the day before Lent (when weddings were not performed) unmarried people used to go in pairs. Also, on the Skelling rocks monks resorted to a particularly sharp amount of laceration during Lent (hence *going to do penance at Skelling*.) *

G61. *Go to the dogs, to*
NQ 1938, 174: 372.

'To go to ruin'. The origin of this well-known phrase is unclear. Is the reference to hunting, baiting, or the slaughter house? OED: 1619.

G62. *Go to the lantern, to*
NQ 1915 XI/12: 100.

'To be hanged'. From the editorial note: "'À la lanterne' was one of the cries of the populace in the French Revolution. Many of the aristocrats were hanged by the lantern ropes to the lantern supports in the streets, and particularly in the Place de Grève." *

G63. *Go west, to*
NQ 1915 XI/12: 6, 391; 1918 XII/4: 218, 280, 337; 1922 XII/11: 168, 413.

'To die'. *Go west* became suddenly popular during the First World War. Opinions on the origin of this phrase differed. Quite wrong is the attempt to derive *go west* from *go (to) waste*. Perhaps the most plausible conjecture refers to the sun: the metaphor is obvious. Later, some punning associations might arise. Thus, in the early seventeenth century, to go west "meant to go westward from the City of London to Tyburn, which was situated close to where the Marble Arch now stands, or, in other words, to be hanged" (XII/11: 168). The belief that the Islands of Blest were situated in the western ocean (XII/4: 218) [may also have some connection with the picture of the sun disappearing in the west]. OED: *a*1532.

G64. *Go wool-gathering, to*
NQ 1875 V/4: 85; 1889 VII/7: 370; 1889 VII/8: 17, 57, 114, 216; 1890 VII/9: 237; 1890 VII/10: 512.

'To indulge in aimless thought, day dreaming, or fruitless pursuit'. The best-known explanation has it that village children were sent to gather wool from ledges for a trivial purpose. But the purpose was not trivial and had nothing to do with day dreaming. The discussion led to no results. It remains a puzzle why the figurative meaning of the phrase surfaced so early, while the attempts to explain it are so late. It was, however, pointed out that gathering tufts of wool could be a remunerative occupation. A certain man was expected to gather wool for the queen. Thus, ancient woolgathering "was no mere gleaning from hedge and busk, but a collection of a sort of rent-charge in wool eligible from tenants." This sense is even farther from day dreaming. The phrase *go wollewarde* existed (so in Shakespeare's *Love's Labour's Lost* V/2 and elsewhere), with reference to wearing woolen clothes next to the skin ("shirtless") [apparently as an outward sign of piety] (NQ V/4, 85), but it has nothing to do with *going woolgathering*. JBK II, 267. OED: 1553 *(were a woll gathering)*.

G65. *Grand old man*

NQ 1890 VII/9: 5, 98, 271; 1897 VIII/12: 288. 435.

The discussion concerned only the chronology of the phrase. At that time, no citation was found predating 1850 (Gladstone, Handel, and the Duke of Wellington were mentioned as being described so). OED: 1838 (about Lord Bacon).

G66. *Grass Widow*

NQ 1870 IV/7: 205; 1883 VI/8: 268; 1884 V/10: 526; Nation 56, 1893: 253–4; NQ 1894 VIII/6: 188, 198, 259, 354, 457; Nation 61, 1895: 223; NQ 1895 VIII/7: 76–7; 1897 VIII/11: 352; 1890 VIII/6: 495; 1899 I/2: 92; ZDW 1, 1900-1:79–80; 2, 1901–2: 347; NQ 1901 IX/7: 268; IX/8: 308–9; 1902 IX/10: 205; ZDW 4, 1903: 298–308; GRM 26, 1938: 71–3; AOAW 1941 79/4: 26–32.

'A woman living away from her husband.' The earliest senses were less neutral: the phrase referred to a woman having children out of wedlock or a woman who lost her virginity before the wedding, or a deserted mistress and was a term of disparagement. German, Dutch, and Danish have exact equivalents of *grass widow*. French *veuve de paille,* literally *straw* (not *grass*) *widow,* could hardly serve as the source of Engl. *grass widow* (though see below). According to one explanation, the modern (innocuous) sense surfaced in the middle of the 19th century in India, with the implication that the men sweated in the heat, while the women waited for them on "greener pastures." The value of this hypothesis is dubious. The main questions are two: whence the variation *straw-grass* and why the change from "dishonored maiden; deserted mistress" to "wife temporarily separated from her husband"? When a man had to work for months from home, his wife was said "to be out at grass." This usage seems to provide a clue. In Germany, *Strohwitwe* 'straw widow' (which competes with *Grasswitwe* 'grass widow') surfaced only in 1715, two centuries after Engl. *grass widow,* but in a German document addressed to pastors, "straw brides" (those who cohabited with a man before the wedding) were mentioned in 1399. The term was used casually and must therefore have been well-known before that date. It looks as though the phrase originated in Germany and spread from there. The brides who came to the altar after losing their virginity (the situation discussed in the 1399 German document) were made to wear a straw wreath, but the wreaths are secondary. The original idea must have referred to a meadow or a bed of straw (the proverbial lovers' tryst) as opposed to the family bed. A meadow is a place of pleasure. Reference to *straw* deprived the situation of its charm and glamour. But straw was not an uncommon synonym for *grass* [hence probably the explanation of how the strawberry got its name]. Attempts to derive *grass widow* and *Strohwitwe* from *strawman* (originally 'scarecrow') and German *Strohmann* should be discarded, because in our texts, *Strohwitwe* preceeds *Strohmann* by many centuries. French *homme de paille* 'man of straw' may have served as a model for the German word. OED: 1529.

G67. *Gray's Inn pieces*
NQ 1916 XII/2: 509; 1917 XII/3: 57.

'Counterfeit money'. The streets near Gray's Inn, as evidenced by an old rhyme, were at one time frequented by prostitutes. Evidently, they were often paid in base coin. [I have not been able to find corroboration of this etymology.] Apperson: 1659 *(Grays Inn for walks, Lincoln's Inn for a wall, The Inner Temple for a garden, and the Middle for a hall).*

G68. *Great Scot*
SNQ 1896 X: 78, 95.

The exclamation was so new at that time that the correspondents (in Scotland!) were not even sure whether *Scot* needed one *t* or two, and on p. 79 an American origin is suggested.[Another euphemism for *God*?] OED:1893. Cf. *Kindly Scot.*

G69. *Greeks have turned Roman Catholics, the*
NQ 1863 III/3: 207.

This is said to someone who is too curious. "One would almost think that the saying must have originated long before the time of modern notions, and modern indifference regarding nicer points of ecclesiastical controversy." *

G70. *Green book*
SNQ 1900 II/1: 144.

"This phrase is a reference to a monastic practice of keeping a book in which are recorded the faults of the members of the establishment, and which had probably been bound in green." OED: 1798.

G71. *Green-eyed monster*
NQ 1900 IX/5: 65, 152, 295, 406.

'Jealousy' (Shakespeare). The point "is that green was well known in Mediæval times as being the special symbol of fickleness and inconstancy, its opposite (as to sense) being blue" (p. 65; Skeat). The article and the discussion that followed are of considerable interest with regard to the symbolism of colors. OED: 1616.

G72. *Grey mare is the better horse, the*
NQ 1880 VI/2: 207, 279; 1881 VI/3: 95–6; 1881 VI/4: 138, 233, 256, 316, 456; 1882 VI/5: 96; 1921 XII/8: 430.

This is said mainly about henpecked husbands. On p. 279 (1880), Macaulay is quoted. He thought that the reference is to "the grey mares of Flanders over the finest coach horses of England." But the proverb can already be found in Ray (as indicated in VI/3:96), which invalidates Macaulay's conjecture. The correspondent who wrote in 1921 cited three more sixteenth-century sources. Other than that, all kinds of worthless stories purported to explain the origin of the saying were quoted. One (1881, pp. 95–6) was invented by the author, the other (1921, p. 430) tells of a crusader and a mare that turned into a woman. Although the following observation sheds no light on the origin of the phrase or the choice of the color word, it may be of some importance: "Mares are seldom used for carriages, and never were. In the middle ages, gentlemen very rarely rode upon them; but they were turned over to servants, and were employed in the work of the farm, and as packhorses, and in other drudgery. In Piers Plowman,

Chaucer, and other early writers, when a farmer's horse is spoken of, it is almost invariably a mare. Numbers of instances might be quoted, but it is needless. Everybody will remember Chaucer's ploughman, 'In a tabard he rode upon a mare.' Probably from force of habit, even to this day homely farmers generally call their animals mares, even when horses" (NQ VI/4: 234). JBK I, 6. EDD: *Grey*; OED: 1529 *(whyther y gray mare maye be y better horse or not)*.

G73. *Grin like a Cheshire cat, to*
NQ 1850 I/2: 377, 412; 1852 I/5: 402; 1852 I/6: 63; 1871 IV/7: 417; 1871 IV/8: 18; 1904 X/1: 365, 513-4.

X/1 contains a survey of the hypotheses offered in the pages of NQ: 1) cheese molded like a grinning cat was at one time sold in Cheshire; 2) the grin of the wolf in the arms of the Earl of Chester is unmistakable (but a wolf cannot be confused with a cat); 3) the lion rampant supposedly resembles a cat (also, a sign on an alehouse was recalled). The author observes that lions, tigers and others are all cats, ". . . and it is this affronté or full-faced attitude of the leopard, as distinct from both the statant and the passant position, that I think, probably suggested the grinning part of the proverb, and this because the mouth of the lion or leopard is generally represented by heraldic carvers and artists with a curve upwards at each extremity" (p. 514). [Funk, p. 126, without citing his reference, mentions "one novel opinion" that "because Cheshire . . . had regal privilege . . . the cats, when they thought of it, were so tickled that they couldn't help grinning."] JBK I, 150-1. See also the next item. EDD: *Cheshire*; OED: 1770.

G74. *Grin like a weasel in a trap, to*
NQ 1909 X/12: 148.

This simile was mentioned without comments among other phrases known in the North Riding in the 1860s. [Can this phrase shed any light on the previous one?] *

G75. *Ground-hog case*
NQ 1915 XI/11: 185.

'A case of vital emergency'. A story is told, allegedly tracing the source of the phrase. US. OED: 1885.

H

H1. *Hair in one's neck*
NQ 1885 VI/11: 266.

'An irritant'. The author of the note suggests that the idiom may refer to the shirt of penance (called *a hair* in Wycliffe). OED: *a*1450, certainly 1817 (from Walter Scott); no later examples.

H2. *Hair of the dog that bit you, a*
NQ 1852 I/6: 316, 565; 1856, II/2: 239, 279; 1865 III/7: 276; 1880 VI/2: 146, 234; 1888 VII/5: 28, 171, 394; 1888 VII/6: 174; 1892, VIII/2: 85; BM 5, 1819: 670.

'A drink to treat a hangover'. As late as 1670, such a hair was recommended to someone bitten by a dog; it had to be put into the wound (II/2: 239). "In Scotland it is a popular belief that the hair of the dog that bit you, when applied to the bite, has a virtue either as a curative or preventive agent" (I/6: 565). The same belief prevailed in Ireland (VI/2: 234). A local (unfortunately, not specified) newspaper is quoted in VIII/2: 85: "This phrase, though now confined to a symbolic and alcoholic interpretation, has an accurately canine origin. In the Caucasus it is still common for any one who is bitten by a dog to lay a handful of hair, taken from the same animal's coat, upon the wound before cauterizing and bandaging it. In some mystic way the hair is supposed to prevent untoward consequences." The efficacy of this usage is referred to by Pliny. The notes in Series VII offer analogs in other languages. [All this is part of the belief that poison is its best antidote and that a monster can be killed only with its own weapon.] Hislop (269). OED: 1546.

H3. *Half rat and half weasel*
NQ 1901 IX/7: 269.

This is said about "close-eyed" people, those whose eyes are set closer together than in most. *

H4. *Half-seas-over*
NQ 1857 II/3: 136; 1888 VII/5: 56; 1887 VII/4: 526; 1896 VIII/9: 125; 1927, 152: 423; 1943, 184: 286.

'Drunk'. The idiom was understood as meaning 'half across the sea(s)'. The note in II/3: 136 derives the sense from the idea of sea sickness; but on p. 526 it is argued that initially the idiom meant, as it is glossed there, 'semi-intoxication'. P. 56 offers some discussion of this conjecture. The *OED* suggests that *seas* was probably a genitive case; *half sea's = half of the sea*. [Funk, p. 175, thought of the gait of an intoxicated man being likened to a ship, with decks half awash. He also mentioned a "theory" that the idiom is a garbled rendition of a Dutch phrase. The same in Hyamson, p. 173: "From a resemblance between the movements of the man and of the ship if the wind is subject to changes. Said to have been derived orig[inally] from Dutch, *up zee zober*, over sea beer," but Dutch *zober* does not exist, and the Dutch for 'over' is *over*. JBK I, 18.] OED: 1551.

H5. *Halifax law*
NQ 1875 V/3: 28, 116, 158; 1895 VIII/8: 368, 410; 1896 VIII/9: 92, 353.

'Hanging first, trial afterwards.' This phrase is often discussed together with Jedwood Justice and Abington Law (at Abington, the Commonwealth Major General Brown first hanged a man, then tried him). *Jedwood* and *Jeddart* are local pronunciations of *Jedburgh*. According to V/3:116, Jedwood justice was "dealt out to moss-troopers by the wardens of the marshes" [*OED: moss-trooper* 'one of a class of marauders who infested the 'mosses' of the Scottish border, in the middle of the seventeenth century; a border freebooter']. According to Halifax Law, if a thief was caught with "cloth, or any other commodity of the value of thirteen pence halfpenny, he shall be . . . taken to the Gibbet and there have his Head cut off from his Body" (VIII/8: 410). Another author (the same page) quotes a 1755 book: "The Halifax law, so much talked of formerly, was made in the reign of Henry VII to put an end to the then common practice of stealing cloths in the night time from the tenters. By this bye-law, the magistrates of Halifax were empowered to pass and execute sentence of death on all criminals, if they were either taken in the fact of stealing, or if they own'd the fact. The value of the thing stolen, however, was to be above thirteen pence halfpenny." The quotation on p. 410 is much longer. The "common litany of the beggars and vagrants" of the parts was: "From Hell, Hull and Halifax, good Lord deliver us." The source of the quotations is *Holinshed's Chronicle* (1587). See also *Abington Law* and *Go to Halifax*. OED: *a*1641 (*Hallifaxe lawe*).

H6. *Hampshire hogs*

NQ 1922 XII/10: 468, 497; 1922 XII/11: 37.

'Hampshire men'. "Wild boars were common, and from them was probably derived the old breed of hogs which was at a very early period identified with this county and from which its jocular name of 'Hoglandia' was derived" (p. 497). EDD: *Hog*; OED: 1622 (*As Hamshire long for her, hath had the tearme of Hogs*).

H7. *Hands full of pancakes*

NQ 1879, V/11: 469.

The phrase was heard in Berkshire. It describes a child fast asleep: "There she lies fast asleep with her hands full of pancakes." *

H8. *Handsome is that handsome does*

NQ 1873 IV/11: 197.

Handsome here means 'skillful' (Skeat). OED: 1689.

H9. *Hanged in an everlasting jacket, to be*

MM 6, 1920: 127 (43).

The phrase was used in the diary of Captain W. F. Hoffman, R.N. (he served from about 1794 to 1820), which was published in 1901 under the title *A Sailor of King George*. The author suggested that the jacket is a coat of pitch, while the reference is to the mutineers of H. M. S. *Hermione*, hanged at Port Royal, Jamaica. *

H10. *Hang (up) one's cap, to*

NQ 1936, 170: 286.

See the comment at *Set the cap, to*. *

H11. *Hang out, to*

NQ 1894 VIII/5: 366; 1894 VIII/6: 34; 1895 VIII/8: 498.

'To lodge, to reside'. The first note is useful because its author is Walter W. Skeat. He was among the few British scholars who took *The Century Dictionary* seriously and pointed to the way *hang out* was used in American English (a relic of earlier British use). In the 1850s, *hang out* was common at Oxford (p. 34). OED: 1846.

H12. *Hang out the broom, to*

NQ 1850 I/1: 384; 1850 I/2: 22, 226; 1851 I/4: 76; 1895 VIII/8: 229, 274-5, 330; 1896 VIII/ 9: 94-5, 435.

Both the phrase *to hang out the broom* 'to invite guests in the wife's absence' (with the implication of inviting another woman?) and the custom of hanging out the broom are or were known in many parts of England. Quite often women used to hang a broom out of the window at the culmination of a bitter quarrel or to announce the spouse's unwanted absence. S. O. Addy (VIII/8: 274-5), with reference to his *Household Tales and Traditional Remains* (David Nutt, 1895), recounted a superstition that was current in the neighborhood of Sheffield (the place of his reference): a girl said to stride over a broom ("besom") handle was destined to have an illegitimate child before the wedding. He accounted for that belief by the magic equation of the broom with the phallus. The custom of hanging a broom on the master-head of a ship (= 'for sale') has also been mentioned. H. Chichester Hart (VIII/9: 95) quoted the Dutch proverb "Zij steekt den bezem uit" ('she hangs out the broom'), that is, 'she wants a husband': "Wanting a new owner is common to the broom at the masthead and the desolate female." According to C. P. Hale (VIII/9: 435), the expression *hang out the broom* was applied to working girls in manufacturing who were about to marry. [A ship is referred to as *she*, so Hart was probably right. Also not implausible is Addy's idea that a broom has phallic connotations, a "Freudian" synecdoche for a male.] Apperson: 1773. Cf. *Put out the besom, to.*

H13. *Hard cases make bad law*

NQ 1940, 178: 426; 1940, 179: 16, 53.

The meaning of this phrase is not quite clear. According to the note in 179: 16, while an average case, dealt with under a given statute, may create little or no notice, a more difficult case arises and ends in a verdict that appears unjust, causing the law itself to get condemned as badly constructed. OED: 1828 (*Hard cases make shipwreck of the law*).

H14. *Hard lines*

NQ 1873, IV/ 12, 67, 174.

"*Hard lines* is a soldier's term, by which is understood hardship or difficulty, possibly derived from duty imposed in the front lines when facing an enemy." It was a term frequently heard in Cambridgeshire in the sense indicated above. "*Line* was formerly synonymous with *lot*. Thus the Bible version of Psalm XVI. V. 6, is 'the lines are fallen unto me in pleasant places; yea, I have a goodly heritage'; while in the Prayer Book we read, 'the lot has fallen unto me in a fair ground; yea, I have a goodly heritage.' *Hard lines* is, therefore, equivalent to *hard lot*." OED: 1695.

H15. *Hard money*

NQ 1885 VI/11: 428.

'Ready money'. This expression is cited as popular in Ireland and explained by the editor as gold and silver, rather than banknotes. [A synonym of hard cash?] OED: 1972.

H16. *Harp and harrow*

NQ 1880 VI/2: 347; 2014, 61: 482–3.

'Things that agree very badly'. The *OED* has three citations: for 1563, 1624, and 1700. The recent discussion does not explain how the contrast originated. The alliteration has always been obvious.

H17. *Haul over the coals, to*

NQ 1853, I/8: 524; 1869, IV/4: 57; 1892 VIII/1: 491.

'To reprimand severely'. "This saying I conceive to have arisen from the custom prevalent in olden times, when every Baron was supreme in his own castle, of extracting money from the unfortunate Jews who happened to fall into his power, by means of torture. The most usual *modus operandi* seems to have been roasting the victims over a slow fire" (I/8, 524). The editor's note quotes Jamieson's explanation: "This phrase undoubtedly [!] refers, either to the absurd appeal to the judgment of God, in times of popery, by causing one accused of a crime to purge himself by walking through burning ploughshares; or to the still more ancient custom, apparently of Druidical origin, of making men or cattle pass through Baal's fire." The *OED* says: "Originally with reference to the treatment of heretics." JBK I, 33–4. OED: 1565 *(to fetche an haeretike ouer the coles)*.

H18. *Have a feast and eat it, to*
NQ 1880 VI/1: 114.

'To stay with the food prepared for the guests who did not show up'. Norfolk. *

H19. *Have a good time, to*
NQ 1869 IV/4: 73.

The author (an American) suggests that *to have a good time* is probably not an Americanism and cites French *le bon temps* to support his opinion, and the *OED* shares this derivation. OED: 1509.

H20. *Have all one's family under one's hat, to*
NQ 1897 VIII/12: 287, 415.

'To be single'. Instead of *family,* words like *fortune* and *possessions* are sometimes used with a similar meaning ('to have nothing but what one has on'). The phrase was known in several regions of England. The *OED* has only *under one's hat* 'concealed', 1885 to the present.

H21. *Have a soul above buttons, to*
NQ 1867 III/11: 356; 1887 VII/4: 227, 333; 1901 IX/8: 423.

'To be upright and honest'. The notes concerned only finding references to the idiom, but nothing was said about its origin. OED: 1795.

H22. *Have got Charley on one's back, to*
NQ 1876 V/6: 168, 258.

Said about an inveterate idler. A correspondent from Worksop adds another meaning to this phrase, namely 'to walk with a stoop' and 'to be prone to idleness'. Cf. *Play the Charley wag.* Common in the North. *

H23. *Have no more use (for something) than a dog* (or *monkey) has for side-pockets, to*
NQ 1880 VI/2: 347, 377; 1881 VI/3: 77.

The phrase has several variants. In Lancashire, they say (or said): "You have no more use for it than a cow has for a ruffled shirt." Cf. *As proud as a dog with side-pockets; As proud as a toad with side-pockets; Side-pocket to a toad.* OED: 1788 *(He has as much need of a wife as a dog of a side pocket).*

H24. *Have sand in one's craw, to*
NQ 1882 VI/5: 65.

'To be determined and plucky'. At that time, slang from the American Far West. OED: 1867 *(he hes lots ove san' in his gizzard).*

H25. *Have the beard upon the shoulder, to*
NQ 1884 VI/9: 389, 453.

'To keep a good lookout for the enemy; to be alert'. The saying has equivalents in other languages and may be of foreign origin. *

H26. *Have the Danes, to*
NQ 1878, V/9: 225.

'To have diarrhea'. The idiom was recorded in the 17th century and is said to have echoed the horror of the Vikings. [Folk etymology? The date makes the reference to the Vikings improbable, unless the phrase was coined as a joke.] The plant *danewort* (= dwarf elder) was also a laxative. *

H27. *Have the French for friends but not for neighbors*
NQ 1863 III/4: 451.

Allegedly, the proverb "dates from the year 803, at which period the Emperor Nicephorus, while treating with the ambassadors of Charlemagne, took the greatest precautions to protect his possessions from the French, who continually menaced them." *

H28. *Hear, hear!*
NQ 1893 VIII/4: 447; 1894 VIII/5: 34; 1894 VIII/6: 518; 1897 VIII/11: 31, 95; 1898 IX/1: 216; 1899 IX/3: 133; ANQ 2, 1888: 6.

'The English parliamentary cry signifying approval'. According to Macaulay's *History of England,* Ch. 11: "In the Commons the debates were warm. The House resolved itself into a Committee, and so great was the excitement that when the authority of the speaker was withdrawn, it was hardly possible to preserve order. Sharp personalities were exchanged. The phrase 'hear him', a phrase which had originally been used only to silence irregular noises, and to remind members of the duty of attending to the discussion, had, during some years, been gradually becoming what it is now; that is to say, a cry indicative, according to the tone, of admiration, acquiescence, indignation or derision" (p. 6). A much longer quotation from Macaulay is given in VIII/5: 34. Several correspondents noted that *hear, hear!* competed with *hear him!* and *hear! EDD: Hear;* OED: 1689 *(hear him, hear him).*

H29. *Hear the bees, to*
NQ 1876 V/5: 408, 499.

'To express one's incredulity concerning the truth of some statement just made'. It probably means 'to hear a hum' (= humbug) and is synonymous with the next. *

H30. *Hear the ducks, to*
NQ 1876 V/5: 499.

One says *we hear the ducks* to express disbelief (*quack,* with a pun on *quack,* noun). U.S. Cf. *Hear the bees, to.* *

H31. *Heart of hearts*

NQ 1871, IV/7: 362, 399, 463, 548; IV/8: 55, 134, 426, 531; 1895 VIII/8: 289; 1896 VIII/9: 92.

The long discussion turned around the question of whether *in one's heart of hearts* is a mistake for *in one's heart of heart*. The allegedly wrong usage has been sanctified by the best writers and may be justified, even if the model is Latin *cor cordium* or Hebrew. OED: 1604.

H32. *Hell for leather*

NQ 1918 XII/4: 186; 1919 XII/5: 25; 1927, 153: 156, 192, 231; 1933, 165: 388.

'To ride at breakneck speed'. The phrase was made popular by Kipling. Improbable derivations from German have been suggested. The opinion predominates that the phrase arose in descriptions of cavalry charges. According to the correspondent in vol. 153, p. 231, it originated among the gunners and means exactly what it says, that is, the fullest strain put on all harness by the dashing forward of the guns at the utmost pace of the horse teams. The phrase *all of a lather* does not seem to provide a clue. Cf. the next idiom. *EDD* gives *fight hell fulero* and *go hell falladerly*. The question on p. 186 is: "Has *fallalderly* any connection with the dialect word *fallalderment*" 'finery'?" The editorial note in 1933, 165: 388 offers a survey of the previous conjectures. OED: 1881 *(Hellfalleero)*.

H33. *Hell in harness*

NQ 1903 IX/11: 187, 338, 417.

Hell occurs in numerous phrases with reference to things done in a violent hurry. Cf. *Hell for leather.* *

H34. *Hell is paved with good intentions*

NQ 1850, I/2: 86, 140; 1852, I/4: 520; 1872, IV/9: 260; 1897 VIII/11: 305, 436; 1897 VIII/12: 231; 1939, 177: 136, 177; 1942, 182: 40.

'Good intentions remain unrealized'. The participants in the exchange discussed what the saying really means and offered uncertain musings about its origin, with references to Boswell's *Life of Samuel Johnson* and the editor's comments on this book (p. 140). On p. 520, the source is said to be Spanish "El infierno es pleno de buenas intenciones." The author quotes from a book "published nearly two hundred years ago" but does not name it. There, an explanation is "that there is no sinner, how bad soever, but hath an intention to better his life, although death doth surprise him." The discussion was resumed in 1897 and contains important references to the version of this proverb in Portuguese and its possible source in the pronouncement of the Spanish bishop Antonion Guevara (esp. VIII/11: 436). OED: 1574 *(Hell is full of good desires.)*

H35. *Here goes!*

NQ 1956 3: 271.

'An exclamation declaring one's readiness to perform a bold action'. Neither the grammar nor the origin of this elliptical phrase has been discovered. The correspondent only found an earlier example than the one given in the *OED* (Richardson's *Clarissa,* 1748). This antedating has not yet been incorporated into the *OED* online. OED: 1829.

H36. *Here's to the mayor of Wigan*

NQ 1897 VIII/11: 187, 273.

The idea of the toast is: "Here's to ourselves" (p. 187). "Legend has it that a bygone Mayor of Wigan attended some meeting in London, accompanied by various other mayors from provincial centres. After the usual banquet, the mayors one by one succumbed and were carried off to bed. The Mayor of Wigan, alone remaining cried out: 'Bring another mayor and another bottle'" (p. 273). Cf. *Bring another mayor and another bottle.* Apperson: 1897. *

H37. *He that will to Cupar, maun to Cupar*

NQ 1880 VI/1: 236, 265; VI/2: 78.

'He who will have his own way will have it'. The reference may be to the town in the county of Fife, Scotland, with an unusual concentration of lawyers, rather than to the Cistercian monastery in Cupar. The saying was used as admonition against litigation. Hislop (152). EDD: *Will/Cupar*; OED: 1816.

H38. *He that would eat a buttered faggot, let him go to Northamton*

The Athenæum 1898, 1: 812.

"There can be little doubt that this proverb refers to the former scarcity of fuel in the country town, and implies that a faggot was a choice delicacy" (Fuller). "Ray, whose collection of proverbs was issued only a few years subsequent to Fuller's 'Worthies', supports Fuller in this view, adding that King James is said to have spoken thus of the Newmarket, but that the saying was more applicable to Northampton, as the dearest town in all England for fuel. There is little question that 'faggot' can mean, as Christopher A. Markham (in his *The Proverbs of Northamptonshire* [pp. 11–2]) says, something like a 'mediæval porcine preparation'; but why any preparation of pig should want buttering is not explained." [Perhaps the phrase and the King's advice have a less complicated explanation. Buttering inappropriate objects (parsnips, among them: see *Fine words butter no parsnips*) seems to have been proverbial. King Lear's Fool (II, 4: 126–8) remembered a man, who "in pure kindness to his horse, buttered his hay." The reference was to the popular genre ridiculing the people who do good things at a wrong time or perform acts of outrageous stupidity. The ship of fools is a classic example. Even more important is the fact that the proverbial wise men of Gotham also resided in Nottingham. In the saying and in the king's advice, faggots probably meant what they always do, that is, 'bundles of branches or twigs,' while the form of the "porcine preparation" only resembles such a bundle. The king seems to have said: "If you want to meet fools, go to Nottingham." King Lear was written in the early seventeen-hundreds, and it is curious that half a century later, neither Fuller nor the well-informed Ray could recognize the allusion.] *

H39. *Hey, Rube*

ANQ 3, 1943: 26, 48.

'A rallying call or a cry for help', (long obsolete) showbiz slang (used by circus carnies); American. The phrase migrated to the circus. The second note lists several little-known synonyms for *country bumpkin.* OED: 1882.

H40. *Higher than Gil(de)roy's kite*

NQ 1887 VII/4: 529; VII/5: 254, 357.

'To be punished more severely than the worst of criminals'. ("The greater the crime, the higher the gallows.") The full phrase is *knocked higher than,* etc. The reference to Gilderoy remains unexplained, but the phrase is (or was) known on both sides of the Atlantic. OED: 1859 *(as high as Mr. Gilderoy's kite).*

H41. *Higher the monkey climbs, the more he shows his tail, the*

NQ 1887 VII/3: 356, 523; VII/4: 132.

This is said about somebody who puts on airs or boasts of prosperity. See other phrases with *tail.* According to the note on p. 523, the proverb originated in Spanish. OED: *a*1594 *(He doth like the ape that the higher he clymbes the more he shews his ars).* Cf. *However far a bird flies it carries its tail with it.*

H42. *Hightem, tightem, and scrub*

NQ 1920 XII/7: 248, 295, 357; 1921 XII/8: 78.

'Holiday, afternoon, and everyday attire'. The variant *highty, tighty, paradighty* is known from a riddle about the holly tree. A common connection with *hoity-toity* has been mentioned, but it does not elucidate the phrase. Obviously, the first garment was "high," the second "tight," and the last good for "scrubbing" (like *scrubs*). *

H43. *Hi, Kelly*

NQ 1883 VI/7: 87, 337; 1883 VI/8: 273.

'Hello'. Recorded in Douglas, Isle of Man. "It is generally understood to be a humorous allusion to the large number of natives who bear the name of Kelly, and is mostly used by the lower order of summer visitors, or 'trippers'. These have so often heard the cry used in earnest by natives calling to members of the prolific clan, that in jest they have repeated it; much in the spirit of the American humorist who, stepping on board a steamer, raised his hat and called to those on shore, 'Good-bye, colonel'; the result being that some score of hats were raised in response, while a hearty 'Good-bye, jedge' was returned. In Wales I have observed 'trippers' amusing themselves by calling aloud in a crowded street, 'Hullo, Mr. Jones!' their object being to arrest the attention of the probably numerous Mr. Joneses within earshot (p. 337). *

H44. *His noble has come down to nine-pence*

NQ 1865 III/7: 219.

This is said about a person who has been brought down in the world and from a state which in his own estimation had been rather an important one. Cf. *Bring a noble to nine-pence and nine-pence to nothing, to* and see *ninepence* in the index. Apperson: 1568. *

H45. *Hitch one's waggon to a star, to*

BM 173, 1903: 719.

'To make a supreme effort'. The phrase is said to have been coined by Ralph W. Emerson. OED: 1870.

H46. *Hit the hay*

NQ 1924, 146: 29, 73.

'To go to bed'. The reference is to the material of which beds were made. The phrase seems to be an Americanism. On p. 73, it is suggested that hay is the favorite bedding of tramps (hence the phrase), but another comment on the same page may be more to the point: "Among the essentials of a seaman's outfit, especially in the old sailing-ship days, was a bed consisting of a bundle of straw stuffed into a coarse cover and sold for 1s. to 1s. 6d. This bed was always termed a 'donkey's breakfast'." OED: 1903 *(crawled into the Hay)*.

H47. *Hobson's choice*

NQ 1880 VI/2: 426; *The Spectator* 1712, No. 509: October 14 (Steele); ANQ 1, 1888: 45; CAM 2009, 58: 18.

'The option of choosing what is offered or nothing'. Cambridge has a hidden waterway, called Hobson's conduit. The reference is to the same Hobson, the carter who gave students "Hobson's choice." He was one of the conduit's planners. For details see Gillian Evan's book *The University of Cambridge: A New History*, 2015. [In his dictionary, Weekley quoted *Hodgson's Choise* (sic), the phrase by a Japanese merchant in 1617, written thirteen years before Hobson's death, and called the accepted theory "very doubtful". Holt, p. 165, took Weekley's remark seriously. SG is rather increduluous of the Hodgson idea.] OED: 1660.

H48. *Hog's Norton where pigs play on the organ*

NQ 1852, I/5: 245, 304; 1922 XII/11: 531; 1923 XII/12: 34, 136.

Perhaps the phrase is sheer nonsense, but Hog's Norton is a village in Leicestershire. In the local church, a pair of organs was found. Upon the end of every key a boar was cut (Ray). Evans, in his *Leistershire Words* says "The true name of the town, according to Peck, is Hocks Norton, but vulgarly pronounced Hogs Norton. The organist to this parish church was named Piggs." The saying was known to Witt (*Recreations*, 1640) (I/5: 245). OED: 1593 *(Hoggenorton, where the pigges play on the organs)*.

H49. *Hokey pokey*

NQ 1885 VI/12: 366, 526.

This used to be the ice vendor's cry in London. On p. 366, the Italian origin of the phrase is proposed (from *Oh! Che poco costa* 'Oh, how cheap'), allegedly, because when "the street trade in ice came in, the Italian was first in the field." On p. 526, the cry is traced to *hocus pocus,* but without explaining the connection. OED: 'a cheap kind of ice cream sold by a street vender' 1884.

H50. *Hold* (or *bear) up oil*

NQ 1880 VI/1: 75, 118, 202; VI/2: 117; 1901 IX/7: 493

'To flatter'. This is a Middle English idiom, and including it in this dictionary could not be expected, but it presents interest because among other contributors to the discussion we find two outstanding scholars (A. L. Mayhew and Walter W. Skeat) and because of the etymology offered in one of the notes. 'To flatter' is the gloss in the *OED*. Skeat (p. 118) suggested that the phrase might refer to the anointing of the kings with oil at their coronation. *Oil* has been recorded as modern slang (1917 and later) with the sense 'glibly pervasive or misleading talk;

nonsense, falsehood' (usually *in the old oil*). On p. 117, a fanciful Celtic etymology of the phrase is offered. It has also been suggested (p. 493) that *oil* in *hold up oil* stands for French *oui* 'yes' [most unlikely]. OED: *a*1387 *(hilde up þe kynges oyl)*.

H51. *Hold tack, to*
NQ 1893 VIII/4: 247, 314; 1894 VIII/5: 38, 253.

'To be a match for; to keep at bay; keep even with' (obsolete). Although the *OED* offers more than what the correspondents unearthed in the 1890s, their examples are still revealing and useful. OED: 1580 *(beare good tack)*.

H52. *Hole and corner with another*
NQ 1885 VI/12: 306.

'A perfect match'. This is the apparent meaning of the phrase. The locality where the phrase was overheard (two workmen were talking) is not given in the note. *

H53. *Hole in the ballad*
NQ 1885 VI/11: 427; 1885 VI/12: 98.

'A lapse of memory during recitation'. Its equivalent in the North is 'a piece torn out'. *

H54. *Honest injun*
NQ 1916 XII/1: 389, 458, 517; 1916 XII/2: 157.

This is an exclamation ('My word of honor'). The derogatory sense is unmistakable: the suggestion was that an "Indian" is never to be trusted ("an honest Injun" is thus a wonder). OED: 1676.

H55. *Hook it*
NQ 1903 IX/11: 348; 1903 IX/12: 33, 156.

The *OED* has the phrase under *hook* 'to move with a sudden turn or twist' (a nautical term). Given this reference, the synonymous idioms *take* (or *sling*) *your hook* remains unaccounted for (p. 33). Compare the following: "One has always been under the impression that this phrase had its origin either in the habit of workmen slinging their bags of tools behind them on ceasing work, preparatory to going home, or in the cessation of the day's work of the harvester, who would sling his reaping-hook over his shoulder on leaving the scene of his labour. . . . Sailors have a similar expression, 'to sling one's hammock'—that is, to make oneself scarce. . . . Again, 'to sling one's Daniels' is to move on, to run away. . . . Or the word 'hook' may apply to the fingers—that is, to pick up one's bundle and depart. In Northamptonshire and elsewhere 'hook-fingered' is dishonest. There is, according to Jamieson, a harvest custom in Scotland called 'throwing the hooks'. The bandster collects all the reaping-hooks, and, taking them by the points, throws them upwards. The direction, whatever it be, in which the point of the hook falls, is supposed to indicate the quarter in which the individual to whom it belongs will be employed as a reaper in the following harvest. If any one of them break in falling, the owner is to die before another harvest" (p. 156). *To take one's hook* is also current in dialects. EDD: *Hook*; OED: *a*1540 *(Hokit)* and 1851 *(hooked it)*.

H56. *Hooky Walker*

NQ 1851 I/4: 424.

This is an expression of ridicule or disbelief. "The history of the renowned 'Hookey Walker' as related by John Bee, Esq. *[Lexicon Balatronicum]*, is simply this:—John Walker was an out-door clerk at Longman, Clementi, and Co's in Cheapside, where a great number of persons were employed; and Old Jack, who has a crooked or hooked nose, occupied the post of a spy upon their aberrations, which were manifold. Of course, it was for the interest of surveillants to throw discredit upon all Jack's reports to the heads of the firm; and numbers could attest that those reports were fabrications, however true. Jack, somehow or other, was constantly outvoted, his evidence superseded, and of course disbelieved; and thus his occupation ceased, but not the fame of 'Hookey Walker'." The story has every trace of a folk etymological explanation. OED: 1811.

H57. *Hope against hope, to*

NQ 1878, V/9: 68, 94, 258, 319, 378; 1902 IX/10: 63, 196.

The phrase goes back to St. Paul. Skeat (p. 94) suggested that the first *hope* means 'expect', as was common in Middle English. However, the Greek original has the same word in both cases. Greek παρ was translated as *contra* into Latin, but the English versions vary (*against* and *contrary*). In any case, there is no need to ascribe different meanings to *hope* (v.) and *hope* (n.) in this now proverbial phrase. Cf. the question asked in IX/10: 196: "Does not this curious phrase arise from a misquotation of Romans iv. 18, 'Who in hope believed against hope' (R.V.)?" OED: 1813.

H58. *Hopping John*

NQ 1909 X/12: 487.

The note runs as follows: "In George Cruikshank's 'Three Courses and a Dessert,' p. 26 (ed., 1830), this term is applied to half a gallon of cider, qualified by a pint of brandy and a dozen roasted apples, hissing hot. The same odd phrase was applied, and perhaps still is, in the southern part of the United States, to a stew of bacon with peas or rice. My references are dated 1838 and 1856. These differing uses would seem to be independent of each other." OED: 1838.

H59. *Hop the twig, to*

NQ 1900 IX/5: 346; 1902 IX/9: 189, 314–5; 1902 IX/10: 16.

'To play truant; bolt'. The sense 'to die' was also common. The original reference must have been to a bird suddenly flying away and eluding the fowler. A character in Walter's *Pirate* (chapter 40) uses the variant *to hop the perch* (pp. 314–5). Some early authors of bilingual dictionaries did not realize how many slangy expressions for 'to die' exist in English and supplied their compatriots with the most inappropriate glosses for this word (p. 16). Similar anecdotes have been told about the occurrence of *kick the bucket* in English-German dictionaries. Cf. *Hop the wag, to*. OED: 1797.

H60. *Hop the wag, to*

NQ 1900 IX/5: 25, 154, 346.

'To play truant'. The phrase has several variants: *hop the twig* (as above), *play the Charley wag,* and simply *hopping it*. OED: 1797 *(hopped the twig)* and 1861 *(hop the wag)*.

H61. *Horn idle*

SNQ 1900 II/1: 93.

'Sinfully idle'. Only a query appeared about the meaning of this rare Scots phrase. The word *horn* in such idioms usually refers to something bad or undesired [because it is so hard?]. Cf. *In a horn.* *

H62. *Horny-handed sons of toil*

NQ 1898 IX/2: 127, 231.

This "hackneyed phrase" (p. 127) was often used about 1850–70. On p. 231, the following is said: "The man who popularized, if he did not make, this phrase, was Denis Kearney, 'Big Dinny', during the well-known meetings on the Sand Lots of San Francisco." OED: 1779 *(rough son of Toil)*.

H63. *Horse and horse*

NQ 1855, I/12: 427.

The phrase was said to be commonly used "in English games when one party wins a game, and his antagonist also wins a game." OED: *a*1859.

H64. *Horse-godmother*

NQ 1888 VII/6: 328, 397; 1889 VII/7: 33.

'A great horse-godmother of a woman' was an every-day expression for a strapping masculine female. *

H65. *Horse sense*

NQ 1897 VIII/11: 149; 1898 IX/1: 487; 1898 IX/2: 32, 131.

"This expression, common all over the United States, is applied conversationally in referring to any individual noticeable for common sense, and knowing, by a sort of instinct, when and how to set about an action without waiting for or seeking the advice of friends and neighbours" (p. 149). OED: 1832.

H66. *How are you off for soap?*

NQ 1860 II/10: 328, 392.

'How are you?' The question has been explained as a joke or with reference to the lack of soap on long voyages. OED: 1834.

H67. *How do you do?*

NQ 1877 V/7: 286.

'A greeting formula'. The intransitive use of *do* in this formula and in the phrases *to do well* and *this will never do* is unusual, but A. Smythe Palmer, ever on the lookout for folk etymology, was wrong in supposing that the second *do* is a reflex of Old Engl. *dugan* 'to thrive'. OED: 1799 *(How'do)*.

H68. *However far a bird flies it carries its tail with it*

NQ 1887 VII/3: 206, 356.

This is said about someone who puts on airs (without being able to hide one's defects). Its provenance seems to be southern England. See other phrases with *tail*. The implication is that exalted rank and prosperity bring the defects of ill breeding into greater prominence. Cf. *Higher the monkey climbs, the more he shows his tail, the.* *

H69. *How goes it?*

NQ 1882 VI/6: 88, 253, 437, 476.

A greeting formula in some parts of England often reduced to *how goa?* Likewise, the French use an exact equivalent of this phrase *(comment ça va-t-il'?),* known as the familiar formula *comment ça va?* EDD: *How*; OED: 1598.

H70. *How's your auntie at Tiverton?*

DCNQ 30, 1965–67: 238.

This is an expression of disbelief in a tall tale (like *tell it to the marines*). Devonshire. A variant of the phrase (also in Devonshire) is *How's your Aunt in at Exeter then?* (DCNQ 30, 1965–67: 252). Sometimes this mocking question begins with *and.* *

H71. *Hue and cry*

NQ 1855 I/11: 185; III/8: 500; 1866 III/9: 40, 83; 1871 IV/8: 21, 94, 209, 309; 1878 V/9: 508; 1878 V/10: 14, 178; 1879 V/11: 99, 357; 1879 V/12: 173; 1888 VII/5: 50, 198; 1895 VIII/ 7: 152.

'An outcry in pursuit of a suspected criminal'. The phrase goes back to legal Anglo-Norman *hu e cri* (*hue-* 'to shoot'), as has been established beyond doubt. The derivation from French *fuite et cri* 'flight and cry' (V/11: 99) is wrong. The long discussion is disappointing, because most of it is devoted to the origin of Old French *haro* (as though *haro* were the source of *hue and cry,* but it is not). The most detailed history of the phrase appears in VII/5: 50 (Frank Chance). OED: 1292.

H72. *Hungry enough to eat brass tacks*

NQ 1931, 161: 105.

'Ravenously hungry'. US. Cf. *Get down to brass tacks, to.* *

H73. *Hunt the clean boot* (or *shoe*), *to*

NQ 1888 VII/6: 485.

Frank Chance quoted an explanation printed in a newspaper: "Burgho has been trained from a puppy to hunt 'the clean shoe'—that is to say, follow the trail of a man whose shoes have not been prepared in any way by the application of blood or aniseed so as to leave a strongly-marked trail." The *OED* gives the same quotation. OED: 1888.

H74. *Hutton roofers*

NQ 1873, IV/11: 214.

This is part of the saying "Waar an' waar (worse and worse), an' then comes Hutton roofers." Its intention is to satirize the inhabitants of a Westmoreland village "in the immediate neighbourhood of Kirkby Lonsdale" (Northwest England). It "is probably explained by the fact of the sequestered situation of the place, in the midst of a waste moorland region, admitting of little communication with the outer world." *

I

I1. *I am in Pimlico with my feet*
NQ 1891 VII/12: 227; 1892 VIII/2: 536; 1908 X/10: 401, 457, 514.

The reference is said to be to poorly shod feet (p. 227). However, another explanation also exists "The expression is probably ironical, as may be inferred from the following passage:—'Not far from this place [the Globe Theatre] were the Asparagus Gardens and Pimblico Path, where were fine walks, cool arbours, &c., much used by the citizens of London and their families, and both mentioned by the comedians at the beginning of 1600. *To walk in Pimblico* became proverbial for a man handsomely drest: as these walks were frequented by none else."—' Nat. Hist. Surrey,' v. 221. This quotation is given in J. Aubrey's 'Remaines of Gentilisme and Judaisme,' p. 243, ed. 1881, Folk-lore Society" (p. 536). And indeed, the Devonshire proverb *to keep it in Pimlico* means 'to keep a house in good order' (X/10: 402–3). Pimlico was also famous for its ale (X/10: 457). See *Keep it in Pimlico, to. ***

I2. *I don't think*
NQ 1915 XI/12: 321, 370, 409, 490.

The discussion revolved around the use of this "tag" at the end of a sentence. No one remembered an earlier example than of Sam Weller's finishing his remark with *I don't think*. *Pickwick Papers* appeared in 1836, but in 1915 the phrase sounded as a colloquial innovation. It has been plausibly traced back to a popular song. OED: 1827.

I3. *I know it, my lord, I know it, as said John Noble*
NQ 1896 VIII/9: 326, 437.

An anecdote is told about the laborer called John Noble, who, when praised for his singing by Lord Dysart, answered with the phrase given here. The answer has a biblical ring ('I know it, my son, I know it"—Genesis XlVIII: 19). The episode became proverbial in Suffolk. *

I4. *I'll have a dag if I lose my spike*
NQ 1870 IV/5: 244.

'I'll attempt, even if I don't succeed'. It has been suggested that the phrase originated with schoolboys playing with dagtops. This *dag* is unrelated to *dag* in *do dags, to,* where *dag* = 'day-work'. There is *dag* (obsolete) 'a pendant pointed portion of anything' and *dag* 'a heavy pistol; a hand gun', also obsolete. The *OED* offers no etymology of this word, except for dissociating *dag* 'pistol' from *dagger*. In an oblique way, *dag* 'pendant' also refers to something sharp. The sense of the phrase must be 'I'll have a small sharp thing, even if I fail to obtain a big one'. Nottinghamshire. *

I5. *I'm a Dutchman*
NQ 1887 VII/4: 25, 158, 256.

The phrase is used in the context of *if I do something, I am a Dutchman,* that is, 'a great fool'. Brewer referred to the rivalry between England and Holland [most negative connotations of *Dutch* are accounted for so]. But another correspondent thought that *Dutchman* is a euphemism for *damned*. OED: 1843.

I6. *In a brace of shakes*

NQ 1862 III/1: 91.

'With great rapidity'. The phrase is an apparent reference to dice. Surrey, Kent. OED: 1841.

I7. *In a fox's sleep*

NQ 1875 V/4: 286, 471.

'Pretending to be asleep'. Frank Chance (p. 286) heard *I was in a fox's sleep* from an Essex man. *

I8. *In a horn*

NQ 1869 IV/3: 480.

An expression of doubt. Cf. *Horn idle*. U.S. OED: 1847.

I9. *In a huff*

NQ 1906 X/5: 448, 497.

The meaning and the sound-imitative origin of *huff*, rhyming with *puff*, was clear to the correspondents. The discussion was started by the occurrence of the phrase in Kent about an old lady dying in a huff. The explanation sounded convincing: *huff*, here, like *puff*, must have alluded to something quick and sudden. Usually *in a huff* means 'in a fit of ill temper' OED: 1599 and 1694.

I10. *In a merry pin*

NQ 1881 VI/4: 513; 1882 VI/5: 94, 137, 237, 377; 1882 VI/6: 16; 1883 VI/7: 58.

'Half-drunk, in a merry humor'. According to Grose (p. 137), the phrase alludes "to a sort of tankard, formerly used in the north, having silver pegs or pins set at equal distances from the top to the bottom: by the rules of good fellowship, every person drinking out of one of these tankards was to swallow the quantity contained between two pins; if he drank more or less, he was to continue drinking till he ended at a pin; by this means persons unaccustomed to measure their draughts were obliged to drink the whole tankard." Grose also gave the synonyms *all upon a merry pin* and *to a merry pin*. Apparently, humorous variations on the main theme sometimes occurred. The correspondent to VI/5: 138 quoted *upon the parish pin*. Grose's explanation seems to be correct. Thus, priests were advised not "to drink to pegs." Brand (in his *Popular Antiquities*) cited the ancient order that "pins or nails should be fastened into the drinking cups or horns at stated distances, and whosoever should drink beyond those marks at one draught should be severely punished" (pp. 237–8). Hence the expression *a peg too high* and *a merry pin*. All the contributors to the discussion agreed on the origin of the phrase, and Chaucer's *on a joly* [sic] *pin* was quoted (p. 16). See also *Nick the pin* and *On a merry pin* [Several idioms with *peg* have the same origin.] OED: c1475.

I11. *In an interesting condition*

NQ 1902 IX/9: 328, 431; 1902 IX/10: 73.

'Pregnant'. According to p. 328, the phrase did not appear in the first edition of the *OED*. Exactly the same phrase occurs in French and German, but the place of origin remains undiscovered. Not too long before 1900, the phrase was considered slang. The correspondents cited several other euphemisms meaning the same: *in a delicate state of health, in the family way, brought to bed of a child,* and *to be in the straw,* but no one dared to use the real word: cf. "as applied to a woman *enceinte*" (p. 431). Cf. *In the straw.* OED: 1748.

I12. *In a twinkling of a bedstaff*

NQ 1858 II/6: 347; 1862 III/2: 18, 359, 477.

'Quickly'; allegedly, in reference to the quality in dusting bedding, carpets, *etc.* A bedstaff used as a hurling weapon may explain the phrase. The most informative note is the last. It refers to an illustration in a 1639 book. *Bedpost* also occurs instead of *bedstaff* (p. 347). OED: 1660.

I13. *Inch breaks no squares*

NQ 1855, I/12: 233, 273.

"What was the square to which an inch was of so little consequence? Possibly some edible sold in squares, so rough at the edges, that breaking off a strip of an inch long left the square as saleable as before" (p. 273). OED: 1698 *(so small a difference breaks no squares).*

I14. *Infants in the porch*

NQ 1925, 149: 330, 431.

The phrase refers to "the exposure of infants in the church porch. In Paris, foundlings were generally deposited in the porch of Notre Dame. The practice of throwing children upon the Church, as it was called, was known as early as the fifth century" (p. 330). *

I15. *In good earnest*

NQ 1879, V/12: 406.

'With a serious purpose'. A. L. Mayhew found an equivalent of the English phrase in the Old High German *Tatian* (*in guota ernust,* Luke XXII: 43). OED: 1477.

I16. *In hot water*

NQ 1872, IV/9: 483, 524.

'In a very dangerous situation'. The first author notes that in 1765 this phrase sounded as a recent coinage, and the *OED* confirms his observation. But as early as 1537 *hot water* meant something like 'trouble' or 'quarreling' (p. 524), which is also confirmed by the *OED.* [I can't help expressing my admiration for C.T. B., who in 1872 knew as much about this phrase as the *OED.*] EDD: *Hot*; OED: 1537 *(cost me hott water).*

I17. *In one's buttons*

NQ 1888 VII/6: 365, 457.

'Perfectly fit'. This is a provincialism recorded in several parts of England. Sometimes 'in one's breeches' occurs as a synonym. OED: a1616.

I18. *In print*

NQ 1908 X/9: 447; 1909 X/11: 176.

James A. H. Murray (p. 447) tells a story about the change of meaning this phrase has undergone since the end of the sixteenth century: *set in print* first meant 'plaited' (about clothes), then 'in proper form'. Murray was not sure of the origin of the second sense. A curious example (*fools in print*; 1633) occurs on p. 176. EDD: *Print*; OED: ?1473 *(in prynte)* and 1598 *(set in print).*

119. *Inside track*

NQ 1869, IV/3: 480.

"This is very generally used now all over the country. When a party has some good luck at the polls, or anything advantageous has happened in its favour, they say that party, or that man, 'has the inside track'. The expression probably was a jockey's, and came from the racecourse." OED: 1857.

120. *In the nick of time*

ANQ 3, 1889: 64, 284.

The following explanation is given (p. 284): "[The expression] arose from a custom in vogue many years ago. Accounts were kept by means of a 'tally', which was composed of two sticks, one retained by the seller and the other retained by the purchaser. Whenever a business transaction took place, corresponding notches were cut in the sticks." [The citations in the *OED* do not confirm this etymology. Hyamson, p. 251, refers to "the former practice of marking time by means of nicks or notches on tallies, while Brewer made a tenuous connection between being "pricked" as present at Cambridge university chapel service if a student arrived *in the nick of time* (did he derive *nick* from *prick*?)] OED: 1610 *(in this nicke of time).*

121. *In the same boat*

NQ 1863, III/4: 370; 1921 XII/8: 432; 1921 XII/9: 298; 1928, 154: 407, 448, 465.

'In the same situation'. Clement's epistle (in Greek) has been quoted, to show the antiquity of the phrase. OED: 1584 *(for in one bote we both imbarked be).*

122. *In the straw*

NQ 1871 IV/7: 407, 482; IV/8: 79, 17; 1905 X/3: 280.

'Pregnant'. *On the straw* also existed. It is suggested on p. 482 "that this phrase had reference to the practice, very prevalent in London before Macadamized roads were made, of laying straw before a house in which a lady was confined." The *OED* doubts this explanation. The idiom is obsolete. On p. 79, two more derivations are cited: "from the uses of the farmyard" (Hotten) and "from the supposed practice of making beds of straw" (Webster). Cf. *In an interesting situation.* JBK II, 17. EDD: *Straw*; OED: *a*1661.

123. *In the swim*

NQ 1901 IX/7: 29, 137.

'Part of the in group'. The explanation given on p. 137 seems acceptable: "A log of fish gathered together is called a *swim,* and when an angler can pitch his hook in such a place he is said to be 'in a good swim'." Hence 'to be among those who know what is going on'. OED: 1869.

124. *In the wrong box*

NQ 1856, II/2: 432; 1859 II/8: 413; II/9: 53; 1860 II/9: 53.

'In a wrong place'. According to II/8: 413, the idiom originated with George Lord Lyttelton, but the note in II/9: 53 suggests that its source is the printers' (compositors') language; this is what the compositor allegedly says when he finds a letter in the wrong place. Formerly, people said *in a wrong box.* The *OED* considers the possibility of an allusion to the boxes of an apothecary. OED: *a*1555.

125. *In touch with*
NQ 1913 XI/7: 188.

For the history of research the following letter from James A. H. Murray will be of interest: "This phrase, with the related 'out of touch with,' 'to keep [or lose] touch with,' &c., seems to be very modern. In the materials collected for the 'New English Dictionary' it appears first in 1884, and becomes all at once immensely run upon, as if it had been then used by somebody of note, and had 'caught on.' It may, of course, appear earlier; but considering that our readers have sent in twenty quotations between 1884 and 1889, and not one before 1884 , it cannot have been very common. Any earlier examples will be useful. But please remember that what is wanted is these phrases, and not merely examples of the sb. *touch,* which has been in use from French since the twelfth century." No answer followed this query. EDD: *Touch*; OED: 1882.

126. *In your own light, like the mayor of Market-Jew*
NQ 1856 II/2: 432; 1859, II/8: 451; 1864 III/5: 275.

The phrase was collected from an old Cornish woman. The pew of the Mayor of Marasion (or Market-Jew) was allegedly so placed that the man was in his own light. Markey-Jew is a sea coast market (as explained on p. 432), but nothing is said about its mayor or the origin of the simile. EDD: *Mayor.* *

127. *Iron curtain*
ANQ 8, 1950: 158.

Before Winston Churchill, Goebbels used this phrase, but the *OED* has a much earlier example. OED: 1794.

128. *It always rains Quaker week*
NQ 1912 XI/5: 467.

The saying originated in the U.S. It was believed that the Friends' (Orthodox) yearly meeting (April or May) invariably brought rain. *

129. *It fair sheds*
NQ 1892, VIII/2: 429; 1893 VIII/3: 15–6, 192.

This is an expression of great surprise (p. 429). In Lancashire, *shed* means 'to surpass; to beat the record' (pp. 15–6); this meaning was obsolete in the 1890s. Can *shed,* it was asked, go back to Old Engl. *scēadan* 'to separate'? *

130. *It's all along o' Colly Weston*
The Athenæum 1898, 1: 812; Spectator, 1917 119: 416, 490, 524, 567.

"It is commonly used when something goes wrong ." This old phrase, recorded by Halliwell, is known in many places. A connection with a village bearing this name is vague. On p. 524, it is suggested that *Colly Weston* is a folk etymological alteration of *galley-west* 'topsy-turvy', common in the US, where it is used literally and metaphorically "by any one and every one"[!]. [To knock *galley-west* means 'to bring to confusion; to knock out'; it is an alteration of English dialectal *colly-west.*] The saying, "has its origin in the excellent and durable character of the Colly Weston roofing stones or slates, which has long been prejudicial to the interests of tiling and thatching." Christoph A. Markham, according to the reviewer in *The Athenæum* "attempts a new and cumbrous explanation." Markham (*The Proverbs of Northamptonshire*, 1897: 23-4) speaks about the roofing slats made from a certain stone at Colly Weston, Northamptonshire. They are beautiful but difficult to fix. Allegedly, "the proprietor of a house covered with these slates, when repaired were heeded exclaiming 'it is all along Colly Weston'." Apperson: 1587. *

131. *It's a long cry to Loch Awe*

NQ 1870 IV/6: 175, 505; 1900 IX/5: 67, 130, 323; 1913 XI/7: 29, 95.

"Originally emanated from a Campbell, who was overpowered by enemies in the distant North, but it ultimately was used to signify the enormous breadth of the Campbells' possessions, inasmuch as any challenge from an enemy could not reach them" (p. 505). *

132. *It is better to wear out than rust out*

NQ 1882 VI/6: 328, 495; 1883 VI/7: 77; 1883 VI/8: 158, 254.

On p. 328, Bacon is said to be the author of the phrase, but no reference is given. This maxim seems to have been a translation from French *(plutôt s'user que se rouiller)* (p. 495). On p. 77, Bishop Latimer (1487-1555) is suggested as the author of this saying, but again, no reference is given. In the *OED*, these words are quoted from the Bishop of Cumberland. OED: 1720 *(A man had better wear out than rust out)*.

133. *It is not every lady of Genoa that is a queen of Corsica*

NQ 1888 VII/5: 487; 1888 VII/6: 79, 177.

"This proverbial saying has, and could have, no reference whatever to the unhappy Westphalian adventurer, Theodore, Baron von Neuhof, king of Corsica in 1736. It goes back beyond his days to the time when the island was a dependency of the republic of Genoa" (p. 177). Though allegedly proverbial, the phrase does not seem to be well-known. *

134. *It is nothing but cork*

NQ 1854, I/10: 128.

"In Oxfordshire, when a child exhibits an overweening fondness for a parent, with a view to gaining some coveted indulgences, it is usually denominated *cork*, or, as it is called by the country people, *cark. It is nothing but cork.*" [In some dialects, a child who feigns great love for the parents, in order to wheedle favors or some good things out of them, is called a fefnicute.] *

135. *It looks dark over Rivington*

LA 1, 1873: 138.

This expression "has come to be commonly applied in these parts [Norwich] to a person's facial indications of an approaching outburst of temper. . . . Whenever the Pike—which stands at an elevation of 1,548 above the level of the sea—may, in metaphorical language, be said to frown or look glum and sulky, the farmers in the neighbourhood surrounding generally calculate upon rain. . . . From distant places, amateur meteorologists look in the direction of the Pike when making observations, and it is proverbial to say, when rain is forecasted [sic], that 'It looks dark over Rivington.'" *

136. *It's not the cricket*
NQ 1948, 193: 366.

'It is unsportsman-like behavior'. A quotation from G. B. Shaw (1904) is given. The *OED* has the phrase *to play cricket* 'to play fairly or honorably' (1902 and later, but in 1987 it occurs in single quotes; does it mean that the phrase is no longer understood by everybody?). OED: 1902.

137. *It's the still (= quiet) sow that eats up the draff*
NQ 1865 III/8: 57.

This is said sarcastically about someone who eats something and disparages the food. The phrase and its variants are known in Scotland and northern England. *

138. *It's time to be off to Turvey*
NQ 1897 VIII/11: 426; 1897 VIII/12: 54.

'To go to bed'. Joseph Wright asked about the word *burvil* in *be off to burvil*. On p. 54, it was suggested that the phrase is akin to *I'm off to Bedfordshire,* with a pun on *bed. Turvey,* which is in Bedfordshire, occurs in this phrase too and might be an alternation of *burvil*. Pembroke. *

139. *It rains cats and dogs*
The Academy 64, 1903: 149; 67, 1903: 150; NQ 1853 I/8: 565; 1857, II/3: 328, 440, 519; 1857, II/4: 18; 1861, II/12: 298, 380; 1877 V/8: 183; 1878 V/10: 299; 1879 V/11: 56, 77; 1904 X/1: 60; 1918 XII/4: 328–9; 1919 XII/5: 108, 166, 326; 1926, 150: 425.

'It pours with rain'. Most of the explanations of this idiom are fanciful. 1) The saying is said to go back not to willow catkins (did someone offer such a conjecture?), but to French *cantaloupe* 'waterfall' [so a product of either a mispronunciation or folk etymology] (II, 1857: 440); 2) Richard S. Charnock, with reference to "Mr. Ford": "When it rains 'cats and dogs', it does so contrary to all reason and experience, 'katà doxas' [as is said in Biblical Greek], which we take to be the true etymon of our cats and dogs" (II/3: 519); the same in II/12: 298; 3) torrential rains allegedly carried along with them the refuse of the streets, including many dead animals (II/4: 18; an often repeated explanation); 4) in "Northern mythology a cat is said to be influenced by the coming storm" (XII/5: 108); [there is no such myth; but one book after another keeps repeating it, for the obvious reason that their authors have no familiarity with Scandinavian mythology, and it never occurred to any one of them to consult the literature on the subject; the derivation was probably borrowed from Trench Johnson's book *Phrases and Names: Their Origin and Meaning* and occurs in Brewer; the expression is thus supposedly due to a combination of popular superstitions and Scandinavian mythology, the cats being transformed witches, and the dogs being the hounds of Odin, the god of storms; however, Odin was neither a thunder god nor a weather god and had no such hounds]; the same author added the following observation: "Has the expression an origin with cats and dogs pattering across a bare boarded floor, strangely resembling the sound of a heavy downpour of rain?"; 5) according to still another conjecture, it is "a corruption of *tempo cattivo* (bad weather), and . . . was introduced into England by Nelson's sailors who had served in Italian waters (XII/5 1919: 166) [of the three folk etymological explanations the author of only one bothers to say something about dogs]; 6) according to XII/5: 326, a note written to *The Daily Express* (no date is given) runs as follows: "The phrase . . . is a corruption of the word *catadupe,* meaning a cataract. The great katadoupeo—the cataracts of the Nile, from katadoupeo—to fall with a heavy sound. It is raining cats and dogs—it is raining cataracts" [the dogmatic tone of the letter is unusual]; the same derivation appears in an anonymous review in *The Academy* 67, 1903: 150: [A. Wallace (*Popular Sayings Dissected,* 1894, p. 32, refers to the Greek word too; apparently, the idea was not his own. No one in the notes given here mentions the preposterous but common explanation that cats and dogs used to sleep in thatched roofs, and heavy rain washed them off (as though dogs ever sleep on or in a roof!).] As early as 1853 (I/8: 565, a correspondent to NQ gave the full text of the saying as *it rained* [sic] *cats and dogs and little pitchforks.* Likewise, in II/12, 1861: 380, the variant ". . . cats and dogs, and pitchforks with their points downwards" was cited. N. E. Toke (NQ XII/4, 1918: 328–9) wrote the following: "The 'New English Dictionary,' under the heading 'cat,' 17, quotes G. Harvey, 'Pierce's Super', 8 (1592), 'Instead of thunderbolts shooteth nothing but dogboltes or catboltes'. This seems nearer the mark, but it is impossible to judge without the context, and this I do not know. By the way, 'dogbolts' and 'catbolts' are terms still employed in provincial dialect to denote, respectively, the iron bars for securing a door or gate, and the bolts for fastening together pieces of timber (see 'English Dialect Dictionary'). A variety of the very popular game of trap and ball was called provincially 'cat and dog'—the 'dog' being the club with which the players propelled the 'cat', that is, the piece of wood which, as in the game of tip-cat, did duty for the ball. If a number of players were engaged in this game and they grew excited, it might easily be said that it 'rained cats and dogs' on the playing-field. Could the expression have arisen in this way? A 'dog' also means a portion of a rainbow, and generally precedes or accompanies squall at sea. In this connexion the 'English Dialect Dictionary' quotes 'It'll mebbe be fine i' t'efternoon if t' thunner keeps off, but there's too many little dogs about' (West Yorks). The connexion of 'dogs' with a downpour of rain is accounted for by this use of the word. Some humorists may have added 'cats', and the phrase, thus originated, may have caught the popular fancy. But this is merely a suggestion, and I should be glad of a less hypothetical explanation." The *OED* offers the closest approximation to the phrase dated to ca. 1652. The quotation from Harvey is now dated to 1593 (at *dog bolt*). The reference to the rainbow is curious, but it does not account for *cats* in the idiom. Also, the evidence of *pitchforks* cannot be shaken off. Apparently, the original idea was that a downpour of sharp objects fell to the ground. Later, *catbolts* and *dogbolts* lost their second elements; the phrase became elegant and senseless. Hazlitt also cites *it rains Boots*; other objects after *it rains* occur quite often. [Cf. also the idiom *it rains by planets* and the following note in Hazlitt, p. 273. *R* refers to Ray's *Proverbs* (1670): "This the country people use when it rains in one place, and not in another: meaning that the showers are governed by the planets, which, being erratic in their own motions, cause such uncertain wandering of clouds and falls of rain. Or that the fall of showers is as uncertain as the motions of the planets are imagined to be.–R. The country people in these days, much less in Ray's, know nothing of planetary influence on the weather, and probably Ray did not know much." Hazlitt also cites *it rains like Old Boots,* about a heavy shower.] Cf. *Lie doggo, to.* JBK I, 12. OED: *a*1652 (*It shall raine. . . . Dogs and Polecats*).

140. *It shines like Holmby mud walls*

The Athenæum 1898, 1: 812.

"Holdenby or Holmby House (afterwards Holdenby palace), erected by Sir Christopher Hatton in a most commanding situation, was for some time the biggest house in all of England. Its great windows, like those of other Elizabethan mansions, were a distinguishing feature, and we can well imagine how, with the sun upon them, they would glisten over many miles of country. This proverb recalls the Derbyshire rhyme: 'Hardwick Hall, more glass than wall'. . . . The cottages at Holmby, until comparatively recent years, were singularly poor, the walls being almost entirely of mud, and a great contrast to the House." Northamptonshire. Svartengren: 224. *

141. *It stands stiff, and but's a mountain*

NQ 1896 VIII/9: 187.

Only a query about this odd saying appeared. [Is it probably a riddle, like many other collected by A. Taylor. *It* refers to the penis, and *butts,* not *but's* or *and [the]* butt *is a mountain,* is meant. This might be the reason why no one sent an explanation, or perhaps no one recognized the truth.] *

142. *It suits to a T*

ANQ 1, 1888: 238.

'To suit perfectly'. ANQ also mentions the hypothesis that "as T is the final letter of the word *suit, suits to a T* means suits completely and absolutely." [Incredible?] See also *Correct to a T* and *Fit to a T, to.* OED: 1771 *(Suited to a tee).*

143. *It will never make old bones*

NQ 1887 VII/4: 165; 1888 VII/5: 454.

The phrase "is used in relation to children small at birth, weak and ailing afterwards" (p. 165). On p. 454, Maupassant is quoted. In *Bel ami,* "Il ne fera pas de vieux os"[*'He will never',* etc.] is said of a man thought to be far gone with consumption. OED: 1821 *(I shall not make old bones).*

144. *It won't hold water*

NQ 1872, IV/10: 352; 1887 VII/3: 228, 317-8, 394.

'The proposition is indefensible'. The editorial note on p. 352 suggests that the idiom goes back to the Vestal Virgin Tutia, who, to prove her innocence, carried water in a sieve, but no evidence of the phrase's antiquity is adduced. On p. 394, classical analogs are cited. Two conjectures in VII/3: 317 and 318 are as follows: 1) "It is merely a coincidence, or is there any connexion between this very common expression and the words of the prophet Jeremiah: 'For my people have committed two evils; they have forsaken me the fountain of living waters, and hewed them out cisterns, broken cisterns, that can hold no water' (Jer. ii. 13)? I merely mention this as a possible origin of the phrase." 2) "It is probable that the saying first had life in the pot-making districts, and arose out of the well-known fact that unglazed earthenware vessels will not hold water for any length of time. Fill an unglazed vessel with water at night, and the next morning it will be found empty." OED: 1622 *(This will not hold water).*

145. *It would puzzle a Philadelphia lawyer*

NQ 1859, II/7: 515.

This is said about "any knotty point proposed for discussion." Strangely, the phrase was known among "the lower orders" in England but not in Philadelphia. Brewer (p. 827) wrote the following: "*You will have to get a Philadelphia lawyer to solve that* is a familiar American phrase. It is said that in 1735, in a case of criminal libel, the only counsel who would undertake the defence was Andrew Hamilton, the famous Philadelphia Barrister, who obtained his client's acquittal in face of apparently irrefutable evidence, and charged no fee. In New England there was a saying the three Philadelphia lawyers were a match for the Devil." [Funk, pp. 708–9, cites a few other uncorroborated suggestions about the origin of the phrase.] OED: 1788.

146. *I wish I had our cat by the tail*

NQ 1909 X/12: 148.

'I wish to be at home'. [A touching tribute to cat lovers.] Yorkshire. *

J

J1. *Jack Pudding*

NQ 1896 VIII/9: 267; 1896 VIII/10: 158.

'A buffoon attendant on a mountebank doctor, a circus clown (Merry Andrew)'. In England, the name was well-known in the past. The notes contain useful references to other clowns, especially German *Hanswurst,* a close analog of Jack Pudding. OED: 1664.

J2. *Jack silver pin*

NQ 1873, IV/11: 524.

This is "an expression much in use in the Bahamas as a taunt to a person, who, having made a present, repents of his generosity and wishes to have the gift returned." No suggestions on the origin of this odd saying appeared. *

J3. *Jack, Tom, and Harry*

NQ 1897 VIII/11: 487.

See *Tom, Dick, and Harry.* *

J4. *Jammed like Jackson*

MM 1, 1911: 253 (58).

A story is told of John Jackson who nearly wrecked the ship in 1787 because he refused to listen to the pilot's advice. The ship struck heavily, and someone on board asked ironically: "How does she go now, Jackson?" Among seamen this saying became common in situations when obstinacy leads to disaster. *

J5. *Jedwood justice*

NQ 1875 V/3: 28, 116, 158.

See *Halifax Law.*

J6. *Jerry-builder*

NQ 1890 VII/9: 507, 10: 116; 1891 VII/12: 376; 1915 XI/12: 482; 1916 XII/1: 299, 415.

'Builder of cheap, trumpery houses.' The following letter from Liverpool is quoted in VII/10: 116: "The origin of the term was the name of two brothers who resided in Liverpool, and who built many of those rapidly-constructed, ill-built, and showy houses which form so large a portion of this city, which are inhabited chiefly by the lower middle classes. The style of the firm, 'Jerry Brothers, Builders and Contractors,' caused the name to become generic for such builders and their work; first in this city, from whence the term spread." This publication was followed by a long rejoinder: [p. 376] "Jerry-Builder (7 S. ix. 507; x. 116).—There does not appear to be the slightest proof that the term *jerry-builder* was derived from the name of any building firm either in Liverpool or elsewhere. I have, therefore for some time held the opinion that the most probable derivation is from *jerry-shop,* which in Lancashire parlance means a low and disreputable beer-house, as opposed to a respectable hotel or public-house. So, I would venture to suggest, the rickety houses built by the bad and low-class builders were called *jerry*-houses, or *jerry-built* houses, as opposed to well and substantially built residences, and the men who ran them up acquired the name of *jerry-builders.* I am not aware that the above suggestion has ever previously been made, and I make it with all diffidence." The note was reprinted in VII/12: 376. [Diffidence is a rare virtue in etymological studies and deserves praise, the more so as the hypothesis sounds quite reasonable. Compare the American phrase *jackall* = *all* (*jack* also occurs elsewhere in some unsavory compounds).] A chance remark in 1901 IX/7: 263 to the effect that the verb *to jerry-build* owes its origin to the infamous brothers' firm made James A. H. Murray write a long letter (1901 IX/7: 305–6; the main text is on p. 306). Below, this letter is reproduced almost in full: "I am glad to see that the Editor of 'N. & Q.' cautions readers against the aprocryphal statement that 'Jerry Brothers, builders and contractors, were a Liverpool firm in the early part of last century.' . . . I may add that, after seeing the original letter to this effect printed in *Truth* in January, 1884 I wrote to its author asking for the evidence on which the statement was made. In his reply, now lying before me, dated 18 December, 1885, the writer admitted that no evidence was producible; he added that he was under the impression of having heard this explanation of *jerry-builder* from the English master at the school which he attended, but he had subsequently searched for authority without finding any; and Sir James Picton, our great Liverpool authority, who had been consulted, had never heard of it. He therefore could not maintain the reliability of the story, and frankly withdrew it. In preparing the articles on the *Jerry* words in the 'New English Dictionary' (section published 1 January last) we made further investigation, with the help of correspondents in Liverpool, and ascertained that no trace of any such name as Jerry in connexion with the building trade could be found. While, therefore, it is quite possible that the cloth-finisher's *jerry,* the compositor's *jerry* on an apprentice completing his time, a jerry-hat, a jerry-shop (or Tom-and-Jerry shop), and a jerry-building may all contain the masculine name Jerry (short for Jeremy or Jeremiah), we are reduced to the conclusion that 'Jerry Brothers' have merely been invented to concoct what, in view of its unsubstantial, pretentious, and deceptive character, we may distinguish as a 'jerrymology' (the *m* being a deceptive insertion in the 'jerry-ology' to make it more like the real thing). We all know how such become current . . . . A glance at the 'Dictionary' will show that the earliest connexion of *jerry* with the building trade is its adverbial use in *jerry-built,* a dialectal expression explained in the 'Lonsdale Glossary,' 1869, as 'slightly or unsubstantially built'. This was also used by Mr. Ruskin in 1875 in 'Fors Clavigera.' As an adjective, qualifying 'builder', 'building', *jerry* appears in 1881-2, when the 'Lancashire Glossary' explained it as 'bad, defective, and deceptive.' In those days it was still written as a separate word; but *jerry builder* and *jerry building* naturally suggested *jerry-build,* which is exemplified in 1890. Earlier dates than some of these may, of course, be found; but on the whole Ruskin's execration of 'jerry-built cottages' in 1875 seems to point to the literary 'coming out' of the word. I need hardly point out that 'jerry-built' is not strictly a verb 'formed out of a proper name'; the verb is *build,* to which *jerry* functions merely as an adverb, as in 'badly built', 'unsubstantially built.' We have not found any verb 'to jerry,' although 'jerryism' appeared in 1885." Since jerry-built houses collapsed almost as soon as they were constructed, some people referred to the walls of Jericho, which fell down at the sound of Joshua's trumpets (p. 482). Still another attempt to explain the compound connects *jerry* with the nautical word *jury* 'temporary', as in *jury-rigged, jury-mast,* etc. (XII/1: 299). [*Jury-mast* appears in the original *OED.* The longest explanation will be found in *The Century Dictionary,* with reference to an entry in Skeat's *Concise;* also *jury-leg* 'wooden leg' (that is, "a temporary leg") is explained in *The Century Dictionary* along the same lines.] *Jerry-building* from *jury-building* does not sound fully convincing, and the derivation from *jelly-builder* (p. 415) seems fanciful. Cf. *Tom and Jerry.* OED: 1881.

J7. *Jibber the kibber, to*

MM 2, 1912: 29 (5), 92 (5).

'To lure a vessel to destruction by giving a false signal from the shore'. The signal, according to folklore, was tied to a horse. *Jibber* is indeed slang for 'horse', but nothing else is known about the origin of the saying. Green cites a few dubious etymological suggestions in which he himself has no trust. *

J8. *Jim Crow*

GM 1875, 771.

'A stereotype black man in a 19th-century song-and-dance act' (dated and now offensive). The story deals with the later history of this figure. OED: 1832.

J9. *Job Johnson's coat*

NQ 1889 VII/7: 308, 358.

'An example of tawdriness'. This is the explanation by Edward H. Marshall: "Job Johnson is a *chevalier d'industrie* ['swindler, crook'], who figures largely in Lord Lytton's novel 'Pelham.' His 'green frock coat, covered, notwithstanding the heat of the weather, with fur, and *cordonné* ['laced'] with the most lordly indifference both as to taste and expense,' is described in chap. lxxix. of that once popular work" (p. 358). *

J10. *John Audley*

NQ 1873, IV/11: 208.

The term refers to 'no person'. "When Richardson, the great theatrical showman, at fairs, thought his actors had played long enough, and saw fresh audiences ready to rush up the steps, he used to put his head between the canvas and call out, "Is John Audley here?" At which the curtain soon fell, and the strollers began to a new crowd of hearers. To John Audley a play still means, in theatrical slang, to cut it down." *

J11. *Johnny Crapaud*

NQ 1852, I/5: 439, 523, 545.

'An ethnic slur for a Frenchman'. On p. 545, reference is made to the fact that three frogs are the old arms of France. OED: 1818.

J12. *John Thomson's man*

GM 14, 1840: 46.

'A hen-pecked husband'. This is a proverbial phrase in Scotland. The conjecture is cited that *John* is "a corruption" of *Joan*. EDD: *Joan*; OED: *a*1513.

J13. *Join giblets, to*

NQ 1887 VII/4: 268, 511; 1888 VII/6: 473.

The phrase denotes a close partnership in Yorkshire, but has an offensive meaning in Lincolnshire. *Giblets* 'inferior parts of poultry' has the figurative meaning 'odds and ends'. The oldest meaning of the phrase was 'to marry'. EDD: *Join/Giblets*; OED: 1681.

J14. *Join the majority, to*

NQ 1879, V/11: 125; 1879, V/12: 216; 1882 VI/6: 225, 352; 1883 VI/7: 136; 1889 VII/7: 305, 432.

'To die'. The phrase is old. *Abiit ad plures* ['went to the majority'] occurred regularly in the second half of the seventeenth century. The source is, most probably, Latin (*ad plures penetrare* ['to reach, join the majority']) and eventually Greek. OED: 1721 *(Death joins us to the great majority)*.

J15. *Join your flats!*

NQ 1924, 146: 193, 259, 294, 422; 1924, 147: 107, 145.

'Do your business properly'. Flats are the halves as are formed by two equal parts pushed from the sides of the stage and meeting in the center. The phrase seems to go back to an incident in the Old Vic, when the back scenes would not meet and somebody shouted from the gallery: "We don't expect no grammar, but you might let the scenes meet," quoted from J. R. Planche's *Recollections and Reflections* (1872 I: 127) (p. 422). *

J16. *Just the cheese*

NQ 1853 I/7: 617; I/8: 89; ANQ 3, 1889: 284.

This is a variant of *That's the cheese*. The note on p. 89 stated that this phrase was some ten or twelve years old. *

K

K1. *Katie, bar the door*

NQ 1992, 237: 376.

"In the United States today there is a vogue for the exclamation, 'Katie, bar the door!' used when any situation seems desperate or things are getting out of hand." The source of the phrase should be a song or a ballad, but it has not been found despite some conjectures. [In the comment on the post of August 29, 2018 (the blog "The Oxford Etymologist"), SG referred to the old variant *Kitty, bar the door,* of British origin.] *

K2. *Keep it in Pimlico, to*

NQ 1863 III/ 4: 327.

'To keep a house in order.' "Pimlico kept a place of entertainment in or near Hoxton and was celebrated for his nut-brown ale. The place seems afterwards to have been called by his name, and is constantly mentioned by our early dramatists." See also *I am in Pimlico with my feet.* Devonshire. Apperson: 1863

K3. *Keep the wolf from the door, to*

NQ 1857 II/4: 51, 115.

'To be barely able to sustain oneself'. The note in II/4: 115 suggests that *wolf* here is a metaphor for "hunger." OED: 1555.

K4. *Keep your hair on!*

NQ 1902 IX/9: 184, 335; 1902 IX/10: 33; 1903 IX/11: 92, 195, 318; 1903 IX/12: 136.

'Stay calm!' Most of the discussion is irrelevant, except the following note by H. Y. J. Taylor (IX/10: 33): "This expression is common or frequently heard in Gloucestershire. Its origin is supposed to be coeval with wigs or the wig period. Irascible and aged gentlemen, 'when mad with passion', have been known not only to curse and swear, but to tear their wigs from their heads, and to trample them under their feet, or to throw them into the fire. Very often when I have manifested symptoms of anger I have been admonished by country fellows, 'Kip thee yar on, maystur!' This expression is synonymous with *keep your temper, or don't get into a rage.* Whenever I have heard the expression, I have invariably associated it with the old country squire who got into a thundering rage and threw his wig off his bald head and trampled it under his feet. Sometimes a similar expression or mandate is used, 'Kip the wig on, ould mon'. I have frequently heard old country farmers and farm labourers say, 'Daz my wig!' or 'Dash my wig if I wool', or 'I dooes'. In the old days, if a man wished in his passion to be emphatic, he threw off his wig." OED: 1883.

K5. *Keep your pecker up*

NQ 1940, 179: 279, 392.

'Keep up your spirit' (*pecker* 'beak; nose' or *pecker* 'penis'). In 1940, the obscene meaning, certainly the most common one current in the US, was not known in England. [But as late as 1955, Funk, see the 1993 volume, p. 628, reproduced this phrase unabashedly and glossed it as 'to maintain one's courage', etc. It also appears that at present (2020) young Americans know *pecker* 'penis' but not the idiom.] On p. 392, examples, including *down in the pecker* 'in bad spirits', from *EDD* are cited. OED: 1845.

K6. *Key of the street*
NQ 1898 IX/2: 88, 234.

To have the key of the street meant 'to have no place to go, no bed to go to, *etc.*' This is evidently an adaptation of the French phrase *le clef des champs.* [The phrase appeared in *The Pickwick Papers* and has never had wide currency. Holt, p. 197, points out that the correspondence between the English and the French phrase is not complete: "The former means to be locked out overnight; the latter, to be free to roam, through the fields, anywhere." The full phrase is *prendre la clef des champs,* figuratively 'to attain freedom'.] OED: 1837.

K7. *Kick the bucket, to*
NQ 1854 I/9: 107; 1904 X/1: 227, 314, 412; 1904 X/2: 75; 1947, 192: 171; LM vol. 7, 1823: p. 442; ANQ 3, 1889: 284.

'To die'. The most common old explanations refer to a man who hanged himself on a beam while standing on the bottom of a pail or bucket; when the noose was around his neck, he kicked the vessel. References to the vocabulary of a slaughterhouse and to a restive cow "kicking the bucket" in the process of milking have also been offered. [As regards such cows, see the commentary on *aroint* in the various editions of *Macbeth* and in Nares.] Especially instructive is the following: "When a butcher slings up a sheep or pig after killing, he fastens to the hocks of the animal what is technically known in the trade as a *gambal,* a piece of wood curved somewhat like a horse's leg. This is also known in Norfolk as a *bucket,* a variation, according to Forby, of *bucker. . . .* To 'kick the bucket', then, is the sign of the animal's being dead, and the origin of the phrase may probably, if not indisputably, be referred to this source" (p. 412). Cf. the remark in X/2: 75: "I suggest that a bucket was suspended to catch the blood of the calves, and sometimes used for a weight. The wooden block that took its place may have got this name. A slaughtered animal surely does not kick." The following [unlikely?] explanation was added as late as 1947: "When friends came to pray for the deceased, before leaving the room they would sprinkle the body with holy water. So intimately therefore was the bucket associated with the feet of deceased persons, that it is easy to see how such a saying as 'kicking the bucket' came about." The 1823 note is a spoof (a German is trying to find a good equivalent of *gestorben* 'deceased, dead'). Attempts to show that *butt,* rather than *bucket,* was the original form make little sense (the material was provided by SG). JBK I, 214. OED: 1785.

K8. *Kick up Bob's a-dying, to*
NQ 1885 VI/11: 208; 1910 XI/1: 150, 258.

'To make a great noise, whether about some physical punishment or pain, or in merriment'. Cf. *Bob's a dying.* OED: 1879.

K9. *Kick upstairs, to*
ANQ 3, 1943: 87.

'To get rid of an official by promoting that person to an impressive post devoid of authority'. Slang. Macaulay is quoted, who gave an example of the phrase in 1684, with Halifax being its possible originator. *

K10. *Kind regards*

NQ 1870, IV/6: 53; 1889 VII/7: 45.

The note on p. 53 contains numerous formulas with which people used to end their letters. Perhaps part of the suggestion made on p. 45 has value "Mr. Albert Gray, in the second volume of his translation for the Hakluyt Society of the 'Voyage of François Pyrard', says in a note, p. 80, 'Port[uguese] *recado,* a message or errand: the plural *recados* is used as our 'compliments'. The expression seems to have been taken up by the English of Bombay and Surat, as in 1675 we find Dr. Fryer (p. 71) stating that a Jesuit near the former place 'sent his *Recarders* with the presents of the best fruit and wines, and whatever we wanted'. Unless Dr. Murray and his coadjutors can give earlier authority, I venture to think we have here the original of our modern phrase 'kind regards'." OED: 1819.

K11. *Kindly Scot*

NQ 1887 VII/4: 168, 311.

Kindly in this phrase means 'native' (a long explanation of the epithet is given on p. 311). [Any connection with *Great Scot*?] OED: 1609 *(kyndlie Scottis men).*

K12. *King cotton*

ANQ 1, 1941: 25.

The question was whether *King commerce* and the like served as the model for *King cotton.* [The correspondent referred to David Christy's 1855 book *Cotton is King,* and an earlier source does not seem to have been found.] OED: 1855.

K13. *King John's man—four feet nothing*

MM 6, 1920: 127 (43).

The note contains only a query about the derivation of this phrase "once used in the Royal Navy" and occurring in the book *A Sailor of King George* by Captain W. F. Hoffman. He served from about 1794 to 1820 and used the phrase 'when speaking of an officer of diminutive stature'. *

K14. *King's highway, the*

NQ 1930, 158: 26; 1933, 165: 226.

At present, the phrase is "a kind of ornament of speech without any clear sense of its historical meaning." But it used to refer to highways enjoying the Crown's special protection. It made the wrongdoer the King's enemy (p. 26). On p. 226, citations antedating those in the original *OED* are given. OED: 1196 *(Ab oriente cyniges heiweg).*

K15. *Knock into a cocked hat, to*

NQ 1878, V/10: 128, 236; 1884 VI/10: 100, 440.

'To beat, smash'. "The allusion is to the field officer's head dress, made to double together and fold flat, so as to be shut up and carried under the arm when not worn on the head." OED: 1833.

K16. *Knock spots, to*
NQ 1888 VII/5: 429, 518.

'To show proficiency'. This is an American phrase, referring to the ability to shoot through any given spot on a card nailed to a tree. It is sometimes used as a synonym for *knock holes* in hunting. OED: 1850 *(to knock (the) spots off)*.

K17. *Knock under the table, to*
NQ 1857, II/3: 369, 433; 1860, II/9: 225.

'To subjugate, get the better of'. Suggestions have been made that *to knuckle under* is the older version of *knock under* and that the phrase goes back to the idea of drinking one under the table. In II/3: 433, it is pointed out that in Devon *knock under* is a term used in sawing. When two people operate a saw the "under one" is called a knocker under, as opposed to the "top sawyer." *The table* looks like a later addition. OED: 1692.

K18. *Know how many beans make five, to*
NQ 1862 III/1: 111; 1885 VI/12: 209; 1886 VI/12: 313; 1886 VII/1: 38.

The phrase refers to a man fully alive to his own interest in dealing. Synonymous with *to know how many go to the dozen* and *is up to a thing or two*. EDD: *Bean*; OED: 1830 *(How many blue beans it takes to make five)*.

K19. *Know how to carry the dead cock home, to*
NQ 1886 VII/2: 506.

This is said of a man who took defeat manfully when beaten in trials of strength or games. The idiom goes back to the pastime of cock fighting. Rural Derbyshire. *

K20. *Know no more than the Pope of Rome, to*
NQ 1863 III/3: 470.

An admission of complete ignorance. Pembrokeshire, current (as of 1863) especially among the middle class; a few inconclusive suggestions on the origin of the saying were given. Apperson: 1663. *

K21. *Know nothing about Diss, to*
NQ 1852 I/6: 303.

Diss may stand for *disputation*. Cambridge, England. Apperson: 1852 *

L

L1. *Lading and teeming*
NQ 1883 VI/7: 485.

'Living from hand to mouth'. *Lade* 'to take out', *teem* 'to pour out'. "A Lancashire woman *teems* out a cup of tea." EDD: *Lade*. *

L2. *Lamb and salad*

NQ 1931, 161: 319, 357, 394; 1932, 162: 34, 89.

'A good thrashing' (slang). *Lamb (lam, lamp)* are well-known regional words for 'beat'. *Sallup* (the same meaning) is also known, but it cannot be shown that such is the origin of *salad*. The confusing part of the story is that in northern England, *lamb and salad* is a synonym of *apple-pie order* and has nothing to do with thrashing. However, the initial inquiry concerned that meaning. *

L3. *Lathom and Knowsley*

NQ 1858, II/5: 211.

"A curious instance of the retention of a proverbial saying long after the occasion of it has passed away, may be instanced in Lancashire. It is a very common expression to say of a person having two houses, even if temporarily, that he has 'Lathom and Knowsley'. Formerly the Earls of Derby had two splendid residences in Lancashire." Apperson: 1858. EDD: *Lathom*. *

L4. *Latins call me Porcus*

NQ 1860 II/10: 350.

The reference is allegedly to someone fond of using hard foreign words. A story about a wolf and a pig is told to justify the saying (the pig calls itself *porcus,* but the wolf eats it despite the Latinism). *

L5. *Lawrence bids*

NQ 1886 VII/1: 269; 1891 VII/11: 212, 415.

This is said about a man falling asleep in his chair or about any idle man. Conversely, "In Mr. S. O. Addy's 'Sheffield Glossary' this expression is given: 'Lawrence bids high wages', with the following explanations: 'Said of a person who is rendered almost incapable of work by the heat of the weather, or who yields to it too willingly about the feast of St. Lawrence, which is the 7th day of August' (Hunter's MS.) 'A proverbial saying for 'to be lazy', because St. Lawrence's day is the 10th of August, within the dog-days, and when the weather is usually very hot and faint' (Pegge's 'Anonymiana,' 1818, p. 237)" (VII/11: 212). South Yorkshire. See *St. Lawrence* in the word index. Apperson *(Lawrence bids one high wages)*: 1784; EDD: *Lawrence.* *

L6. *Lay a ship by the walls, to*

MM 1, 1911: 30 (2); MM 41, 1955: 77 (2).

'To lay up a ship by the dockyard wall, condemned to uselessness'. An example dating to 1780 is given in vol. 1. In vol. 41, the idiom is antedated to 1760 *(to keep the ship by the walls)*. See *Lie by the wall.* *

L7. *Lay figure*

NQ 1876 V/5: 436.

'A wooden model of the human body'. *Lay man* preceded *lay figure*. Bailey's and Wedgwood's explanation still stands: from Dutch *lee-man,* for *lede-man* (*led* 'joint'): "a figure with movable joints, a contrivance doubtless imported from the Netherlands" (Wedgwood). Other suggestions are wrong (from the verb *lay,* and the like). OED: both *lay-man* and *lay figure*: 1688.

L8. *Lay-overs for meddlers*

NQ 1858, II/6: 481; 1859, II/7: 38, 138, 225; 1869, IV/ 4: 507; 1870 IV/5: 25, 257; 1945, 188: 191, 240.

This is an answer to over-curious people. Whoever hears this phrase is sure to ask its meaning. The answer invariably returned is "Pitch-plasters over thy mouth, to stop thy talking and meddling" (p. 25). In vol. 188: 191, *rare-over* and *lorries* are cited as variants (a warning to children not to touch what they oughtn't to). See a longer version of this phrase below. For *rare-overs* see also IV/4: 507. Apperson: 1690. EDD: *Lay-overs**

L9. *Layers for meddlers, and crutches for wild ducks*

NQ 1902 IX/10: 307, 475; MCNNQ 5, 1884: 317, 329.

This is an answer to over-inquisitive children. In MCNNQ 5: 317, *layers* is derived from *lay-holds* by one author and from *layo'ers* by another. On p. 329, French *leurres* ['bait, deception' (pl.)] is suggested and rejected. The correspondent explains: "*Layover for meddlers* over things laid over, put by for meddlers, and meddlers like myself were not to meddle with them or ask any more questions." NQ IX/10: 475 cites numerous variants of this phrase and suggests their origin in a hoax or a fool's errand. Cf. *Crutches for lame ducks* and *Lay-overs for meddlers*. Apperson: 1690. *

L10. *Lazy Lawrence*

NQ 1891 VII/11: 4, 115, 212, 415; 1897 VIII/11: 189, 235.

The following curious explanation is quoted from the *Dialect of Craven* (1828): "When a person is remarkably idle, he is often thus addressed, 'I see lang *Lawrence* hes gitten hod on thee'. May not this expression allude to those who are frequently prostrated at the shrine of a saint, when they should be engaged in the useful and active duties of life? But if an idle person, laid immovably at his full length, be compared to *St. Lawrence,* fixed with stretched-out limbs upon the gridiron, preparatory to his atrocious and unmerited sufferings, it is a cruel and unfeeling comparison!" There is no certainly that Lawrence is St. Lawrence, but such is the belief of those who use the phrase (pp. 78 and 299), and the following legend looks like the foundation of this belief: "A traditional tale has been handed down from age to age that at his execution he bore his torments without a writhe or groan, which caused some of those standing by to remark, 'How great must be his faith!' But his pagan executioner said, 'It is not his faith, but his idleness; he is too lazy to turn himself'. And hence arose the saying, 'As lazy as Lawrence'." (VII/11: 212.) See *Get (St.) Lawrence on the shoulder, to* and *As lazy as Laurence's dog. EDD* offers no explanation, but calls Lawrence a "genius" of business. EDD: *Lawrence*; OED: 1796.

L11. *Leap in the dark*

NQ 1876 V/6: 29, 94, 151, 273; 1877 V/7: 252, 358; 1877 V/8: 237; 1891 VII/12: 328, 394, 452; 1903 IX/11: 466; 1910 XI/2: 86, 154.

'A dangerous action with unclear consequences'. The long exchange dealt only with the earliest occurrences of the phrase. In V/7: 252, a 1694 (!) citation is given. OED: 1697.

L12. *Leaps and bounds*

NQ 1892 VIII/1: 86; 1894 VIII/5: 32; 1896 VIII/9: 427.

'Precipitously'. The discussion centered on whether this binomial is tautological. The difference between the words was explained (the hare leaps, while the ball bounds), and a few quotations showed that the best poets had not been afraid of using the idiom. In VIII/5: 32, the suggestion is made that the source of the idiom is French *par coups et par bonds* 'by fits and starts'. If so, in adopting this idiom, English changed its meaning. OED: 1720.

L13. *Learn by heart, to*

NQ 1851 I/3: 483; I/4: 75; 1926, 150: 296.

'To learn by rote'. The origin of the idiom has been sought in Luke I: 66 and II: 19 (p. 483) and in French (p. 75), with reference to "Quitard, a French writer on proverbs" [Piere-Marie Quitard, 1792–1882; probably his *Dictionnaire etymologique. . . . des proverbes. . . .*, 1842, is meant]. OED: c1405.

L14. *Leave is light*

NQ 1855, I/12: 233.

'Permission, if asked, is easily granted'. The phrase is either an aphorism or a proverb. The correspondent's sanctimonious comment runs as follows: "It is but the expense of a little breath, and therefore they who are under command are very much to blame to hazard disobliging their superiors by not asking. If this neglect proceeds from a diffidence, it is the more inexcusable, because that seems, in some measure, to imply a conviction of what we have to ask being unreasonable." OED: 1546.

L15. *Let every herring hang by its own tail*

NQ 1862 II/2: 304.

'Let every thing occupy its proper place'. The allusion is to the drying of the fish. Irish. OED: 1672 (*Every herring must hang by its own neck; gills*).

L16. *Let George do it*

NQ 1923 XII/12: 492.

'Let someone else do it'. The following query from the New York Public Library may be of interest, even though it was not answered: "The expression 'Let George do it' has in the last ten or dozen years become current in America. Especially during the [First World] War was it in common use. The phrase meaning, of course, 'Let the other fellow do it'. We are interested to learn if there is any foundation to the statement that this phrase is of English origin. We know that the French have employed for several centuries a very similar expression, 'Laissez faire à George, il est home d'âge,'['Let George do it, he is a grownup man'], which they trace back to the time of Louis XII. Has such an expression been used in England, and if so, is there any explanation of its origin known to you or your readers?" OED: 1909.

L17. *Let sleeping dogs lie*

NQ 1897 VIII/11: 29, 209, 417.

'Don't trouble trouble until trouble troubles you'. The question was asked about the Greek analog of the proverb. Everybody cited μή κίνει Καμαρίναν (*ne moveas camarinam* ['Don't move it']): Apollo's advice not to drain or cleanse ("move") the swamp Camarina became proverbial. The advice was neglected with catastrophic results (the swamp was drained and allowed the Roman troops to reach the town of Camarina and destroy it). Hence the implication "let good enough alone." More to the point is F. Adams's long article (VIII/11: 209). He cites the older and more popular variant of the English phrase (in English, from Chaucer on): "It's ill to wake [*or* don't waken] sleeping dogs," from several languages. The saying may be Scottish, for it occurs in Hislop (p. 209). OED: 1823.

L18. *Let the cat out of the bag, to*
NQ 1879, V/12: 336; MM 1, 1911: 189 (87).

'To reveal a secret'. The following explanation has been given: "Formerly dishonest country-men practiced the trick of substituting a cat for a suckling pig, and bringing it to market in a bag; so that he who, without examination, made a hasty bargain was said to 'buy a pig in a poke', and might 'get a cat in a bag'. And the discovery of this cheat originated the expression 'Letting the cat out of the bag'" (p. 336). [Allen, p. 136, finds this explanation totally incredible, given the cat's aversion to confinement.] It has also been conjectured that a cat of nine tails is meant and that originally the idiom meant 'to cause trouble'. JBK I, 39–40. OED: 1760.

L19. *Level best*
NQ 1894 VIII/5: 47, 130.

'(One's) very best'. The suggestion that the phrase *to do one's level best* was an Americanism seemed unlikely to some because it occurred in British dialects. On p. 131, a correspondent suggested that *level* in *level best* might owe its existence "to the sport of athletic running: to do one's level best = to do one's best on the level." OED: 1851.

L20. *Lick into shape, to*
NQ 1880 VI/2: 486; 1881 VI/3: 212, 517; 1881 VI/4: 378, 395; 1919 XII/5: 69, 129.

'To put into shape' and 'to knock into shape'. The ambiguity of the phrase is due to the slangy sense of *lick* 'to beat', but the long and sometimes acrimonious discussion showed that *lick* here has its direct meaning and that the phrase goes back to the fact or the belief that bear cubs are born shapeless (or perhaps with membranes covering the body) and are indeed licked into shape by the she bear. *

L21. *Lie at the catch, to*
NQ 1852 I/6: 56; 1853 I/7: 132; 1854 I/10: 135.

The phrase is used in Bunyan's *The Pilgrim's Progress*. He explains it himself (see the quotation on p. 56, with reference to those who try to outwit God), but the metaphor can have its origin in the position of the fowler waiting, cord in hand, for the unwary bird (p. 135). OED: 1608.

L22. *Lie by the wall, to*
NQ 1858, II/6: 325, 440.

'To be dead'. The phrase seems to be confined to East Anglia. [The suggestion that *wall* is "a corruption" of OE *wæl* 'death', p. 440, is hardly worth considering.] According to the *OED*, the reference is to a ship lying on one side, unused, etc. A 1789 example is given of the citation applied to a person dead but not buried. Norfolk, Suffolk. The *OED* marks it as obsolete, but it may be current in regional speech; in any case, it was still known in 1858. See *Lay a ship by the walls, to.* OED 1579.

L23. *Lie cold-floor, to*
NQ 1881 VI/3: 448; 1881 VI/4: 74.

'To lie in the house before burial' (said of a corpse). The phrase was recorded in South Lincolnshire (p. 448) and compared with Scots *to lie in the could* (sic) *bark* (p. 74). *

L24. *Lie doggo*
NQ 1896 VIII/9: 266.

'To lie quiet, remain hidden'. This idiom (slang) occurred in the past, rarely (only in British English), and is now all but forgotten. Its synonym *to play doggo* also exists. James A. H. Murray discovered an 1882 citation and wondered whether *doggo* was a mock ablative of manner. The dictionaries that risk suggesting the etymology of *lie doggo* say only that *doggo* is *dog + o* and refer to dogs' sleeping habits or to dogs in concealment. However, among the many words with the suffix -*o* (*typo, weirdo, cheerio,* and commercial names like *Drano = Draino*), animal names do not occur. Some light on the origin of *lie doggo* may fall from the Modern Icelandic idioms *sitja upp við dogg* 'to sit or half-lie supporting oneself with elbows', *sitja eins og doggur* 'sit motionless; look distraught', and *vera eins og dogur* 'to be motionless'. In some German dialects, the diminutive forms *dodel, doggel,* and *tiggel~teckel* have been recorded. Two of the basic meanings of those words seem to have been 'round stick' and 'doll', with reference to the animal name ("dog"). They look like baby words, and the animal name *dog* may have the same origin. The attested forms of Icel. *doggur,* which, unlike Engl. *doggo,* have currency outside a few collocations, do not antedate the eighteenth century. Engl. *dog* can also mean 'device, implement'; the recorded forms go back to the Middle period. Perhaps Engl. *doggo* also contains the name of some device that was current not too long ago in the European itinerant handymen's *lingua franca.* The overall image of *lie doggo* looks nearly the same as in the phrase *as dead as a doornail,* which seems to have been coined in allusion to nails driven deep into the wood and remaining immobile. Naturally, folk etymology associated *doggo* with the animal name, but the jocular Latinization, suggested by Murray, need not be dismissed. Confusion between animal names and the names of tools in idioms is not uncommon. Funk, pp. 7–14, came to this conclusion, while investigating the origin of the phrase *as independent as a hog on ice.* See *Sharing the Rings of the Scandinavian Fellowship: Festschrift in Honor of Ērika Sausverde.* Vilnius: Vilnius University Press, 2019, 204–5 and 209–10. OED: 1882. Cf. *It rains cats and dogs.*

L25. *Life of Riley*
ANQ 4, 1944: 55.

'An easy and pleasant life'. The correspondent suggested two hypotheses of the idiom's origin: "1) that it sprang from the carefree and idling spirit of James Whitcomb Riley's 'barefoot boy'; 2) that the Riley is a characterization of Irish gaiety, love of pleasure, etc." However, he added: "Neither is convincingly documented, nor does the plausibility of one seem any greater than that of the other." [Funk, pp.170–1, traced the phrase to a song, popular in the 1880s, that is, to a date much earlier than 1911, when it was first attested in print. He referred to the comic song "Is that Mr. Reilly" by Pat Rooney.] OED: 1911.

L26. *Lightly come, lightly go*

NQ 1921 XII/8: 488.

'What is obtained easily is lost easily'. The note offers an antedating of this saying offered in the original edition of the *OED* (from 1624 to 1538), where a 1538 synonym is also given: "it is but trick and go." EDD: *Lightly*; OED: 1624.

L27. *Like an owl in an ivy bush*

NQ 1900 IX/6: 328, 397; 1901 IX/7: 16, 116; 1902 IX/9: 157.

'Well-hidden'. The phrase is proverbial in north Lincolnshire, but it is also widely known elsewhere and occurs in Ray. Its origins in the prayer book is doubtful. Brewer (p. 1790 at this phrase) noted that "owls are proverbial for their judge-like solemnity," while ivy, the favorite plant of Bacchus [not Athena!] "was supposed to be the favorite haunt of owls." Svartengren: 211. OED: *a*1625.

L28. *Like a thresher*

NQ 1899 IX/4: 106, 171, 234.

Thresher in this reinforcing simile means 'flail', and the phrase, obsolescent at the end of the 19th century, was used approvingly with the vague sense 'forcefully'. One could work like a thresher and even sing like a thresher. A thresher could also be used as an offensive weapon. Svartengren: 124. *

L29. *Like chips in porridge, neither good nor harm*

NQ 1881 VI/3: 246, 276, 375, 396.

This is said about someone of little promise. Occasionally altered into *like chicken porridge*. The phrase was known to the correspondents from the south and west of England. OED: 1880 *(the proverbial chip in porridge, which does neither good nor harm)*.

L30. *Like death on a mop-stick*

NQ 1880 VI/1: 375; VI/2: 34, 117.

"In old days, children amused themselves by making a death's head by scooping out a turnip, cutting three holes for eyes and mouth, and putting a lightened candle-end inside from behind. A stake or old mop-stick was then pointed with a knife and stuck into the bottom of the turnip, and a death's head with eyes of fire was complete. Sometimes a stick was tied across the mop-stick, and a shirt or sheet stretched over it, to make it ghostly and ghastly" (p. 117). Cf. *Cry mapsticks, to.* *

L31. *Like Hicks's horses, all of a snarl*

NQ 1878 V/10: 6.

This is (or was) a saying in Somersetshire used when a skein of thread is entangled. "A bystander will remark, 'Oh, that is like Hicks's horses, all of a snarl'; and, by way of parenthesis, adds, 'They say that he had only one'. It is then explained that the said horses or horse got entangled in the harness." *

L32. *Like Hunt's dog, neither go to church nor stay at home*
BrA February 9–11, # 105: 2.

The British Apollo offers the following explanation, without referring to its source: "One Hunt, a labouring Man, at a small town in Shropshire, kept a mastiff, who was very fond of following his master up and down. Now Hunt was a religious man, and every Sunday in the afternoon went to church with all his family, and lock'd his mastiff in the house till he came back again. The dog, it seems, unwilling to be left alone complain'd in melancholy notes, of such a dismal sound, that all the village was disturb'd by his incessant howling; This made Hunt resolve to take his dog to church next Sunday. The dog however, who perhaps had formerly been beaten by the sexton for disturbing the congregation, cou'd be brought no further than the church door, for there he hung behind, and tug'd the string by which his master held him. Hunt grew angry at the obstinacy of his mastiff, and after having beat him soundly, and let him go, and with uplifted hands and zealous accent, cried, half-weeping, 'Oh! What will this world come to? My very dogs have learn'd to practice wickedness, and are neither contented to go to church, or stay at home, good Lord deliver us.' The people, pleas'd to see a man so serious upon such occasion, laugh'd poor Hunt and his dog into a common proverb." [All such etymologies should be taken with a huge grain of salt.] *

L33. *Like lucky John Toy, he has lost a shilling and found a two-penny loaf*
NQ 1856, II/3: 327; 1864 III/6: 6.

"At Penryn, in West Cornwall, this proverb [was frequently] applied to any one who rejoiced over a small gain, though purchased at the expense of a greater loss." A retarded man called John Toy was known, but the author of the note (p. 327) doubted that that person had anything to do with the idiom, [and indeed most characters in such idioms may not have had living prototypes]. Apperson: 1864. *

L34. *Like Madame Hassell's feast*
NQ 1856 II/1: 313; II/2: 339.

The full text of the phrase is "Like Madam Hassell's feast, enough, and none to spare" (said about a spare dinner). It allegedly goes back to the custom of a certain Mrs. Casely's boarding house. Irish. *

L35. *Like one o'clock*
NQ 1900 IX/6: 198, 305, 376, 473.

'Quickly'. No convincing explanation was offered, though the following may be worth noting: "Of all the hours that clocks strike the hour of one is naturally the shortest and the soonest over" (p. 473). Svartengren: 406. OED: 1847.

L36. *Like station*
NQ 1892 VIII/1: 231.

A correspondent from Cincinnati, Ohio, wrote: "Thirty or forty years ago, in northern New England, 'acting like statia' was in somewhat common use to describe the unruly, mischievous, or excited conduct of a child." EDD: *Station.* *

L37. *Like the curate's egg, good in parts*

NQ 1909 X/11: 70, 134, 356.

See *Curate's eggs.*

L38. *Like the Dutchman's anchor at home*

NQ 1912 XI/5: 330, 435; 1916 XII/1: 396.

'An object that would have been useful in this situation, but it was, unfortunately, left at home'. The story cited as the source on p. 435 was almost certainly invented in retrospect. It is one of many phrases "often with an opprobrious or derisive application, largely due to the rivalry and enmity between the English and Dutch in the 17th century" (OED). The writer on p. 396 adds *Dutch tandem,* "heard in the West Country, which is applied to a person driving a single horse with another tied to the tail of the cart." *

L39. *Little bird told me*

NQ 1852 I/4: 232, 284, 394; 1869, IV/4: 292; 1881 VI/4: 366.

'I've heard it from someone'. A humorous reply meaning "I won't tell you from whom I have this information." The note on p. 232 [quite unconvincingly] traces the idiom to the Koran and the New Testament. "Does not the phrase come from the world-wide story of a bird—a parrot or magpie—telling tales out of school to the betrayal of a wife's infidelity?" (p. 292) (A few parallel versions are given in the note.) JBK I, 63. *

L40. *Little Englander*

NQ 1921 XII/8: 474; 1925, 148: 262, 305.

'A term of reproach against those opposed to the expansion of the empire'. "In 'Joseph Chamberlain,' by Alexander Mackintosh (p. 402) 'Little Englander' is traced to a question in *The Pall Mall Gazette* in 1884, which asked 'the advocates of a Little England, where are they now'? It was at that time under Mr. W. T. Stead's regime that the *Pall Mall,* a Liberal organ, was demanding an advanced foreign policy in the Soudan and elsewhere. In Montgomery & Cambray's 'Dictionary of Political Phrases and Allusions' published in 1906 the *Pall Mall Gazette* is also credited with the phrase, which had attained wide currency during the Jameson Raid, and the Boer War" (p. 305). "A phrase first applied by the *Pall Mall Gazette,* then a Liberal paper, to those persons in the country who disagree with 'Imperialism', and are usually found in opposition when the Government are engaged in disputes and wars; the 'peace at any price' party. Sorry I cannot give date. The phrase 'Little Englanders' also occurs in the *Westminster Gazette* for Aug. 1, 1895, and 'Little Englandism' in *The Times* for Jan. 20, 1899" (p. 474). OED: 1833.

L41. *Little old ladies in tennis shoes*

ANQ 15, 1976: 59.

"This phrase was first used in a political speech by then-Attorney General of the State of California Stanley Mosk in the mid-1960s, possibly coined by Mosk's speechwriter of the time, Tom McDonald, to describe ultra-conservative critics of liberal legislation proposed by the Democratic Party. It was popularized by the syndicated cartoonist Phil Interlandi (Los Angeles *Times* Syndicate)." *

L42. *Little summer of St. Luke*
NQ 1888 VII/5: 507; 1888 VII/6: 50, 374.

"A recurrence of warm weather of a milder kind, the duration of which is usually about ten days or a fortnight, takes place nearly every year in the middle of October; and as the 18th of that month is St. Luke's Day, this is generally called by us St. Luke's summer" (p. 50). The expression "is not likely to be very old, since before the reformation of the calendar St. Luke's Day in England corresponded to what is now the 29th of October, whereas the warmer weather usually occurs about the middle of that month, near the time when St. Luke's Day is now kept." (p. 50). OED: 1824 *(St. Luke's Little Summer).*

L43. *London paved with gold*
NQ 1882 VI/5: 429; 1882 VI/6: 153, 299, 496; 1884 VI/9: 358, 398, 457.

The correspondents quoted several songs glorifying London, where streets are said to be paved with gold. However, the reference, it was proposed, might have been to "the golden shower which fell upon Farinelli in 1734." This reference is to James Carey's ballad. In 1735, "Handel was deserted and conversely, driven away, and 5,000 £. a year paid to Charles Broschi, commonly called 'Farinelli'." Farinelli was the stage name of Carlo M. N. Broschi (1705–1782), a famous Italian castrato singer. On p. 457, it is suggested that the phrase goes back to the tale of the credulous Dick Whittington, who believed that in London the streets are indeed paved with gold. The *OED* shares this opinion. OED: 1798. *

L44. *Long and the short of it, the*
NQ 1897 VIII/12: 388, 452, 497; 1898 IX/1: 91.

'The gist of the story, all that need to be said; the general effect or result'. It was noted that Shakespeare used this phrase with *long* and *short* in reverse order (not an uncommon phenomenon in such idioms: cf. the older variant *from post to pillar*, p. 497). The phrase "exists in French with a difference of meaning; thus *le court et le long d'une affaire* means 'all the ins and outs of a matter" (p. 497). OED: 1622.

L45. *Look (or stare) like a throttled earwig, to*
NQ 1909 X/12: 148, 218.

'To have this is said about someone with a startled or any unusually fixed look.' But the phrase is also applied to people dressed in new clothes or wearing high collars, and a bad singer is "sometimes described as having 'a voice like a throttled earwig'." Northern England. EDD: *Earwig.* *

L46. *Look nine ways for Sunday, to*
NQ 1861, II/12: 309, 357.

'To be completely at a loss'. On p. 357, the suggestion is made that the phrase is pugilistic in origin, with Sunday representing the rest the spent fighter requires. *Two* is sometimes substituted for *nine* [but *nine* is a formulaic number]. Lancashire. EDD: *Sunday*; OED: 1832 *(looking about six ways for Sunday).*

L47. *Lose face, to*
ANQ 6, 1946: 120.

'To be shamed in public'. The note offers an early (1847) citation of the phrase. The *OED* gives an 1834 citation in which *lose face* is called 'so obviously unfamiliar' and an 1835 one with *lose face* still in quotes. Both refer to China. OED: 1834. Cf. *Save face, to.*

L48. *Lynch law*
NQ 1909 X/11: 445, 515.

'Execution without due process'. "Not only was 'Lynch's law' the original form of the term, but it was the only form known until after 1830. Moreover, though the term 'Lynch's law' is first found in 1817, yet the practice was known here before the outbreak of the Revolutionary War. . . . The term 'Lynch's law', as originally used, did not mean to put to death, but merely indicated punishment in some milder way—sometimes by driving a wrong-doer (or alleged wrongdoer, for mistakes were often made) out of a district, sometimes by tarring and feathering, but generally by applying thirty-nine lashes. It was not until about 1835 that any one was put to death under lynch law. Of the many persons named Lynch—some imaginary, some real—who have been proposed as the putative father of lynch law, the only one who deserves serious consideration is Charles Lynch of Virginia who was born un 1736 and died on 29 Oct., 1796." But this conclusion has been contested. The author of the note is Albert Matthews, an outstanding expert in the area of American realities. OED: 1811.

M

M1. *Make a crutch of one's cross, to*
Academy 64, 1903: 149.

'To endure suffering to strengthen one's character'. The reviewer of F. Edward Hulme's book *Proverb Lore* says: "To us it is the last word of smugness to affliction which it does not propose to alleviate." *

M2. *Make a hand of, to*
NQ 1886 VII/1: 449, 517; 1886 VII/2: 33, 138.

'To destroy'. The phrase occurs in some editions of Bunyan's *The Pilgrim's Progress* and alternates with *make an end,* but *hand* does not appear to have been a mistake, for *make a hand* occurs elsewhere and in the modern dialect of Lancashire (pp. 517 and 33). EDD: *Hand*; OED: 1569.

M3. *Make a leg, to*
NQ 1881 VI/3: 149, 337, 375; 1881 VI/4: 215; 1882 VI/5: 57, 175, 297.

'To bow and scrape'. The phrase is archaic. In the words of one of the correspondents, "Fashions change. More lately the 'bow' is the principal mark of courtesy, the scrape of the foot merely an accessory; but my contention is that in olden days the scrape, or rather genuflection, was the marked and principal sign of respect or homage, the 'bow of the head' either accessory to it or wanting" (p. 375). The contributors to the discussion gave many examples of "making a leg." EDD: *Leg*; OED: 1548 *(makest wery legges)*.

M4. *Make a long arm, to*
NQ 1911 XI/4: 44, 118, 158, 215, 498; 1923 XIII/1: 468; 1924, 146: 17.

'To help oneself to something far from the place where one it sitting'. Many people knew this phrase on both sides of the Atlantic (though in the United States, only on the East Coast), and believed that it was their family quip. Although used rather widely, it left few traces in printed sources. OED: 1593.

M5. *Make a shaft or a bolt of it, to*
NQ 1862, III/1: 59.

'To make one use or other of the thing spoken of'. *Ivanhoe* is quoted: "The bolt was the arrow peculiarly fitted to the crossbow, as that of the long-bow was called a shaft. Hence the English proverb, 'I will make a shaft or bolt of it'." The *OED* glosses the phrase as 'make the venture'. It compares the phrase with "either make a spoon or spoil a horn." See it above. OED: 1616.

M6. *Make buttons, to*
NQ 1908 X/9: 467; 1908 X/10: 13, 158.

'To fidget'. This phrase, which meant 'to be in great fear' was still current in provincial English at the beginning of the 20th century. OED: *a*1565.

M7. *Make children's shoes, to*
NQ 1855, I/11: 184.

This East Anglian phrase is explained as meaning 'to trifle, do nonsense'. EDD: *Children*. *

M8. *Make love, to*
NQ 1881 VI/4: 347.

'To indulge in amorous pursuits'. According to John Lily's novel *Eupheus and his England* (1580), the phrase was new and smacked of shopkeepers' usage. Even so, the phrase is a calque of French *faire l'amour*. OED: 1567.

M9. *Make no bones, to*
NQ 1887 VII/3: 408, 523; 1887 VII/4: 137, 210.

'To do something without scruple'. The exchange is valuable only because James A. H. Murray took part in it (p. 210). People indulged in guesswork, as though the *OED* did not exist. Murray explained that eleven out of the fifty-five quotations known to his team had been included in the entry and showed the progress of the idiom with various prepositions. The earliest form of the idiom was *to find no bones in,* where *bones* alluded to difficulties. EDD: *Bone*; OED: 1571.

M10. *Make one's parish, to*
NQ 1910 XI/1: 206, 254, 315.

According to an old law (the example is from Devonshire), a man was considered a resident of the parish in which he served out the last forty days of his apprenticeship. Hence the phrase, which means 'to serve out this period of time in a certain place'. *

M11. *Make up one's mouth, to*
NQ 1888 VII/5: 387; 1888 VII/6: 38.

'To eat a little bit after the main meal' (so in Shropshire). The phrase is obsolete, and at one time, it (also?) meant 'to finish a speech'. The figurative meaning seems to have been 'to make profit'. OED: 1606 ('to finish speaking').

M12. *Man alive*
NQ 1886 VII/1: 249, 375.

According to one explanation (p. 375): "This is an old Rugby School phrase . . . . an exclamation of impatience: 'Man alive, what are you doing that for?' that is, 'You, a living man with your wits about you, haven't you more sense than to do that?'. . . . It is interesting, as one of the comparatively few cases in which, in ordinary English, an adjective follows, instead of preceding, the substantive. These instances are often of a religious kind; as, 'God Almighty', 'Life eternal', 'Faith unfeigned', 'Court Christian'; but some are secular, as, 'Court martial', 'Theatre royal'." [The place of the adjective goes back to French usage.] EDD: *Man*; OED: 1839.

M13. *Man and a brother, a*
NQ 1887 VII/3: 288, 356, 394, 466.

The phrase was adopted as a seal by the Anti-Slavery Society of London. In 1768, Wedgwood produced a medallion "representing a negro in chains, with one knee on the ground and both hands lifted up to heaven" (p. 356). In a printed book, it appeared in 1799 (p. 394). "The design for the seal of the Society for the Abolition of Slavery was modelled by Hackwood under Wedgwood's directions, and was laid before the committee of the Society on Oct. 16, 1787. It being approved of, 'a seal was ordered to be engraved from it; and in 1792 Wedgwood, at his own expense, had a block cut from the design as a frontispiece illustration for one of Clarkson's pamphlets'." OED: 1787.

M14. *Man in a quart bottle*
NQ 1909 X/12: 289; 1910 XI/1: 136.

The phrase refers to people's credulity. The whole affair arose "out of a wager between the Duke of Montague and Lord Chesterfield, the latter of whom is reported to have said: 'Surely, if a man should say that he would jump into a quart bottle, nobody would believe that'. The Duke accepted the challenge. An advertisement duly appeared 10 Jan., 1749, stating that at a certain specified time and place a person would get into a tavern quart bottle and perform other extraordinary feats . . . . On the 16th of January, 1749, a crowded audience filled the Haymarket Theatre, London, to witness a conjuror perform several astonishing feats, among them that of jumping into a quart bottle. The conjuror, of course, failed to appear, and a formidable riot was the result, the theatrical property being wholly destroyed by the dupes whose credulity had victimized them. An account of the affair was printed in *The General Magazine* for January, 1749, a copy of which is now before me" (p. 136). OED: 1764.

M15. *Man in the street*
NQ 1881 VI/3: 69; 1898 IX/2: 7, 131; 1902 IX/10: 107; 1903 IX/11: 73; 1906 X/5: 167; 1909 X/11: 196; *The Spectator* 1904: 290, 413.

The suggested definition was 'one who speaks with confident knowledge having none'. An 1831 example is cited (p. 290), but the phrase was known as early as in 1648 (p. 413). "Emerson seems to have been one of the first, if not the first, who brought this phrase into literary use. In his essay on 'Self-reliance' he writes: 'The man in the street does not know a star in the sky'. This appeared in the first series of his essays, published, I think not long after the date indicated by Mr. Parry. Again in 'the conduct of Life', Article VI., on 'Worship', referring to Free-Trade, has this sentence: 'Well,' says the man in the street, 'Cobden got a stipend out of it.' These passages will be found in Routledge's edition of Emerson's works, 1883, pp. 20 and 402" (p. 413). The *OED* defines the idiom as 'the ordinary or average man (person); known at the end of the 18th century as distinguished from the expert or specialist'. Emerson's *Eloquence* (1854) is quoted. The same explanation appeared in *NQ* IX/2: 131. OED: 1770.

M16. *Man of one book*
NQ 1886 VII/1: 349, 495.

Apparently, Thomas Aquinas suggested that concentration on books prevents the mind from being distracted (p. 495). Conversely, there is an adage to the effect that a man of one book lacks perspective and is dangerous (p. 349). *

M17. *Man of straw*
NQ 1872, IV/9: 457, 495; 1933, 165: 387.

'An imaginary adversary, *etc.*' The phrase was said to go back to the custom in the seventeenth century of "witnesses carrying straw in their shoes as a sign to inform the public where a false oath might be procured for half-a-crown." According to IV/9: 495, such people offered themselves not as witnesses but as persons ready to go bail (for payment) for another. The explanations bear every sign of folk etymology and are at odds with the date now known. OED: 1599.

M18. *Man of wax*
NQ 1927, 152: 17, 70.

'A term of emphatic commendation'. It occurs in *Romeo and Juliet*. The short discussion centered on the meaning of *wax*. Could the reference be to cobbler's wax, a substance with which the threads used from sewing were greased? Or does the phrase *to be in a wax* 'to be furiously angry' have anything to do with the obscure phrase? (The origin of *wax*: 'anger' is also unclear.) EDD: *Wax*; OED: 1503.

M19. *Man proposes, but God disposes*
NQ 1872 V/11: 206; 1878 V/10: 306, 436; 1882 VI/5: 98; 1883 VI/8: 7, 97, 254; 1919 XII/5: 232; 1944, 187: 18.

This saying, which exists in several languages, may go back, according to the correspondents, to "the well known tractate of Thomas à Kempis, *De Imitatione Christi*. The Latin phrase is quoted "Nam homo proponit, sed Deus disponit." Hislop: 221. OED: *c*1500 (*the fole proposeth & god dysposeth*).

M20. *Mantle-maker's twist*

NQ 1918 XII/4: 272, 334.

'Stirring the brew in the teapot to make it stronger'. The following explanation is given on p. 334: "This expression, though now less frequently heard than formerly, is, to my knowledge, still used (though generally in a humorous sense) by old-fashioned people. I invariably hear it spoken of as the 'mantua-maker's twist', a proof of its bygone origin. Eighty or a hundred years ago tea was an expensive luxury, though much appreciated as a beverage by seamstresses, mantua-makers, and other sedentary workwomen, who drank tea at frequent intervals during each day. When the brew became weaker it was a general custom not to make fresh tea, but to pour more water upon the tealeaves, and not to 'stir' the infusion, but, under the impression that greater strength was effected by the process, to take the teapot in both hands and give it several rapid twirls before decanting the brew." *

M21. *Many a mickle makes a muckle*

NQ 1888 VII/6: 389; 1892 VIII/2: 205, 278, 369; 1893 VIII/3: 348; 1893 VIII/4: 19, 158; 1906 X/6: 388, 456; 1907 X/7: 11, 112, 215; 1908 X/9: 338; 1908 X/10: 286; *The Spectator* 137, 1926: 380.

'A large sum or amount'. Long before the appearance of the article in *The Spectator,* a correspondent to *NQ* wondered how the saying can make sense, both *mickle* and *muckle* meaning 'much'. According to some comments, the "correct" form of the saying was allegedly *many kittles make a mickle* (VIII/3: 348); other correspondents cited the variant *mony a pickle makes a mickle* ("it rhymes, and it is altogether Scotch"); (VIII/2: 278; X/6: 456), unknown to the other contributors to the discussion. The Scotch variant is *mony a little macks a meikle* (VIII/4: 158), though it was pointed out (X/6: 456) that the proverb is English, with the Scotch variants being modifications of it. There was a suggestion that *mickle-meickle* refers to quantity, while *muckle* indicates size (X/7: 11), but facts disprove it. The Greek "model" is close to the English analog (VIII/4: 19). OED: 1793.

M22. *March of intellect*

NQ 1889 VII/8: 87; 1889 VII/8: 154, 354.

Bartlett traced this phrase to Southey's *Collection, on Progress of Society* (p. 154). At one time it was made fun of (p. 87). Carlyle used it in 1828 (p. 354), and a year later it occurred in a comic song (also p. 354). OED: 1775 *(The march of the human mind)* and 1818 *(march of intellect).*

M23. *Married by the hangman*

NQ 1860 II/9: 487; 1866 III/9: 267.

'Marked as a prostitute' is a more likely gloss on this phrase than a cant term for being chained or handcuffed together. The source of the second interpretation is Grose (p. 487).

M24. *Meat and mense*

NQ 1871, IV/8: 284, 380, 465; 1873, IV/11: 455; 1927, 153: 424, 465; 1928, 154: 15.

Meat and mense occurs in Scotland and is part of the phrase *to have one's meat and one's mense* and *to have neither meat nor mense.* The overwhelming opinion was that *mense* is English, not Latin, and that it is related to *man.* The word means 'good manners, discretion'. The saying *to have one's meat and one's mense* "is applied to a person who has invited another to dine with him who has refused, or failed to make his appearance; meaning that you have both the meat [food] he would have eaten, and the honour of having invited him." (IV/8: 284). The *OED* confirms the etymology suggested above (*mense* is from the obsolete noun *mensk,* from Scandinavian: Old Icelandic *menska* 'humanity'). In vol. 153: 465, several versions of the saying are given. EDD: *Meat*; OED: 1628 *(I have my meate and my mense).*

M25. *Meg's diversions*

NQ 1914 XI/9: 208, 254.

'Mischievous pranks'. Of the two explanations on p. 254, the second is right, but the first one is also curious: 1) "The Meg from whom this phrase originated was "Long Meg of Westminster," who in 'A Dictionary of the Noted Names of Fiction,' &c., by William A. Wheeler, M.A. (1870), is described as follows: 'A 'lusty bouncing romp' and procuress of the sixteenth century, whose 'Life and Pranks' were 'imprinted in London' in 1582, and subsequently. She is often alluded to by the older English writers." 2) "Meg was Margaret Crow in Craven's play 'Meg's Diversions,' produced at the New Royalty in 1866. It had a long and successful run, and figured on the bill with Burnand's inimitable burlesque of 'Black-eyed Susan,' which drew the whole town to the little house in Dean Street, Soho. Miss M. Oliver impersonated Meg, and, in the language of her father, Jasper Pidgeon, the village carpenter, was her 'diversion'." EDD: *Meg*; OED: 1807.

M26. *Melverley, God help me*

NQ 1850, I/1: 325.

See the notes on *Binsey, God help me*; *Crowley, God help us*; *From Lincoln heath, God help me*; *Saffron Walden, God help me,* and *Tickhill, God help me.* *

M27. *Mend or end*

NQ 1884 VI/10: 246, 296, 474; 1892 VIII/2: 391, 525; 1894 VIII/5: 486-7; 1894 VIII/6: 11, 277, 437; 1895 VIII/7: 18; 1895 VIII/8: 512; 1897 VIII/12: 477; 1898 IX/2: 424; *Spectator* 1923 131: 461, 499, 558.

'Kill or cure'. In 1923, the correspondents discussed the origin of the phrase without having looked it up in the *OED,* and L. R. M. Strachan (p. 558 in the *Spectator*) set the record straight, but the reference to Walter Scott (p. 461) and Hermann Cohen fills the gap between 1680 and 1884. However, consider the following: "That the phrase is at least as old as 1584, appears by the following passage from Lyle's 'Alexander and Campaspe,' published in that year:— 'Painters now coveting to draw a glancing eye, now a winking—still mending it, never ending it'" (VIII/5: 487) and "From 'Life and Letters of Erasmus,' by J. A. Froude, new edition, 1894:— 1518. 'That frigid, quarrelsome old lady, Theology, had swollen herself to such a point of vanity that it was necessary to bring her back to the fountain, but I would rather have her mended than ended'.—p. 215. 19 Nov., 1521. 'I have no more to do with Luther than with any other Christian. I would sooner have him mended than ended'.—p. 300" (VIII/8: 512). OED: 1578 *(It hathe mended as manye as it hathe ended).*

M28. *Merry Andrew*

NQ 1852, I/5: 128.

'A buffoon'. The note quotes Hearne, whose statement is said in the *OED* to be lacking solid evidence. According to Hearne (1735), the phrase was originally applied to Andrew Boorde (*a* 1490–1549), English physician and author. JBK 129–30. OED: 1677.

M29. *Mind one's P's and Q's*

NQ 1851 I/3: 357, 463, 523; I/4: 11; 1860 II/9: 53; 1876 V/5: 74; 1897, VIII/12: 220; 1926, 150: 100, 143; 1940, 178: 124; MCNNQ 1, 1878: 309; SNQ 3, 1889: 80; ANQ 2, 1889: 291-2.

NQ I/3: 357 cites the most often repeated derivation of this idiom: "From the ancient custom of hanging a slate behind the alehouse door, on which was written *P.* or *Q.* (i. e. *Pint or Quart*) against the name of each customer, according to the quantity which he had drunk, and which was not expected to be paid for till the Saturday evening, when the wages were settled." On p. 463 of the same volume, another popular explanation is offered: "*'Mind your toupées and your queues,'*—the *toupée* being the artificial locks of hair on the head, and the *queue* the pig-tail of olden time." Finally, on p. 524, a third origin is proposed: "I was told by a printer that the phrase had originated among those of his craft, since young compositors experience great difficulty in discriminating between the types of the two letters." (The same in 1860 II/9: 53 and, with a few details added, in 1851 I/4: 11.) Vol. 150, p. 100, contains a survey of the previous discussion of this idiom in *NQ*. On p. 143 (the same volume), reference to French *pieds* ('legs') and *queues* ('wigs') during the reign of Louis XIV is added, which is a variation on *your tou-pées and queues* (above). Vol. 178 gives quotations dated to 1602, 1616, and later. Reference to a teacher instructing his pupils about not confounding p's and q's may have some foundation in fact, but is unlikely to be the origin of the idiom. ANQ 2, 291-2 lists six hypotheses. Here is one: "French was for so long the legal language, entirely or in part, that the caution might have been given in stating the defending a cause, 'Mind you are ready with the *parceque* [why] when the *pourquoi* [because] is asked'—Be ready with your reasons, the 'because' for the 'why?' I think the term is now never used but as regards conversation. 'We must not talk at random, we must remember our P's and Q's.' 'Take care what you say, mind your P's and Q's.'" Another hypothesis that has not surfaced elsewhere runs as follows: "Punch used to be sold in bowls of two sizes; the P size was a shilling and the Q size sixpence". The *OED* does not suggest an etymology, but cites several more conjectures in addition to those listed above. The writer in MCNNQ 1: 209 gives a survey of three explanations and supports the idiom's derivation from the injunction of master printer to apprentices. OED: 1756.

M30. *Minnesota jog, the*

ANQ 2, 1889: 179.

"Few people, who consult the map of the United States, have failed to notice the triangular strip of island extending some distance north of the parallel which constitutes the boundary line between the west central parts of Canada and the United States. This territory is, for the greater part, situated in Lake of the Woods, but it includes also a small strip of land. The area in question is called the 'Minnesota Jog'." *

M31. *Mint state*
NQ 1931, 161: 335, 377, 430-1.

'Perfect original condition'. The term was first used in numismatics. Later, philatelists began to use it, and still later bibliophiles, when portraying the conditions of first editions, etc. On pp. 430-1, an especially detailed explanation by a professional coin collector appears. OED: 1901.

M32. *Money makes the mare go*
ANQ 2, 1889: 118; ANQ 5, 1890: 188.

"In Caleb Bingham's *American Preceptor,* published in 1794, is a dialogue called *Self-Interest* in which an English rustic, named Scrapewell, makes all sorts of false excuses to avoid lending his mare to a neighbor; but afterwards, finding that the loan was to be profitable to himself, he takes back all the excuses and lets the mare go." The suggestion is made that the proverb derives from this text. Chronology does not justify this explanation. "Sir Penny" is said in a fourteenth-century poem to make full many go in rich clothes and ride on horseback (perhaps with reference to this idiom; ANQ 5). JBK I, 4-6. OED: 1573 (*Money makes the horsse to goe*).

M33. *Monkey on the chimney*
NQ 1904 X/1: 288, 396.

'There is mortgage in the house' (regional). *House* for *chimney* also occurs. *The house is in pop* means the same. No explanation of why *mortgage* is called 'monkey' has been offered. Compare *Pay in monkey's coin.* *

M34. *Monkey's parade*
NQ 1910 XI/1: 225, 276.

'A noisy promenade of adolescents (not rowdies) frequenting a main road as aimless wanderers'. The writer on p. 276 knew the phrase as early as 1880. OED: 1910.

M35. *Month's mind*
GM 35, 1765: 137; NQ 1876 V/6: 63, 232; 1877 V/7: 29, 192; 1882 VI/6: 205, 251, 352, 374, 410, 458, 516-8; 1883 VI/7: 115, 298; 1883 VI/8: 312; 1900 IX/6: 104, 195, 295; 1904 X/2: 487; 1905 X/3: 54; MCNNQ 1, 1878: 302.

Month's mind was a service performed for the dead, one month after their death. In this phrase *mind,* as the explanation goes, means 'remembrance'. "The unabridged 'month's mind', the *trentana,* the French *trentel,* the English *trental,* is, to those who know anything of the ceremonials of the Roman Catholic Church, a daily service for thirty consecutive days. So to speak, it is a ceremonial of thirty days' length, as implied by the singular number of *trentana,* or other designation for it. Such a ceremonial, which both mourners and priests performed not merely 'in memoriam', but with a deep longing for the safety of the soul of the deceased, that safety being confirmed or accelerated through it, would most naturally be applied to any continuous or fixed longing, especially when its users had become Protestants" (VI/6: 205). In IX/6: 104, 195, and 295, the meaning of the word *trental* is discussed. The older authors explained the phrase *month's mind,* synonymous with *trental,* as a celebration in remembrance of dead persons a month after their decease. *Week's mind* and *year's mind* (or *twelvemonth's*) have also been recorded. The earliest commentators detected an additional meaning, namely 'continuous and eager longing'. The controversy centered on whether *a month's mind* meant a mass once a month or thirty masses on thirty consecutive days. "Those who assume that a trental always meant thirty masses on thirty consecutive days should remember that the most famous trental, St. Gregory's, consisted of three masses on each of the ten chief feasts of the church. . . ." (F. J. Furnivall in VI/6: 251). Furnivall confirmed his old view on p. 374: the phrase "simply means one day's service, a month after a man's death or burial, in mind or memory of him," but in VI/8: 312, he admits that "in the case of very rich folk, the successive thirty-day service" could happen. The conclusion does not invalidate the idea of the transferred meaning 'earnest longing or desire'. Furnivall's opinion was contested on several grounds, including the role of St. Gregory: "a month's mind had no other meaning than prayers for thirty consecutive days" (VI/6: 518). The discussion lasted for quite some time, and a few ambiguities do not seem to have been resolved. [Hyamson, p. 243, defines the phrase as 'a great desire' and cites two explanations, without giving his sources. 1) "By saying that they have a month's mind to a thing, they undoubtedly [!] mean that, if they had what they so much longed for, it would do them as much good as they believe 'a month's mind' or service in the church said once a month, would benefit their souls after their decease." 2) According to another suggestion, the allusion is to a woman's longing during the first month of pregnancy"—surely, a fanciful explanation.] OED: 1467.

M36. *More than Carter had oats*
ANQ 15, 1976: 59.
'Very much'. This phrase that has some variants (e.g. *hay* for *oats*) is known in many places in the US. An apocryphal tall tale about a farmer who had to move his fence to find room for stacking the bundle is all that is known about the mysterious Carter. *

M37. *Mother Carey's chickens*
NQ 1932, 62: 333.
'A storm petrel, thought by sailors to be a harbinger of bad weather'. Only one explanation seems to be known: the phrase is allegedly a corruption of *madre cara,* that is, the Blessed Virgin. The editor calls it unconvincing. JBK I, 35. OED: 1767.

M38. *Mothering Sunday*
MCNNQ 5, 1884: 212.
The same as *Carling Sunday.* EDD: *Mothering.* OED: 1783.

M39. *Mother of dead dogs*
NQ 1906 X/5: 509; X/6: 32, 95; 1907 X/7: 457; 1909 X/12: 406; 1910 XI/1: 325
'The Thames'. The phrase is a familiar quotation, though only technically so, because hardly anyone would recognize it today. It occurs many times in Carlyle, who was read, revered, and constantly quoted in his day. His coinage would perhaps not have been worthy of inclusion in a dictionary if it had not been pointed out that *the mother of tomcats* appears to have been a French slang term for the Seine (XI/1, 1910: 325). *

M40. *Mother-sick*
NQ 1891 VII/11: 189, 318, 355, 435, 496.

This word (or phrase), reminiscent of *homesick* has (or had?) some currency in several parts of England. Its implications varied from 'longing for one's mother' (about babies) and 'homesick' (about bigger children) to 'violently hysterical'. Therefore, some correspondents called the word touching and others repulsive. OED: 1618 ('hysterical'), 1748 ('pining for one's mother').

M41. *Moulden's bridge*
NQ 1875 V/3: 145.

'A threat'. "Many years ago there used to be a bridge near Warwick called by some such name as 'Moulden's bridge', over which it was absolutely necessary for the north Warwickshire folk to pass on their way to the country assizes and county jail. The yeomen, farmers, and tradesmen of the northern division of the county, whenever they had a hired servant or apprentice who evinced symptoms of becoming refractory, were accustomed to address them thus: 'I tell you what it is, sir, if you don't mind what you are about you'll get over Moulden's bridge', which always had the desired effect. The saying, I believe, has now quite died out." *

M42. *Moulton images*
The Athenæum 1898, 1: 812.

The saying "is supposed to reflect on the lack of beauty among the inhabitants of that large village, but seems in reality to be a pun on *molten*". Northamptonshire. *

M43. *Move the previous question, to*
NQ 1872 IV/9: 486.

This is the editor's note: "The origin of the phrase is parliamentary. When it is considered advisable to get rid of any motion or question without directly negativing it, the 'previous question'—namely, 'that this question be *now* put' is moved, and if carried the motion or question objected to is not put, and so got rid of without being negatived by a direct vote on its merits." OED: 1849.

M44. *Mutual admiration society*
ANQ 1, 1888: 46, 59; 1899 IX/4: 417.

"The name was first applied by American newspaper humorists to a friendly circle, self-styled the 'Five of Clubs', which George S. Hillard, Henry R. Cleveland, Prof. C. C. Felton, Charles Sumner, and H. W. Longfellow established at Cambridge in 1836. The point of the jest lay in the fact that as literary men they all had good chances, of which they liberally availed themselves, to speak well of each other's books in the reviews" (so explained on p. 46). The date of the earliest citation in the *OED* (1845) seems to confirm this explanation.

M45. *My eye and Tommy*
NQ 1859, II/8: 491; 1911 XI/4: 207, 255.

'Nonsense'. The phrase resembles *all my eye and Betty Martin* and suggests the idea of a "substitution table," with *my eye,* followed by a more or less arbitrary name for 'rubbish, fiddlesticks'. OED: 1810.

N

N1. *Nail one's ears to the pump, to*
NQ 1911 XI/5: 428; 1912 IX/6: 76.

'To punish, while using a measure ironically suggested as inadmissible'. Allegedly, some unfortunate debt collector was nailed to a pump at Trinity College, Dublin. *

N2. *Nail the colors to the mast, to*
NQ 1926, 150: 115, 196.

'To stick to one's position; refuse to budge'. The correspondence is devoted to Jack Crawford, who at the Battle of Camperdown did nail the color to the mast of his ship. OED: 1800 *(saw a man nail the French ensign to the stump of the mizzen-mast)* and 1808—*(nailed her colours to the mast).*

N3. *Needle's eye*
MCNNQ 3, 1881: 120, 123, 125, 135.

All correspondents were in agreement that the Biblical *needle* was a narrow passage, gate, or doorway (perhaps in the court of a temple, thus closed to the camel, an unclean animal—so on p. 135). OED: *a*1384.

N4. *Neither barrel, better herring*
NQ 1885 VI/11: 393.

More often *never a barrel, better herring* (see it below). 'Nothing to choose between two equally good things' (= whichever barrel you pick, you won't find a better herring.) OED: 1546.

N5. *Neither my eye nor my elbow*
NQ 1907 X/8: 7, 137, 254; 1908 X/9: 15.

The idiom refers to the speaker's ignorance of the subject, though in Derbyshire it means 'neither the one thing nor the other' (a comment on an unsatisfactory answer, promise, or arrangement): p. 7. Both *eye* and *elbow* could once mean 'arse' ('ass'). The phrase is obsolete, and, when used, speakers are unaware of those senses. [Cf. a similar treatment of the outwardly innocent *nitty-gritty.* Is there some implied but lost connection with *never touch your eye with your elbow*?] Apperson: 1894 *(not to know one's arse from one's elbow).* *

N6. *Nettle in, dock out*
NQ 1851 I/3: 133, 201, 205, 368, 463; 1855 I/11: 92.

The phrase occurs in Chaucer's *Troilus and Cressida* and puzzled commentators. All the publications state that this charm (or cure) defying the sting of the nettle is still widely known in rural England. EDD: *Nettle*; OED: 1374.

N7. *Never a barrel the better herring*
NQ 1865 III/8: 540.

'What's sauce for the goose is sauce for the gander'; or 'the choicest herrings are not packed in barrels'; or 'there will be better herrings for consumption on the spot, when there are no barrels to pack them for conveyance to distant lands.' Cf. *Neither barrel, better herring.* OED: 1546 *(Neither barrel better hearryng).*

N8. *Never touch your eye but with your elbow*

NQ 1884 VI/9: 289, 396.

A jocular way of saying: "Never touch your eye at all." Several synonymous expression are known. Cf. the question after *Neither my eye nor my elbow* *

N9. *New terror to death*

NQ 1876 V/6: 126, 195, 236, 293, 416.

'A posthumous biography published soon after the person's death and vilifying him'. The phrase has been attributed to Sir Charles Wetherell (1770–1846), an English lawyer, politician, and judge, Lord Lyndhurst (1772–1863), and Lord Brougham (1778–1868). But Swift used it as early as 1703 (see p. 236), and John Arbuthnot, Alexander Pope's friend did too (see p. 126). The reference is to the damaging recollections, published shortly after a person's death. *

N10. *Next the heart*

NQ 1877, V/7: 288, 417; NQ 1877, V/8: 18, 137.

'In the morning, fasting'. This phrase is said about the good affects (clearly, *effects* is meant) of drinking before breakfast. In the notes, the phrase was traced to at least as early as 1520. *The OED* does not tie it to drinking. The gloss there is 'on an empty stomach'. The phrase is said to be rare, now regional, and used without *the*. OED: c1440 *(nexte thy herte)*.

N11. *Nick the pin*

NQ 1894 VIII/6: 7, 76, 117, 174; 1901 IX/8: 264.

'To drink to the pin, that is, a certain amount, as indicated'. A pin is a four and a half gallon of ale or beer. According to p. 174, "so called from its being little larger than the huge wooden *pin* tankards used at the old German drinking parties, when each drinker drank down to a pin, generally of silver, in the side of the tankard." On p. 264, E. Cole's *English Dictionary* is quoted: "Nick the pin, drink just to the pin placed about the middle of a wooden cup. This caused so much debauchery that priests were forbidden to drink at or to the pins." On p. 175, two suggestions are offered about the origin of *pin*: from the cask's resemblance to a skittle pin and from being related to *penny*, that is, one-twelfth of a shilling. "If *pin* equals one-twelfth, it means one-twelfth of a hogshead of fifty-four gallons." [Hazlitt, p. 306, adds the following note to the entry *Make a pearl on your nail* (it has some relevance to the phrase above): Nash's *Pierce Penniless*, 1592, repr. Collier, 1868, p. 57. This phrase is connected with a convivial custom known as 'drinking *supernaculum*.' Supernaculum is, according to the most reasonable etymology, derived from Lat. *super*, and Germ. *nagel*, the nail, agreeable to a barbarous practice of coupling words taken from two distinct languages; unless it is to be supposed that the word is compounded of *super* and *nagulum*, a kind of jargon or loose Latinity, as Nash prints *super nagulum*. In a marginal note to his text, Nash observes, 'Drinking super nagulum, a devise of drinking, new come out of Fraunce; which is, after a man hath turned up the bottom of the cup, to drop on hys nayle, and made a pearle with that is left; which if it slide, and he cannot make stand on, by reason ther's too much, he must drinke againe for his penance.' See also *Notes and Queries*, 4th S., i. 460, 559, *Sussex Arch. Coll.*, xiv., 15, and my *Faiths and Folklore*, 1905, p. 574."] Cf. *In a merry pin*. OED: 1655.

N12. *Nimble ninepence is better than a slow shilling*
NQ 1851 I/4: 234; 1890 VII/10: 208, 314.

The reference is to the fact that people are reluctant to spend large sums but spend small amounts easily. The *OED* cites *nimble ninepence* (1801) occurring outside this phrase but only marks the phrase as rare and 'chiefly U.S.'. Its definition is given as 'quick return, circulating briskly'. For comparison see *ninepence* in the index. EDD: *Nimble*; OED: 1801 *(The 'nimble ninepence' being considered 'better than the slow shilling').*

N13. *Nine days wonder*
NQ 1852, I/4: 192; 1861 II/11: 249, 297, 478; 1877 V/7: 128; 1886 VII/1: 520; 1886 VII/2: 55, 154; ANQ 8, 1891: 6.

According to the editor's note (I/4: 192), the phrase goes back to "Kemp's *Nine Daies Wonder,* performed in a Morrice Daunce from London to Norwich, wherein euery dayes iourney is pleasantly set downe, to satisfie his friends the truth against all lying ballad-makers; what he did, how he was welcomed, and by whome entertained." Whether a short-lived miracle or one that lasts a whole nine days, Heywood used it in 1549 (II/11: 478). But the phrase is much older. The *OED* says: 'The brief time for which a novelty is supposed to attract attention'. [Hyamson, p. 251: "Said to be derived from the interest and excitement of children over the nine days' blindness of a newly born kitten"—a startling etymology.] OED: *a*1450 *(For this a wonder last but dayes nyne).*

N14. *Nine of diamonds and the curse of Scotland*
BrA 1707, GM 56, 1786: 301-2, 390-1, 410, 536, 968, 1122; 61, 1786: 141; NQ 1849, I/1: 61, 90; 1851, III/1: 22, 253, 423, 483; 1870, IV/6: 195, 289; 1875, V/6: 20, 97, 118; OID 1882; NQ 1893, VIII/3: 367, 398, 416, 453; 1893, VIII/4: 537; 1894, VIII/5: 11, 113; 1894, VIII/6: 185; 1895, VIII/7: 274; 1899 IX/4: 39; 1907, X/8: 114.

The question is: "Why is nine of diamonds called the curse of Scotland?" It will be seen from the bibliography above (and the list is certainly incomplete, even if we disregard the dictionaries and popular books that mention this phrase) that the mysterious role of the playing card *nine of diamonds* in the history of Scotland has bothered people for more than two centuries. As early as 1707, no one knew the answer, which is buried in the depths of (Scottish?) folklore. The number nine is a favorite of Eurasian oral tradition, along with *three* and *seven* (see *nine* and *ninepence* in the word index), which makes a search for the origin of the proverb in question nearly hopeless. These are the hypotheses discussed in various publications. 1) Every ninth king of Scotland was a tyrant (perhaps so, but why diamonds?). 2) On April 16, 1746, the battle of Culloden took place. It was between the forces of the Jacobites and of the government. Each leader—Charles Edward Stuart (Bonnie Prince Charles) and Prince William, the Duke of Cumberland, but more often the Duke, reportedly instructed his followers to give the enemy no quarter. The instructions were said to have been written on reverse of a playing card (nine of diamonds). This card was never found and probably did not exist. 3) Another relevant battle is the Massacre of Glencoe (February 3, 1693). On that day, the clan MacDonald of Glenco was attacked and treated with great cruelty. Later, Lord Stair, Secretary of State for Scotland, played the major role in concluding the 1701 Treaty of Union between the Kingdom of England and Kingdom of Scotland. In Scotland, many people looked upon this treaty as a disaster. Lord Stair's coat of arms did contain nine lozenges, but whether this fact throws light on the proverb is unclear. The *OED* finds the connection probable. 4) There is a card game called Pope Joan. It was possibly introduced to Scotland in the first half of the sixteenth century. In the game, the nine of diamonds, or the Pope, is the winning card, and the story goes that many Scottish courtiers were ruined because of their addiction to that game. It has been suggested that the antipapal spirit of the Scots caused the pope to be called the Curse of Scotland. Such conjectures cannot be verified. 5) It has often been said that *curse of Scotland* is an alteration of *cross of Scotland,* with reference to St. Andrew's cross (St. Andrews is the patron saint of Scotland). But the form of St. Andrew's cross resembles five more than nine. And the old question arises: Where do diamonds come in? 6) According to one version, the proverb derives from the coat of arms of Daniel Campbell of Shawfield, M.P. for Glasgow, who was responsible for the introduction of the highly unpopular malt tax into Scotland. Contrary to some assertions, his coat of arms does not contain nine diamonds. Daniel Campbell was not alone reportedly having had such a coat of arms, but in every case the information turned out to be false. 7) There is a legend that, when Robert Bruce was in flight on the water of Cairn in the Galloway district, the heel of his boot became loose. The treacherous or careless Rob McQuechan mended the boot and wounded Bruce badly in the heel. The proverb commemorating this event mentions half an inch, but Robert Burns seems to have spoken about nine inches. 8) A certain George Campbell attempted to steal the crown out of Edinburgh castle, but succeeded only in abstracting nine jewels from it. To replace the diamonds, a heavy tax was laid on the whole kingdom; hence allegedly, *the curse of Scotland.* At one time, the nine of diamonds was indeed called George Campbell. It will be seen that the historical background of the phrase remains a matter of rather uninspiring speculation. The *OED* quotes from a book with the dates 1715–47.

N15. *Ninepence, Nanny! Two groats and a penny!*
NQ 1886 VII/2: 266.

An evasive answer to somebody's question: "What did so-and-so say?" Numerous phrases of this type are known in dialects. Very few of them have been included in this dictionary, but *ninepence* plays such a noticeable role in English idioms that this one has been spared. Two groats and a penny make up a very small sum. Does the response mean 'your question is not worth answering'? Derbyshire. *

N16. *Nine tailors make a man*
BrA March 21–6 #30: 2, NQ 1852 I/6: 390, 563; 1853 I/7: 165, 557–5; 1868, IV/2: 437, 587; 1869, IV/3: 84; 1871, IV/8: 36; 1877 V/7: 164; 1923 XII/12: 318; 1926, 150: 390, 427; 1926, 151: 15; BM 25, 1829: 343.

This is a much discussed phrase. The earliest correspondent to *NQ* (I/6: 390) says: "I have heard it stated, that this saying originated in the custom, at the close of the passing bell, of tolling *three times three* in the case of a *man*; whereas for women and children, the number of the closing strokes upon the bell is respectively fewer." This is the most often repeated explanation. Half a century later, James Curtis, the author of the survey "Number 'Nine', Chiefly Considered in its Historical Aspects" (*Transactions of the Royal Society of Literature of the United Kingdom,* Second Series, vol. 20, 1899: 237–59) repeated that note almost verbatim: "[The saying] perhaps originated in shameless peeping Tom the tailor; or perhaps from the following. The departure of an adult has sometimes been announced by the tolling of church bells, formerly practised from a belief in their efficacy to drive away evil spirits. It may possibly be that tailors in the above phrase is a corruption of 'tellers' or strokes tolled at the end of a knell. In some places the death of an adult was announced by nine strokes in succession; six for a woman, three for a child. I have heard that at Wimbledon now it is still the custom to toll nine times for a man" (p. 251). The editorial note to *NQ* I/6: 390 offers a long story: "This saying, we believe, had its origin in the following manner:—In 1742 an orphan boy applied for alms at a fashionable tailor's shop in London, in which nine journeymen were employed. His interesting appearance opened the hearts of the benevolent gentlemen of the cloth, who immediately contributed nine shillings for the relief of the little stranger. With this capital our youthful hero purchased fruit, which he retailed at a profit. Time passes on, and wealth and honour smile upon our young tradesman, so that when he set up his carriage, instead of troubling the Heralds' College for his crest, he painted the following motto on the panel: 'Nine tailors make me a man'." In I/6, a 1682 poem is reproduced: there, nine tailors are said to have pulled together their resources to rescue a destitute draper. The note in I/7, 1853: 165 reprints a fanciful story from *The British Apollo* (1726, I: 236) about a bellicose woman overpowering *eight* tailors. The same saying is known in northern France, but its source there is not discussed (from France to England or from England to France?) (I/7, 1853: 557–8). An analog in German also exists. There are anecdotes about eighteen tailors addressed as "both" (indicating that nine tailors are equal to one person) and the similie *Like the nine tailors going a-fox hunting at Astleys.* Cf. *There's nothing like leather.* OED: 1607 *(They say three Taylors go to the making vp of a man, but Ime sure I had foure Taylors and a halfe went to the making of me thus.)* See also *Fox's wedding* [it is emphasized there that tailors were for a long time objects of ridicule] and *Whip the cat, to.*

N17. *Nip and tuck*
MM 38, 1952: 153 (26), 331 (26).
'Neck and neck' (that is, 'a close result in a race or a contest'). The American origin of the idiom has been confirmed. *Tack* and *chuck* have been recorded in place of *tuck,* as well as the 1832 sentence 'There is not a nip of brandy between them'. OED: 1832 and more certainly, 1845.

N18. *No fore royal, no morning coffee*
MM 58, 1972: 473 (26); 58, 1973: 352 (26); MM 60, 1974: 332 (26).
Royal means 'royal sail'. "Captain George Browne had the following to say about a Swansea copper-ore brig (or snow) in which he served about 1875 and which seems to provide a factual basis for the saying: 'She also had a stump fore-topgallant mast, which the sailors said was a trick of the owner to deprive them of their morning coffee—there being no fore royal to stow made her an easy job, and they should not merit coffee'" (58, 1973: 352). *

N19. *No great shakes*
NQ 1852 I/5: 443; 1862 III/2: 52; 1877 V/8: 184; 1879 V/12: 473; 1899 IX/3: 169, 277, 352, 493; 1911 XI/3: 129, 173, 257, 338; ANQ 3, 1889: 284.
'Not a big deal, nothing much'. The editor's note in I/5: 443 suggests a connection with a *handshake.* In some way, the story cited in the article "Odd Phases in Some Popular Phrases" confirms the handshake idea, though it sounds like pure fiction: "*No great shakes* is an expression

of opprobrium often used toward ill-conditioned persons. The belief was and is current that the character can be estimated by the manner of shaking hands, hence the phrase." NQ V/12: 473 quotes Brewer "The *shake* is the common, or stubble, which poor men were by law empowered to use for their hogs, sheep, or cattle, between harvest and seedtime, hence a privilege. It is quite a mistake to derive the word from the French *chaque* or Persian *shuck* (a thing)" [an equally fanciful derivation is from German *Schatz* 'treasure' (IX/3: 352)]. Brewer does not say who derived *shakes* from French or Persian. In V/8: 184, an American correspondent refers to Worcester's dictionary in which *shake* is defined as 'one of the staves of a hogshead taken apart' and adds that in California it means a larger-sized shingle for roofing buildings, "and, taking it in that sense, the slang expression becomes perfectly clear, and indicates that a poor bargain, or a person or things of little account or value, is in the same relation to a good one that a shingle is to a shake. The distinction between a shake and a shingle probably still exists in the shingle-using counties of England, and was doubtless formerly exported thence to America." XI/3: 129 quotes the explanation about shingles but finds more probable Admiral Smythe's suggestion (in *Sailor's Word-Book*) that the idiom is derived from taking to pieces of a cask and packing up the parts, which are then termed "shakes." In the Midland counties, "they say *to shake* (for shuffle) cards, also to shake the dice. Hence a good deal or throw is called a good shake, and metaphorically anything that is of little worth *no great shakes*" (IX/3: 277). Still "another explanation is that the phrase is an allusion to the practice of shaking walnut trees to dislodge the fruit so that where the crop of walnuts is scanty there will be 'no great shakes'" (IX/3: 352, quoted from W. S. Walsh's *Handy Book of Literary Curiosities* [quite incredible]). A. Smythe Palmer, the author of a still useful book on folk etymology (as long as it is consulted with caution), suggested the following explanation: "It is probably that *shakes* here is identical with the provincial word *shake,* to brag, which must be of ancient usage, as we find '*schakare,* or cracker, or boost maker, jactator, philo-compus' in the 'Promptorium Parvulorum,' about 1440. . . . Thus *no great shakes* would mean nothing to make a noise or brag about. Otherwise we may look for it in the provincial *shakes,* a bargain, comparing Danish *skakkre,* to peddle, or huxter; Icelandic *skakka,* to balance" (p. 257). [Both explanations seem wide of the mark; also, such a Danish word does not exist; *skakka* is correct but has nothing to do with *shake.*] JBK I, 28. OED: 1819. The idiom is late, and the *OED* says: "Perhaps alluding to shaking of dice."

N20. *No love lost*
NQ 1868, IV/1: 29, 158, 279; 1868, IV/2: 213; 1869, IV/4: 133; 1870, IV/5: 163; 1890 VII/9: 126, 336; 1892 VIII/1: 229, 498; 1892, VIII/2: 51, 98, 170; 1896 VIII/9: 307, 431.

The phrase used to mean the opposite of what it means today, namely, 'they are friends' [= no love has been lost in their relations]. In IV/1: 158, it is suggested that "there was not so much love between them that there was a surplus which could go to waste." The correspondent in IV/1: 279 says: "Love may be said to be lost, or thrown away, when it is exhibited by one person towards another who neither values nor returns it. So that when of both it can be said that there is no love between them, it may fairly be said that there is no love lost, or thrown away, on either side. Very near akin this to the old Latin proverb *perit quod facis ingrato*" [that is lost (*or* dies) which you do without receiving gratitude.'] In VIII/2: 51, we find the following: "There is none on either side, therefore none can be lost. It means they are not friends." In the last notes in Series VIII, no one says anything new, and only VIII/9: 431 deserves attention because it is by G. L. Apperson. OED: in a positive sense (1600); in a negative sense (1622).

N21. *No penny, no paternoster*
NQ 1890 VII/10: 308, 434; 1891 VII/11: 15.

This sixteenth-century proverb of course appears in Whiting, with reference to Heywood, but without any explanation (the proverb is made use of in Samuel Butler's *Hudibras*). According to Robert Greene's *Menaphon,* the paternoster, which used to fill a sheet of paper, was reduced to the compass of a penny. Hence the ironic implication "no payment, no prayer." The alliteration made the phrase memorable. OED: 1528 ('you want a thing, you must pay for it').

N22. *Nose of wax*
NQ 1853 I/7: 158, 439; 1854 I/10: 235; 1907 X/8: 228, 274, 298; 1908 X/10: 437; 1912 XI/5: 7; 1916 XII/2: 150.

The phrase is used not only about a pushover but also about anything too pliant and accommodating, especially with regard to faith and legal matters. According to Nares (as quoted on p. 158), the metaphor was "originally borrowed from the Roman Catholic writers, who applied it to the Holy Scriptures, on account of their being liable to various interpretations." On p. 235, the author refers to an episode in Apuleius's *Metamorphoses* II, in which sorceresses cut off a sleeping man's nose and ears and replaced them with those made of wax. A *nasus cereus* ['nose of wax] was perhaps easier to move in any direction than the one made of flesh and blood. OED: ?1533 (The phrase is called rare).

N23. *Nos(e)y Parker*
NQ 1932, 162: 10, 52, 87, 215.

'An overinquisitive, prying person'. This slang phrase may have had its origin in theaters and music halls. Possibly, it was first applied by comedians to female characters. OED: 1896.

N24. *Not a patch on it* (or *someone*)
NQ 1886 VII/1: 508; 1886 VII/2: 77, 153, 218, 277; 1897, VIII/12: 67, 137; 1898 IX/1: 175.

To be not a patch on something or somebody means 'not to be the object's or person's equal'. In VIII/12: 137, three explanations are offered. 1) *Patch* in this idiom is a term of reproach, from *patch* 'fool' (the reference is to jesters' multicolored clothes); 2) patches of black sticking plaster were once used to improve the skin (*not a patch* would then be inferior, as not to be usable even for such a purpose); 3) since a patch should be similar to the garment on which it is to be placed, *not a patch* would mean something quite useless. [2 and 3 refer to approximately the same situation]. EDD: *Patch*; OED: 1860.

N25. *Not enough room to swing a cat*
NQ 1914 XI/9: 187, 237; 1925, 148: 315, 358.

The reference is to very confined space. Allegedly, cats were swung from the branch of a tree as targets, or the phrase may be a remnant of naval slang *(cat = cat-o'-nine-tails).* The latter hypothesis is heavily criticized on p. 187, and indeed, this instrument of punishment postdates the idiom. OED: 1665 *(They had not space enough to swing a cat in).*

N26. *Not my cup of tea*

NQ 1938, 175: 335.

It is not my cup of tea 'it is not my business', etc. No explanation has been offered, but the phrase cannot be older than the first years of Charles II's reign, for it is then that tea became a novelty, as evidenced by Pepys. Cf. the next item. Judging from the citations in the OED, the phrase is surprisingly recent. OED: 1932.

N27. *Not my pigeon*

NQ 1938, 175: 374.

It's not my pigeon 'it is not my business'. Perhaps the reference is to *pigeon* 'a dupe', but a suggestion has been made that the phrase originated in India, where *pigeon* stood for *Pidgin English*. Cf. the previous item. *

N28. *Not to care a fig*

NQ 1854, I/9: 149; ANQ 1, 1888: 180.

'Not to care at all'. The English idiom has analogs in several European languages. The note on p. 149 traces it to Italian and Friedrich Barbarossa's time. OED: 1632.

N29. *Not to care a twopenny damn*

NQ 1879 V/12: 126, 233, 257; 1887 VII/3: 232, 326, 462; 1887 VII/4: 32; 1897 VIII/12: 92; 1903 IX/11: 425; 1918 XII/4: 238.

'Not to care at all'. The phrase was apparently coined by the Duke of Wellington. A. L. Mayhew (p. 126) wondered whether *damn* 'a small Indian coin' *(dâm)* was meant (if so, the Duke's expression was not an oath). But the phrase had the variant with *three-square damn* (on p. 233, the Indian origin of even that variant has been suggested). On p. 257, the correspondent wrote that the phrase was "no more than an ornamental variety of a 'twelvepenny curse', that is, a curse for which a man was liable to be fined twelvepence by a justice." Cf. *Not worth a rap.* *

N30. *Not to have a halfpenny to bless oneself with*

NQ 1974 192: 171.

"To bless oneself is to make the sign of the cross, and the saying refers to the old pious custom of a person doing this with the first piece of money he had received that day. The recipient crossed himself with the coin, before putting it into his pocket." *

N31. *Not to know a B from a bull's foot*

NQ 1872, IV/10: 425; 1883 VI/8: 364, 476.

'To be an utter fool'. The first note is by J. A. Picton, an etymologist, well-known at that time but not always reliable. In a comment explaining Hamlet's *I know a hawk from a handsaw,* he cited *hawk* 'a builder's tool' and quoted the proverb given here (p. 427); it indicates extreme stupidity. However, except for the underlying formula, the two phrases have little in common. EDD: B; OED: 1401.

N32. *Not worth an old song*

NQ 1858 II/6: 148, 213-4, 279; 1880 VI/2: 287.

'Worthless'. *Song* 'a trifle' is recorded in the *OED* (*song,* 5), along with this idiom, but without an explanation. In 1858 II/6: 213-4, Thomas Boys, a frequent and knowledgeable contributor, tells a story about the corruption of old church songs and the effort of the authorities to rectify the situation. Allegedly, old songs became worthless. Hence also *to buy something for a song,* with *old* left out. [The explanation is long and in some places confusing.] Boys also cites examples from Romance (*chansons!* etc.), with the word for "songs" meaning 'nonsense'. In II/6: 279, it is suggested that the saying originated in the abundance of old songs produced before the 19th century (even new songs were sold a penny a piece). JBK I, 75. OED: 1728.

N33. *Not worth a rap*
NQ 1897 VIII/11: 368, 454.

'Worthless'. The suggestion that *rap* here refers to a counterfeit coin appears to be correct. The short discussion concerned only the provenance of the coin. Cf. *Not to care a twopenny damn.* OED: 1862.

N34. *Not worth a thirteen*
NQ 1930, 158: 150, 196, 281, 322.

'Worthless.' If *thirteen* here is the same as *thraneen* (the word has several variants) 'straw', then the phrase is an equivalent of 'not worth a straw'. Ireland. *

N35. *Not worth a cress*
NQ 1935, 169: 441; 1936, 170: 11.

'Of minimal worth (significance).' The phrase *not worth a curse* is known much better. The unanswered question is whether *curse* is a metathesis of *cress*. Indeed, phrases like *not worth a straw, a fig,* etc. exist. *Kerse* 'a small sour wild cherry' would fit the pattern well, but, as the *OED* notes, the chronology remains a problem. *Not worth a cress* turned up in texts between 1377 and 1400, while no citation of *not worth a curse* predates 1768. OED: 1377. Cf. the next item.

N36. *Not worth a tinker's curse*
NQ 1897, VIII/11: 345, 452, 496.

'Of minimal worth (significance).' The most informative note is the last (by F. Adams), for it contains a detailed reference to *curse* in the *OED*. Whether *curse* is an alteration ("corruption") of *cress* is doubtful. It is also unclear whether *tinker* contains reference to the itinerant worker who mended pots and pans (tinkers swore a lot but not more than some other groups of people). Elsewhere, *cobbler* is used in this idiom. A similar ambiguity characterizes the phrase *tinker's dam* (*dam* 'a wall of dough raised around a place which a plumber desires to flood with a coat of solder'; *dam = damn*?) OED: *(a tinkler's curse)* 1824. See also the previous item.

O

O1. *Ob and soller*
NQ 1891 VII/11: 428; 1891 VII/12: 18.

"In the theological controversies of the time, one disputant made an ob(jection) to the argument of his adversary, who replied by a sol(ution). Such wranglers are ob-and-sol-ers" (p. 18). The phrase occurs in Samuel Butler's *Hudibras* and for some time was recognized by many. OED: 1588 *(ob and sol).*

02. *Odds and ends*

NQ 1875 V/3: 165, 315, 514; 1875 V/4: 59.

'Miscellaneous pieces or remnants'. Skeat's opinion is cited that *odds* in this idiom stands for 'crumbs'. Speakers in many areas (in the *r*-less dialects of England) say *orts and ends,* [but this is probably a folk etymology of the phrase; yet indeed, the noun *odd* (sg.) does not exist. According to the *OED,* perhaps of dialectal origin, for earlier *odd ends* (*ends* 'fragments').]. OED: *a*1740.

03. *Odor of sanctity*

NQ 1901 IX/8: 483; 1902 IX/9: 54; 1902 IX/10: 298, 358.

"This phrase refers to a belief which has prevailed that the dead bodies of persons who were remarkable for the holiness of their lives and saintly deaths have emitted a miraculous odour of surpassing sweetness—whether immediately after death or on long-subsequent uncovering of their remains" (p. 54). OED: *c*1684.

04. *O dear no!*

NQ 1908 X/10: 395, 434–5, 516; MLQ 1902: 174 (reprinted in *Verbatim* 23/2, 1996: 18)

An exclamation. Below, the exchange between Walter W. Skeat (p. 395) and A. L. Mayhew (pp. 434–5), two distinguished philologists, sometimes collaborators, sometimes opponents, is reproduced almost in full. Skeat: "The quotations show that the formula 'Oh! dear!' is the oldest. It was not till later that it became 'Oh! dear Lord!' &c. ; that is, it was misunderstood. It was simply borrowed from Old French; even Cotgrave gives *déa*, which he explains by 'yes, verily'; and he thinks that it once meant 'a God's name'. But here he is wrong. It is fully explained in Godefroy's Old French dictionary, which gives *dea, dia,* as an exclamation, particularly in the phrase *hé dia,* used to express great astonishment and the like. To understand this, examine all his examples; there is a whole column full of them. There can be little doubt that *dea* and *dia* are shortened forms of the O.F. *deable* and *diable.* There is no mystery at all. The phrase 'Oh! dear!' is an English substitution for the O.F. *hé déa,* which simply meant 'Oh! the devil!' It is well known how oaths come to be 'minced'. Cotgrave had the right idea, but did not discern who was invoked." Mayhew: "There is no evidence that the O.F. *dea!* ever crossed the Channel. Does the interjection *dea!* occur in any English text, or even in any Anglo-Norman text? How is the final *-r* in 'Dear me!' 'O dear no!' to be accounted for? This use of 'dear' is comparatively modern—not earlier than the seventeenth century; but in the seventeenth century final *-r* would not have lost its full consonantal value. Even now *idea* and *dear* would not be considered perfect rimes. The identity of E. *dear* with O.F. *dea* must be rejected on phonetic as well as on historical grounds. The interjectional use of 'dear' is due to an ellipsis of the divine name. This is suggested in 'N.E.D.' *[OED]*, and is abundantly corroborated by dialectal usage, as may be seen in 'E.D.D' *[EnglishDialect Dictionary].* Compare the following phrases: Dear be here! Dear bless you! Dear help you! Dear keep us! Dear kens! Dear knows! Dear love you! Dear me! (Dear God, save me!). The earliest example of 'O dear!' in 'N.E.D.' is taken from Congreve's 'Double Dealer'. . . . How is it possible to connect this late usage with an Old French word obsolescent in the sixteenth century? No, there is nothing diabolic in the innocent exclamation 'O dear!'" OED: 1694.

05. *Of a certain age*

NQ 1888 VII/5: 447; 1888 VII/6: 36, 130, 274.

James A. H. Murray asked for the exact meaning of the phrase. "Is it not, in English use, always said of women?" The answers confirmed his understanding of the phrase, which seems to be a borrowing of French *d'un certain âge,* but in French, at least at that time, the collocation was applied to both men and women and meant 'rather advanced in years' (p. 447), that is, forty for a woman and sixty for a man (p. 274). OED: 1823 (Byron).

06. *Of course*

NQ 1879 V/12: 344, 394, 515.

'Certainly'. This sense of the phrase goes back to the first decades of the twentieth century. It is not entirely clear if the phrase is a calque of Latin *de cursu.* The 1879 notes do not address this question, but they show the attitude of some people at that time toward the overuse of the phrase and make instructive reading. *Of course* may be redundant or contain overtones from aggression to humility. EDD: *Of;* OED: 1541.

07. *Of sorts*

NQ 1913 XI/7: 10, 56, 117, 136, 197, 274, 417, 454; 1914 XI/9: 174.

'Of a certain kind'. The phrase need not always have the depreciatory sense 'of an inferior type'. *Of sorts* often occurred in inventories. Two correspondents pointed to the use of this word group in Shakespeare. It enjoyed great popularity in Anglo-Indian and possibly became familiar because Kipling used it. Earlier, people said *of a sort. Of sorts* was also the latest slang at Cambridge in the 1880s. In the words of one correspondent, "The phrase is a qualifying one, indicating that the substantive to which it is appended is not to be understood too literally. This may be due to a lack of precise information on the part of the speaker or writer, but at the time referred to [the late 1880s in India] I think 'of sorts' was frequently tacked on as a conversational garnish, to which the speaker attached no very definite meaning" (p. 197). OED: 1597.

08. *Old Cole's dog*

NQ 1873, IV/12: 317, 482.

Nothing seems to be known about the namesake of the legendary king (or is the reference to that merry old soul?) and his dog. The saying exists in several forms. Two are given in the notes: "The pride of old Cole's dog, who took the wall of a lung-cart, and got his guts squeezed out" and "Pride and ambition were the overthrow of old Cole's dog." See also *As proud as old Cole's . . . dog.* The contributors to Series IV missed the 1850 publication. *

09. *Old Harvey*

NQ 1877 V/8: 269.

'The large boat (the launch) of a line-of-battle ship'. The query about the origin of the name has not been answered. *

010. *Old lady of Threadneedle street*

NQ 1910 XI/1: 89, 177.

'The Bank of England'. The common opinion refers to the temporary stopping of cash payments on the 26th of February, 1797, one-pound bank notes being issued in March the same year. According to the book *Sheridan* by Walter Sichel, 1909, p. 16: "To Sheridan is due, as we have seen, the accepted figure of the Bank of England as an old lady. Speaking on the stoppage of its cash payments in the spring of 1797, he compared it . . . 'to an elderly lady in the City, of great credit and long standing, who had lately made a *faux pas* which was not altogether inexcusable'" (p. 177). OED: 1797.

011. *Old maids lead apes in hell*
NQ 1876 V/5: 178; 1885 VI/12: 415.

F. J. Furnivall (p. 415) referred to a late 16th-century tale in which *ape* can be understood as meaning a dishonest bachelor trying to marry a widow. [Hyamson mentions the idiom twice. At *Apes in Hell, To lead* (p. 17), he writes: "From the monkish story that women married neither to God nor to man will be given to apes in the next world." He offers no reference to the story. On p. 218, at *Leads apes in hell, To,* he adds: "The supposed fate of old maids, esp. those who were coquettes while alive. (!) Ape was sometimes a synonym for fool."] JBK I, 236. OED: 1605.

012. *Old mother Damnable*
NQ 1913 XI/8: 69.

"A writer in *The Observer* of 22 June, 1913, stated that this epithet—designating the Church of England—was attributed by the late Father Bridgett to Father Persons, S.J., of the time of Queen Elizabeth." No one responded to the question whether this statement is credible. *

013. *On a merry pin*
See *In a merry pin.*

014. *Once and away*
NQ 1883 VI/7: 408; VI/8: 58, 133, 253; 1884 VI/9: 297, 336.

'For this occasion only' or 'immediately'. The discussants could not agree on the meaning of the phrase. Those who understood it as 'immediately' cited the command in the games: "Once and away, twice and away, thrice and away." Likewise, there was no consensus on whether *once and away* is a late variant of *once in a way* and whether *once in a way* and *once and away* are synonyms. Modern dictionaries give *once in a way* with somewhat contradictory glosses: 'now and again; occasionally; exceptionally rarely', which is indeed different from *once and away*. The *OED* offers two glosses: 'and giving away again' and 'once' (*once in a way* with only three examples for 1583 and 1655).

015. *Once in a blue moon*
NQ 1880 VI/2: 125, 236, 335; 1888 VII/5: 248; 1927, 152: 189, 229, 461; SNQ 1905 II/7: 14.

'Extremely seldom'. No explanation of the idiom has been offered, but probably it was coined as an example of an absurdity, like the belief that the moon is made of green cheese. However, consider the following: "*The Times* of June 14 [1927] says in speaking of the delayed arrival of the monsoon at Bombay—'A curious and rare phenomenon was observed last night when the moon was seen to be distinctly blue. *The Times of India* says that the colour appeared to be between Cambridge blue and turquoise.' Can it be said that the expression 'once in a blue moon' has its origin in the rareness of this phenomenon?" (1927, 152: 461). OED: 1833.

016. *Only too thankful*
NQ 1902 IX/9: 288, 370, 457; 1902 IX/10: 13, 151, 171.

'Very grateful'. James A. H. Murray (p. 288) asked: "What does *too* here mean? And what does *only* mean? Why *too*? And why *only* too? When a man is 'only too glad' to get something to do, why is he *too* glad; and if he is 'too glad' to refuse it, why is he *only* too glad? What does the 'only' limit or exclude? Or is it ironical in its origin, like 'Has he lost anything?' 'Only his life; that's all', or 'Did he speak long?' 'Only till everybody was asleep'." All kinds of rather confusing interpretations of the phrase were offered. OED: 1610 (*Thankfull* [sic]).

017. *On the broad level*
NQ 1869 IV/3: 480.

'An offer to sell at the lowest price'. U.S. *

018. *On the cards*
NQ 1887 VII/4: 507; 1888 VII/5: 14, 77, 495.

'Likely or probable'. "That which is 'on the cards' may be a game, a stake, or a trick; and the adoption of the phrase in common parlance seems easy and natural" (p. 14). OED: 1813 (*out of the cards*) and 1849 (*on the cards*).

019. *On the carpet*
NQ 1889 VII/7: 344, 432, 476; 1889 VII/8: 35.

'Laid on the carpet for consideration'. *To carpet someone* 'to scold, *etc.*' is probably connected with the beating of carpets. The idiom is explained in the *OED* as an analog rather than a translation of French *sur le tapis*. OED: 1726 (originally US).

020. *On the fly*
NQ 1916 XII/2: 69.

'A prolonged bout'. "Before the days of the Licensing Act of Bruce, passed in 1872, when a prolonged and continuous drunken bout could be indulged in at public-houses with much greater freedom than now, a participator in such was said in North-East Cornwall to be 'on the fly'." OED: 1851.

021. *On the high seas*
NQ 1887 VII/3: 265, 482.

'Stormy waters'. The note on p. 265 suggests that the English phrase "does not refer to the high waves seen at sea, but is a mistranslation of the Italian 'in alto mare' (French 'en haute mer'),— for *alto* in Italian (as *altus* in Latin) means either high or deep, according to circumstances." (p. 265). On p. 482, an analog from Greek is given. OED: at least as early as 1300, but the phrase may have been current in Old English.

022. *On the putty*
MM 96, 2010: 221 (2).

'Getting stuck' (slang) The correspondent suggests a concrete shoal that could have given rise to this phrase. OED: 1902.

023. *Oppressive respectability*

NQ 1870, IV/5: 399, 430, 477.

The exchange is interesting in that it reveals the source of what became for a short time a familiar quotation. It seems to have originated with Hotten, the author of *The True Story of Lord and Lady Byron* and was immediately noticed and used by Dickens. *

024. *Orthodoxy is my doxy*

NQ 1896 VIII/9; 406.

The note is worthy of attention only because it was written by James A. H. Murray, who asked for the earliest citations of this phrase. In the *OED, doxy* 'opinion' is dated to 1730.

025. *Ossing comes to bossing*

NQ 1907 X/7: 69, 135.

'Effort leads to success'. *To oss* 'to try' is a widely-known and much-discussed verb in many dialects; *to boss* means 'to command'. Hence, if you try, you'll be at the top. But the original sense of *boss* was 'to kiss', so that the saying apparently meant to encourage wooers. Cheshire. OED: *a*1450.

026. *Our mutual friend*

NQ 1888 VII/5: 206, 298, 517; 1888 VII/6: 192, 396; 1894 VIII/5: 326, 450, 492; 1894 VIII/6: 77, 154, 514; 1895 VIII/7: 13.

Discussion of this phrase flared up and died out with great regularity. Allegedly, if two people love each other, they are "mutual friends" (p.192). This statement is ridiculed on p. 396. *Mutual,* it is said, presupposes reciprocity, but sharing a friend does not make this person mutual. However, the phrase *our mutual friend* was known long before Dickens, and no effort is likely to make people stop using it. OED: 1658.

027. *Our swineherd*

NQ 1870, IV/6: 458.

'A man of St. John's College, Cambridge'. A query about the age of the phrase (known as early as 1573?) has never been answered. *

028. *Out for a thing (to be)*

NQ 1912 XI/6: 409, 494; 1913 XI/7: 35, 52.

To be out for a thing means 'to be intent on obtaining something'. On p. 409, the phrase is compared with German *auf etwas aus sein*. Some people thought it was an Americanism. [If this suggestion is true, the German model begins to look probable.] On p. 52, the writer wonders whether the phrase originated in sportsman's slang, but cites no evidence. *

029. *Out in the cold*

NQ 1876 V/5: 228.

The full phrase is *to leave out in the cold,* that is, 'to neglect intentionally'. The correspondent noted that the phrase had been much used "of late" in political circles. He quoted Fuller's *Good Thoughts in Bad Times* (1645), where the phrase *let him out of the cold* occurs. OED: 1839.

030. *Out of God's blessing into a warm sun*

The Athenæum 1903, 2: 220.

'Going to the worse from the better condition'. The author of the note suggests that "the opposition originally lay between those who duly entered the cool cathedral for service and those who sat on the ale-bench outside. It may be traceable to some more southern country." OED: 1546.

031. *Out of the dice*

NQ 1940, 179: 262.

'Not improbable'. Walter Scott used this phrase, but the correspondent wondered whether such an idiom existed. The *OED* does not give the phrase or quote Walter Scott. *

032. *Out of the horse's mouth*

NQ 1939, 177: 484; ANQ 7, 1948: 158; ANQ 2, 1963: 41; ANQ 10, 1971: 72.

'Directly from a reliable source'. The phrase goes back to the custom of looking a horse in the mouth. The phrase "is probably an assurance that a tip on a horse race is trustworthy" (p. 158). OED: 1928 *(Straight from the horse's mouth)*. Cf. the next item.

033. *Out of the nosebag*

ANQ 7, 1948: 158.

The phrase is synonymous with 'out of the horse's mouth', given in the note in the form *right out of the nosebag*. OED: 1874. Cf. the previous item.

034. *Out of the top drawer*

NQ 1927, 153: 156, 195.

'First-rate'. The correspondent (p. 156) notes that the phrase often occurred in 1927 (also in the negative form *not out of the top drawer*), but he had never seen it earlier. OED: 1905.

035. *Outrun the constable, to*

NQ 1921 XII/8: 29, 58, 97, 117, 157.

'To exceed one's financial resources'. Most probably, it is a familiar quotation traceable to Samuel Butler's *Hudibras*. JBK I, 64. OED: 1600.

036. *Over against*

NQ 1895 VIII/7: 129, 278.

The question concerned the meaning of the phrase, and the discussants agreed on 'opposite, in front of'. OED: c1450 *(oueragayn)*.

037. *Over the left*

NQ 1854 I/10: 236; 1860 II/10: 304; 1869 IV/3: 480.

'Not at all'. On p. 236, a 1705 example of its use in Hartford, CT is given. The reference is to a game. The *OED* explains that *over the left* is the shorter variant of *over the left shoulder*. It does not confirm the notion that the phrase is an Americanism or that it originated in games. OED: 1640.

O38. *Over to Gilbert*

MM 2, 1912: 63 (24).

"The expressions *over to Gilbert* and *hard as Gilbert* have been in use for many years, and are often heard now, meaning that something is awry. It is possible that these expressions came into use since the production of *H. M. S. Pinafore,* etc., by Gilbert and Sullivan, and that they are closely allied to the adjective *Gilbertian* meaning topsy-turvy." *

P

P1. *Paddington spectacles*

NQ 1876 V/6: 308; 1877 V/7: 314.

Here are both the query that aroused surprise and the answer: "If those who are troubled with Newgate cramps and Tyburn convulsions would wear the Paddington spectacle for half an hour, they would be cured." "I presume that by this phrase is meant the cap pulled over the eyes of the convicted criminal on the scaffold at Paddington, the old place for capital executions. Its use in *Poor Robin's Almanack* in connexion with Newgate and Tyburn points to this as the most likely, if not the only, explanation." *

P2. *Pad the hoof, to*

NQ 1867 III/11: 443.

'To walk'. The author of the note explains: "One of the minor punishments in our cavalry regiments is still called 'pad drill'; where the culprit for a certain time walks back and forwards on a limited portion of the barrack yard, carrying not only his own but also his horse's accouterments." Cf. *Beat the hoof, to.* OED: 1683.

P3. *Paid down upon the nail*

NQ 1854 I/9: 196, 384; 1890 VII/9: 366; 1890 VII/10: 31, 214; 1897 VIII/12: 83 1906 X/6: 365, 416; 1912 XI/6: 47, 212; MCNNQ 5, 1884: 33.

The source seems to have been Latin *in ~ ad unguem* (cf. French *sur l'ongle*) (VII/9: 366). "A well known half-slang phrase used for a cash payment" (VII/9: 366); *on the nail* 'ready money'. See the main discussion at *Cash on the nail*.

P4. *Paint the lion, to*

NQ 1892, VIII/2: 106, 194; 1911 XI/4: 109; 1912 XI/5: 297; MM 41, 1955: 388 (38).

The reference is to a barbarous custom. A woman coming on board a ship is stripped naked, smeared over with tar, and thrown in the river. A horrifying example dated to 1794 is quoted: "This day a woman going on some occasion on board a ship on the river, some of the crew took it in their heads to paint the lion, as they called it; which was performed by stripping the woman quite naked, and smearing her over with tar, and in that manner threw her into the river, where she was nearly drowned" (p. 106). The same quotation was rediscovered on p. 109. *

P5. *Paltock's inn*

NQ 1882 VI/6: 268, 455.

'A place where no worthy people live'. "This proverbial expression may perhaps be derived from the French *paltoquet,* a boor. In Littré we find that in the dialect of Burgundy *paltoquai* means a peasant, from *paletoc* or *paletót:* 'Celui qui est vétu d'une casaque' ['he who wears a cloak'.] And *paletoquier* is found in Cotgrave in the sixteenth century. Paltock's Inn would therefore mean an abode or resort of boors or disorderly persons" (p. 455). OED: 1579 (obsolete); it suggests a probable derivation from the genitive of a personal name and *inn.*

P6. *Paper over the cracks, to*

NQ 1961, 206: 103.

The reference is to a temporary expediency. The phrase seems to have originated with Bismarck. A nautical explanation is given as well. The reference to Bismarck also appears in the *OED* (1865).

P7. *Parson's nose*

NQ 1896 VIII/10: 496; 1897 VIII/11: 33, 92; 1897 VIII/12: 58; 1901 IX/8: 113; 1930, 158: 243, 286.

'The tail of a roast fowl'. The same part is sometimes called *the pope's nose.* The exchange contains several amusing phrases of this type, for instance, *the pope's eye* 'the gland in the leg of mutton', *the bishop's nose* (the same as *the parson's nose*), *the bishop's mitre,* a synonym of *bishop,* and *alderman's walk,* the same part of the joint. Compare the comment on p. 58: "May not the resemblance in shape between the 'caudal appendage' of plucked fowls and some forms of mitres, once used by bishops and abbots, account for the names 'pope's nose', &c.?" OED: 1836.

P8. *Part brass-rags, to*

NQ 1916 XII/1: 268, 317.

'To fall out; to part on bad terms'. The following explanations appear on p. 317: "It is a custom in the navy for two men in a gun's crew, or otherwise, to have a common supply of rags and other cleaning material; if they quarrel sufficiently badly to dissolve partnership, they are said to "'part brass-rags'." "'Parting brass-rags' is, or was a few years ago, a 'lower-deck' expression used when two friends 'fall out'. The term 'raggy' is lower-deckese for 'chum'—blue-jacket 'pals' being wont to share their 'cleaning-rags'." OED: 1898.

P9. *Pass one's persimmon, to*

NQ 1896 VIII/10: 295.

'To be beyond one's comprehension'. The quotation from De Quincey (given in the note) is also the earliest in the *OED.* All the others (1845, 1945, 1995) are from American authors. No explanation of the idiom has been offered. OED: 1839.

P10. *Pass the time of day, to*

NQ 1880 VI/2: 85, 135, 293; 1881 VI/3: 195; 1899 IX/3: 427; 1899 IX/4: 72, 427; 1899 IX/4: 72.

'To exchange perfunctory greetings' (without further attempts to cultivate the acquaintance). "The expression was a very common one in old coaching days. In fact, it was the vernacular in which coachmen expressed their mode of salutation when meeting on the road, which was performed by raising the elbow on the whip hand, with perhaps a nod or sidelong glance over the right shoulder. It was quite 'the thing' or 'down the road'" (p. 135). The old watchmen "passed" or "called" the hours of the night; "may not the phrase have come from the old time night custom?" (IX/4: 72). OED: 1835.

P11. *Pay in monkey's coin, to*
NQ 1896, VIII/9: 429, 494.

Brewer (1894), at *monkey's money*, explains the old saying as meaning to pay "in goods, in personal work, in mumbling and grievances." It was suggested that dealing with monkeys in France might be at the root of the proverb. *Monkey's allowance* (slang) meant 'blows instead of alms' and is not synonymous with *monkey's coin,* but can there be a connection with *Monkey on the chimney?* *

P12. *Pay off creditors with the foretopsail sheet, to*
MM 64, 1978: 285 (19); 65, 1979: 89 (19).

'Not to pay creditors'. The reference is to the flag (the Blue Peter), a signal for departure, hoisted on this sheet. The creditors, by implication, will stay behind empty-handed. *

P13. *Pay the piper, to*
NQ 1884 VI/9: 248; 1905 X/3: 468; 1922 XII/11: 287.

'To bear the unfavorable consequences of one's actions'. Ever since Brewer referred the idiom to the legend of the Piper of Hamelin, his explanation has been repeated many times. The correspondent to *NQ* (p. 248) had every right to doubt Brewer's derivation. England, he said "had from early times pipers who lived by their piping, the expense of which was, doubtless, on frequent occasions defrayed by one out of the many that had enjoyed the pleasure of the dance." The French say *payer les violons,* used in the sense of paying the expense of something of which others have all the profit or pleasure." [Note also the idiom *he who pays the piper calls the tune.* The Dutch legend was hardly known in England before Browning composed his poem.] JBK II, 28. EDD: *Pay*; OED: 1681.

P14. *Pay through the nose, to*
NQ 1850 I/1: 335, 421; 1850 I/2: 348; 1872 IV/9: 311; 1876 V/6: 134; 1898 IX/2: 48, 231, 457; 1939, 177: 443; 1951, 196: 64, 108; MCNNQ vol. 1, 1878: 73.

'To pay an exorbitant price'. [One could also be "bored through the nose," that is "cheated."] The early explanations have often been repeated in popular books: *nose* is allegedly a mispronunciation of *noose,* or the reference is to Odin's laying a "nose tax" on every Swede. The note in IV/9: 311 cites a distant French analog: "to extract the maggots from a man's nose, that is, to pump him, to extract his secrets, *tirer les vers du nez à quelqu'un,*" while the note in IX/2: 231 suggests that *nose* stands for 'an improper channel'. In *NQ* 177, p. 443, the idea is expressed that the original phrase was applied to extortionist Jews known for their "stout noses." In 1898 IX/2: 457, Richard Edgcumbe wrote: "This was originally a common expression on board ship: 'pay out the cable', 'pay out handsomely'. The nose of the ship is, of course, the bow; its nostrils are the hawse holes on either side. Now, it does not seem very difficult (at all events, for a sailor) to associate extortionate disbursements with handsome payments—such, for instance, as paying out a chain cable (through the nose), especially when the order is conveyed in such language as this, 'pay out handsomely'. At all events, I can speak on this matter from personal experience as a midshipman. To my mind 'paying through the nose' for anything has always been associated with the rattling of a 'payed out' chain cable, after the anchor has gripped the ground." The 1951 notes add nothing new and were written without reference to the older discussion. A correspondent to MCNNQ cites the variant *pay through the eyes and nose.* V/6: 134 contains a long 1599 quotation about the origin of the Scottish saying *to take one by the nose.* It has nothing to do with paying through the nose. JBK I, 28. The *OED* offers no explanation; its first example is dated to 1666.

P15. *Pecking order*
NQ 1966, 211: 464.

'Order of precedence'. An illuminating example from Richardson's *Clarissa* is quoted, but it only describes a scene of chickens pecking one another. The phrase as now known is late: the *OED* has no earlier citations than 1927 (about animals) and 1930 (about any hierarchy).

P16. *Pence a piece*
NQ 1856, II/2: 66, 99, 118, 219, 299, 338; 1857, II/3: 337.

Strictly speaking, it is not an idiom, but a common market phrase. Although the query (why *pence,* rather than *penny*?) has not been answered, the correspondents attested to the broad currency of the phrase in the 1850s. EDD: *Pence;* The *OED* has *sights to be seen for pence a piece* (*a*1658).

P17. *Penny plain, twopence colored*
NQ 1932, 162: 150.

"It is impossible to say exactly when this phrase became current, but there is no difficulty in deciding what is its origin. During the first half of the last century certain firms in London published many thousands of portraits of popular actors and actresses in 'costume' parts, and the price of each of these was a penny each plain, and twopence each coloured." The entire article is worth reading. Among other things, the author mentions references to such portraits in the works of Robert Louis Stevenson. OED: 1854.

P18. *Penny saved is a penny got, a*
NQ 1907 X/7: 48, 97; 1984, 229: 372.

"The credit for the most familiar phrasing of the proverb should be given to John Dunton, the bookseller-publisher-author of the late seventeenth and early eighteenth centuries" (p. 372). The *OED* has the variants with *got* and *gained* (for *saved*) going back to 1633 and 1659 respectively. On p. 97, equivalents in several European languages are given. OED: *a*1633 (*A penny spar'd is twice got.*)

P19. *Pick up the church lights, to*
NQ 1925, 149: 208, 286.

'To maintain church light'. "Young men and maidens of a congregation associated themselves together for the purpose of obtaining gifts to defray the expenses incurred in providing lights (almost invariably candles) in their churches, as, in the same way, such bands of workers accepted gifts of sheep, bees, etc., for general church expenses" (p. 286). Somersetshire. *

P20. *Pig and whistle*
Time (NS), 1888, VIII: 581; SNQ 1902 II/4: 47, ANQ 2012: 75–7

'The name of the tavern sign'. The occasional phrase *gone to pigs and whistles* might mean 'ruined by intemperance'. Max Müller thought that *pig* in the sign goes back to Danish *piga* 'girl', with *whistle* being a salutation (*waeshael* that is, middle English *wæs hæil* the etymou of Modern Engl. *wassail*). Brewer connected *pig* 'a small bowl' with *piggin*. The contributor who mentioned those hypotheses wrote: "I suggest that the phrase originated in order to explain the way in which the wood of some soft-grained tree, instead of being devoted to the forma-tion of some permanently useful and valuable article of furniture, was used up by boys and youths in the whittling of pegs and whistles. That is to say, 'gone to pigs and whistles' means reduced to some mean and trifling service" (p. 47). Without mentioning his sources, the cor-respondent to the *Time* "knew": "The old pig or pot (a contraction of the Gaelic 'pigean' and of the Irish 'pigen') and wassail bowl originated the sign of the Pig and Whistle." Bill Bryson (*The Mother Tongue*. New York: Avon Books, 1990, p. 200) writes: "The Pig and Whistle is said to have its roots in peg (a drinking vessel) and wassail (a festive drink)." He gives no reference. His ex-planation must be due to folk etymology. The Contributor to *ANQ* (2012) was unaware of the discussion presented above and based his etymology on *wissel* 'change,' with *pigs and wissels* being "originally the succession of jugs or pitchers of beer or wine paid for in turn by members of a party of drinkers," like the modern *pints and rounds* (= dissipation). Highly speculative. EDD: *Wissel*; OED: 1903.

P21. *Pigeons of Paul's*
NQ 1873, IV/12: 259.

'Pigeons of Paul's' had a certain reference to birds about the Cathedral (that is, St. Paul's). It was the London slang of the Plantagenet times for the "scholars of Paul's." Those boys, in re-turn, called the scholars of St. Anthony's Hospital "Anthony pigs." *

P22. *Pigs can see the wind*
Time, 25. 8: 584–5; NQ 1889 VII/8: 367, 457; 1890 VII/9: 14; 1916 XII/2: 289, 358, 435.

It has been observed that pigs are afraid of the wind. Samuel Butler noted this fact in *Hudibras* (III/2: 1105). "Pigs do not like wind and they are known to run away from it squealing." Allegedly, any wind feels hot to them (p. 358). The notes contain a few references corroborat-ing this observation. *

P23. *Pigs might fly*
NQ 1870, IV/6: 398; 1871, IV/7: 41; 1894, VIII/6: 344.

The origin of the saying which refers to an impossible situation, has not been ascertained. Ray and Hazlitt give "Pigs fly in the air with their tails forward." [The variant "when pigs grow wings" was not mentioned in the exchange.] Apparently, sometimes an addition occurs ". . . if they had wings." OED: 1732 (*That is as likely as to see an Hog fly.*)

P24. *Pin a day is a groat a year, a*

NQ 1869 IV/4: 363.

This is a proverb encouraging frugality. The note contained a suggestive question: "Did this proverb originate when pins were much more costly than now, or is it a saying of modern invention?" OED: 1712.

P25. *Pin money*

NQ 1943, 184: 286, 383.

In the past, the phrase designated a sum allotted to a woman for clothing, etc. P. 383 specifies the phrase as an old law term (so in 1725). OED: 1640 *(Rent I haue bestowed on my daughter Mary to buy her pins.)*

P26. *Pin one's faith upon somebody else's sleeve*

NQ 1858, II/ 6: 130; 1920 XII/7: 268.

'To follow someone blindly'. The phrase (p. 130) is often used as part of the admonition not to pin one's faith on somebody else's sleeve. The author of the note suggests that this saying may go back to the days of heraldry. Family badges were sewn on the servants' sleeves. But in times of strife they could be fabricated, and one was advised not to trust them. [Can there be any connection with *Sleeveless errand?* OED: 1585 *(for pinning themselues vpon mens sleeues).*

P27. *Pipe-clay one's weekly accounts, to*

MM 2, 1912: 63 (24).

The *OED* glosses *pipeclay* as 'to settle or put in order'. The note calls it navy slang and gives only three citations (1806, 1834, and 1853). The phrase occurs in *Peter Simple,* Chapter 2. The editor suggests that perhaps *to pipe-clay* in this sense was borrowed from the Marines and meant 'to make fit for muster'. A pipeclay is the same as a claypipe.

P28. *Piper's news*

NQ 1876 V/5: 297.

'A piece of old news'. Perhaps "the information circulated by such persons in their peregrinations soon becomes common property." Scotland. Cf. *Tinker's news.* OED: 1602.

P29. *Play all sharps, to*

NQ 1880 VI/1: 56, 104.

'To try one's utmost'. The phrase was given with reference to a servant but without specifying the location. It was new to the correspondent. *

P30. *Play Hal* (or *hell) and Tommy, to*

NQ 1861 II/12: 167, 332; 1872 IV/9: 118, 184.

'To use extreme violence in a quarrel'. *Hell* supposedly stands for *Hal,* the reference being to Harry (that is, Henry) VIII and Thomas Cromwell, Earl of Essex, and their dissolution of the monasteries. Another form of the phrase is *to play hell and Tommy with one.* Hal has also been understood as Old Harry 'the Devil' or as 'congenial agent', Henry VIII's sobriquet being *Old Hairy.* Northern England. EDD: *Hell*; OED: 1825.

P31. *Play Hamlet, to*

NQ 1897 VIII/12: 308; 1898 IX/1: 14; 1909 X/11: 237.

'To make a disturbance; sulk' (said about children), p. 237. The phrase was still popular in South Yorkshire in 1897 (p. 308). The same note mentions Brewer's reference to Icelandic *amlod* [that is, Amlóði, which is quite unnecessary]. Cf. *Raise Cain* and *Raise Hamlet on one*. EDD: *Hamlet*. *

P32. *Play (up) Old Gooseberry, to*

NQ 1867 III/12: 208; 1881 VI/3: 429; 1881 VI/4: 54, 417; 1898 IX/1: 147, 293, 452.

'To make mischief; to make a mess of it'. In the note on p. 208, the reference is said to be perhaps to gooseberry wine, but see *Do gooseberry*. EDD: *Gooseberry*; OED: 1796.

P33. *Play possum, to*

ANQ 5, 1890: 126; ANQ 6, 1890: 68, 94.

'To feign death, (to save oneself)'. The notes cite examples of several creatures, including the fox [cf. Brer Fox!] playing this trick. Some naturalists believe that the opossum really faints with terror. OED: 1807.

P34. *Play the bear, to*

NQ 1876 V/5: 485; V/6: 36, 294; 1879, V/12: 106, 217, 478; 1890 VII/10: 285; 1891 VII/11: 354.

'To destroy, wreak havoc'. The phrase was known in many parts of England. The correspondents offered vague attempts to trace the idiom to a specific event or a circus bear that broke free. EDD: *Bear*; OED: 1579 ("to behave rudely and roughly").

P35. *Play the charley (wag), to*

NQ 1895 VIII/7: 7, 153; 1895 VIII/8: 32, 77; 1897 VIII/11: 294–5; 1900 IX/5: 154.

'To play truant'. In VIII/8: 32, a 'popular rhyme' from Halliwell is quoted: "Charley wag, ate the pudding and left the bag" (in VIII/7: 153, *swallowed* is given for *left*). In VIII/8: 77, the correspondent made the following curious statement: "I heard a person remark that she could not think how parents who gave a child the name of Charles could expect it to turn out well—a prejudice which may have originated in ancestral experiences of the Stuart line." The most detailed note, signed by C. P. Hale, appeared in VIII/11: 294–5. Hale reproduced the story he had heard from a Mr. H. Bourn, of Whickham. It was published in the *Newcastle Weekly Chronicle* in July 1895 [these pages are, unfortunately, inaccessible in the US], where the phrase was the object of a lively discussion but supplied no information except for the reference to H. Bourn, who wrote the following: "When conversing with an old man at Swalwell the other day, he informed me that, when he attended school in that village eighty years ago, if a scholar left the school for a few minutes, a plummet, suspended from the ceiling by a string, was set in motion, and should the scholar not return before the plummet ceased to vibrate or wag he was told by the master he had been 'playing the wag' (during the wagging of the plummet), for which he was punished. May not the phrase 'Playing the wag' have been afterwards applied to the scholar who absented himself from school against the command of his parents?" He was not sure how important Bourn's story was, [and indeed, the spread of the idiom remains unexplained. Could that wag be invented under the influence of the phrase?]. Cf. *Have got Charley on one's back, to.* OED: 1861 *(play the wag).*

P36. *Play the dozen,* to
ANQ 1, 1942: 156, 168.

'To exchange insults'. The notes trace the game of dozens to Black English [nowadays much more is known about the subject], but the origin of the game and its name were [and still are] unclear. OED: 1933.

P37. *Play the goat, to*
NQ 1901 IX/ 8: 302, 510.

Suggestions were offered modifying the definition in the *OED* (the same in the *OED* online): not 'to frolic foolishly' but 'to betray; to lead a dissolute life'. OED: 1841.

P38. *Please the pigs, to*
GM 60, 1780: 876. NQ 1850 I/2: 423; 1852 I/5: 13, 91, 436-7, 450; 1884 VI/9: 149, 232;

'If circumstances allow'. The hypotheses cited in *NQ* have often been repeated: *pigs* from *pixies* or from *pix (pyx),* or even from *piga* 'the virgin', but Old Engl. *piga* is a ghost word. The *OED* says cautiously that there is no evidence for such hypotheses; *The Century Dictionary* calls them (and more of the same type) absurd. On p. 437, several stories are told about changing the place of the church to be built through the actions of animals, including pigs; one such story concerns Winwick, Lancashire. The author suggests the folklore base of this saying. The full text of the saying is *an't please the pigs*; *an't = if it.* Considering how obscure the origin of the phrase is and how unlikely it is that it goes back to *pyxies* or *pyx,* the following note by Alfred Gatty is perhaps worth considering: "I think it possible that the pigs of the Gergesenes (Matthew viii. 28. *et seq.*) may be those appealed to, and that the invocation may be of somewhat impious meaning. John Bradford, the martyr of 1555, has within a few consecutive pages of his writings the following expressions: 'And so by this means, as they save their pigs, which they would not lose (I mean their worldly pelf), so they would please the Protestants, and be counted with them for gospellers, yea, marry, would they'.—*Writings of Bradford,* Parker Society, ed., p. 390. Again: 'Now are they unwilling to drink God's cup of afflictions, which He offereth common with His son Christ our Lord, lest they should love their pigs with the Gergenites'. P. 409. Again: 'This is a hard sermon: 'Who is able to abide it?' Therefore, Christ must be prayed to depart, lest all their pigs be drowned. The devil shall have his dwelling again in themselves, rather than in their pigs'. P. 409. These and similar expressions in the same writer without reference to any text upon the subject, seem to show, that men loving their pigs more than God, was a theological phrase of the day, descriptive of their too great worldliness. Hence, just as St. Paul said, 'if the Lord will', or as we say, 'please God', or, as it is sometimes written, D.V. [Deo volente 'with God's will'], worldly men would exclaim, 'please the pigs', and thereby mean that, provided it suited their present interest, they would do this or that thing" (p. 423). [The additional difficulty in tracing the origin of the idiom is the alliteration (*p.* . . . . *p*). Sometimes an alliterating word is chosen only for the euphonic effect.] JBK I, 105. OED: 1683.

P39. *Pluck a crow with somebody, to*
NQ 1864 III/6: 390, 524; 1898 IX/1: 367, 438; 1898 IX/2: 155; 1941, 181: 20.

'To disagree' or 'to settle a small affair'. Synonyms were cited and the French origin was suggested and rejected. The conjectures about the origin are fanciful (e.g. "when you pluck a crow, nothing remains," or *crow* is said to be an alteration of the French word for "moustache"). *I have a goose to pluck with you* occurred in the same sense in 1659. [Hyamson, p. 103, cites *to pluck (pull, pick) a crow,* which he glosses as 'to have a quarrel', and explains that "originally the phrase meant to concern oneself in a matter of little importance, a crow being considered of no value."] OED: *a*1500 *(We haue a craw to pull.)*

P40. *Point of war*
NQ 1907 X/8: 8, 96, 313.

"Although originally applied as a general term for the various trumpet calls and drum beatings in the last field, still I think that at least for the last 150 years 'point of war' has been used in a restricted sense for one particular call, as is certainly the case at the present time. . . . I think the term 'point' originally meant a point to be remembered—one of the things necessary to be known to every soldier" (p. 313). This is an extract from a longer note by S. C. Harris. OED: 1578.

P41. *Poke borak, to*
NQ 1887 VII/3: 476.

This is the text of the query: "In Stormonth's *English Dictionary* I read, '*Al-borak,* the winged creature having the face of a man, on which Mohammed is said to have journeyed or flown to heaven'. Is there any connexion between this word and the phrase 'to poke borak', applied in colonial conversation to the operations of a person who pours fictitious information into the ears of a credulous listener? If not, what is the derivation of the expression? Is *borak* the correct spelling?" *OED*: *borak* 'nonsense, *etc.*' (1845). Australian and New Zealand slang. Aboriginal Australian. The verb *barrack* (apparently, originally Australian) means 'to shout jocular or derisive remarks. . . . as partisans against a person. . . .'; Wright *(EDD)* has *barrack* 'to brag'. OED: 1882 *(poking borak).*

P42. *Policy of pinpricks*
NQ 1899 IX/3: 46, 115, 238, 278; 1902 IX/10: 372, 412, 518; 1903 IX/12: 15, 295; 1906 X/5: 366.

'Wearing down an opponent by a series of instants'. The phrase was discussed as a term of diplomacy and traced to French *coups d'epingle.* The authorship of the phrase was tentatively ascribed to Alphonse Daudet, but it is older than *Tartarin.* In the note of 1906, James A. H. Murray quoted the entry, shortly to appear in the *OED,* and explained how the phrase traveled between France and England. OED: 1853 *(A combat of pin-pricks.)*

P43. *Poor Jack*
NQ 1892, VIII/2: 529; 1893 VIII/ 3: 76.

"Poor Jack seems obviously the same as Poor John, a kind of dried coarse fish, a common article of diet, constantly referred to by the Elizabethan writers. Several quotations are given in Nares's *Glossary*" (p. 76). VIII/2: 529 contains a 1769 quotation of *eat poor Jack.* OED: 1623.

P44. *Pop goes the weasel*

NQ 1905 X/3: 430, 491; 1907 X/7: 107; 1916 XII/1: 400.

The question was about the origin of the nursery rhyme. Two answers appeared on p. 491: 1) "This phrase certainly refers to a purse made of weasel-skin, which opened and closed with a snap. The 'popping of the weasel' in the song (I believe a sort of music-hall ditty of the fifties [1850s]) is the opening of the purse, and consequent spending of money, as the context shows. 'Bang went sixpence' is a verbal, not real, parallel." [Note *certainly* in the first sentence.] 2) "'Weasel,' I believe, is (or was) the technical or slang name for a narrow iron implement which is used by tailors in cutting out their cloth, and without which it is impossible to carry on their trade. A certain tailor, residing, presumably, in the vicinity of Islington, was in the habit of travelling with too great frequency 'up and down the city road' for the purpose of going 'in and out' a certain public-house entitled the 'Eagle'. His object in doing so is implied, but not expressly stated. In any case, 'that's the way the money goes', and to such an extent does the said 'money go' that he is ultimately reduced to the dire necessity of 'popping' (that is, pawning) his 'weasel'. This is clearly his last resource, as without his 'weasel' he is unable to earn his living, so that the poem evidently represents a man reduced to the last extremity, and comprises a somewhat laconic, but impressive sermon on the evils of drink . . . . I was not aware that there was any doubt on the subject" (p. 491). [Now note the last sentence.] A year and a half later, the following letter by James A. H. Murray appeared: "I should be glad of any information as to the origin, history, and date of this phrase, as applied to a dance or otherwise. I can distinctly remember seeing, some time in the fifties [1850s], in a provincial musicseller's catalogue, the advertisement 'The new country dance 'Pop goes the Weasel,' introduced by Her Majesty Queen Victoria; the new [some term I forget] 'La Napoléonienne,' introduced by her Imperial Majesty the Empress Eugénie'. This was, I think, about the end of 1854 or in 1855, but the tune was already by that time whistled or yelled about the streets, and it was the august patronage ascribed to it that fixed the advertisement in my mind. Was the phrase introduced with the dance, or had it any previous history? Has any one a dated copy of the original dance music? I shall be thankful for prompt answers, or indications where they can be seen in print" (p. 107). In the editor's words (p. 400), "no conclusion was arrived at." OED: 1853.

P45. *Possession is nine points of the law*

NQ 1879 V/11: 447; 1879 V/12: 33, 378; 1889 VII/7: 248, 393; 1907 X/7: 167; 1925, 149: 461; 1926, 150: 29.

Especially well-known is the end of the phrase *nine points of the law* [p. 378]. But, as explained on p. 33, there are really eight points, which are listed. "This probably was first applied to actions of ejectment, in which the plaintiff must recover on the strength of his own title, the defendant's possession being presumed to be legal until the contrary is shown." The variant with *eleven* for *nine* also exists (VII/7: 248). In X/7: 167 the following note by James A. H. Murray appeared: "In connexion with this quasi-legal maxim, I think the question was asked some time ago. 'How many points has the law, and what are they?' The question did not show much appreciation of the meaning of the maxim; but it may perhaps be answered according to its wisdom, by saying, 'The law (like anything else) has just as many points as you choose to attribute to it for the purpose of stating a proposition. When you say (as most people do at present) that possession is *nine* points of the law, you suppose 'the law' to have ten points; but if you say, in accordance with earlier usage, that possession is *eleven* points of the law, you suppose 'the law' to have twelve points; while, if you say, as has also been said, that possession is *ninety-nine* points of the law, you suppose 'the law' to have a hundred points'. In other words, the question is not how many points 'the law' has, but what proportion of all the points possession is equal to. The actual purport of the maxim, of course, is that, in a dispute about property, *possession* is (or used to be, when the saying arose in the fifteenth century) so strong a point in favour of the possessor, that it might outweigh nine, or eleven, or ninety-nine points that might legally be pleaded in behalf of some one else. The historical illustration of the expression will be found in the next issue of the 'Dictionary,' in which 'point' will form one of the important articles." OED: 1616.

P46. *Potato and point*
NQ 1880 VI/1: 236, 443-4; VI/2: 36-7.
The reference is to a meager meal (potatoes and nothing or almost nothing else). This is the editorial comment on p. 236: "We have heard that 'potato and point' is a meal consisting of a large dish of potatoes and a very small piece of meat; the potatoes are eaten, but the meat is only pointed at." *

P47. *Pour oil upon the troubled waters, to*
ANQ 1, 1888: 151; ANQ 3, 1889: 36. NQ 1881 VI/3: 69, 298; 1881 VI/4: 174; 1882 VI/6: 97, 377; 1884 VI/10: 307, 351; 1885 VI/11: 38, 72; 1887 VII/3: 285, 482; 1890 VII/10: 386; 1902 IX/9: 107; 1903 IX/11: 520; 1903 IX/12: 389; 1916 XII/2: 87, 159;
'To bring quiet amid a storm; to appease conflict or disturbance.' The origin of the phrase is lost, but the effect of oil on stormy waves is a well-known fact. [Twice used in the development of the plot by Jules Verne.] OED: 1774 *(to still the waves in a storm by pouring oil into the sea.)*

P48. *Present in Halgavor Court*
NQ 1863 III/4: 19; 1864 III/5: 276.
This is supposedly an allusion to "a carnival formerly held on Halgavor Moor, when those who had in any way offended 'the youthlyer sort of Bodmin town-men' were tried and condemned for some ludicrous offence." *

P49. *Pretty kettle of fish*
NQ 1872 IV/9: 102; ANQ 3, 1889: 59; NQ 1889 VII/8: 63.
'An unpleasant situation'. The idiom has been explained with reference to eating fish near a salmon river and, conversely, to the way of catching fish. In VII/8: 63, it is suggested that *kettle* in this phrase means 'kettleful', that is, 'a piled, higgledy-piggledy assortment of fish, such as one would have either in a large and well-filled kettle or cauldron or in a kettle-net'. JBK I, 31. OED: 1742.

P50. *Pride of the morning*
NQ 1877 V/8: 396.
See *Cry of the morning*. EDD: *Pride*; OED: 1777-8.

P51. *Proved up to the hilt*

NQ 1888 VII/5: 228, 312, 351, 495.

'Entirely'. Perhaps the best explanation of this rather obvious phrase is as follows: "As the argument—like a problem or theorem in Euclid—is without flaw throughout, and may be relied on to settle the question, so a sword thoroughly proved or tested by a recognized authority can . . . be well tempered and without flaw, and therefore to be relied on in fight" (p. 351). OED: 1944 (but *to the hilt* 'completely' occurred in 1862).

P52. *Psychological moment*

NQ 1908 X/10: 488; 1909 X/11: 13, 54, 94, 138.

'A moment of great expectation'. This phrase, according to James A. H. Murray, "has been much run upon of late" (p. 488). It seems to have been an import from French, where it was also recent (p. 94). But, according to the suggestion on p. 13, "it was first used by Bismarck towards the end of his career." OED: 1871.

P53. *Pull Devil, pull baker*

NQ 1857 III/3: 228, 258, 316; 1953, 198: 286; 1886 VII/1: 16, 96; ANQ 4, 1889: 31; Spectator 1923 130: 550, 588, 665.

Two tales have been cited to explain the phrase. According to one, an evil baker supplied a ship's crew with bad biscuits. On the voyage back, the ship suddenly stopped, and the sailors saw the culprit fighting with the Devil, who was trying to pull his victim down. But the baker fought so valiantly that the sailors forgot their chagrin and, depending on who was winning, shouted: "Pull Devil, pull baker" (NQ III/3: 316). Another tale has it that a baker is detected making short weight. The Devil enters and carries off the light bread and ill-gotten gold. The baker pursues the Devil, and the tug of war begins. This is the content of an old play (ANQ 4, 1889, 31). In both versions, the Devil wins, and both go back to puppet plays. An Elizabethan ballad "The Devil and the Baker" was known, so that the characters in popular performance may be medieval. In NQ VII/1: 16, the question is raised whether the struggle ever formed an episode in the Punch drama. The most informative article on the subject is by G. Speaight in *NQ* 198, 1953. OED: 1764 *(Pull baker, pull devil)*.

P54. *Pull garlick, to*

NQ 1859, II/8: 229.

'To submit tamely to ill treatment'. The note deals with the word *pill-garlic,* discussed in NQ I/3: 42, 74, 150. A pill-garlick (with *pill* here understood as *peel*) is someone left in the lurch, forsaken by everybody. [Nothing is said about the relations between *pill (peel)* and *pull.* They seem to have been taken for interchangeable synonyms.] JBK I, 49. OED: *a*1529 *(pyllyd garleke).*

P55. *Pull one's leg, to*

NQ 1913 XI/7: 508; 1913 XI/8: 58, 158, 213.

'To trick, deceive'. Strangely, considering the date in the *OED,* the phrase was new to most writers. [At one time, *leg* was supposed to be an "indecent" word. Can this be the reason few people knew the phrase even in 1913?] On p. 158, it is called a Scotticism. Yet it was, though foreign to newcomers, widely used in India in the 1870s (p. 213). OED: 1821.

P56. *Pull prime, to*

NQ 1856, II/2: 431; 1857, II/4: 496; 1875 V/3: 67, 155, 332, 333, 379.

It is a dicing term, as explained in the last two references. "To pull" is to draw from the pack. "Prime," in primero, is a winning hand of different suits. It is also a card term: 'to draw for a card to try and get a prime'; obsolete. Other explanations of the idiom (from French, from pulling the bell for prime, that is, the first economical hour succeeding to lauds; or milkmaids' morning operations) are wrong. As noted in II/4: 496, the variant *pull for prime* also exists. OED: 1631.

P57. *Pull the rug (from under), to*

ANQ 7, 1968: 57.

'To ruin someone's prospects'. Peter Tammony, an outstanding student of slang and local idioms, gives several earlier synonymous phrases, namely, *pull the switch* (19ᵗʰ-century usage), *pull the pin, pull the chain,* and *pull the plug,* some of them obviously going back to mechanical processes. OED: 1928. The dates for the synonyms from OED: *pull the pin* (1860), and *pull the plug* (1923).

P58. *Put a Dutchman in, to*

ANQ 3, 1889: 153, 204.

"The phrase is used by builders and cabinet-makers where a small piece of wood has to be inserted to make a bad joint good." The correspondent to ANQ 3: 153 suggests: "In Germany there is a province called Swabia, and old German carpenters make use of the expression to *put a schwab in.* Might not the word *schwab* in America have come to be *Dutchman*?" The author of the note on p. 204 says: "I am told by a builder that German carpenters and cabinet-makers have a habit of fitting joints and mortises very loosely, and then making their work tight and firm by inserting small wedges. Hence the phrase current among the building fraternity *to put a Dutchman in*—that is, where a joint does not fit perfectly, to insert a small bit of wood, after the German fashion." [*Dutch* could indeed mean 'German': cf. *Pennsylvania Dutch.* The original *OED* notes this sense of *Dutchman* but provides no etymology. Its source is an 1874 dictionary.]

P59. *Put a sneck in the kettle crook, to*

NQ 1860 II/9: 446.

This is said on being surprised by some extraordinary event or novelty. The kettle crook is "a piece of solid iron with a hook at its end, fixed by the upper end to an iron bar placed across the chimney-vent, and that suspended by the bows on which are hung in their turn the mettle pot, saucepan, or whatever other utensil may be used for the cooking of the food." A sneck is the latch on a lid. Northern England and Scotland. * See also *Give one sneck posset, to*

P60. *Put a spoke in one's wheel, to*

NQ 1853 I/8: 269, 351, 522, 576, 624; 1854 I/9: 45, 601; 1854 I/10: 54; 1901 IX/7: 128, 258.

'To destroy one's plans'. According to the first note (p. 269), some people understood the idiom as meaning 'to afford help', for what is a wheel without spokes? This sense of the idiom was confirmed by an American who used the phrase "I'll give you a spoke" (= help). No other correspondents knew the phrase endowed with a positive sense: everybody suggested that *spoke* stood for 'bar', 'stick' (p. 522) or 'spike' (p. 576). Also, on p. 576, it is suggested that *spoke* is an ignorant perversion of *spike,* and the Dutch analog *en spaak in t'wiel steeken* [which the *OED* believes to be the source of the English saying] is cited. Still another interpretation (p. 45) runs as follows "This phrase must have had its origin in the days in which the vehicles used in this country [England] had wheels of solid wood without spokes." The author describes a "vehicle used in the cultivation of the land on the slopes of the skirts of Dartmoor in Devonshire; [it] has three wheels of solid wood; it resembles a huge wheelbarrow, with two wheels behind, and one in the front of it, and has two long handles like the handles of a plough, projecting behind for the purpose of guiding it. As the horse is attached to the vehicle by chains only, and he has no power to hold back when going down hill [sic], the driver is provided with a piece of wood, 'a spoke', which is of the shape of the wooden pin used for rolling paste, for the purpose of 'dragging' the front wheel of the vehicle. This he effects by thrusting the spoke into one of the three round holes made in the solid wheel for that purpose." [Brewer's comment is a condensed version of the text quoted above.] Some agreement was reached after the following explanation appeared in print (p. 601): "I have always understood the 'spoke' to be, not a radius of the wheel, but a bar put between the spokes at right angles, so as to prevent the turning of the wheel; a rude mode of 'locking', which I have often seen practiced. The correctness of the metaphor is thus evident." But to *put in one's spoke* means 'to attempt to give advice' (*OED*: 1580); [possibly hence the now obsolete association with *speak,* as in *spoke* 'remark' (*OED*: 1594, 1599, 1615 and *spokesman*).] The brief discussion in 1901 added nothing new and was carried on in ignorance of the earlier notes. JBK I, 68. OED: *a*1625.

P61. *Put in one's motto, to*
NQ 1897 VIII/11: 468.

'To enter rashly into a conversation or to summarize circumstances sententiously' (slang). The unanswered question concerned the possibility that the phrase might be a borrowing from Italian. In the Italian text of Matthew XVII: 4 *fece motto* 'said unto Jesus' occurs. *Fece* is the past tense of *fare* 'to do, make'. [The hypothesis carries little conviction, but *motto* is indeed a borrowing of Ital. *motto*]. *

P62. *Put one's foot into it, to*
NQ 1853, I/8: 77, 159.

'To make a grave error'. The note on p. 77 contains a most improbable reference to a legal dispute in Hindostan. On p. 159, a dubious source in Greek is cited. [Isn't *it* a genteel euphemism?] OED: 1796 (the *OED* compares this phrase with *put one's foot in one's mouth*).

P63. *Put one's monkey up, to*
NQ 1874 V/1: 248, 295; 1912 XI/5: 325.

'To enrage a person'. Reference to an analog in Welsh is given, but Welsh *mwnci* means 'horse collar'. A classical Greek analog (p. 325) might perhaps be considered as the source. OED: 1833 (no origin is suggested).

P64. *Put out the besom, to*

NQ 1884 VI/10: 526; 1885 VI/11: 78, 178.

See *Hang out the broom.*

P65. *Put side on, to*

NQ 1891 VII/11: 107, 173, 313.

'To put on airs'. Barrère and Leland suggest the origin in billiards or sailing, or an animal's walk; side 'front' explains the phrase too. The *OED* cites this phrase as a term in billiards (1858) but gives no figurative meaning.

P66. *Put the kibosh on, to*

NQ 1874 V/2: 53, 478; 1875 V/3: 173; 1885 VI/12: 148; 1901 IX/7: 10, 276; IX/8: 87; 1925, 148: 393; 1924, 147: 244; 1937, 173: 113; CoE 2018 48/1: 2-23; 2019 48/4-5: 17-33; 48/8: 2-50; 49/3: 21-36; 2020 49/6: 2-13.

'To put an end to something'. Now that *Origin of Kibosh* by Gerald Cohen, Stephen Goranson, and Matthew Little is available in book form (Routledge, 2018), there is no need to give a detailed survey of all opinions. The authors defend the idea that *kibosh* goes back to *kurbash* 'lash'. The material offered in the book is persuasive; however, one sense of this word may need an additional comment. The idea in the supplement to Volume 3 of *The Century Dictionary*, 2nd ed. may also have merit. Not improbably, *kurbash* 'lash' was identified by the lower classes of London speakers as beginning with *ker* in *kerslap, kerplunk, kerfuffle ~ kurfuffle,* and even *curmudgeon,* and ending with *bosh* 'nothing, stuff, nonsense'. Without the help of folk etymology *kurbash ~ kibosh* would probably not have survived. Several conjectures discussed and rejected in the book should be buried with other "noxious guesses with which the soil of English etymology is cumbered," as James A. H. Murray put it in a different context (1897). Especially popular are the Yiddish and the Hebrew derivations. Allegedly, the word means 'eighteen pence', and reference is to small auctions in Petticoat Lane, where, "an eager purchaser, to cut the proceedings short, will call out *Khai Bash!* And the article will promptly be knocked down to him" (see a full account in the book, pp. 124–9). Another often-cited etymology connects *kibosh* with Irish *caidhp bháis* 'cap of death'. The connection between the Irish phrase and *kibosh* is tenuous, especially because the judge who pronounced the sentence of death put it on his, rather than the defendant's, head (pp. 98–102 in the book). *Kibosh,* the name of a tool used in clog-making, is a regional northern word. Although a colloquialism could spread south from the north of England (for example, this is what happened to the noun *slang*), the semantic and chronological difficulties connected with this derivation of the phrase are considerable (pp. 91–5 of the book). Still another derivation of *kibosh,* from the French *caboche* 'head (informal)' via the verb 'to cut off a stag's head behind the ears as a trophy' looks uninviting because the path from the French word to an item of nineteenth-century English criminal slang would be hard to trace. For completeness' sake, a few more guesses may be added. "The *kywash* was a figure of a seated man, carved in wood, placed by the Southern American Indians to keep guard over their burial-places . . . . Is any connexion between the two words possible?" (VI/12: 148). The answer is no. "*Kybosh* is a widely known trade word. I have heard it used, practically every day, for the last forty odd years—not in one locality only, but in all parts of England . . . . *Kybosh* is Portland cement; *to kybosh* is to throw with blowpipe and with brush, this dark dust into the deep recesses of carved stonework . . . ." (IX/7: 277). But, as noted in the book, the use of the term *kybosh* in architecture, even if it could be confirmed, throws no light on the word's origin. James Platt, Jun. (his contribution is also discussed in the book) indicated that *kybosh,* in criminal slang, could mean 'to make an object perfect, to add finishing touches to an already good piece of work' (also IX/7: 277). This sense is close to the one, allegedly used at one time by architectural sculptors (by kybosh-ing the shadows of carved stonework "may become intensified, and thus augment the gen-eral good effect of the ornamentation"). The semantic development is rather obvious. *Kibosh* means 'to finish; to finish off', and the process of finishing may presuppose destruction or striving for perfection. Platt knew *kybosh* 'nonsense', and so did Thomas Ratcliff, another fre-quent and learned contributor to *NQ,* who remembered (the same page) that in his school-days *kybosh* meant either 'nonsense' *(blarney)* or 'beating' *(I'll give him kybosh).* 'Beating' goes well with putting the kibosh on one, but why 'nonsense'? In 1877, Charles Mackay, a knowl-edgeable word historian and poet of note, published out of pocket *The Gaelic Etymology of the Languages of Western Europe. . . ,* a volume purporting to show that thousands of English words are adaptations of Irish words. His findings aroused the indignation of specialists, but occasionally he guessed well. Thus, he was probably right in suggesting an Irish etymon of *curmudgeon.* At *kybosh,* he wrote: "Gaelic *cià* 'what', *baois* 'idle talk'. The exclamation *cia baois,* pronounced as *ci-baoish,* means 'what idle nonsense' or 'what indecency'. This is a fan-ciful conjecture. Perhaps 'nonsense', which cannot be derived from any sense of *kybosh* in *put the kibosh on,* is a different word, unless it can be traced to the equation *end, extinction = nonsense.* The contributor to NQ 173, 1937: 113 "would suggest that this Cockney expression originated with the Italian ice-cream merchants . . . . It is synonymous with *to put the tin lid on,* the *tin lid* being originally a candle-extinguisher, and called *capoce* or *capuce . . . .* There is also a well-known idiom for extinction 'That fair puts the cap on it'" (a guess on a par with *kywash,* cited above). Especially pervasive, as already mentioned, is the idea that *kibosh* is "pure Hebrew". Even Ernest Weekley, who did mention the association with *bosh,* found this idea worthy of consideration. As late as 1989, Isacc Mozeson in the book titled *The Word* (a col-lection of wild fantasies) cited Webster's *keibe* 'carrion' from Yiddish, but preferred Hebrew *kobhush* 'to master, subdue' as the etymon of *kybosh.* At the moment, *kurbash* as the etymon of *kybosh* has the greatest potential. Not unlikely, *-bosh* in *kybosh,* without being the word's source, helped it to survive and spread. The Yiddish-Hebrew origin of *kybosh* has nothing to recommend it. The same holds for the Irish *cap of death* idea and several others, based on the chance similarity between *kybosh* and some words of other languages. Judging by the avail-able material, *put the kybosh on* enjoyed considerable popularity on both sides of the Atlantic (it was sometimes even taken for an Americanism), got a second lease of/on life with the music hall song "We'll put the kibosh on the Kaiser" during World War I, and has receded into the background; now not everybody, at least in the United States, even recognizes the phrase (and those who do tend to pronounce *kibosh,* as though it was *kibbosh*). A semantic parallel to *kibosh* 'lash' would be *scourge*: from "whip" to "affliction". OED: 1836.

P67. *Put to buck, to*

NQ 1874 V/1: 228, 293; 1874 V/2: 76, 138, 279.

'To be delayed or hindered'. All kinds of suggestions have been offered, e.g. *buck* 'sweat', *bucking* 'sweating', *buck* 'buckle', *to buck = aback,* or *put to buck = put to book* 'make a witness swear'. Most likely, the phrase is connected with *buck* 'to wash, soak'. EDD: *Buck.* The *OED* has *to drive the buck* 'to carry through the process of bucking' (not in a figurative sense: 1648).

P68. *Put to the horn, to*

NQ 1894 VIII/5: 328, 375, 415.

See *Come out the little end of the horn, to.*

P69. *Put up with*

NQ 1874 V/2: 388; 1875 V/3: 14.

'To endure'. Verb-adverb collocations (like *give up* and *do in*) are not included in this dictionary because their origin is hardly ever discussed outside special sources. *Put up with* is an exception. On p. 14, the suggestion is made that the original idea and form of this collocation was to put up the wrong in one's pocket and keep it there. Another suggestion will be found on p. 388: "Richard Baxter, in his autobiography, speaking of his preaching before Cromwell, says, 'the plainness and nearness, I heard, was displeasing to him and his courtiers, but they *put it up*'. This appears to be another, possibly an older, form of expression of the same idea." OED: 1641.

Q

Q1. *Quarrel with one's bread and butter, to*

NQ 1920 XII/7: 189.

'To give up' ['risk the loss of, or complain about one's means of livelihood without good reason']. This is not an Americanism, as was once suggested. OED: 1738.

Q2. *Quite the (clean) potato*

NQ 1888 VII/6: 366; 1889 VII/7: 457; 1889 VII/8: 74, 237.

'The very pink of perfection'. Only examples were cited, but no one offered an "etymology." The *OED* derives the phrase from Australian usage (1822).

R

R1. *Rag upon every bush*

NQ 1866 III/9: 474

'Two-timer', explained in the note as 'a young man courting several women'. *

R2. *Raise Cain, to*

NQ 1918 XII/4: 77, 146.

'To create disturbance'. The obvious reference is to a scene of great violence. Cf. *Raise Hamlet on one, to.* [Funk, p. 42, doubts the biblical origin of the reference to Cain and suggests that *cain* or *kain,* or *cane* 'the rent of land, payable in produce' was meant. As he adds, there is evidence supporting this hypothesis, but he does not cite it.] OED: 1840.

R3. *Raise Hamlet on one, to*
NQ 1909 X/ 11: 65, 137, 237.

'To become angry and violent'. The phrase is synonymous with *to raise Cain* and many other similar phrases. Cf. *Play Hamlet, to* and *Raise Cain, to.* *

R4. *Raise Ned, to*
NQ 1906 X/5: 8.

'To disrupt things habitually but without malicious intent'. *Ned* must be a taboo word for the Devil. To *raise Harry* also exists, and *Harry* is indeed the Devil. U.S. slang, now rare. OED: 1848 *(raisin' promiscoous Ned.)*

R5. *Raise the wind, to*
NQ 1852 I/6: 486; 1853 I/7: 27.

This is said by "seamen who whistle at sea to raise the wind, or by 'fast men', who seek the assistance of money lenders or pawnbrokers for a similar purpose." Cf. *Whistle for the wind, to.* JBK I, 19. OED: 1722.

R6. *Rank and file*
NQ 1890 VII/9: 5, 198.

'Ordinary soldiers, as contrasted with officers' (often used metaphorically). "Rank is the breadth and file depth [cf. *in single file*] in speaking of the rank and file of a body of men" (p. 5). OED: 1598.

R7. *Rare-overs for meddlers*
NQ 1870 IV/5: 257.

'An answer to over-curious people'. Sometimes the following is added: "and crutches for lame ducks." See also *Lay-overs for meddlers* and *Layers for meddlers, and crutches for wild ducks.* *

R8. *Receive the canvas, to*
NQ 1887 VII/4: 469; 1888 VII/5: 116, 398.

'To get the sack, to be fired'. The explanation is the same as the one always suggested for *get ~ give the sack* (see them above): "The phrase (= to be dismissed) is taken from the practice of journeymen mechanics who travel in quest of work, with the implements of their profession. When they are discharged by their masters they are said to receive the *canvas,* or the *bag;* because in this their tools and necessaries are packed up, preparatory to their removal'.—'The Brothers,' II. i., vol. i. p. 20" (p. 116). (The reference is to Gifford's edition of *Shirley.*) Instead of *get the canvas* the verb *to canvas* is sometimes used in the same sense. OED: 1652, glossed as 'repulse, rejection'.

R9. *Red tape*
NQ 1883 VI/8: 349, 393.

'Excessive adherence to rules and formalities'. Red tape was a well-known article as early as the middle of the seventeenth century, but the correspondents to *NQ* did not refer to the fact that in Government offices documents were tied into bundles with red or pinkish tape, which gave rise to the notion of official obstruction. OED: 1658.

R10. *Regular mull*

NQ 1851 I/3: 449, 508; 1852 I/5: 165.

'A disagreeable predicament'. The story of King Mûl has been suggested as the source of the phrase; or perhaps in the past not only wine was mulled; or it is "a corruption of *muddle.*" The author of the note on p. 165 refers to the derogatory name *mull* given to the residents of Bengal, Bombay, and Madras. [If the phrase is English, *mull* may be a word for 'rubbish']. *

R11. *Remember Tod*

NQ 1932, 163: 45, 85.

A begging formula. "In some parts of England it is, or was, the custom for children, in the month of June, to ask for pennies or gifts with the phrase 'Remember Tod' like that other memory of St. James in August, 'Remember the grotto'" (p. 45). The question was about the meaning of *Tod.* It is not clear whether *Tod* or *tod* is meant. No explanation was received. *

R12. *Return thanks, to*

NQ 1902 IX/10: 26, 79.

This is the comment on p. 26: "One of the oddest and most out-of-place phrases is that of 're-turning thanks' which appears in tradesmen's business announcements and notices. It is understood to be the tradesman's way of thanking his customers for their past favours. Giving thanks would, perhaps, be better, for his customers would scarcely thank him for allowing them to deal with him." However, on p. 79, the correspondent objects: "A return may be made that is not a return in kind; and I hold that a customer has often as much occasion to thank a tradesman for the attention he has given to his wants as the tradesman has to thank the customers for his patronage." OED: ?1570.

R13. *Rhyme rats to death, to*

NQ 1852 I/6: 460, 591.

In addition to a vague reference to "runic" songs, a passage from *As You Like It* has been quoted. Rosalind says (III: 2, 187–89) "I was never so be-rimed since Pythagoras' time, that I was an Irish rat, which I can hardly remember." [Annotated editions of Shakespeare's play explain in detail the superstition connected with exorcising rats.] The allusion may be to an old Irish belief that witches who assume the shape of rats can be "rhymed to death." Can there be a connection with the simile *As dead as a rat?* OED: 1656.

R14. *Ride bodkin, to*

NQ 1854 I/10: 524; 1855 I/11: 52; 1889 VII/8: 27, 76, 116; 1890 VII/9: 74; 1897 VIII/11: 267, 354, 429; 1897 VIII/12: 114; 1901 IX/7: 228, 376.

'To occupy a seat on a coach, wedged in between two other passengers'. The reference is to a narrow dagger. *To sit bodkin* has also been recorded ('to be wedged in between others'). "It has recently been suggested to me that a place in which to set a sword (or bodkin) used to exist in the old travelling coach or chariot between the two occupants of the 'front seat'" (VIII/11:

267). "The 'sword-case' in old carriages was not a perpendicular socket, but a horizontal recess in the upper part of the back, the full width of the carriage" (p. 354). On p. 429, the *OED*'s explanation of the idiom is challenged by F. Adams, who points out that in the earliest examples there is no connotation of wedging in between two others. OED: 1638 *(be Bodkin bitch-baby must ye.)*

R15. *Ride hell-for-leather, to*
Spectator 1912 109: 643, 747.
'To ride at breakneck speed'. Frank Taylor explained how he used this phrase in his poem and referred to Kipling's 1889 ballad "Shillin' a Day." His tentative explanation runs as follows: "He who rides 'Hell-for-leather' is he who rides in a fashion very deleterious to the human cuticle." (Cf. *Hell-beat for leather*). OED: 1881 *(Hallfalleero)*.

R16. *Ride in the marrow-bone stage, to*
NQ 1857 II/4: 115.
'To walk'. According to the correspondent, the phrase is "a ludicrous corruption of *mary-le-bone.*" The *OED* at *marrowbone stage* makes no mention of this odd etymology. The earliest citation is dated to 1820. JBK II, 75.

R17. *Ride the breeze, to*
SNQ 1895 I/9: 160; 1896 I/9: 174.
'To run a race on horseback'. "Those who are at a wedding, especially the younger part of the company, who are conducting the bride from her own house to the bridegroom's, often set off, at full speed, for the latter. He who reaches the house is said to *win the bruise.* This means nothing more than riding for the *brose, broth,* or *kail,* the prize of spice-broth, allotted in some places to the victor. For fuller particulars see Rogers' 'Social Life in Scotland', I., 113." Scotland. *

R18. *Ride the high horse*
NQ 1911 XI/4: 490; 1912 XI/5: 15, 54, 114.
'To put on airs'. The epithet *high* seems to have alternated with *great* in this idiom, which must go back to the time of chivalry, when strong horses were needed to carry a knight in full armor. The phrase is probably a translation from French: *montrer sur ses grands chevaux* (thus, 'great', not 'high'). OED: 1782

R19. *Right away*
NQ 1880 VI/2: 223, 416; 1881 VI/3: 77; 1881 VI/4: 117, 176.
'Immediately', but also 'directly'. In British English, *right away* might suggest not a short time but a long distance, and indeed, on p. 77 we read: "This appears to be used as the technical expression for the final order to start a goods train, at least on the Great Eastern Railway, when the tedious process of shunting is completed. This seems to involve the idea of continuity of distance." Some people thought that the phrase had originated in America ("the purest of Americanisms"), but its use in northern England and Ireland runs counter to this suggestion. OED: 1734.

R20. *Ring the changes, to*

NQ 1926, 150: 44, 106.

'To substitute bad money for good; to give wrong change'. Only three examples (1678, 1749, and 1828), in addition to those from dictionaries of slang, are given. No one offered an explanation of the origin. [*Changes* from *change*?] The phrase is called 'now rare.' OED: 1614 ('to repeat essentially the same word') and 1786 for the first meaning above.

R21. *Rising of the lights*

NQ 1859, II/7: 58, 138; 1905 X/4: 66, 135.

It was a living phase, as of 1859 and later, in some parts of England referring to "a sense of fullness or suffocation about the chest." In regional American English, it was also current. In the note (p. 138), the case is described in detail. OED: 1630.

R22. *Roast a cat, to*

NQ 1892, VIII/1: 514; VIII/2: 212, 277.

'To expose to severe criticism'. The phrase is said to refer to the custom of throwing cats into the fire for religious purposes. It was still common in the 16th century. The note in p. 277 quotes Hampson's *Medii Ævi Kalendarium,* pp. 297–8, on burning cats in the Middle Ages as a part of the festival of St. John (June 24), but the connection between the rite and the idiom remains tenuous. * See also *cat* in the word index.

R23. *Rob Peter to pay Paul, to*

NQ 1874 V/2: 320; 1883 VI/7: 255; 1912 XI/6: 46; ANQ 5, 1890: 147; ANQ 8, 1892: 162.

In V/2: 320, the following is said: "The proverb of 'Robbing Peter to pay Paul' was applied in 1550, on the occasion of the appropriation of some of the estates of Westminster to fill up the needs of London." Another correspondent mentioned its use in Thomas Nashe's *Have with You to Saffron-Walden,* 1596 (IV/12: 166); but Canon Robertson has pointed out that a similar, though not exactly the same, expression is found generally applied as far back as the twelfth century:—"Tanquam si quis crucifigeret Paulum ut redimeret Petrum" [Like one who would crucify Paul, so that he could redeem Peter] (Herbert of Bosham, 287). The note on XI/6: 46 suggests that the saying originated at some feast of Peter and Paul (June 29), requiring the transfer of garments from one statue to the other as part of a regular ceremony. OED: *a*1400

R24. *Robin Hood's pennyworths*

NQ 1861 II/11: 310; 1875 V/3: 369, 455; 1900 IX/5: 73.

'To sell at half-price'. *To see Robin Hood's pennyworths* supposedly means 'to sell goods under half their value'. Fuller's *Worthies* (1662) is cited on p. 455, to justify the meaning given. Fuller says in his *Worthies* that *to sell Robin Hood's pennyworth* "is spoken of things sold under half their value, or, if you will, half sold, half given. Robin Hood came lightly by his ware, and lightly parted therewith; so that he could afford the length of his bow for a yard of velvet." OED: 1582.

R25. *Robin Hood wind*

NQ 1891 VII/11: 248, 311, 352; 1922 XII/10: 378, 411.

'A cold wind during a thaw'. The phrase is especially common in the region where Robin Hood is supposed to have been active. In Yorkshire, it is often said that Robin Hood could stand any wind but a thaw wind. The reference is to the bitter north and east winds from the direction of Blackstone Edge, a predominant feature of which hill is Robin Hood's bed. Apperson: 1855. *

R26. *Rock-bottom prices*

NQ 1902 IX/10: 26, 154.

'Prices at the irreducible minimum'. In 1890, *rock-bottom* was considered slang, and as late as 1902 some people found the phrase unusual. The expression is apparently an Americanism. OED: 1873.

R27. *Rod in pickle*

NQ 1856 II/2: 400.

This is said allegedly in reference to soaking rods as instruments of punishment, to make them supple. EDD: *Rod*; OED: 1625.

R28. *Roper's news*

NQ 1915 XI/11: 110, 174.

'Old news'. The collocation was also known to a correspondent in Cornwall in the saying: "Roper's news—hearing the crier." In the same county, *Mr. Roper* was used in reference to the hangman. The same as *Duck's news,* above. Apperson: 1879. *

R29. *Round robin*

NQ 1896 VIII/10: 392; 1897 VIII/11: 127, 130-1.

'A petition with signatures written in circle to conceal the order of writing' (and several other more or less similar senses). In the thirties of the eighteenth century, the term was applied facetiously to a sacramental wafer and seems to have meant 'a piece of bread' or 'cookie', which corresponds to *round robin* 'small pancake' in Devonshire' (VIII/11:127). Frank Chance (VIII/11: 130-1) believed that *robin* here is a specific use of the name Robin, like *Jack* in *flap-jack,* another regional name of a pancake. Robin rolls were sold in Oxford shops (VIII/11: 131). Perhaps a baker named Robin was the originator of some such dainty. It has often been said that round robins had their origin in the navy as an alteration of French *ruban rond* 'round ribbon'. But French *ruban rond* would have become *robin round*; besides, French dictionaries do not cite such a phrase. Despite the uncertainty, it is perhaps better not to separate *round robin* 'petition' from *round robin* 'pancake; cookie'. If the phrase was first applied to the document by natives of Devonshire, the possibility remains that it did originate in Devonshire, "that county having been well represented in the navy" (VIII/10: 392). Then a round robin is simply a round object. OED: ?1548.

R30. *Rule of thumb*

NQ 1857, II/4: 147, 315-6.

'Rough measurement'. II/4: 147 reports that brewers dip their thumb to measure the temperature of ale. In II/4: 315-6, a story is told about calculations made on the nail of the thumb.

Another suggestion on the same page perhaps sounds more realistic: "Amongst country labourers, whose hands and fingers are enlarged by griping their tools hard at work, I have often seen the measure of length roughly taken (where no other means were at hand) in this way. Giles or Jim will very knowingly place his thumb close and firm on the surface of the thing to be measured, then his other thumb in front of the first, and so on alternately from one end to the other. 'There', says he, 'that's so many inches: my thumb will just cover an inch'. 'Rule of thumb' means, therefore, a *rough measurement*." Allen, p. 624, cites more "fakelore" about the origin of this phrase. EDD: *Thumb*; OED: *a*1658.

R31. *Rule the ring, to*
NQ 1881 VI/3: 477; 1881 VI/4: 112.

'To take the lead'. According to the suggestion on p. 477, the phrase is "a metaphor taken from dog-fighting or bull-fighting." In the 1820s, in several towns in Yorkshire, "the usual form of a challenge to fight was either the shaking or the turning over of the bull-ring" (p. 112). OED: *a*1529.

R32. *Rule the roast, to*
NQ 1857, II/4: 152; 1858, II/ 6: 338, 489; 1859, II/7: 58; 1881 VI/3: 127, 169, 277, 396, 432, 477, 495, 512; 1896 VIII/10: 295, 365, 423, 503; 1897 VIII/11: 273, 358, 477.

'To be in authority'. The initial query was about whether this saying is a "corruption" of *rule the roost*. The contributors to *NQ*, it appears, gave the correct answer: the two idioms are not connected. The editorial comment in II/4: 152 quotes improbable explanations by Cleland and Webster. Johnson's etymology (*roast* from *roist*), cited in II/6: 489, is also useless. Equally groundless are Brewer's derivation of *roast* from the nonexistent Danish form *roadst* 'council' (VI/3: 127) and tracing *roast* to *rostrum*. Wedgwood (in his dictionary and in VI/3: 169) traced *roast* to *rod*, an ingenious but indefensible etymology. Richardson's suggestion (see II/6: 338) that *roast* means 'feast' makes sense, and the *OED*, though it says that the origin of the phrase remains unclear, features it under *roast* 'meat'. In both *rule the roost* and *rule the roast*, alliteration must have played an important role (II/7: 58). OED: "In common use from *c*1500 onwards, but none of the early examples throw any light on the precise origin of the expression."

R33. *Rump and dozen*
NQ 1890 VII/10: 48, 134, 178, 332, 472; MCNNQ 5, 1884: 209.

This archaic phrase refers to a good dinner (a steak and twelve oysters or perhaps a dozen bottles of wine); common as a bet. OED: 1778.

R34. *Rump and kidney man*
NQ 1868, IV/1: 414.

The phrase was found in an Anglo-French-German dictionary and glossed as 'village musician, fiddler'. No one seems to have heard it. A similar definition is in the *OED* ("a fiddler who plays at local events and dines on leftovers"), which gives a single 1699 example from Nares.

R35. *Run amuck*

GM 38, 1768: 283; GM 40, 1770: 564; EMLR 37, 1800: 110; NQ 1865 III/8: 89; 1898 IX/2: 406.

'To run in frenzied thirst for destruction and murder'. Not the origin of the phrase but the etymology of *amuck,* formerly spelled *a muck,* was at issue. The note on p. 283 suggests the etymology of *amuck,* recognized at present (from Portuguese: 'frenzied Malay'), but wonders whether the word has something to do with Mecca. The response on p. 564 gives a more detailed description of a man running amuck. The author of a long note in *The European Magazine* cited *amoca* 'revenge' (from East Indies), which he found in a 1623 book. According to another unreliable explanation, cited in III/8: 89, *a-mocca ~ a-muck* in the Malay language means 'killingly'. With regard to chronology, compare the following note: "According to Mr. Mason Jackson in his work 'The Pictorial Press' (p. 50), there is extant an illustrated pamphlet, bearing the imprint 'London: Printed for T. Banks, July the 18, 1642', which contains a long and minute narrative of some murders on shipboard by a native of Jaba, who, immediately before the crime, 'upon a sudden cries' *a muck,* which in that language is a hazard or run my death; and mention is made of what occurred 'after the muck'" (IX/2: 406). *Amuck ~ amok* is from Malay *amoq* 'fighting blood'. EDD: *Run*; OED *(he runs a mucke)*: 1672.

R36. *Run a rig, to*

NQ 1877 V/7: 237.

'To deceive'. According to the note, the phrase might be connected with the so-called running agriculture. Kent. *Rig* 'wanton, *etc.*' remains a word of unknown origin. EDD: *Run*; OED: 'to play a prank or trick' (obsolete): 1764.

R37. *Run like a skeiner, to*

NQ 1891 VII/12: 206.

The phrase was "obviously derived from the woolen manufacture, which used to give employment in the district." West country. The *OED* has *skeiner* 'one who or that which makes yarns into skeins', but no examples before 1921. The note provides a noticeably earlier date (1831).

R38. *Run milk, to*

NQ 1925, 148: 208, 305.

"A milkman will advertise that there is 'wanted a boy to run milk', which means to deliver milk." In the dairy trade, phrases such as *milk-run, milk-walk,* and *milk-round* (in the US, *milk-route*) were common. They meant a milkman's regular round for the sale of milk. OED: 1909.

R39. *Run of his teeth*

NQ 1904 X/1: 388, 436.

"This phrase is current in conversation, especially in connexion with the appointment of a club secretary who has an annual income and the right to take his meals in the house" (p. 388). On p. 436, it is suggested that "this is a phrase of Canadian origin, employed in reference to one's board or boarding expenses, *e.g.,* 'He pays so much for the run of his teeth'." EDD: *Run*; OED: 1801.

S

S1. *Sabbath day's journey*
NQ 1911 XI/4: 429; 1912 XI/5: 15.

The phrase is of Biblical origin and specified the shortest distance the Jews were permitted to walk on foot on the Sabbath (p. 15 offers a detailed explanation), but in later English, it began to designate the opposite: a journey of great length or one that involved undue exertion. OED: 1526.

S2. *Sacred cow*
ANQ 7, 1947: 30.

'The designation for the president's (US) plane'. According to one version, this name was invented during a Big Three meeting at Teheran or Yalta. According to another account, the air force men called their heavily guarded planes this. [But the phrase was known long before World War Two and meant an object of veneration among Hindus.] OED: 1891.

S3. *Saffron Walden, God help me*
NQ 1851 I/3: 167.

"Many of the mendicants who ramble the county of Suffolk in search of relief, when asked where they come from, reply in a pitiful tone, 'Saffron Walden, God help me'. No more detailed explanation has been offered. Several phrases of the same type are known. Cf. *Binsey/ Crowley/ Melverley/From Lincoln heath, God help me.* *

S4. *St. Boniface's cup*
NQ 1857 II/3: 188.

"This proverb is explained in the curious book *Ebrietatis Encomium [In Praise of Inebriation]* (cap. 11.) by a legend that Pope Boniface instituted indulgences for those who should drink a cup after grace. It is further explained in a postscript, that this cup was to his own memory, or that of the Pope for the time being, under the phrase *'au bon pére'* ['to the good father']." *

S5. *St. Pawsle's and St. Pawsle's e'ens*
NQ 1877 V/7: 120, 236.

This phrase recorded in Yorkshire means, according to W. W. S. [= Walter W. Skeat's] and a Yorkshire speaker's explanation, *St. Apostle* (unnamed). The evening or day is understood as the greatest holiday imaginable. *

S6. *St. Peter's fingers*
NQ 1861, II/11: 128.

The full phrase is *he has got St. Peter's fingers.* It seems to refer to burglars. All is "Fish that comes to net with them, who are termed Saint Peter's children, as having every finger a fish hook." [Can there be a connection with *St. Peter's fish,* alluding to the touch of St. Peter's thumb and finger when he caught the fish whose mouth contained the tribute money? *(OED).*] EDD; *Peter*; OED: 1857.

S7. *Same old two-and-sixpence*

NQ 1858, II/5: 187.

"When a person has been absent from his friends for some considerable time, and is thought to be unchanged when they meet again, it is common for them to say, 'you are the same old two-and-sixpence'. Sometimes he says of himself, 'I am the same old two-and-sixpence'. The expression is most commonly applied to the manners, habits, and modes of thought and speech; seldom, if ever, to the bodily appearance." The author of the note is an American and cites a story about an American Indian who offered his furs to two people and was offered the same price. *Two-and-sixpence* was not an uncommon phrase. *

S8. *Save face, to*

NQ 1900 IX/6: 308, 398.

'To retain respect'. This is the opposite of *lose face* and has the same origin. The discussion shows that in 1900 the expression was not common, except in "Pidgin English" (p. 398), where it had universal currency. OED: 1870.

S9. *Save one's bacon, to*

NQ 1850 I/2: 499; 1898 IX/2: 407, 497; 1899 IX/3: 33, 472.

'To escape injury to one's body'. The note in I/2: 499 offers the following improbable explanation: "I venture to suggest that this phrase has reference to the custom at Dunmow, in Essex, of giving a flitch of bacon to any married couple residing in the parish, who live in harmony for a year and a day. A man and his wife who stopped short when on the verge of a quarrel might be said to have 'just saved their bacon'; and in course of time the phrase would be applied to anyone who barely escaped any loss or danger." The author of the note in IX/3: 472 quotes this idiom from a 13th-century Latin version of a story in which the wolf has eaten the bacon and thus "saved it." IX/2: 407 also refers to French *sauver son lard* ['to save one's bacon'], but "[t]his expression has such a thoroughly English ring that *sauver son lard* hardly sounds like native French. And yet it is not likely that it is borrowed *argot*. The French phrase is not . . . so familiar as English. Littré does not give it, but in citing the figurative locution *manger le lard* ['to eat one's bacon'], he says that it may have arisen from the charge brought against persons guilty of eating bacon or other forbidden viands on fast days . . . . *bacon* was a term applied to a section of an old top that was placed in the smaller of two rings as a forfeit by a player whose top, when spun, had remained within the boundary formed by the larger circle. It became the prize of the player who pegged it out of its small enclosure." JBK I, 147–8. EDD: *Save*; OED: 1654.

S10. *Save the mark*

NQ 1861, II/11: 429; 1872, IV/9: 350; 1874 V/2: 169, 215, 335–6, 437; 1878 V/9: 426; 1894 VIII/5: 363; 1894 VIII/6: 345, 431–2; 1895 VIII/7: 118, 373.

God save or *bless the mark* attracted so much attention because it occurs five times in Shakespeare, where it seems to mean "God forgive me for swearing." "The phrase has been explained as referring to archery. When the archer was seen to have aimed and shot well, and while the arrow was speeding in its course, the spectators, in their excitement, exclaimed, 'Save the mark!' or 'God save the mark!', intimating thereby that the mark was in imminent danger of being hit" (II/11: 429). Several interpretations can probably be disregarded, but the following note presents some interest: "It is a phrase which one hears frequently in Ireland, and the sense in which it is used exactly tallies with the two Shakespearean examples. It is employed sarcastically—also, I should say, in derisive mockery of pretensions ridiculously claimed, or the association of objects diametrically opposed or incongruously related . . . . I have extracted this explanation from 'Words, Facts, and Phrases,' by Eliezer Edwards: 'These words are connected with an old Irish superstition. If a person, on telling the story of some hurt or injury which another has received, should illustrate his narrative, by touching the corresponding part of his own, or his hearer's body, he averts the omen of similar injury by using as a sort of charm the words, *God save the mark*" (VIII/6: 345). A similar explanation appeared in V/9: 426, and the reference to an ironic sense was given in the editorial note in II/11: 429. In VIII/6: 432, several examples of the phrase are quoted. The author of the note finds the reference to archery plausible but disagrees with Brewer's explanation that people cried out, when an archer shot well, "God save the mark" to prevent any one coming after to hit the same mark, with people applying the formula ironically to a novice whose arrow is nowhere. This is the conclusion offered in V/2: 335–6: "Our ancestors conceived that by mentioning a calamity they rendered themselves liable to a visitation of it, and, therefore, tried to avert it by some pious ejaculation. 'God save the mark!' will, then, be equivalent to the *quod abominor* ['may it pass me by'] of the Roman." Perhaps, the author of the note writes, "during the visitations of the plague, our ancestors were in the habit of saying 'God save us from the mark!' meaning thereby the mark of the cross on the door, which indicated that the house was infected; that hence, in course of time, the expression came to mean God save us from any evil, whatever evil it might be the speaker was speaking of; also that in time 'God save me from the mark!' was corrupted into 'God save the mark!'?" The *OED* refutes the reference to archery and explains the phrase as a formula that originally served to avert an evil omen. It summarizes the note in VIII/7: 373, according to which midwives formerly said: "God bless (save) the mark at the birth of a child bearing a birthmark." Here is a more complete version of W. A. Henderson's explanation: "Among the superstitions of the past, birth-marks, &c., were regarded as prognostic of evil, and I am told that among the old school of female accoucheurs [midwives] it is still the custom at the birth of a marked child to use the phrase . . . . This I submit as a more reasonable explanation than that 'derived from the butts,' and, what is more, substantiated by actual evidence. The difficulty is, I think, in tracing the metamorphose of the blessing into a sarcasm. Guessing is to be reprehended, but I will venture. It is a common practice among ill-natured people to taunt and gibe at deformed humanity. May not this phrase, originally moulded for a prayer, in the mouth of these scoffers and jeerers have become as a very shibboleth of derision and mockery?" (p. 373). However, *mark* did have the sense 'omen'. OED: 1598.

S11. *Say bee to a battledore, to*
NQ 1870 IV/ 6: 164, 184, 262.

'(Not) to say boo to a goose'. *Bee* here stands for the letter B. The battledore may be the cardboard primer that succeeded the hornbook; *bee* is then the name of the letter. See *Cry bee to a battledore, to.* This explanation seems to be correct. OED: 1570 *(Hee knew not a B. from a battledore).*

S12. *Say nothing and saw wood, to*
ANQ 6, 1891: 197.

"During the past year or two the expression, 'say nothing and saw wood', has come into general use, the idea conveyed by it being to do a great deal of active work in a secret manner. It is used with regard to political work more than any other." The correspondent wondered where this recommendation could come from. The *OED* gives *to saw wood* (American slang) 'to attend to one's own affairs, to continue working steadily' and offers 1894, 1909, 1913 and 1933 citations.

S13. *Scarborough warning*
LA I, 1873: 306; NQ 1873, IV/12: 408; 1880 VI/1: 394; 1880 VI/2: 17, 258; 1887 VII/4: 308; 1915 XI/11: 46, 95, 136, 158, 233.

'Something falling without giving warning to those below; no warning at all' (as defined in VII/4: 308). It is an obsolete phrase of which two explanations are known. "One is that Thomas Stafford, 1557, with a few troops seized on Scarborough Castle, before the townsmen knew that he was near the place at all. The second is, that if ships passed the castle without saluting it, by lowering colours or striking sails, a shotted gun was fired into them by way at once of warning and penalty" (IV/12: 408). The first explanation going back to Fuller is disproved by chronology *(OED)*. In view of the correct date, the statement quoted in XI/11: 46 cannot be correct either but has some historical value: "In his 'History of Scarbrough'[sic], Joseph Brogden Baker notes that the sudden surprise of the castle in 1554 'gave rise to the proverb known as Scarbrough warning" (p. 69). The date (1546) was established by Vincent Stuckey Lean (XI/11: 158). The author gives several early quotations. The problem of origins is complicated by the existence of the phrase *a Skyreburn warning* (Galloway). The Skyreburn, as is clear from *-burn*, is a river. It is notorious for its unpredictable swelling, but it remains unclear how (if at all) the two phrases interacted. [It seems that MM III: 241, identified *Scarborough Warning* with *Halifax Law*. According to them, in Scarborough, Yorkshire, an offender caught in the act was summarilty dispatched, usually by hanging. Is there any connection with *Scotch Verdict*?] OED: 1546.

S14. *Schoolmaster is abroad*
NQ 1858, II/5: 107; 1888 VII/5: 108, 175, 335.

"This saying originated with Lord Brougham, and is thus reported in one of his speeches: 'Let the soldier be abroad, if he will; he can do nothing in this age. There is another personage abroad—a person less imposing—in the eyes of some, perhaps, insignificant. The schoolmaster is abroad; and I trust to him, armed with his primer, against the soldier in full military array'" (p. 107). The reference is to Lord Henry Brougham (1778-1868). The most detailed version is told on p. 175. [Hyamson, p. 307: "'Knowledge is universal'. The original meaning of the phrase was, however, the opposite, *viz.,* that the schoolmaster had packed up and left the country. The phrase was popularized by Lord Brougham in the House of Commons on the 29th January, 1828. See Knowles 2006, p. 74, on Oscar Wilde's punning treatment of this phrase.] OED: 1828.

S15. *Scoggins's heirs*

NQ 1869, IV/3: 484.

A quotation from Gerarde's *Herball* (1597) is given. The reference is to the stinking goosefoot *(Chenopodium vulvaria)*: "The whole plant is of a most loathsome savour or smel; upon which plant, if any should chance to rest and sleepe, he might very well report to his friends that he had reposed himself *among the chiefe of Scoggins' heirs.*" The following amusing editorial note follows the query: "The origin of the expression will be found in *The Jests of Scogin* (see Shakespeare Jest-Books, Second Series, p. 93). It is entitled "How Scogin and his Wife made an Heire," and is too ill-flavoured to be reproduced in the salubrious pages of *N & Q.*" Scoggins was a court fool to Edward IV (reigned from 1462), and this name became proverbial from 1573 on. *

S16. *Scotch prize*

NQ 1873, IV/12: 495.

An American correspondent to *NQ* quoted the following passage written by an officer in the army of the United States during the revolution in an account of the battle of Long Island: "We took Major Moncreiff, their commanding officer prisoner, but he was a Scotch prize to Ensign Brodhead, who took him, and had him in possession for some hours, but was obliged to surrender himself." The question about the meaning of the prize was not answered. The *OED* defines the phrase as 'taken in error, found to be worthless, or liable to cause problems for its captors'. [The use of *Scotch* is obviously derogatory. Cf. the next item.] The American provenance of the phrase seems likely. OED: 1776.

S17. *Scotch science*

NQ 1911 XI/4: 250.

'Main force and stupidity combined'. Apparently, slang, and a typical ethnic slur (Cf. the previous item), "well understood by mariners, particularly those of the deep sea, as distinguished from coasting men." The query about the origin of the phrase was not answered. *

S18. *Scotch verdict, a*

NQ 1896, VIII/9: 66.

The author, a Scotsman, never heard this American phrase. [Does it mean 'guilty'? Cf. *Seaborough warning.*]

S19. *Scrape (an) acquaintance, to*

NQ 1889 VII/7: 406; ANQ 3, 1889: 284.

'To worm oneself into somebody's acquaintance'. In ANQ, a story is told about a Roman soldier in a public bath scraping himself with a piece of tile and noticed there by the emperor Hadrian, *etc.* The anecdote is borrowed from "an interesting article" titled "Odd Phases in Some Popular Phrases," but the Latin phrase is not given. [Typical folk etymology.] The phrase may have originated "in bowing and scraping" to a person, in order to curry favor with him (as suggested in VII/7: 406). OED: 1600.

S20. *See the lions, to*
NQ 1855 I/11: 405.

'To see the most interesting sights'. The reference is to the menagerie in London (the most memorable sight in the capital for visitors from the provinces). Allegedly, the lions in the menagerie in the Tower of London were the first attraction shown to strangers (the same explanation in the *OED*); hence the verb *lionize*. OED: 1629.

S21. *Seldom comes a better*
NQ 1898 IX/2: 135, 266.

In *The Porter's Lodge,* this phrase is quoted as meaning approximately 'enjoy what you have', allegedly a "very sooth [true] proverb" (p. 135). On p. 266, the same proverb is given with reference to an old ballad (published in 1784) with *the* before *better*. OED: 1546 *(Seldom cometh the better).*

S22. *Send farthingales to broad gates in Oxford*
NQ 1859 II/8: 8.

Verdingale is an older (French) variant of *farthingale* 'broad hoop worn under a woman's dress'. The proverb mocked Pembroke College (Oxford), which received the name *Broad Gates* for the wide form of its entrances. Apperson: 1562.

S23. *Send Jack after yes, to*
NQ 1859 II/8: 484; 1860 II/9: 34.

The note on p. 484 says: "In the southern counties if a person in haste accidentally knocks down any article, and the fall of this knocks down a second, they say 'that's sending Jack after yes'. I should fancy it meant sending after yeast, which is often done in a hurry at baking times, if the haste only were alluded to; but why should it be only employed when one thing knocks down another?" Suprisingly, the idea that *yes* means *yeast* may be correct, for the author of the later note (p. 34) quotes Fielding's *Tom Thumb,* where sending Jack for mustard has a similar sense. [Or is it a case of folk etymology, an attempt to justify an incomprehensible word?] *

S24. *Send one to Coventry, to*
NQ 1852, I/6: 589–90; 1853, I/6: 318; 1874, V/1: 400; LA 2, 1874: 56–7; NQ 1878, V/10: 266; 1899 IX/4: 264, 335; 1922 XII/10: 251; 1925, 149: 8, 33.

'To ostracize'. In I/6: 318, the following explanation is offered. "If a soldier was found to be a coward he was sent to Coventry, as being a central town of England, and a place where he was least likely to be exposed to the terrors of an unfriendly army." According to another conjecture (also I/6: 318), *Coventry* is a folk etymological alternation of French *couvent* 'convent' (one is allegedly sent there for seclusion). The editor adds his own hypothesis: "The best explanation of this expression is that given in *The Beauties of England and Wales,* vol. xv. Part ii. P. 168. 'The inhabitants of Coventry were formerly most decidedly averse from any correspondence with the military quartered within their limits. A female known to speak to a man in a scarlet coat became directly the object of town scandal. So rigidly indeed did the natives abstain from communication with all who bore his Majesty's military commission, that officers were here confined to the interchanges of the mess-room; and in the mess-room the term of 'sending a man to Coventry', if you wish to shut him from society, probably originated.' [No evidence is given for either explanation.] In I/6: 589–90, Hutton's *History of Birmingham* is quoted: "The day after Charles I left Birmingham, on his march from Shrewsbury, in 1642, the parliamentary party seized the carriages, containing the royal plate and furniture, which they conveyed for security to Warwick Castle. They apprehended all messengers and suspected persons, and frequently attacked and reduced small parties of the Royalists, whom they sent prisoners to Coventry. Hence the expression respecting a refractory person, *send him to Coventry*." The correspondent writing in 1899 (p. 264) found the quotations in the *OED* insufficient and offered the following: "It occurs in a letter from Marlborough to Harley, of 29 Aug., 1707, among the Marlborough despatches at the Record Office: 'If Mons de Focsani be weary of Coventry, where he has been alone I believe these tenn months, I know no reason why he may not remove to Lichfield if the Queen please to allow it: he desired himself to be sent to Coventry to avoid being with the French'." The same query appeared in 1925. It produced one response, namely that *Coventry* stands for *quarantine.* [It is not improbable that the phrase was coined with reference to some such word (*coven tree* or *quareanteen*), wich was later "folk etymologized" into *Coventry.* Cf. the history of *Scarborough warning* and the next item. The Internet offers another array of derivations. One is obviously sent to Coventry or Putney for punishment. The *OED* mentions "numerous ingenious conjectures" and favors the one given in 1703: "At Cromichan, a town so generally wicked, that it had risen upon small parties of the kings, and kill'd, or taken them prisoners, and sent them to Coventry [then strongly held for the parliament]." JBK II, 5. OED: *a*1691.

S25. *Send one to Putney, to*
NQ 1925, 149: 9.

See *Send one to Coventry, to.* One can also be sent to Putney on a pig. [*Pig* might have been added for the sake of alliteration.] *

S26. *Service is no inheritance*
NQ 1854 I/9: 20, 41.

"This proverbial saying has evidently arisen from the old manorial right, under which the lord of the manor claimed suit and service and fealty before admitting the heir to his inheritance, or the purchaser to his purchase. On which occasion, the party admitted to the estate, whether purchaser or heir, 'fecit fidelitatem suam et solvit relevium'['swore his fealty and paid his relief']; the relief being generally a year's rent or service" (p. 20). The *OED* gives two citations from 1631 and 1745.

S27. *Set the cap, to*
NQ 1935, 169: 391, 427; 1936, 170: 214, 268, 286, 305; 57, 2010, 336-7.

'The phrase used by a woman about a man when she wishes to become engaged to him'. According to Weekley's etymological dictionary, this is one of many nautical metaphors (French *mettre le cap sur* 'to turn the ship'). Likewise, *to hang (up) one's cap* is said about a wooer who begins to pay court to a woman (it can also be applied to a woman having matrimonial intentions), but there does not seem to be any connection between the two phrases.

EDD: *Cap*; The *OED* gives nearly the same definition and adds: *colloquial* ("said of a woman who sets herself to gain the affection of a man"). The earliest citation for *to set the cap* is dated to 1823. The 2010 note is a sad example of modern etymologizing. The author offered the same explanation as Weekley and presented it as a novel idea.

S28. *Set the Thames on fire, to*
NQ 1865 III/7: 239; 1870 IV/6: 39, 101, 144, 223; 1873 IV/12: 80, 119, 137; NQ 1883 VI/8: 446, 476; 1884 VI/9: 14, 156; 1885 VI/12: 360; 1888 VII/6: 166; 1894 VIII/6: 502–3; 1895 VIII/7: 69; 1921 XII/8: 331, 378, 416; LA 1, 1873: 208; MCNNQ 1, 1878: 271.

'To work wonders; to distinguish oneself'. In the saying *he will never set the Thames on fire,* some people took *Thames* for *temes* 'sieve', and the variant emerged *he will never set the sieve on fire.* This odd interpretation gave rise to a long and fruitless discussion about the flammability of sieves. In VIII/6: 502–3, F. Adams gives numerous analogs of rivers on fire in other languages. JBK II, 15. OED: 1720.

S29. *Set up one's rest, to*
NQ 1907 X/7: 53, 175; 1912 XI/6: 347.

'To make up one's mind; to pause for rest, to halt' (probably obsolete). Skeat comments: "Fully explained in Nares's 'Glossary.' From the game of primero, meaning to stand upon the cards you have in your hand, in the hope that they may win. In playing *vingt-un* a player is similarly said 'to stand'. It means then to be satisfied with, to rely upon as sufficient, to be content . . . . Nares gives fifteen examples" (p. 53). On p. 347, the rules of the game are explained in detail. OED: 1572.

S30. *Seven and nine*
NQ 1909 X/11: 497.

"The American phrase 'seven-by-nine' is generally applied to a laugh or smile of latitude more than usually benignant, as if measuring the length and width thereof and at the same time playing upon the word *benign*." Cf. the next entry. *

S31. *Seven by nine politician*
NQ 1909 X/11: 410; 1909 X/12: 38.

This appears to be an Americanism: 'a politician who cuts some figure'. "In old times window-panes were made of this size in inches, and this may be the case now" (p. 410). The definition quoted above came from an Englishman. But on p. 38, a correspondent from Connecticut gave an apparently more precise explanation. A seven-by-nine politician is a man "of too limited abilities, force, or outlook to cut much of any. The phrase refers to the old-fashioned window-panes, before the time when glass filling the whole or half of the sash was common; these were 'seven by nine' in hundreds of thousands of farm or village houses . . . . Its nearest synonym is 'peanut' politician, that is, bearing the same relation to large political ideas and plans as a peanut vendor, or huckster of peanuts and roast chestnuts in a pushcart, does to large mercantile activities. Neither name implies a low position or importance: only the pettiness of the issues which form the staple of the activities . . . . Similar names are 'two-cent' or 'two-for-a-cent' ('ha-penny' comes just between) or 'huckleberry' (whortleberry) politician:

the last having the same implication as 'peanut'—one who peddles huckleberries by the quart." Cf. the preceding entry. *

S32. *Sham Abraham, to*
NQ 1850 I/5: 442; 1907 X/7: 469; 1907 X/8: 293, 395, 477; 1908 X/9: 37, 417; 1912 XI/6: 269.

'To feign madness or sickness'. The 1752 citation in the *OED* explains: "A cant sea phrase when a sailor is unwilling to work on pretence of sickness." Up to here the editor's note refers to *Abraham-man* 'a logger claiming to have been released on license from the hospital of St. Mary of Bethlehem in London . . . or any similar institution . . .' (that is, from Bedlam) (NQ I/5, 442). Abraham seems to have been the name of the ward in which deranged patients are confined, "It is said that on certain occasions, as of holidays, those inmates who were not too incapacitated had permission to visit their friends outside the hospital, while those who had no friends begged about the streets. The ridicule to which the latter class were subjected by the young and ignorant excited pity on their behalf, and to be an Abraham Man was soon found by the vagrant to be a profitable vocation, with the results that idiocy, and the Bethlem dress which indicated it, became too fashionable, and unscrupulous persons were said to 'sham Abraham', until the offence was punished by the whipping-post and confinement in the stocks. In 'King Lear' the country gave Edgar 'proof and precedent of Bedlam beggars' when he borrowed 'Poor Tom's' dress for the purpose of disguise (Act II. Sc. III). But it has yet to be explained. Why the particular ward in Bethlem Hospital was named the Abraham ward. Who was this Abraham? Or was the name of the ward adopted in allusion to the beggar Lazarus being 'carried by the angels into Abraham's bosom'?" (X/8: 293). The following may also be of interest: "During the year 1752 this expression became a familiar catchword. At the Old Bailey Sessions, which began on 18 February, one James Lowry, captain of the merchant ship Molly, was condemned to death 'for the murder of Kenric Hossack, on board the said ship, by whipping him to death'. Two other sailors had been flogged to death by this cruel skipper, who was wont to salute his dying victims with the remark, 'He is only shamming Abraham'. Lowry was hanged at Execution Dock on 25 March, 1752, in the presence of a furious mob, who taunted him with the cry, 'He's shamming Abraham'" (X/9: 417). OED: 1752.

S33. *She's the cat's mother*
NQ 1878 V/9: 402, 494; 1878 V/10: 77, 239; 1879 V/12: 396.

This facetious phrase was used when a child spoke of some woman without naming her. It is like asking: "Who's she?" But in Yorkshire, the same phrase was used "for confusion of reference" and considered vulgar. *Aunt* and *grandmother* were occasionally substituted for *mother,* and on p. 396 *he's the cat's father* is cited. OED: 1878.

S34. *Ship-shape and Bristol fashion*
NQ 1885 VI/11: 26, 118; 1914 XI/9: 446; 1923 XIII/1: 358; MM 30, 1944: 166 (2); MM 31, 1945: 46 (2); MM 32, 1946: 127 (2).

This is the greatest praise of a ship known and is current on both sides of the Atlantic. MM 31: 46 (2) gives reference to NQ XIII:1. In vol. 32, the following is added: "This river at . . . low tide dries out to 6 in. As a result of this, ships which were built at Bristol, and indeed any ships which were likely to have to go up to Bristol for loading, were built with extra stout timbers to withstand the structural strain resultant on drying out at the wharves. This was known as building ships 'Bristol fashion'; doubtless the full expression 'All shipshape and Bristol fashion' was merely a touch of local pride, bearing in mind the preeminence of Bristol as a port at the period in question." *Shipshape* is often spelled as one word. The hotels Bristol on the continent were apparently named after the marqueses of Bristol. EDD: *Ship*; OED: 1840.

S35. *Shoe the goose, to*
NQ 1871 IV/8: 335.
'To trifle away one's time' (not 'to be tipsy' as it is sometimes understood). The phrase is obsolete. EDD: *Shoe*; OED: 14 . . .

S36. *Shoot one's bolt, to*
NQ 1939, 177: 334, 412.
'To have done all that one can do'. The bolt (NQ 177, p. 334) "is doubtless—originally—the quarrel of the crossbow (should not the full phrase be 'shoot his last bolt'?"). The *OED* has a similar phrase dated to *a*1100. [The proverb *a fool's bolt is soon shot* goes back to at least *a*1225].

S37. *Shoot the guy, to*
NQ 1884 VI/10: 426.
'To ring the bell on the fifth of November' (in commemoration of the Gunpowder Plot). EDD: *Shoot.* *

S38. *Shoot the moon, to*
NQ 1869 IV/3: 383; 1903 IX/12: 107.
'To run away without paying'. The *OED* definition is 'to remove household goods by night in order to avoid seizure for rent'. The correspondent to *NQ* (1869) wrote that the Swiss have an identical slang expression (in French): "Il a fusillé la lune ('He shot the moon')"; however, he offered no explanation of the phrase. EDD: *Moon*; OED: 1812 *(bolt the moon)*.

S39. *Shoot the sun, to*
MM 86, 2000: 88 (2); 332 (2); 476 (2).
'To take the solar meridional altitude with a sextant or a quadrant'. The earliest reference to this measurement is said to go back to 1580. Quite probably, Coleridge, while writing his *Rime of the Ancient Mariner,* knew it too. OED: 1861.

S40. *Short-day money*
NQ 1877 V/7: 66.
'The money given to poor widows as alms on St. Thomas's Day, the shortest day of the year'. (Possibly, individual usage.) *

S41. *Show must go on, the*
ANQ 2, 1942: 73; ANQ 2, 1943: 159.
'Regardless of what happens, the show will not be cancelled'. This cry is said to have been coined in the circus (US), but the date of its origin remains unknown. OED: 1862.

S42. *Show the white feather, to*

NQ 1857 II/3: 198, 237.

'To show cowardice'. "The appearance of a white feather in the fine plumage of a gamecock was considered as evidence against the purity of his breeding. Hence the stigma." On p. 198, it is argued that fear makes people and animals turn white (hence, allegedly the saying). JBK I, 168. The *OED* confirms the first explanation (initially given as slang by Grose, 1785: *he has a white feather, he is a coward*). OED: 1829.

S43. *Side-pocket to a toad*

NQ 1873 IV/12: 385, 435; 1874 V/1: 18.

'Something useless'. This is part of the phrase *no more use than a side-pocket to a toad*. Also, *he is as proud as a toad with a side-pocket* has been recorded. Gloucestershire. Cf. *Have no more use (for something) than a dog (or monkey) has for side-pockets, to*. OED: 1828 (this phrase with *dog* instead of *toad* is dated to 1788).

S44. *Sing old Rose and burn the bellows*

NQ 1860 II/9: 72, 264; 1870 IV/7: 187, 272; 1892 VIII/2: 527; 1893 VIII/3: 77, 173, 256.

'A call to rejoicing amid an accident'. Only two uncertain conjectures on the origin of the saying appeared (*Bellows = Bella* or *old rose* 'the name of a horse'). The *OED* quotes a passage from 1780, which is also reproduced in the note on p. 264, copied from *The British Apollo*. In the West of England, it used to be one of the "commonest expressions of jollity, or devil-may-care hilarity" (VIII/3: 256). Consider the following discussion "[It] is a general expression for depraved and drunken conduct. Its origin is involved in considerable obscurity, but has been attributed to the name of one George Rose, sometime M.P. for Christchurch, 'equally celebrated for his vocal abilities and his wanton destruction of furniture when in a state of excitement.' It has been further suggested that it is the outcome of the cries of schoolboys, when holidays are announced: 'Let's singe old Rose and burn libellos'; that is, 'Let's singe the hair of old Rose the schoolmaster and burn our books'—make high holiday, in fact. Others seem inclined to believe that a reference is made to the hostess, Old Rose, of an inn, the 'Ram' at Nottingham, noted at one time for the convivial excesses of its frequenters." Brewer (at *Sing Old Rose*) also suggested that *burn the bellows* was the boys' "perversion" of *burn libellos* ('burn the books'). JBK II, 121. OED: 1766 (the full phrase).

S45. *Sing Whillelujah (or Willalew) to the day-nettles, to*

NQ 1875 V/3: 328, 454; 1875 V/4: 336; 1876 V/4: 336.

This expression was used in Ireland when speaking disrespectfully of someone who is dead. *Day-nettle* is apparently an alteration of *dead-nettle* (Ulster), believed to cause a disease in cattle. *Willalew* (elsewhere in Ireland, *pullalew*) is the "Irish cry" at funerals. EDD: *Whillaloo; Day-nettle ~ dead-nettle* appears in the *OED*, along with *dea-nettle,* but not in connection with this phrase. *

S46. *Sit between two stools, to*

NQ 1872 IV/10: 181.

'To vacillate between two different courses of action'. The note discusses several possible meanings of the idiom, cites analogs in modern and old languages, and compares *sit between two stools* and *fall between two stools*. The *OED* has *between tou Stoles*: 1390 and; *fall*: 1857.

S47. *Sixty-four dollar question*

ANQ 4, 1944: 64.

'A crucial question expressing the basic issue on a problematic subject'. This phrase "originated with the form in which questions are asked in 'Take It or Leave It,' the raido feature sponsored by Eversharp, Inc. Seven questions are posed, and if answered correctly, they pay the contestants in a rising (doubling) scale—that is, one dollar, two, four, eight, sixteen, thirty-two, and finally sixty-four dollars. The first Eversharp Columbia Network program presenting 'Take It or Leave It' took place on Sunday, April 21, 1940." OED: 1942.

S48. *Skeleton in every house*

NQ 1850 I/2: 231.

In the editor's note, the phrase is derived from an Italian story. The *OED* notes that *"a skeleton in the closet,* etc. was brought into literary use by Thackeray [1845] but known to have been current at an earlier date." Cf. the next item. OED: 1845.

S49. *Skeleton in the cupboard*

NQ 1889 VII/8: 347, 413; 1947, 192: 524.

'A family secret'. The note on p. 524 questions the idea that the phrase originated with doctors. In VII/8: 347, a note by James A. H. Murray appeared: ("What is the origin of the expression?"). Cf. the previous item. OED: 1859.

S50. *Skyreburn warning*

NQ 1915 XI/11: 95, 136, 158.

See *Scarborough warning.*

S51. *Sleep like a top, to*

NQ 1859 II/8: 53, 97–8; 1874 V/2: 200, 220, 354.

'To be fast asleep'. A spinning top looks immobile, and this fact has often been cited as explaining the idiom (II/8: 97–8). Another etymology connects *top* with Italian *tope* 'mouse', also 'doormouse' (thus, 'sleep like a dorrmouse' (II/8: 53), and the French also say *il dort comme un taupe,* but *taupe* means 'mole' (the French for "dormouse" is *loir*), while *top* is 'toupie' in French (V/2: 220). Both II/8: 97–9 and V/2: 220 cite the French simile *il dort comme un sabot* (*sabot* 'wooden shoe' and 'whipping top'). OED: 1693.

S52. *Sleep the sleep of the just, to*

NQ 1887 VII/4: 408; 1888 VII/5: 47, 96, 176, 235, 373; 1889 VII/7: 469; 1889 VII/8: 39, 358; 1903 IX/12: 131.

Strangely, the origin of this familiar phrase has not been found. It does not occur in this form in the Bible. OED: 1848 (Thackeray).

S53. *Sleepy hollow*

NQ 1893 VIII/4: 347; 1894 VIII/5: 273.

This place was made famous by Washington Irving. Here is part of the description given by a correspondent from New Brighton, N. Y., on p. 273: "Lying on the east bank of the Hudson River, about twenty-five miles from New York City . . . it is situated within the bounds of the village of Tarrytown, a mile and a half from that station. A gentle declivity in the road leads one down into the hollow, where are found Sleepy Hollow Cemetery and Church. I cannot say how long the place has been known as Sleepy Hollow, but it is certainly for more than a century, perhaps for more than two—the name having been first given by the old Dutch settlers." OED: 1820.

S54. *Sleeveless errand*

NQ 1850 I/1: 439; 1852 I/5: 473; 1855 I/12: 58, 481, 520; 1887 VII/3: 6, 74, 391; 1887 VII/4: 38; 1895 VIII/7: 227; 1912 XI/5: 445; 1912 XI/6: 16, 73–4; *The Athenæum* 1903, 2: 220.

'A useless endeavor'. The phrase was discussed in old dictionaries in the entry *sleeveless*. Todd in Johnson-Todd added to the literal sense ('wanting sleeves') the following: 'Wanting propriety; without a cover or pretense'. Horne Tooke wrote the same: 'Without a cover or pretense' (I/5: 473). The note in I/12: 58 cites Chaucer's *sleevelesse wordes* and other authors. The correspondent referred to *sleeve* 'to divide or separate', but he confused *sleeve* with *sleave* 'to divide by separation into filaments'; *sleeve* goes back to *sliefe ~ slefe*. Consequently, his etymology is worthless. In VII/3: 74, Walter W. Skeat confirmed the antiquity of the adjective and showed that *sleeveless* had not always gone with *errand*. He suggested "a reference to the herald's tabard or sleeveless coat, with the idea that the message on which a herald was sent was of no avail." And indeed, *sleeveless* meant 'useless'. Sleeves, that is, sleeve pockets, were used equally with hose pockets for placing valuables and other matters (VII/3: 6), so that *sleeveless* might have signified 'devoid of value' (VII/3: 391). The sleeve was a significant part of a knight's apparel. The example is "the Norman baronial family of Hauten-Coigniers, who bore a maunder, or sleeve on their shield." (VIII/7: 227.) The correspondent to *The Athenæum* referred to the "custom associated with envoys, to which reference is made" in the *Mabinogion*: "Now this was the guise in which the messengers journeyed; one sleeve was on the cap of each of them in front, as a sign that they were messengers, in order that through what hostile land soever they might pass no harm might be done them." Ernest Weekley (XI/5: 445) suggested an original connection of *glove* and *errand,* because "the sleeve as a symbol was interchangeable with the glove." The reference was allegedly to a reward, especially that given to a messenger in the shape of a pair of sleeves. He wrote "I do not see any great difficulty in supposing that *sleeveless errand,* that is, fool's errand, for which the messenger receives derision or ill-treatment in place of the regular reward, is connected with this French *manche* or Italian *mancia,* but I should like to be able to strengthen my hypothesis by an instance of a 'pair of sleeves' used for a 'pair of gloves' in the sense of gratuity." In his dictionary, the word *sleeveless* does not appear. [In chapter 6 of Wolfram's *Parzival,* one sleeve of Obilot's gown is removed as a gift to Gawan. If this gift reflected widespread practice, a *sleeveless errand* might refer to an adventure in which a knight received no reward.] Though probably of not much use, the following comment may be noted: "If, as Todd says, 'sleeveless' means 'wanting reasonableness, propriety, solidity', may it not be connected with an expression I used to hear in my boyhood, which, I think, came from the Royal Navy, which characterized talk deficient in those respects as 'like a soldier's coat without sleeves'?" (XI/6: 74). [Holt, p. 292, after mentioning Brewer's explanation, writes the following: "Others have found that the French have used their word for sleeve, *manche,* to mean a tip, just as the expression 'a pair of gloves' has been (this is supported by an Italian equivalent for *poverboire, mancia* 'a penny for drink') or that a Teutonic root for 'sleeve' meant dull, inactive, blunt [What word could he have in mind?]. The most plausible explanation I have seen is that envoys used to wear sleeves on their helmets, just as knights often wore similar tokens in honor of their girl-friends. An envoy without an identifying sleeve, his "credentials," was likely to be turned back with his errand unaccomplished." He says that the phrase was popularized by being the title of a recent novel. In his book, he made wide use of *NQ,* that "unique little magazine" and the "clearing-house of very miscellaneous information" (p. VI of the preface) but, unfortunately, hardly ever indicated the pages he used. His mention of chivalry does not quite replicate the information in *NQ.* The novel by Morah R. C. James (he does not mention the title) was banned in England as obscene, which contributed to its popularity. Needless to say, *bootless* in the phrase *bootless errand* has nothing to do with boots!] Cf. *Pin one's faith upon somebody else's sleeve.* JBK I, 107–8. EDD: *Sleeveless;* OED: 1546.

S55. *Smell a rat, to*
NQ 1918 XII/4: 187; 1929, 156: 295, 339.

'To suspect treason'. Vol. 156, p. 339 warns against "folk etymology" in the study of the origin of idioms and proverbs. A curious instance of the similarity in sense and also in sound: Engl. *rat* ~ German *Unrat* is cited on p. 187: German *Unrat wittern* (*Unrat* 'garbage'). [Hyamson, p. 279: "In allusion to a cat smelling the proximity of a rat."] JBK, 128. OED: *a*1540.

S56. *Smile like a basket of chips, to*
NQ 1871 IV/7: 9, 132.

This is said about smiling of habit and unconsciously. Another version has *bundle* instead of *basket.* It "was a very common saying in south-east Cornwall from thirty to forty years ago. The words 'under a dog's arm' were not unfrequently added to it." OED: 1788 *(He grins like a basket of chips).*

S57. *Smother in the lode and worry in the hose, to*
NQ 1877 V/8: 408, 433; 1878 V/9: 74; 1878 V/10: 273; 1879 V/11: 117.

'To nip in the bud'. The phrase is probably from the use of mining terms: *worry* 'to choke', *hose* 'the shaft by which the mineral is brought to the open surface'. *Lode* means 'drain' (explained in detail in V/11: 117), a term, used chiefly in Lincolnshire and Norfolk (perhaps preserved as Load in some place names). *Hose* is said to be the same word as *hause* 'gorge, neck' (p. 273). The author of the note on p. 273 glosses the idiom as meaning that "the conspiracy was stifled in its secret progress, as if rolled along in a drain; rendered nugatory, but not finally crushed till at the outlet, by violent seizure, tearing, and throttling, as vermin by dogs and ferrets." The reference to the conspiracy was in answer to the phrase quoted on p. 408: "and that complot likely to be smothered in the loode and worried in the hose." (The explanation on p. 433 is irrelevant: *loode* allegedly meaning *loags* 'stockings'). *

S58. *Soft sawder*
NQ 1857, II/3: 108, 139.

'Flattery'. Explained correctly as *soft solder* (II/3: 139). "Coppersmiths and brass workers, as well as goldsmiths, have two descriptions of *solder*: one of hard metal, which is the genuine article; one of the *soft* amalgam, which only holds together for the moment, but yields to the first strain. Flattery, like 'soft solder', or as it is vulgarly pronounced, *sawder,* is the mere deception meant to be implied by the figure, which has pressed this term into its service." The earlier comment (II/3: 108) suggests that *sawder* means *sawyer* and quotes the journal *Assamblée Nationale* to this effect ('a sawyer who leans lazily on his saw and gets through very little work'). [This is a groundless suggestion], but the *OED* confirms that the phrase was introduced by Judge Halliburton in his *Sam Slick* and thus originated in the US or Canada. OED: 1836.

S59. *Soft words butter no parsnips*
NQ 1893 VIII/4: 480; 1894 VIII/5: 174.

See *Fine words butter no parsnips.*

S60. *Sold down the river*
ANQ 2, 1942: 85, 138; ANQ 3, 1943: 46.

'Betrayed and deserted'. The question was asked in connection with the baseball expression *sold down the river* (meaning 'retired from a major league'). The answers unanimously pointed to the time when slaves were auctioned to plantations in the southern states and transported down the Ohio River and the Mississippi. Perhaps the popularity of the phrase is due to the description in *Uncle Tom's Cabin.* OED: colloquial, originally U.S., 1921.

S61. *Sole is the bread and butter of fish*
NQ 1897, VIII/11: 448.

"The meaning is that, as every one likes bread and butter, and returns to it with pleasure after partaking of other food, so in regards to sole, it is a fish which suits all tastes, and to which people, after tiring of salmon, turbot, whitebait, often revert, and never tire of having it put before them at their meals." The saying was known to the correspondent from Cornwall, and he wondered whether it had any currency elsewhere. *

S62. *So long*
NQ 1921 XII/9: 419; 1925 148: 210, 232.

'Good-bye'. The notes deal only with the dating of the phrase. "It was the invariable formula of leave-taking among young people in Dundee by 1875 at the latest" (p. 210). "I heard this expression first early in 1875, when in Colombia (S.A.). It was in constant use amongst the Cornish, Welsh and English miners as an equivalent to *Hasta luego,* the usual Spanish form to taking leave" (p. 232). The phrase may perhaps have a foreign origin, but hardly German. The first edition of the *OED* wrote: "Compare German *so lange,*" but *so lange* means only 'as (so) long as.' The following note appeared in 1921: "About twenty years ago I was told that it is allied to Samuel Pepys's expression 'so home', and should be written 'so along' or 'so long', meaning that the person using the expression must go his way." OED: 1865.

S63. *Sow one's wild oats, to*
NQ 1852 I/5: 227, 306; 1956 II/12: 229.

'To leave the excesses of one's young days behind'. On p. 306, the correspondent writes: "In Kent, if a person has been talking at random, it is not uncommon to hear it said, 'you are talking *havers*', or *folly*. Now I find in an old dictionary that the word *havers* means *oats*; and therefore I conclude, that the phrase *to sow one's wild oats* means nothing more than 'to sow folly'." [*Haver* does mean 'oats,' but no evidence points to *oats* as a common synonym for 'folly'.] The note on p. 229 cites the Danish proverb *Loki is now sowing his oats,* equivalent to *The Devil is sowing his tares.* The proverb was known to Jacob Grimm [and is often mentioned in later works on Scandinavian mythology and folklore.] Could it really be that *wild oats* 'mischief' is of Scandinavian origin, with reference to a person who once behaved like the evil god Loki but his misdeeds belong to the past? Is this the reason the phrase cannot be used in any other tense form, such as *He will grow up and will stop sowing his wild oats* or *Many people sow their wild oats and repent*? [Hyamson, pp. 323–4: "The word 'oats' has two allusions: (1) to the spirit given by a diet of oats to horses; (2) to the parable of the sower." It is unclear how either allusion sheds light on the idioms that Hyamson glosses as 'to give free rein to the calls of youth'.] JBK I, 200. OED: 1576.

S64. *Speak by the card, to*
NQ 1862 III/2: 503; 1863 III/3: 38; III/4: 56

'To express oneself clearly'. The phrase first turned up in *Hamlet* V.1:134 and has been discussed in all annotated editions of the play. It is not known whether Shakespeare coined the phrase and whether *speak by the card* is an idiom. But *by the card,* most probably, is. The reference might be to the shipman's card or *card* 'chart'. To *speak by the card* has been compared with *speak by the book.* *

S65. *Speak in lutestring*
NQ 1851 I/3: 188; 1853 I/8: 356, 523; 1879 V/12: 287, 413; 1880 VI/1: 121–2; VI/2: 256.

As explained in the *OED, lutestring* 'a string of a lute' was "assimilated to *lustring* ' a glossy silk fabric'. The enigmatic phrase appears only in the Junius letters (Letter 47, May 28, 1771), and, since no one else seems to have used it, it was probably Junius's neologism. The meaning, as the *OED* states, is obscure. It is impossible to decide whether the reference is to the chords of two instruments sounding in unison or to the fabric. Therefore, the allusion could be to the speech of an imitator or (ironically) to suspicious sweetness. Both senses probably would come out as ironic. OED: 1771.

S66. *Spick and span*
NQ 1851 I/3: 330, 480; 1852 I/5: 521; 1869 IV/4: 512; 1900 IX/6: 307.

'Bright, clean and tidy; spruce, neat'. This phrase appears in all etymological and explanatory dictionaries at the first word. Its analogs mean 'brand-new', as though "fresh from the fire (mint)," rather than "spruce." Numerous improbable derivations of both *spick* and *span* have been offered, including some from Italian and Latin. But the phrase is Germanic. *Span* means 'chip, splinter', and the idea must have been 'fresh as a chip sawed off from a block of wood'. *Spick* is an archaic doublet of *spike,* perhaps 'bright, shining as a new nail'. The English phrase is very close to the Swedish and strongly reminiscent of the Norwegian one, but those may not be native, for Old Icelandic had only *spánnýr* (*spán* corresponds to Engl. *span* in the idiom; *nýr* 'new'). It is Dutch that has *spijk* in this phrase. Yet it remains unclear how *spijk* made its way into Scandinavian and English, unless we assume that the phrase became part of the lingua franca of migratory workmen (carpenters? joiners?), a hybrid of two compounds. Among the older suggestions, the one referring to spinning ("freshly spun") enjoyed special popularity, but it lacks foundation. The string *spick and span new* must have been too long, so that *new* was discarded, and only *spick and span* remained, with a changed meaning. Analogous binomials occurred in late Middle English, but *spick and span* in this form goes back to the 17th century. [Hyamson, pp. 324–5, lists five etymologies of the idiom. The last two are: (4) "from spike, a sixteenth part of a yard, implying therefore, of a suit of clothes, fresh from the tailor," and (5) "from the spannans (stretchers) and the spikes (hooks) on which cloth was hung."] OED: 1665.

S67. *Spit(ten) image*

NQ 1894 VIII/5: 200; 1895 VIII/7: 487; 1895 VIII/8: 53, 213. AS 5, 1930: 209; 79, 2004: 33–58. Verbatim: 1976, 3/3: 12.

'A nearly indistinguishable likeness.' Most often the end of the phrase is *of his (her) father.* The discussion centered on which variant is correct or at least preferable: *spit image, spitting image, spittin image, spit and image,* or even *spit and spirit.* Laurence R. Horn (2004) examined the relevant material and concluded that the most likely initial form was *spitten image,* with *spitten* being an irregular past participle of the verb *spit.* The collocation *spitten image* could be easily reanalyzed as *spittin' image* and *spit an' image. Spit and spirit* is then a late alteration. [No one seems to have noted that in Shakespeare's days and some time later *spirit* was pronounced as the monosyllable *sprit* and could be confused with *spurt*; hence *spirit* 'sperm' as in Sonnet 129 and elsewhere. *Spit and spurt* looks like a plausible tautological binomial of the *safe and sound* type.] With regard to the origin of the phrase, Horn refers to spittle being equated with semen (therefore, always of . . . *father,* but never . . . *mother*). This leaves the shortest variants *the spit image of* or simply *the spit of* unexplained. Mossé (1930) derived the English phrase from French *c'est lui tout craché de son père* (*cracher* 'to spit': 'he is the very spit of his father'). Horn missed the discussion of the phrase in *NQ* and *Verbatim,* while Norman R. Shapiro (in *Verbatim*) missed Mossé and cited the same French analog. The article in *Verbatim* gives sixteenth- and seventeenth-century examples, though not exactly of the same phrase, in French, Spanish, and English, but of the same idea (*as like him as if he had been spit* [sic] *out of his mouth*); equating expectoration and ejaculation occurred to people quite naturally. The French phrase turns up in Voltaire (NQ VIII/5: 200) and much earlier (1665) in La Fontaine (Horn, p. 47). Horn (pp. 45–6) cites almost identical phrases from a dozen European languages, and the letter in NQ VIII/8: 53 also cites a few. [It is quite unlikely that they should have been coined independently everywhere, though the image, with reference to other bodily fluids, notably, to mucus (so in the Scandinavian languages) and (!) excrements (in some parts of

Germany), as indicated by Horn, is easy to explain. Not improbably, unless the source happens to be found in Greek, Latin, or some popular religious sources, the phrase was coined in France and spread in several variants far and wide.] EDD: *Spit*; OED: 1878 *(Spitten picter)*.

S68. *Spoil the ship for a ha'porth of tar, to*

NQ 1897 VIII/11: 307, 331, 515; 1912 XI/5: 468; 1912 XI/6: 54; 1925, 149: 99; 1967, 212: 189; MM 1912 II/: 88; MM 3, 1913: 253 (50).

'To spoil an enterprise by trying to save in a small matter of detail'. Most authors suggest that *ship* is the local pronunciation of *sheep,* the fact highlighted by dialectologists and the authors of fiction. The note in vol. 212 gives Sheridan's (1811) version of this idiom. As late as 1897 (VIII/11: 307), James A. H. Murray was not sure whether *ship* in this saying should be understood as *sheep*. In the responses, the merger of *ship ~ sheep* in some dialects was confirmed, and a quotation with a pun from *Love's Labour's Lost* (II: 1, 219) was given. However, the author of the note in VIII/11: 307 insisted that the idiom originated in the nautical rather than agricultural milieu. MM also addresses an example of the pun on *sheep ~ ship* from *Love's Labour's Lost*. OED: "Originally referring to the use of tar to protect destructive attacks of fleas. (*Sheep* is dialectally pronounced *ship* over a great part of England)." OED: 1631 *(Rather . . . to lose ten sheepe, than be at the charge of a halfe penny worth of Tarre)*.

S69. *Spring captain*

NQ 1884 VI/10: 89, 233, 315; 1885 VI/11: 13.

The phrase is so explained on p. 233: "'An old salt', who through age or sickness is only able to follow his avocation at sea during the summer season. Many of these men command excursion steamers, which are laid up during the winter months." But the phrase could have broader ramifications, as follows from the note on p. 315: "Some twenty years ago this term was familiar to me as applied to young men, especially military officers, who came up to London in the spring for the Epsom and Ascot races, cut a dash during that period, and then disappeared, usually owing money for racing debts. As well-dressed young men were the commonly styled 'Captain' when spoken to by book-makers offering to make bets, the origin of the expression seems obvious, while the circumstances generally attending their departure will account for the contemptuous way in which it is used." Perhaps there was a vague European background for the phrase, because (as pointed out on p. 13) "in the Prussian army the officer of the Landwehr and of the Reserves, summoned for the duty in their respective regiments during six weeks in summer, used to be called 'summer Lieutenants'." Thackeray used the phrase in a contemptuous sense (p. 89). *

S70. *Square head*

NQ 1881 VI/3: 108, 294.

To have a square head on one's shoulders means 'to be a smart man'. The idiom has a counterpart in French, but was known in popular speech in England. The reference could be to *square* 'fair, of good quality'. OED: 1890.

S71. *Stabbed by a Bridport dagger*
NQ 1856 II/1: 323.

'Hanged'. "Originated from the quantity of hemp which was formerly grown in that part of the county of Dorset." *

S72. *Stand buff, to*
NQ 1860, II/9: 5.

'To stand firm'. It "alludes to the thick leather jerkin which served as a defence." The *OED* gives the phrase under *buff* 'a blow' and suggests tentatively that this is what *buff* here means (*a*1680).

S73. *Stand in another's shoes, to*
NQ 1856 II/2: 187, 278, 339.

'To occupy another person's place'. The correspondent to II/2: 187 quotes a 1834 book, according to which the phrase goes back to a custom in medieval Scandinavia. Allegedly, an adopted person (in the ritual of adoption) stood in the shoes of the one who adopted him. [This is pure fancy, for the phrase is postmedieval, and no evidence for the alleged custom has been given.] The other notes offer only examples of the idiom. *

S74. *Stand like a Stoughton bottle*
NQ 1906 X/6: 8.

'To stand stupidly immobile'. Possibly, the phrase originated in the 1870s as theatrical slang, but the reference remains unexplained. *

S75. *Stand the racket, to*
NQ 1897 VIII/11: 365; 1897 VIII/12: 72; 1900 IX/5: 316, 422.

'To put up with consequences; to pay compensation'. The note on p. 365 suggests that *racket* corresponds to ancient *Scotch racket* 'ransom of a thief'. A different derivation is offered on p. 422: "*Stand* in this phrase is evidently an abbreviation of *withstand* and a *racket* is a noise resembling that produced by playing the ball with the racket in the game of tennis. Hence it has apparently acquired the meaning, not only of endurance or resistance of tumultuous noises, as confused talk, superabundant street noises, &c., but also that of bearing any specific burden, such as financial responsibility." OED: 1789.

S76. *Steal one's thunder, to*
ANQ 1, 1888: 6; 1897 VIII/12: 286.

'To achieve success by preempting someone else's attempt to impress'. The notes give the story that seems to be the only one in circulation: "John Dennis, the English critic and dramatist (1657–1734), upon finding that the manager of the Drury Lane Theater was using in *Macbeth* some artificial thunder which he had invented for a play of his own, which the same manager had rejected, exclaimed, 'They won't act my tragedy, but they *steal my thunder*'. OED: 1900.

S77. *Stew in one's own grease, to*
NQ 1870 IV/7: 187, 272; NQ 1887 VII/4: 366, 397, 475; 1894 VIII/6: 269, 318, 411; 1895 VIII/7: 391; 1909 X/12: 206.

'To suffer from self-inflicted troubles'. The idiom occurs in many variants, with synonyms for *stew* and *grease*. As pointed out in IV/7: 187, it was borrowed from some cook(ery) book. Its alleged French source is *cuire dans son jus* (IV/7: 272). In the exchange of 1894, much was made of Bismarck's use of the phrase. [In French, German, and English, the idiom means the same: one is in a bind and has only him- or herself to thank for it. But in Russian, the reference is true to its culinary spirit: people stew in their own juice when they are doomed to remain in a narrow group of ever the same people, shut off from external influences.] OED: numerous synonyms of *stew* (*frye inne oure owne gres*: 13..).

S78. *Stick a fork in the beam, to*
MM 59, 1973: 109 (3); 61, 1975: 413 (3).

'The (once) accepted notice to youngsters to vacate the gunroom or the mess and turn in' [nautical use]. The origin of the custom has not been explained. *

S79. *Stick to one's tut*
NQ 1909 X/11: 307, 417; 1909 X/12: 15.

'To show unswerving perseverance'. The reference seems to be to *tut,* a base in the game of rounders (an English game akin to baseball). The phrase referred to the criminals who refused to yield to the pressure of the authorities. According to one explanation, "No player must leave his 'tut' until the next one takes the run, and once away from a 'tut' he must not return, but go on to the next" (p. 417). *

S80. *Still and on*
NQ 1895 VIII/7: 204, 475; VIII/8: 77.

The Scottish phrase means 'nevertheless', but it occurred in a poem with the sense 'continuously', which was known to Jamieson (he glossed it 'without intermission'). [Apparently, a tautological binomial, with both elements meaning the same: *still* 'constantly', as in Shakespeare and the King James Bible, and *on* as in *on and on.*] OED: *a*1616 (*Still and anon*).

S81. *Stoke the Dutchman, to*
NQ 1887 VII/4: 348, 452.

'To keep the steam up'. This was said with reference to the Flying Dutchman, the fastest train on the great Western Railway. *

S82. *Storm in a teacup*
NQ 1910 XI/2: 86, 131, 173, 255.

'A lot of commotion about something trivial'. In 1910, James A. H. Murray had no examples of the idiom predating 1872. In the exchange that followed, many variants were cited: *tempest* for *storm,* and *teapot,* etc. for *teacup.* No one could give a date earlier than 1854, but the adage goes back to Cicero, who already referred to it as old (*ut dicitur* ['as is said']). His storm occurred in a ladle. OED: 1678 (*a storm in a cream bowl*).

S83. *Sunday side*
NQ 1903 IX/11: 128, 338.

The phrase "refers to the undercut of a sirloin of beef, and was a very common expression a quarter of a century ago (and may be still), probably owing to Thackeray's allusion to it. The application of the term to this part of the joint is unmistakable. In small families, where economy was desirable, the joint was roasted for Sunday, and the undercut eaten hot on that day—the other side being cold meat for the rest of the week. By leaving the 'week side' uncarved when hot, it was rendered more juicy and palatable as a cold collation" (p. 338). The *OED* has *Sunday joint* (1844) and *Sunday roast* (1826), but, apparently, no *Sunday side.*

S84. *Sun is over the fore yard*
MM 51, 1965: 262 (3).

'The time has now come when it is permissible to partake of refreshment'. The phrase, of nautical origin, "was properly only applied to a ship on an easterly course, when the sun might well be over the fore yard about 11.00 am." OED: 1839.

S85. *Swallow the anchor, to*
MM 50, 1964: 328 (26).

"Years ago the inference was usually one of giving up the career or premature departure from sea-going rather than of normal retirement. To-day the wide sense is much more general." OED: 1907.

S86. *Swallow a yard of land, to*
NQ 1875 V/3: 108, 174, 217, 373, 478.

'To get drunk'. This is a bantering expression addressed to a heavy drinker. Probably not older than the middle of the 19th century. The implication is that a good drink costs as much as a yard of land or that the drinker can now lie "in a yard of land." The last-named correspondent (p. 478) offered a citation going back to 1849 (the phrase must have been quite new). Lancashire. *

S87. *Sweetness of light*
GM 1876, 255; 1889 VII/7: 285.

A familiar quotation rather then an idiom. It was unanimously attributed to Matthew Arnold, but it originated with Jonathan Swift. Walter W. Skeat's note runs as follows: "This is a meaningless expression unless we know the context. It may, therefore, be useful to give it. In Swift's 'Battle of the Books' there is a dispute between a spider and a bee. Afterwards Æsop takes up the cause of ancient authors, whom he likens to bees, and says that 'instead of dirt and poison [such as are collected by modern authors or spiders] we have rather chose [*sic*] to fill our hives with *honey* and *wax,* thus furnishing mankind with the two noblest of things, which are *sweetness* and *light*" (p. 285). *

T

T1. *Tace is Latin for a candle*
NQ 1850 I/2: 45; I/3: 456; 1888 VII/5: 85, 235, 260, 393; 1910 XI/1: 380.

'An expression of disapproval' (so, apparently, understood in the 18th century): see VII/5: 85. Swift, Fielding, and other authors used the phrase. *Tace* 'be silent' (Latin): "[a] humorously veiled hint to any one to keep silent about something" (the excerpt from Camden, 1605, does not explain the joke). Some vague connection between throwing a candle and silence or an association between candles and a dying man, or some other rite in the Roman Catholic countries (VII/5: 393) may be worth considering. OED: 1605 (there, the phrase is explained as 'a humorously veiled hint to any one to keep silent about something'.) Several correspondents knew the variant with *horselock* instead of *candle,* but no explanation of it appeared.

T2. *Tag, rag, and bobtail*
NQ 1861, II/12: 110; 1891 VII/12: 5, 93, 194.

'The rabble'. The phrase once had a longer form, namely, *tag and rag, cut and long tail,* as indicated by George L. Apperson (VII/12: 93), who also cited a few other variants. OED: 1645 (each word in the phrase means 'riffraff').

T3. *Take a rise*
NQ 1895 VIII/8: 126, 175, 237.

'To use a situation as a favorable opportunity, *etc*'. Many examples from old writers were quoted. One of the explanations was that the metaphor had been taken from fly-fishing. The *OED* gives two glosses: 'to make (a person) the butt of a joke involving some form of pretence or dissimulation (now *rare*)' and 'to provoke an angry or irritated response from (a person), esp. by teasing'. The earliest citation there is dated to 1703.

T4. *Take a salad, to*
NQ 1877 V/8: 269.

"When an officer on board ship is wakened and fails to obey the summons, but has another nap, it is called 'taking a salad'." *

T5. *Take French leave, to*
NQ 1879 V/12: 87; 1882 VI/5: 347, 496; 1883 VI/8: 514; 1884 VI/9: 133, 213, 279; 1887 VII/3: 5-6, 109, 518; MCNNQ 3, 1881: 115, 119; ANQ 3, 1889: 181.

'To leave unobtrusively or without permission'. The comments contain only a survey of several previous interpretations of the phrase, all of which arrive at more or less the same conclusion. The Germans have an exact analog; the French call it 'English leave'. The most detailed discussion was by Frank Chance (VII/3: 5-6 and 518), but no one explained the reference to *French* or *English*. The explanation given in *MCNNQ* 3:115 is wrong: the author traces the phrase to the Napoleonic wars, but the *OED* has earlier examples. On p. 119 of *MCNNQ* 3, *franchir* 'to get over *or* away', *franchise* 'freedom', etc. are suggested as etymons. A similar improbable interpretation occurs in VII/3: 109. There we read: "*French* from *Frank* 'free', as in *frankincense* and *franklin*: 'A result of our forefathers' taking leave of one's host or hostess, was customary (not rude)." Of some interest is the long note in VI/9: 133: "When a soldier or servant takes 'French leave', he, for a time at least, absconds. If one jocularly remark of something which he is in search of and cannot find, 'it has taken French leave', he means that it has been unduly removed, or possibly purloined. When a person is said to take French leave, the phrase invariably presupposes that he is subordinate, bound to seek leave from a possibly only temporary superior. Its origin probably arose either from the old-fashioned contempt of the English, and especially of the English sailor, for the Frenchman, who was thus taunted for being unexpectedly absent when everything seemed to promise an unpacific 'meeting', or from the escapes of French prisoners of war." In the later usage, especially at school, *leave* means 'permission' rather than 'absence' (VI/9: 213). OED: 1751.

T6. *Take it in snuff, to*

NQ 1869 IV/4: 36-7; ANQ 3, 1889: 193.

'To take offence'. The correspondent to *ANQ* writes: "The phrase 'to take it in snuff' = to take offense is probably derived from the Anglo-Saxon *snoffa* = dudgeon, allied to *chaff,* (Spanish, *chufeta* = jest)." [Old Engl. *snoffa* is now usually glossed 'nausea' and has nothing to do with *chaff*.] The *OED* cites several variants of this phrase: *to take . . . in (the) snuff, to snuff, to take snuff,* and *snuff* and explains: "The original reference was no doubt [!] to the unpleasant smell proceeding from the smoking snuff of a candle, but there may also have been association with *snuff* 'an (*or* the) act of snuffing, especially as an expression of contempt or disdain." John Addis's (IV/4: 36) earliest example goes back to the 17th century. He explained the idiom so: "Whatever was the date of the introduction of tobacco snuff, it seems clear [!] that medicated snuffs were used at an early period . . . . Doubtless [!] the nose-powder took its name from the act of *snuffing up* by which it is inhaled. And it seems almost as certain [!] that 'snuff' = 'dudgeon' . . . comes from the *sniffing,* the expansion of the nostrils, which is a sign of sudden passion. The connection which seemingly exists between the snuffing of a candle and the blowing of the nose is more puzzling . . . . Can the connection arise from the like action of the finger with thumb in both cases, before snuffers and pocket-handkerchiefs were invented? But not only in Teutonic [= Germanic] languages do we find this connection. The Latin *emungo* has the double meaning ['to blow one's nose' and 'to cheat'], and so the French *moucher,* &c." Edmund Tew also quotes Greek and Latin authors and draws the following conclusion: "This saying . . . has no connection with 'powdered tobacco'. . . . The act of drawing up the nostrils is *sniffing* or *snuffing,* as expressive of disgust, contempt, scorn, or ridicule, naturally produces wrinkles on the nose; and this, no doubt [!], from being so common a way of exhibiting these feelings, first suggested the idea and gained for it such acceptance, that even by Plautus it is spoken of as 'vetustum adagium' [very old adage]'." [However, no author quoted in the note uses a phrase like *take it in snuff*. This saying as well as *up to snuff,* seems to have had a common European foundation: cf. German *mir ist es Schnuppe* 'I cannot care less' and Russian *delo—tabak* 'the affair has gone awry' (literally, this business is tobacco)]. *Take it in snuff* (with a preposition) is not in the *OED,* but *to give one snuff* 'to punish' is (1890).

T7. *Take the cake, to*

NQ 1892, VIII/1: 69, 176, 364; 1892, VIII/2: 215; 1893 VIII/3: 234; 1955, 200: 357; ANQ 1, 1888: 147.

'To carry off the honors'. The custom is supposed to have Irish roots. The Irish seem to have taken the phrase to America, where it contributed to the creation of cake walk dance. The cake walk dance hypothesis was suggested in 1892 and in 1955. The contributors cited a Greek analog. Games with a cake being the prize were common in rural England (pp. 69 and 215). The article in *ANQ* confirms the reference to Irish and supplies a few details. OED: 1847 *(take the cakes),* 1884 *(take the cake).*

T8. *Take the pearl from a piper's eye, to*

NQ 1885 VI/12: 189, 277, 298.

Pearl is a white spot in the eye, so that the whole means 'enough to make a blind man see'. The alliterating word *piper* remains unexplained. *

T9. *Talk like a Dutch uncle, to*

NQ 1853 I/7: 65; 1863 III/3: 471; 1880 VI/2: 309, 473; 1925, 148: 28, 88; 1939, 177: 88; 1943, 184: 28, 268; ANQ 2, 1943: 151, 174, 14.

The reference is to a well-meaning person pestering people with good advice (see the first citation). The author of the note in vol. 184: 28, suggests that *uncle* in this phrase means 'any interfering senior' or 'an officious guardian'. In the US (at least in Nebraska), *I'll be your Dutch uncle* was said (1939) in coaxing someone to do a thing. In a comment on this use of *Dutch uncle* in Nebraska, it was suggested (184: 268), that in the US the phrase goes back to Pennsylvania Dutch (that is, German), in which *German* is synonymous with 'insisting on strict discipline'. However, the usual notion is that the idiom can be traced to the time of England's rivalry with the Netherlands and has a vague reference to anything disagreeable. The note in III/3: 471 is the longest but uninformative. *Dutch* is there explained as *deutsch* 'German'; in Protestant Germany, one's uncle had the role of the Roman *patruus* 'severe reprover'. However, the derogatory connotations of *Dutch* are also noted (*Dutch* 'of inferior quality', as in *Dutch myrtle* 'a weed' and the like.) The notes in *ANQ* reproduce the discussion in *NQ* for 1943 and add nothing new. [In the past, different words existed for "paternal uncle" and "maternal uncle"; the difference is still observed in Modern Scandinavain and elsewhere in Germanic. The use of the generic term for *uncle* here shows that in this form the idiom cannot be ancient.] OED: 1838.

T10. *Talk through one's hat, to*

NQ 1916 XII/2: 449; 1921 XII/9: 449; 1923 XII/12: 233, 276, 313, 417, 457, 478.

'To talk insincerely *or* nonsense'. The saying has been traced to the custom of standing for a short time in church and praying into a hat, but, as pointed out in XII/12: 478, that would be rather talking *to* one's hat. According to another explanation, the phrase is an Americanism; it originally meant 'to talk big'; this derivation is supported in the *OED*. OED: 1888.

T11. *Tamson's mare*

NQ 1913 XI/7: 9, 54.

'Going on foot'. R. L. Stevenson used the phrase in *Catriona*. The following explanation was offered on p. 54: "This, no doubt, is a variant on 'Shanks's nag, naggy, or 'naigy', a well-known Scottish term for going on foot . . . . In the days of the 'makaris' (see Dunbar's poems) to be 'John Thomson's man' was to be guided in action by one's consort: and possibly this proverbial phrase may be represented in the equivalent for Shank's nag. Stevenson's Scotch is frequently provincial, and sometimes inaccurate." *

T12. *Tappit hen*

MCNNQ 3, 1881: 23, 30, 33.

'A drinking vessel containing a Scotch quart'; the direct meaning is 'a hen having a crest or topknot', equal to three English quarts. Possibly, it was a tin pot with a knob on the top resembling a crested hen (p. 23). The rest of the correspondence concerns itself with people's drinking habits and the appearance of crested hens. OED: 1721.

T13. *Tea and turn-out*
NQ 1911 XI/4: 170, 235, 336.

'A light meal after which one was expected to leave the table.' In this phrase, *turn-out* means 'leave'. The old-fashioned people were reluctant to reconcile themselves to the afternoon tea, a habit that replaced a more substantial meal, and the phrase contained a note of disapproval. OED: 1806.

T14. *Tear limb* (or *Lymm*) *from Warburton, to*
NQ 1882 VI/6: 27, 157.

'A formula expressing threat'. Lymm and Warburton are two neighboring parishes that, despite some rivalry between them, cannot be separated. To try to do what is suggested in the phrase is a hopeless enterprise, and no one is advised to do so. *Limb* appears to be a folk etymological alteration of *Lymm*. Cheshire. Apperson: 1901. *

T15. *Tell tales out of school*
NQ 1907 X/7: 407; 1907 X/8: 55.

'To divulge the information not meant for outsiders'. In the past, *of* instead of *out of* was used, but if *of the school* were used, the meaning would be immediately clear. OED: 1556.

T16. *Tell that to the marines*
NQ 1867 III/12: 78; 1922 XII/10: 72; MCNNQ 2, 1879: 276; MM 14, 1928: 90 (2), 286 (2). AS 36, 1961: 243-57.

'A mocking expression of disbelief'. Allegedly, the phrase goes back to the animosity between professional sailors and ignorant "marines" (hence *marine* 'an empty bottle'). The implication is that a marine will believe any nonsense. In MM 14: 90, an 1833 example is given. In MM 14: 286, only two examples going back to 1801 and 1806 are added. A similar attitude was described by an officer of the Royal Navy, who in 1829 expressed his disagreement so: "'You may tell that to the marines, but the sailors won't believe it'. Marines at that time were regarded by sailors not with kindly feeling and as inferior in position." Albert J. Moe in *AS* traced the origin of the phrase on both sides of the Atlantic and of the legends (including hoaxes) connected with the phrase: OED: 1806.

T17. *That beats Ackytoashy, and Ackytoashy beats the Devil*
DCNQ 12, 1922-23: 48, 76, 133.

The phrase is said of something almost incredible. Another variant has *Acky Baugh* instead of *Ackytoashy*. *Acky* is decipherable. It is short for *Hercules* and *Archelaus,* both names having been occasionally used in the country and sometimes confused. But *Toashy* remains unexplained, and nothing is known about his deeds. *Acky Baugh* looks like a variant of *Akebo,* whichever came first. Cornwall. Cf. the next two items. *

T18. *That beats Akebo*

NQ 1874 V/1: 148, 255, 317, 476; V/2: 157.

'An expression of great surprise'. Judging by a citation in Hotten, Akebo (or Akeybo) was someone who outwitted the Devil, unless some place name is meant. Ireland, but not exclusively there. Cf. the previous and the next item. *

T19. *That bangs Banagher, and Banagher beats the world*

NQ 1872 IV/9: 513; 1882 VI/6: 369; 1883 VI/7: 56; VI/8: 409

Something unbelievable is implied when this phrase is used. The legend tells about the miraculous qualities of the sand in the churchyard surrounding a tomb erected to the memory of St. Muireadach O'Heney. On p. 513, a story is related about horse racing: the horse sprinkled with this sand was supposed to win, and, if it lost, the winner was said to bang Banagher. Anthony Trollope heard another legend: Banagher was said to have conquered everything, including the Devil (p. 409). Whatever its origin, the expression follows the same model, as seen in the idioms beginning with *that beats*; they refer to outwitting the Devil. Etiological explanations could be added easily in retrospect. In this case, alliteration *(b . . . b)* is also immediately noticeable. Cf. the previous two items. OED: 1830 *(but that bates Bannagher)*.

T20. *That's basing*

NQ 1881 VI/6: 86; 1882 VI/6: 521.

'A card term used when clubs are turned up'. Perhaps the saying has "some reference to clubs having been turned up as trumps when the news arrived of Basing House being taken by storm by the parlimentarians, Oct. 16, 1645" (p. 521). *

T21. *That's the cheese*

NQ 1865 III/7: 397, 465, 505; III/8: 39; 1888 VII/6: 267, 453; ANQ 3, 1889: 169; The Academy 64, 1903: 149.

'That's the real thing' (allegedly, popularized by comedian David Rees). The Anglo-Indian origin of the phrase was suggested as early as 1864 and is now recognized by all (though the *OED* says: "probably"). Other explanations testify to the richness of people's imagination and the power of folk etymology. An anecdote has often been repeated about a dimwitted boy who ate a piece of soap and thought it was cheese. Also, *cheese* has been traced to a low courtesy made by whirling the gown or petticoats around until they are inflated like a balloon or resemble a large cheese. A witty Englishman has been conjured up, who instead of saying *c'est une autre chose* 'that's a different thing' said *that's the cheese*. The idea that *cheese* in the idiom is related to *choose* has nothing to recommend it either. Cf. *Just the cheese.* OED: 1840.

T22. *That's the ticket*

NQ 1857 II/3: 407; NQ 1872, IV/9: 463; 1886 VII/1: 409, 494; ANQ 3, 1889: 169.

'That's the proper thing'. The phrase was qualified as slang in 1886. The *OED* has citations between 1838 and 1866, one of them from Thackeray (1853), who was fond of the most recent slang. It suggests the origin from the sense *ticket* in politics or from the winning ticket in a lottery. The question was asked whether the phrase goes back to the double meaning of French *etiquette* (II/3: 407). That etymology is unlikely, because the full phrase seems to have been *that's the ticket for soup* and may have had its origin in soup kitchen distributions (VII/1: 494). See also *Give somebody the ticket for* soup. OED: 1838.

T23. *There must be rules*
ANQ 2, 1942: 118.

This phrase is used as a comment on apparently purposeless rules and regulations. The author writes: "If my memory is correct, I first came across the phrase in a story of someone who went into a store one morning to buy some cloth, let us say. He was told that this particular material was sold only in the afternoon. When he asked the reason, he received the reply 'There must be rules'." *

T24. *There's nothing like leather*
NQ 1882 VI/6: 515; 1883 VI/ 7: 232; 1883 VI/8: 337; 1900 IX/6: 426, 510.

'A formula recommending allegedly the best material'. The phrase is believed to go back to the folk tale in which a mason, a carpenter, and a cobbler were consulted about the best material to defend the town in danger of a siege. Each suggested the material he worked with (stone, wood, and leather). It is not clear how credible the following source is—"that a certain leather merchant, having amassed a fortune by his trade, used to drive about in a carriage with a leather hood to it, and that people used to point at him and it and remark, 'There is nothing like leather'" (IX/6: 426). [The tale is suspiciously like the one told about the saying *Nine tailors make a man*.] OED: 1767.

T25. *Thin red line*
NQ 1894 VIII/6: 379; 1895 VIII/7: 57, 115, 191; 1925, 149: 445.

This phrase, with reference to the British army, originated from the Battle of Balaclava, during the Crimean war on October 25, 1854. However, the original dispatch mentioned streak, not *line* (Knowles 2006, p. 112). OED: 1829 *(long red line of Britons)* and 1855 *(thin red line)*.

T26. *Third degree*
NQ 1930, 158: 29, 69.

'Certain methods of extorting confessions by police officers'. The only explanation offered runs as follows: "The 'third degree' was originally an American slang or cant term, now in common use both in England and the United States. It is believed to have been suggested by the third masonic degree, that of a master mason, which is conferred with considerable ceremony" (p. 69). However, the original dispact mentioned *streak,* not *degree* (Knowles 2006, p. 112). OED: 1880.

T27. *Thirteen to the dozen*
NQ 1868 IV/2: 464; 1880 VI/2: 308, 417.

To give (offer) thirteen to the dozen means 'to offer a reward for a deal or for one's pains'. Skeat (IV/2: 464) cited a 1588 example, in which this expression is paraphrased. Perhaps it originated in bakers' trade: "The retailers of bread from house to house were allowed a thirteenth loaf by the baker as a payment for their trouble." See *Baker's dozen*. OED: 1588.

T28. *This day eight days*
NQ 1859 II/8: 531; 1860 II/9: 90, 153, 353.

'A week ago'. The phrase has an exact counterpart in French and goes back to the Roman Catholic church, where the "octave" of a feast is mentioned (p. 531). OED: 1664. (OED: *week, twelve months,* etc. occur in place *eight days.*)

T29. *Three on a match*
ANQ 4, 1944: 10, 28.

The reference is to lighting three cigarettes in a row with one match and the bad luck connected with it. According to one explanation (p. 10), the phrase originated "in the trenches, where holding a match—while three men lighted cigarettes would allow too long a glow: a sniper might get the third man." The conjectures on p. 28 look less plausible: "The idea originated with a Russian burial service in which three candles surround the corpse, one to the right, one to the left, and one over the head. According to custom, all three of these must be lit with one taper" and "some say the idea was fostered, if not originated, by the Swedish match king Ivar Kreuger, who acted on the theory that the mustard left on the plate is the mustard that makes the profits—and he thereby brought on an appreciable increase in the sale of matches." *

T30. *Throw a bonnet (cap) over the windmills (mill), to*
NQ 1900 IX/5: 268, 421; 1926, 151: 262.

'To compromise oneself' (usually said about a woman). Apparently, from French: *Jeter son bonnet par-dessus les moulins* ['to go to all lengths']. OED: 1916.

T31. *Throw dust in the eyes, to*
NQ 1885 VI/11: 166, 313.

'To deceive'. The notes cite episodes from Greek and Latin sources in which dust was thrown in the eyes of the opponents during the war; the action worked well as an artifice. If so, the idiom may go back to the use of dust in ancient warfare. OED: 1581.

T32. *Thrown over the rannal-bawk*
NQ 1880 VI/2: 368; 1881 VI/3: 16.

'To have one's banns published in church'. "A *rannal-bawk* is an iron beam in a kitchen chimney, from which kettles, &c., are suspended by means of *reckans*" (p. 368). Similar colorful phrases occur elsewhere, e.g. *thrown out of the desk in church*, p. 16. *Bawk* is 'balk'. The *OED* has *rannal-balk* in texts from 1781. The compound is a variant of *rantle-tree* (OED: 1685).

T33. *Throw the thirteens about one, to*
NQ 1880 VI/2: 287, 418; 1885 VI/ 12: 386, 452; 1886 VII/1: 77.

'To display great generosity'. A *thirteen* was the name for a silver shilling in Ireland before 1825–26. The reference is to the distribution of medals on the occasion of Queen Victoria's coronation and of throwing about coins by candidates-elect.

T34. *Tib's eve*
NQ 1883 VI/8: 256; 1893 VIII/4: 507; 1894 VIII/5: 58, 132, 193, 298, 438; 1902 IX/9: 109, 238, 335.

'Never'. The idea seems to be that there is no such saint, for Tib's eve is neither before nor after Christmas; or perhaps it is the day of judgement (so in Ireland). (Actually, a seventh-century St. Tibba existed, and St. Tibb's Row, Cambridge, is presumably named after him; see VIII/5: 298.) Brewer derived St. Tib from St. Ubes [but the derivation looks unconvincing]. VIII/5: 438 contains a long note about this saint, but his identity remains questionable (IX/9: 238). Among the many synonyms of this phrase, *when three Thursdays meet, in a month of Sundays, tomorrow come never* and *Johny Pyot's term day* have been mentioned. Also, the obscure synonym *Latter Lammas* is known (VI/8: 256). OED: 1785.

T35. *Tickhill, God help me*
NQ 1850 I/1: 247, 325, 422; I/2: 452; NQ 1851 I/3: 340; 1854, I/10: 223.

Several names alternate with Tickhill (see the reference below). The phrase seems to be part of a formulaic exchange about a place where things either go badly or well. When asked about where the person is from, if things go badly, the resident answers: "From Tickhill, *etc.,* God help me." When things go well, the response is: "From Tickhill, *etc.,* and what do you think?" The story told in I/1: 1850, 422 is typical: "Near to the town of 'merry Lincoln' is a large heath celebrated for its cherries. If a person meets one of the cherry growers on his way to the market, and asks him where he comes from, the answer will be, if the season is favourable, 'From Lincoln Heath, where should 'un?" However, the correspondent to I/10: 1851: 223 notes that the castle of Tickhill, or Tichil, was besieged more than once in the Middle Ages. Cf. *Binsey, God help me; Crawley, God help us; From Lincoln heath, God help me,* and *Saffron Walden, God help me.* EDD: *Tickhill.* *

T36. *Tidy mess*
NQ 1881 VI/4: 205.

'A fair, average attendance' (its synonym is *a goodish few*). The phrase depends on a regional sense (or pronunciation) of *mass* as *mess.* *

T37. *Tiler's law*
NQ 1882 VI/6: 346, 524.

The phrase occurred in a 1648 text and is explained on p. 524 so: "Surely the expression 'Tyler's law' must have drawn its origin from Wat Tyler, of Dartford, whose prompt and righteous sentence of death passed and executed upon the tax-collector in 1381 has made him as classically heroic among English fathers as ever Virginius was among Romans. The royalist writer of 1648 (regarding Wat only as the leader of the peasant revolt, which murdered the archbishop, defied the king, and insulted the Princess of Wales) probably refers to Tyler's violent death at the hands of Walworth, the valiant lord mayor." *

T38. *Till the cows come home*
NQ 1907 X/8: 507; 1925, 149: 315, 354; 1928, 155: 424, 466.

'Never'. The only suggestion about the origin of this phrase appeared in vol. 155: 424 "In a recent issue of the *Sunday Times* the meaning of the above phrase was asked, and correspondents in reply state: *(a)* that it is an Anglicised misrendering of the refrain of James Hogg, the Ettrick Shepherd's song: 'When the kye come hame; when the kye come hame;/ Twixt the gloamin' and the mirk, when the kye come hame;' *(b)* that Jonathan Swift, who died twenty-five years before Hogg was born, wrote in his 'Polite Conversations,' Dialogue ii., 'I warrant you lay abed till the cows came home'." However the use of the phrase in 1610 runs contrary to these explanations, except that they make the context clear: cows "come home" in the evening; hence possibly "late," "very late," and "never." OED: 1610.

T39. *Tinker's dam*
ANQ 5, 1890: 169; The Spectator 1926 137: 380.

This word group is used in the phrase *not to be worth* (or *care*) *a tinker's dam*. The correspondent to *ANQ* compared *a tinker's dam* with *a continental damn*. That damn referred to continental money, which had become worthless towards the end of the Revolution. He understood *dam* as a coin. The first edition of the *OED* noted the low status of itinerant workers in former times and spelled *dam* as *damn*. In the blog "Oxford Etymologist" for November 30, 2016, a correspondent remembered an etymology of *tinker's damn* proposed in an English newspaper in the 1950s: *"Dam* is a small piece of dough or rolled up bread crumbs used by a tinker as a base for applying solder to a hole in a saucepan." This is, apparently, a traditional explanation. The *OED* online also spells *damn* and refers "to the reputed addiction of tinkers to profane swearing." That tinkers' language is especially profane can hardly be demonstrated. It mentions "an ingenious but baseless conjecture" (called this by James A. H. Murray) to the effect that *tinker's dam* was a wall of dough raised around a place which a plumber desires to flood with a coat of solder. A version of *a coat of solder* is *a wad of moistclay,* later "tossed away as a worthless bit of something or other." OED: 1839.

T40. *Tit for tat*
NQ 1854 I/10: 524; 1858, II/5: 247; 1861 II/12: 380; 1893 VIII/4: 525.

'A retaliatory return'. Latin *quid pro quo*. The editorial note (I/10: 524) refers (unwisely) to John Bellenden Ker, the author of improbable "Low Saxon" etymologies, who gives *dit vor dat* as the source. In II/5: 247, a 1713 text is quoted in which the speaker says *tint for tant* (a play upon *tintum pro tanto*?). Walter W. Skeat explained *tit for tat* as "blow for blow" and called it a corruption of *tip for tap,* where *tip* is a slight tap. F. C. Birkbeck Terry (VIII/4: 525) quoted Heywood (1546), who knew the phrase in the form *tat for tat*. The *OED* tentatively sides with Skeat. JBK I, 43. OED: 1546 (Heywood: *tyt for tat*).

T41. *To a cow's thumb*
NQ 1897, VIII/12: 487.

'Fashionably'. The phrase was known as early as 1671 (Skinner). Apparently, it is a jocular or ignorant alteration of French *à la coutume* ['with perfect propriety']. The author of the note is Joseph Wright. OED: 1681.

T42. *Toad under a harrow*
NQ 1873 IV/12: 126, 339, 437; 1874 V/1: 16; 1891 VII/12: 260; 1897 VIII/11: 367; 2014 LXI/4: 482–3.

The phrase expresses silent submission or a condition in which there is no peace. In American English (as of 1874), it was also used about a person wearing an unbecoming headdress. JBK I, 39. EDD: *Toad/Harrow*; OED (*toad-under-a-harrow,* a north-country word): 1825.

T43. *To a merry pin*
NQ 1881 VI/4: 513; 1882 VI/5: 94, 137, 237, 377; 1882 VI/6: 16; 1883 VI/7: 58.

See *In a merry pin.*

T44. *Toko for yam*
NQ 1880 VI/ 1: 455; VI/2: 56, 277.

'Quid pro quo; an Oliver for a Roland'. The phrase was common in the navy. *To get toko for yam* 'means to get punished'. The phrase possibly originated in the West Indies. *Toko* meant 'flogging', while *yam* was an almost generic term for any food. OED: 1823 (*Toco instead of yam,* the same etymology).

T45. *Tom and Jerry*
NQ 1886 VII/2: 189, 256.

'A pub, a tavern of the lowest class'. The reference is to the characters of Corinthian Tom and Jerry Hawthorne in Pierce Egan's *Life in London* (1821). Cf. *Jerry-Builder.* OED: 1836.

T46. *Tom Coxe's traverse*
MM 6, 1920: 127 (43), 188 (43).

'To do things in a long, round-about way'. The phrase occurs in the diary of Captain W. F. Hoffman, R.N. (he served from about 1794 to 1820), which was published in 1901 under the title *A Sailor of King George.* "'Three turns round the long boat and a pull at the scuttle butt' in 1878 and thereabouts in merchantmen, said of a loafer during his watch on deck." The *OED* quotes the same passage from the 1867 edition. "It means the work of an artful dodger, all jaw, and no good in him."

T47. *Tom, Dick, and Harry*
NQ 1894 VIII/6: 244; 1897 VIII/11: 487; 1912 XI/6: 268; 1926, 151: 460.

'Any three randomly chosen representatives of the populace'. On p. 244, Frank Chance offers equivalents of the phrase in several languages. The correspondent, apparently associated with the *OED,* offered a few characteristic quotations on p. 487. In XI/6: 268, James A. H. Murray wrote: "The earliest instance of the English use of this comprehensive phrase sent in for the 'New English Dictionary' is accidentally of 1865. But we have examples from the United States of 1815 and 1818. Will readers try to furnish English examples earlier than these, or in the interval between 1815 and 1865? I seem to remember it in colloquial or newspaper use before 1860." OED: ?1563 (*Every Hick and Tom making himself a capitan*).

T48. *Tom Tiddler's ground*

SNQ 1901 II/2: 144 (p.1090).

'The ground or tenement of a sluggard'. Brewer is quoted: "Tidler is a contraction of 'the idler' or 't'idler.' The game so called consists in this: Tom Tidler stands on a heap of stones, gravel, &c. ; other boys rush on the heap, crying 'Here I am on Tom Tidler's ground,' and Tom bestirs himself to keep the invaders off." The author of the note comments: "My own impression is that modern usage has widened the meaning of the phrase, which is now applied to land or territory the ownership of which is uncertain or debatable ; the phrase, in fact, I think, has become equivalent to 'No man's land'." The Centenary edition of Brewer deleted the improbable etymology of *Tiddler* from *the idler*. The identity of Tom Tiddler remains unknown, but the alliteration is obvious. OED: 1816 (with reference to the children's game) and 1834 ('a forbidden place', 'a no man's land', etc.).

T49. *Too little and too late*

ANQ 2, 1942: 71.

"In the New York Times, July 6, 1942, Fred E. Baer attributed the phrase to Allan Nevins, who had used it in an article called "Germany Disturbs the Peace" (*Current History,* May, 1935, p. 178): 'The former Allies had blundered in the past by offering Germany too little, and offering even that too late, until finally Nazi Germany had become a menace to all mankind'." But the phrase is much older. OED: 1847.

T50. *Toss or buy, to*

NQ 1901 IX/8: 324, 426; 1902 IX/9: 12, 172, 515; 1921 XII/9: 449, 494, 536; 1922 XII/10: 53.

The reference is to the once popular attraction. All the correspondents remembered approximately the same, for example: "Stall was a circular dish of wood, of about seven or eight inches in diameter, on which were imbedded twelve or fourteen farthings, alternately head and tail. Round a pivot in the centre there worked a metal arrow which revolved very easily, and when a boy gave a halfpenny this arrow was turned rapidly round. If the point stopped in accordance with what the boy called, heads or tails, he got a piece of cake (or a pie); but if not, then he got nothing" (p. 426). The pieman's call was: "Toss or buy! Here am I! Pies, pies, all hot, all hot! Heads, I win" (p. 494). Dickens often referred to street piemen ("'Heads', as the pieman says," occurs in the *Pickwick Papers*. See *The Dickensian* 10, 1914, pp. 209 and 250.)*

T51. *To the bitter end*

NQ 1870, IV/6: 340, 427, 516; 1871, IV/7: 23, 85; 1881 VI/3: 26, 193, 334; 1881 VI/4: 238, 277; 1900 IX/6: 346, 453; MM 1, 1911: 56; Spectator 115, 1915: 367.

'To the absolute end of something, however grim it may be'. The Biblical and Talmudic origin of the phrase has been suggested, [but the analogs are not close]. The curious part of the correspondence (IV/6: 340 and the first response) is its emphasis on "stock phrases," that is, the use and overuse of what is now called buzzwords. It follows that *to the bitter end* was a trite idiom as early as 1870. The nautical origin of the phrase has been pointed out, and many years later the following note was published: "*To follow a thing to the bitter end,* that is, 'to pay out cable till there is no more left at the bitts'. As *bitter-end* is given in the dictionaries as a nautical term, the above derivation at first sight seems plausible, and for aught I know may be correct" (IX/6: 346). However, the author suggests a Biblical origin, with reference to Sam. II. 26 [the connection looks tenuous]. In IX/6: 453, the nautical context is confirmed, and it is pointed out that "the very words *bitter end* constitute a sea-phrase meaning 'that part of the ship's cable which is abaft the bitts, and therefore within board when the ship rides at anchor'. Sailors say, "Bend to the bitter end," when they would have that end bent to the anchor; and when a chain or rope is paid out to the bitter end, no more remains to be let go. So that the word *bitter* in this conjunction, although generally understood to convey the sense of harshness to the taste, has strictly no such meaning, this sense being acquired from the association of the word with the sense in which it is used in scripture." OED: ". . . the history is doubtful" (1849).

T52. *Touch cold iron*
NQ 1894 VIII/5: 160, 235, 354; 1894 VIII/6: 155.
"The words may be comparatively modern, but the idea carries us back to a remote pre-Christian time. The sentence runs, 'Tick tack, never change back, touch cold iron'. It is, we are told, the 'binding sentence upon the completion of an exchange or a swop by boys, at the same time touching a piece of cold iron with the finger'. In far-off days iron was a sacred metal. Here we find it used to confirm a promise—a survival, no doubt, of the time when it was used to add solemnity to an oath" (p. 160). The quotation is from Jesse Salisbury's *A Glossary of the Words and Phrases Used in S. E. Worcestershire* (1893). Some of the comments that followed are irrelevant, but the idea seems to be clear (if a boy wants to retrieve an object given of his free will, he will be killed with a "cold weapon"). Several correspondents knew the formula. The *OED* has one 1834 mention of the phrase, but it has nothing to do with the idiom (just touching cold iron). Cf. the next item.

T53. *Touch wood*
NQ 1906 X/6: 230-2.
The American version of this phrase is *knock on wood*. It is traced to some superstition: touching wood may prevent a disaster. Cf. *Touch cold iron*.

T54. *Tread on one's coat-tails, to*
NQ 1890 VII/9: 127, 255.
'To provoke or challenge to fight'. In the 1880s and 1890s, the phrase was synonymous with *to trail one's coat-tails*. The suggestion on p. 255 points to the Irish origin of the phrase. The challenger would invite those present to tread on the tail of his coat. The *OED* lists several similar phrases, but none with *tread* or *trail*. It also refers to Irishmen at Donnybrook Fair. The *t-t* alliteration is unmistakable.

T55. *True blue*
NQ 1851 I/3: 27, 92, 289; 1860 II/9: 289; 1924 146: 228.
'Loyal to a good cause'. "Everybody has heard and made use of the phrase 'true blue'; but everybody does not know that its first assumption was by the Covenanters in opposition to the scarlet badge of Charles I, and hence it was taken by the troops of Lesley and Montrose in 1639" (p. 228). The same explanation was given as early as 1851 (see pp. 27 and 289), and the

chronology makes it plausible. [The dissenting opinion (p. 92: "blue as the type of immutability" has hardly any merit.] OED: ?1636 (no explanation is offered).

T56. *Truff the ducks*
NQ 1886 VII/1: 257.

'A nickname for a tramp or a beggar (*truff* 'steal')'. The comment runs as follows: "As ducks wander further afield than fowls, they are more easily picked up by tramps." The sayings is Irish (the correspondent wrote from Belfast), but that verb is a borrowing of French *truffer* 'to fill up'. EDD: *Truff.* *

T57. *Tub to the whale*
NQ 1853 I/8: 304, 328.

The full phrase is *to throw out a tub to the whale* 'to create a diversion, especially in order to escape a threatened danger'. The correspondent correctly identified the source as Swift's *Tale of the Tub*: "It is to the effect that sailors engaged in the Greenland fisheries make it a practice to throw overboard a tub to a wounded whale, to divert his attention from the boat which contains his assailants." The *OED* gives a long quotation from Swift (1704). OED: 1730 *(throwing out the Tub)*.

T58. *Tune the old cow died of*
NQ 1915 XI/11: 248, 309, 443, 501; 1952: 130.

In XI/11: 248, the following query by James A. H. Murray appeared: "This phrase is humorously applied to a grotesque or unmusical succession of sounds, or an ill-played piece of music. The earliest instance of its use I have is in a letter of Lady Granville's in 1836. But Hotten's 'Slang Dict.' (1865) says: 'originally the name of an old ballad, alluded to in the dramatists of Shakespeare's time'. Brewer, 'Reader's Handbook,' gives the words of the ballad, but without any reference. If any reader of 'N. & Q.' can give me a reference to the Shakespearian dramatist alluded to, or furnish an earlier example of the use of the phrase than 1836, I shall be glad." One of the comments runs as follows (p. 309): "Among the peasantry of Scotland and the north of Ireland [the phrase] usually retains its original meaning of a homily in lieu of alms, and is a reference to the old ballad of the cowherd who, having no fodder for his cow, sought to assuage her hunger by a comfortable and suggestive tune. This is how the ballad begins: 'Jack Whaley had a cow, and he had naught to feed her; He took his pipe and played a tune. And bid the cow consider'." OED: 1820.

T59. *Turn the cat in the pan, to*
GM 24, 1754: 66; GM 88, 1818: 512; NQ 1863 III/3: 191, 314; 1877, V/8: 148, 454, 520; 1878, V/9: 417.

'To change one's views from motives of interest'. Attempts have been made to trace *cat* to *cate* 'cake', actually, 'pancake' (a hypothesis at variance with chronology: *OED*). It is found in Bacon's *Essays* 22. The notes in 1877 added no new ideas on the origin of the saying but made it clear that *to turn the cat in the pan* can also mean 'to turn sides'. The *OED* does not record the meaning given above as the first. [After mentioning "a cookery metaphor; from *cate*, cabe," Hyamson, p. 77, mentions another incredible derivation "from the Catipani, a south-Italian race, notorious for its perfidy. Yet another derivation is from the French, *tourner cote en peine,* to turn sides in trouble.] JBK I, 51. EDD: *Cat*; OED: ? *a*1430 or ?1383.

T60. *Turn the tables, to*
NQ 1851 I/3: 276; 1855 I/11: 94; 1903 IX/12: 128.

'To bring about the reversal of fortune'. On p. 276, a fanciful explanation by William Bingley (in his book *Useful Knowledge*) is reproduced, with reference to a Roman custom, and on p. 94 the reference to the game of backgammon is given (the same in the *OED*). The game was formerly called "The Tables," "where the tables are said to be turned, when the fortune of the game changes from one player to the other." JBK I, 23. OED: 1612.

T61. *Twopence for manners*
NQ 1902 IX/9: 129.

The following quotation from an article by the Rev. E. J. Hardy [no reference is given] explains this curious phrase: "Formerly in Ireland twopence, or a penny, or a few pieces of turf were brought to the schoolmaster each week by every scholar in payment for tuition in manners. Accordingly it would be said of an uncourteous boy, 'Oh! he never paid his twopence.' I am afraid in some Board schools twopennyworth of manners is not imparted in the year. You will hear them [children], as they rush out of school, calling passers-by nicknames, and making remarks about their personal appearance as rude as were those of the young people who said to Elisha, 'Go up, thou bald head!'" In 1885: VI/12: 454, two articles deal with the history of the Societies for the Restoration of Manners (but *twopence for manners* is not mentioned there). Cf. *Victor penny.* *

T62. *Twopence more and up goes the donkey*
NQ 1898 IX/1: 328, 475.

The phrase is discussed in detail in Farmer and Henley. P. 475 provides a full description of the entertainment. "From what I remember of it, the origin of the phrase was due to a travelling showman with whom 'Lord' George Sanger, the famous equestrian and circus proprietor, began his showman's career. Part of the performance used to consist in the hoisting of a donkey on a pole or ladder—a part of the programme very popular with the spectators. But before the due performance of the act a certain amount by way of subscription was always requested of the bystanders, and generally 'twopence more' was demanded. And so arose the saying 'Twopence more and up goes the donkey'. In the newspaper article—it appeared in the *Daily Mail,* some two months ago—Mr. Sander, as already stated, claims the origin of the saying for his then employer . . . . But the expression caught on, and was very soon known all over London and elsewhere. Naturally, the business was copied by other itinerant entertainers, and to quote the 'Slang Dictionary', which noticed the phrase, it became 'a vulgar street phrase for extracting as much money as possible before performing any task'." OED: 1841 *(one penny more, up goes the donkey).*

U

U1. *Ugly mug*
NQ 1899 IX/4: 268, 402.

'A repulsive appearance'. This is what the correspondent on p. 268 says: "In a note to George Daniel's 'Merrie England, chap. XXVII., it is stated that 'the mugs out of which the violent politicians of Charles the Second's time drank their beer were fashioned into the resemblance of Shaftesbury's face. Hence the common phrase 'Ugly mug'. Where is there any contemporary authority for this? Are any such mugs in existence?" [This is a passage from *The Columbia Viking Desk Encyclopedia*. Anthony A. Cooper Shaftesbury (1621–1683): "Distrust of autocratic rule caused his support to fluctuate between Stuarts and Parliament. Helped restore Charles II, but urged leniency for the regicide, *etc.*"] The response (p. 402) calls this explanation into question. Such mugs do not seem to have existed. He asks: "Is it not probable that George Daniel refers somewhat loosely to the stoneware jugs of that period, upon the neck of which is depicted an ugly mask, the mouth being especially ugly and repulsive?" OED: 1798.

U2. *Under the table*
SNQ 1903 II/5: 59.

'Drunk'. "This phrase is often used to imply that a man had got so drunk that he slipped off his chair and lay under the table. Burns, however, makes a dead drunk man fall *beside* his chair. The phrase really means dead. It refers to an old practice once general in Ireland and the Highlands of Scotland, and partially also in the Lowlands, of holding lykewakes over dead persons. The coffin containing the corpse was placed on the floor, under a table, round which sat his friends all night. For their entertainment the table was loaded with bottles of whiskey and ale, cheese and bread, pipes and tobacco. The deceased was not mentioned by name, but spoken of euphemistically as the man under the table." OED: *a*1636.

U3. *Under the weather*
NQ 1858 II/5: 216; 1897 VIII/11: 246, 338; 1897 VIII/12: 34.

'Slightly indisposed'. The phrase was explained tentatively in the editor's note (p. 216) from the phrase *under the wind,* that is, 'protected from the wind'. On p. 338, several phrases connecting *weather* and human disposition are cited. EDD: *Under*; OED: 1827 (no etymology; said to be originally U.S.).

U4. *Unearned increment*
NQ 1899 IX/4: 109, 153, 235, 258.

'Such increase in the volume of land or property as taken place without labor or expenditure on the part of the owner'. "The term, very slightly varying in one word, will be found in Mill's 'Political Economy,' book V. chap. Ii. Sec. 5, thus:—'This would not properly be taking anything from anybody: it would be merely applying an accession of wealth, or part of it, created by circumstances, to the benefit of society, instead of allowing it to become an unearned appendage to the riches of a particular class'. Mr. John Morley, M. P., a political disciple and close friend of Mill, said in the House of Commons, 1890:—'The question of unearned increment will have to be faced before many years are over. It is unendurable that great increments which have not been earned, by those to whom they accrue, but have been formed by the industry of the community should be absorbed by those who have contributed nothing to that increase'. The policy indicated, however, is advocated in Adam Smith, though the term itself may have come to Mill through Bentham, or the elder Mill, or Ricardo. Mr. W. L. Courtney, in his 'Life of Mill' ('Great Writers Series'), alludes to 'the unearned increment', and quoted the term as being 'a direct deduction [by Mill] from Ricardo's theory of rent' (p. 99)" (p. 235). OED: 1871 (two years before J. S. Mill).

U5. *Unspeakable Turk*
NQ 1899 IX/3: 68, 177, 235.

The phrase has been traced to Carlyle's 1831 essay on the *Nibelungenlied*: "How they [that is, Kaiser Ortnitt and little King Elberich] sailed with Messina ships into Paynim lands; fought with that unspeakable Turk, King Machobol" (p. 177). The same in the *OED*: 1831.

U6. *Up and Down*
See *Down to the ground.* EDD: *Up.*

U7. *Up at Harwich*
NQ 1866 III/9: 325-6.

'In a state of confusion; at sixes and sevens'. The phrase was (still is?) current in the eastern counties. "Harwich was formerly one, if not the chief, port of embarkation for the continent, and at the same time tedious of access. From Norfolk and Suffolk the whole counties must be crossed, and boat finally be taken before getting to Harwich. From London and Essex, all Essex must be crossed before you reach the extremest point of land in the whole county, till you approach the town and harbour *in the corner*; and when once there, there is 'nillye willye,' the stormy sea before you. Hence, when any one drifted into an unpleasant position, and had, if any, only an unwelcome alternative, he was said to be 'All up at Harwich!'—a phrase denoting his consequent perplexity and embarrassment of mind" (pp. 325-6). However, the other correspondents, including Walter W. Skeat (p. 325), believed that *Harwich* was a folk etymological variant of *harriage,* from the verb *harry* (compare *marriage* and *carriage*). *Harriage* is a well-attested legal term meaning 'service done by the tenant with his beast of burden' (ultimately from Old French). Yet the phrase *at harriage* never existed. [The derivation by Skeat and his allies might be a scholarly folk etymological alternation of *up at Harwich,* rather than the other way around!]*

U8. *Up corn, down horn*
NQ 1886 VII/1: 192.

'When corn [grain] is dear, beef is cheap, because if people have to spend more of their money for bread, they have the less to spend on meat'. The saying is (or was) common among farmers. * Cf. *Down corn, down hops*

U9. *Up to scratch*
NQ 1894 VIII/ 6: 426; 1895 VIII/7: 34-35, 153.

'To be ready to start a race, *etc.*; to be ready to embark on an enterprise'. Despite the improbable suggestion that the idiom is connected with witch trials, the origin is not in doubt. It "originated in pugilistic slang, the combatants, when preparing to begin, having to tow a line drawn in the centre of the ring. This was otherwise called 'toeing the scratch'" (VIII/7: 35). EDD: *Scratch*; OED: 1821 *(to the scratch)*.

U10. *U P K spells goslings*

NQ 1867 III/11: 161.

'A boyish phrase to insult a loser at play'. The procedure is described, but the abbreviation remains unclear despite the reference to Brady's *Varieties of Literature*. *Gosling* in the North corresponds to *April's fool*. Apperson: 1791. *

U11. *Upon a merry pin*

See *In a merry pin*.

U12. *Up to snuff*

NQ 1868 IV/2: 226, 284; 1869 IV/3: 597; IV/4: 36; 1876 V/5: 336, 436; 1880 VI/1: 153, 484; 1880 VI/2: 256; ANQ 3, 1889: 193.

'Up to the required standard; shrewd'. Todd (in Johnson-Todd) thought that the idiom refers to the person's acute sense of smell. Another derivation connects it with the time when snuff came into general use: someone who knew different kinds was allegedly said to be up to snuff. E. Cobham Brewer (V/5: 436) suggested that *snuff* in this idiom is connected with the Scandinavian words for 'cunning' *(snu, snue)* and 'snort' *(snofle)*. According to IV/4: 36, the "phrase 'up to snuff', is curiously suggestive of Horace's "homo emunctæ naris" [literally,'a man with the nose free from snot' and figuratively 'a man of great wit and sagacity'] and of the uses of *nasus* and *nasutus*. Has 'snuff' in this case anything to do with the A.-S. [Anglo-Saxon, i.e., Old English] *snytro, snoter* ['wisdom, wise'], and Mœso-Gothic [= Gothic] *snutro*? [a typo for *snutrs* 'wise']." [There should be some connection between *up to snuff* and *take it in snuff*, but it does not seem to have been discussed.] *OED*: 1810.

U13. *Upwards of*

NQ 1902 IX/9: 20, 446, 516; 1902 IX/10: 38, 138.

The phrase is ambiguous. In some dialects, it means 'close, approaching to' not 'more (than)'. EDD: *Upwards*; OED: 'above' (1853); 'more than' (1721); used erroneously for 'nearly, not quite' (chiefly dialectal), 1902.

V

V1. *Very well dice*

MM 51, 1965: 187 (8), 366 (8).

'An order to steady a ship's head in any given direction'. The reference is to sailing close-hauled. *Dice*, alternating with *thrice*, is said to be a variant of *thus*. *Dice, no higher* is an order to the man at the wheel to be on his guard against bringing the ship any closer to the wind. The *OED* gives *dyce* as the main spelling, mentions *thus* ("assumed to mean 'thus'") and concludes: "History unclear." OED: 1867.

V2. *Victor penny*
NQ 1911 XI/4: 474.

"Under-paid schoolmasters in the seventeenth, eighteenth, and nineteenth centuries augmented their incomes by the receipt of 'Victor penny' from their pupils. This was apparently paid for the privilege of celebrating the result of a contest in cock-fighting or throwing at cocks by some sort of procession, in which the owner of the victorious bird in the one case, or the most successful thrower in the other, was conducted from the scene of battle in triumph: this practice is called 'rydyng aboute of victory' in Dean Colet's 'statutes for St. Paul's School'." Cf. *Pence two for manners.* OED: 1525.

W

W1. *Walk width and stride sidth*
NQ 1881 VI/3: 470; VI/4: 95; 1882 VI/6: 115.

Walter W. Skeat (p. 95) explains the phrase, now only dialectal, with reference to *wide and side* 'wide and long'. *

W2. *Walk your chalks*
NQ 1859 II/8: 490; 1860 II/9: 63, 112, 152, 289.

'Go away!' This was said to a person whose company is no longer wanted, possibly with reference to an intoxicated person unable to walk straight or walking off without paying (p. 289). Another author (p. 152) suggested a slave market in Rome, where slaves newly arrived from abroad had to stand with their feet chalked until someone bought them off. OED: 1835.

W3. *Warm the bell, to*
MM 39, 1953: 70 (24).

The note runs as follows: "This expression would appear to come, by association, from 'warming the glass', namely the half-hour sand-glass by which the sounding of a ship's bell was timed, for there was a belief in the old sailing days that when the glass was warm the sand ran through quicker, thus shortening the watch. Midshipmen on watch were reputed to nurse the glass between their hands, or under their jackets, to stimulate the flow of the sand." OED: 1924.

W4. *Warm the cockles of one's heart, to*
NQ 1887 VII/4: 26; ANQ 2, 1889: 261, 312; ANQ 3, 1889: 8, 117, 228, 260.

'To gladden'. "The phrase is never heard except as used jocosely" (VII/4: 261). As late as 1864, Hotten called it vulgar. The question about its origin resolves itself into the meaning of *cockle* (a shell? a weed?). The *OED* suggests tentatively that the reference is here to the spiral conformation of the fibers of the heart. Other than that, *cockle* has been traced to Latin *corculum* 'little heart' (so A. S. Palmer, as quoted in ANQ 2, p. 261) and *kógne* 'a bone-like cavity; shell' (ANQ 3, p. 117); both sources are to be rejected. OED: 1671 *(rejoice the Cockles of his heart).*

W5. *Watch how the cat jumps, to*
NQ 1891 VII/11: 448; 1891 VII/12: 51, 154; 1911 XI/4: 106.

'To be on the lookout'. Apparently, of modern origin. According to one suggestion (p. 154), the reference is to the game called tip-cat, rather than to a real cat. OED: 1827.

W6. *Weakest goes to the wall, the*
NQ 1873 IV/11: 109, 184–5, 263, 334, 352, 434, 533; 1914 XI/10: 27, 78; 1919 XII/5: 177, 222; 1947 192: 171.

The conjectures on the origin of this phrase are many. 1) In Scots, *worse* is pronounced as *war*; hence *the weakest go to the war* (IV/11: 109; a fanciful derivation, refuted by the next correspondent). 2) Perhaps the reference was to the wall side of the street as the safer one. But on extraordinary occasions, when there is a crowd and a crush in a street, one is not eager to be upon the wall side, whether the wall be represented by plate glass windows, closed shutters, iron railings, or the sides or corners of narrow passages or gateways. Then the weakest do 'go to the wall' with a vengeance, and realize to the fullest extent the meaning of the phrase. The author of this note is Frank Chance, who cites French *mettre quelqu'un au pied du mur, acculer quelqu'un contre la muraille* = 'to get one with one's back against the wall, so that he cannot move or defend himself, but commonly used figuratively' = 'to reduce one to extremities'." Engl. *drive to the wall* and Scottish *back at the wa'* [= wall] mean 'unfortunate, in trouble' (IV/11: 184–85). 3) Possibly derived from the custom of our ancestors, when their beds stood at the side of the room, to put the youngest and feeblest of the family on the inside, the place of warmth and security; while the father, as the strongest, lay on the outer side, where a stock or post fastened to the floor kept the whole party compact and comfortable. On the same page (IV/11: 352), we read: "The expression 'tenir le haut du pavé' is exactly translated by the Scottish 'to keep the cantle o' the causey,' or 'the crown o' the causey.' In former days, before the invention of *trottoirs,* the street was raised in the middle, and had gutters at the sides, consequently, the middle of the street was the best walking.—"When he's fou ['drunk'] he's crouse ['bold, cheerful'] an' saucy, keeps the cantle o' causey";—and the weakest would then be thrust to the wall, and into the gutter too. 'Back at the wa'[ll] has quite another meaning, and refers to a man being beset by numbers, and in extremity, when he would try to get his back to a wall, so as to prevent his being attacked behind, and oblige his assailants to meet him in front. Hence it comes to mean, 'in evil case, in extremity'. However, F. Chance (IV/11: 352) explained that *tenir le haut du pavé* does not refer to "the crown of the causey," because in France the street was raised in the middle and raised at the side. With regard to Shakespeare's *I will take the wall of any man or maid of Montague's* (*Romeo and Juliet* I, 1), quoted by F. Chance, E. L. Blenkinsopp commented in IV/11: 533: "This would happen in all street fights, which used to be common enough; the victorious party would rush on in the middle of the narrow street, driving the conquered against the houses and walls. Especially would this be the case in Scotland, where it was a point of honour to 'keep the causey'." 4) Of note is the idiom *to lie by the wall* 'to be dead' (IV/11: 334). The discussion resumed in 1919, but no one remembered the exchange in 1873 and nothing new was said. In 1947, a correspondent suggested that the saying perhaps can be traced to the time when people knelt on the floor in churches and benches stood only near the wall; old and feeble people are said to have gone to those benches (vol. 192: 171). This hypothesis is close to what was suggested in XI/10: 27: "I lately heard as explanation of the origin of this proverb which is new to me. In former days there were no seats in churches, but several of them had (and have) stone benches running along the walls. It is averred that they were intended for the use of such people as were too weak or infirm to stand during the whole service." XI/10: 78 supported this idea. The editorial note on p. 27 is fully applicable to all three publications: "This explanation seems an instance of misplaced ingenuity, for it does not fit in with the actual use of the phrase, which implies the very contrary of protection or consideration." OED: 1597.

W7. *Wear the breeches, to*
NQ 1856 II/1: 283, 343; 1898 IX/1: 403.

'To usurp the authority of the husband'. P. 283 contains fifteenth-century references to the same idea in French and English. On p. 343, the equivalents in Dutch and German are given. An oblique reference to the problem of who should wear the breeches in the family can be found in an Italian 1540 book (p. 403). [In medieval Iceland, the husband was allowed to divorce his wife if she wore breeches.] With regard to the phrase in German see Stefan Ettinger "Haben die Männer am Gril die Hosen an?" Phraseologie und Sprachwirklichkeit" In: *Theorie und Praxis der idiomatischen Wörterbücher* (Carmen M. Blanco, ed.), Tübingen: Max Niemeyer, 2009, 45–64. EDD: *Wear*; OED: 1553 (*As though the good man of the house weare no breeches*).

W8. *Wee Willie winkie*
SNQ 1896 10: 47.

About this character in a nursery rhyme Charles Mackay in his *Dictionary of Lowland Scotch* (as quoted on p. 47) wrote: "A term of somewhat contemptuous endearment to a diminutive and not overintelligent child. The Jacobites of 1688 to 1715 long applied to it to William III. 'The Last Will and Testament of *Willie Winkie*' is the title of a once popular Jacobite song." OED: 1888 (The only citation is from Rudyard Kipling).

W9. *Weep Irish*
NQ 1916 XII/2: 328, 456; 1917 XII/3: 13

'To feign sorrow'. [An ethnic slur?] No explanation was offered in the correspondence, and none is given in the *OED*. *OED:* 1577 (no citation after 1882).

W10. *Weigh anchor, to*
NQ 1892 VIII/1: 375, 477.

'To take up the anchor, so as to sail away.' The evidence in the *OED* shows that *weigh* in this phrase has always meant 'to lift.' On p. 477, the suggestion that the original phrase sounded as *the anchor is a-weigh,* which later became *a-weight,* was refuted. OED: *a*1400.

W11. *We shall live till we die, like Tantrabobus*
NQ 1890 VII/10: 447; 1891 VII/11: 97, 272, 393.

Of interest is the passage from M. A. Courtney's *Glossary of West Cornwall*: "*Tantrum-bobus, Tantra-bobus,* applied to a noisily playful child, often used thus:—'Oh, you *tantera-bobus.*' There is a proverb, 'Like *tantra-bobus,* lived till he died.' Sometimes, like *Tantra-bobus*' cat" (p. 97). *Tantrabobus* (sic) is also the name of the Devil in Devon (VII/11: 97). On p. 272, the onomatopoeic origin of the similar-sounding *Tantarbobus* and its [not unlikely] connection with *tantrum* are suggested, but this suggestion does not explain the idiom. It is also doubtful that *Tantrabobus* contains an allusion to the regional word *tantels* 'idle people' (? = 'we'll vegete like idle people') (p. 393). [Was there a tale of some noisy evil creature called Tantarabob(u)s who died of anger like Rumpelstilzchen?] Cf. *Get one's dander up, to.* *

W12. *What cheer?*

NQ 1893 VIII/3: 66, 94, 236.

'A salutation formula'. By some it was felt to be slangy and modern, but it is very old. In Newcastle-on-Tyne, it was used on the street as the only equivalent of *how do you do?* The formula has been immortalized because it was adopted as the motto of Providence (Rhode Island). [*Cheer,* from Latin *cara* 'face; mood' also had this meaning in Middle English, and *what cheer* retains it. The verb *cheer* is of the same origin.] EDD: *Cheer*; OED: *a*1450.

W13. *What the dickens*

NQ 1883 VI/7: 252; 1901 IX/8: 252; 1910 XI/1: 160; GM 271, 1891: 196; TAPA 26, 1895: 83.

'An explanation expressing astonishment, *etc.*' Predictably, the discussion centered on the origin of the word *dickens,* a synonym or euphemism for 'devil'. The correspondents to *NQ* quoted several sources (including dictionaries). According to one suggestion, *dickens* emerged as a contraction of *devilkins* or *odd bodikins.* Congreve used the indefinite article in this phrase ("What a dickens . . ."); *dickens* alternated with *dickons.* The interjectional word used in Scotland is *diakins. Deus* 'God'(Latin) is a different word. In *GM,* the derivation from *devilkins* was repeated, but the *OED* found it unlikely. The most detailed discussion appeared in Charles P. G. Scott's essay in *TAPA.* He rejected the derivation from the nonexistent *devilkins, daikins* and, like Wedgwood, mentioned Low German *düker.* In his opinion, *Dicken* is a diminutive of *Dick,* with *s* added for emphasis. [The emphatic *s* is indeed common: compare animal pet names like *Cuddles* and *Sniffers; Withers,* a character in *Dombey and Son;* slang words like *digs,* etc. Germanic family names meaning 'devil' are not too rare: cf. not only *Dickens* but also German *Düwel* and *Waldteufel*]. OED: 1599.

W14. *What you but see when you haven't a gun*

NQ 1908 X/9: 108, 217, 493; 1908 X/10: 38, 255; 1912 XI/5: 378.

'If I could but get that, I would be happy'. The phrase "is brought in when a tale is being told in which the teller lost an opportunity through lacking the wherewithal for taking advantage of it" (p. 108). The correspondent to X/9: 108 gives evidence that, contrary to the opinion of many, the phrase did not originate in America, [and this is probably correct]. He cites two phrases that refer to the situation described in the proverb. *

W15. *Wheedled as children with a penny in the forehead*

NQ 1901 IX/8: 104, 189.

The phrase is explained in light of various practical jokes. This is what is said on p. 189: "The perpetrator selected an unsophisticated youth from several present and induced him to allow a coin to be placed on his forehead. When this was firmly pressed, it adhered to the brow, and the company were invited to look intently at the experiment. Under pretense of adjusting it more firmly the operator then deftly removed the coin. But the sensation produced by the pressure of the piece remained after the coin was gone, and the youth imagined that he still carried the coin itself in his forehead. He was then told to show the spectators the tenacity of the supposed adhesion by wrinkling his brow, shaking his head, etc. The grimaces made in doing this provoked much merriment and it was not until the laughter of the audience became immoderate that the nature of the joke revealed itself to its dupe." The *OED* confirms this explanation and has examples between 1602 and 1734. Apparently, the game was still remembered in 1901.

W16. *When my ship comes home*
NQ 1896 VIII/9: 244; MM 3, 1913: 180, 217.

'One day when I am in luck'. "It is less generally known that formerly the phrase had a legal value, e.g.—'I promys and me bynd to pay within xx daies after the save aryving of the said good shipe into the river of Temys the port of here ryght dyscharge' (1536) in Marsden's "Select Pleas in the Court of Admiralty," p. 55.' OED: 1548 *(Doubting not to bring his ship to the porte desired)*.

W17. *When the maggot bites*
NQ 1853 I/8: 244, 304, 353, 526.

This was said about a thing done for a seemingly fanciful reason. On p. 353, similar references in French and German to biting creatures in one's head are given. [Russian too has a similar phrase]. OED: only two examples are given, from 1684 and 1687.

W18. *Whether or no*
NQ 1871 IV/7: 142, 286, 378, 485; IV/ 8: 33.

This is not, properly speaking, an idiom, but the exchange is curious in that it juxtaposes archaic and modern usage. Some people believed that only *whether or not* is correct. Their opponents referred to Shakespeare and older authors. The phrase expressed the negative in an alternative choice or possibility. OED: 1650 *(whether or no)*.

W19. *Whip the cat, to*
NQ 1860 II/9: 325; 1902 IX/10: 298, 455; 1903 IX/10: 205; 1903 IX/11: 276, 353; 1908 X/9: 5, 317, 494; 1928, 155: 11; 1935, 168: 316, 357, 392; DCNQ 17, 1932–33: 233.

The saying used to be an expression current among itinerant tailors. It seems to have had some reference to the tailors' hangover, but this explanation sounds like a folk etymological fantasy (IX/10: 205). The broad folkloric background (1935: 357) is instructive (see *tailor* in the word index and *Fox's wedding*) but does not shed light on the tailors' role. Traveling tailors were sometimes called flogcats (X/9: 5). The commentary in IX/11: 276 supplies reference to whipping other animals all over the English-speaking world. The games and customs, including those Grose mentioned, have nothing to do with tailors. The recorded senses go all the way from 'vomit' to 'loaf'. In vol. 168, p. 357, L. R. M. Strachan offers numerous quotations from Wright's *English Dialect Dictionary,* but the origin of the idiom remains unclear. Were tailors called cats because of their parsimonious habits? *To whip the cat* has been recorded with the sense 'to practice the most pinching parsimony' (X/9: 317). Itinerant shoemakers, carpenters, and saddlers were also known "to whip the cat." The game of whipping the cat, described by Wright, does not account for various journeymen's occupations. The *OED* lists numerous meanings, some of them reconstructed tentatively from short and vague sentences. There is no certainty that the phrase originated among tailors. Of special interest are the uses of the idiom that have nothing to do with itinerant handymen. In the Australian bush, *to whip the cat* or *to flog pussy* means 'to cry over spilt milk'. In the royal navy, *to whip* (or *flog*) *the cat* had a similar meaning: one is told not to whip the cat when a bad thing for which no amends can be made causes late remorse. French has *il n'y a pas de quoi fouetter un chat* 'there isn't a cat to whip', that is, 'it's not worth a tinker's dam(n)' (X/9: 317, 494), but the implication is obscure. In DCNQ 17, the following editorial note appeared: "Professor Max Förster calls attention to the dictionary meanings of 'Whipping the Cat', all of which seem to imply something derogatory of the person concerned: to get drunk, to lay the blame of one's offences on another, to play practical jokes, to practice extreme parsimony, to shirk work on Monday, etc." Unfortunately, no reference is given. [Wherever the idiom originated, could it mean 'to do an obviously useless thing, to lay blame' (Foster's gloss), 'gad about', etc.—all derogatory—and then be transferred contemptuously to tailors and others? Hyamson, p. 77, says: "After a standing joke played on stupid country men in parts of England." His only definition of the idiom is 'to play a practical joke'.] JBK I, 94. EDD: *Cat*; OED: 1622.

W20. *Whistle for the wind, to*
NQ 1854 I/10: 306.

"Sailors, when becalmed, have a practice of whistling for the wind." The suggestion is made that the idiom may have something to do with the saying *you may whistle for it,* that is, wishing something when there is little chance of getting. Cf. *Raise the wind, to.* *

W21. *Whistling woman and a crowing hen*
NQ 1850 I/2: 226; 1873, IV/11: 353, 394, 475; Iv/12: 39, 157, 216, 482; 1897, VIII/12: 67, 149.

The note in p. 353 gives numerous misogynistic rhymes of this type. In IV/11: 353, several analogs are cited and the French origin (after Hazzlitt) is suggested. Hens sometimes crow, and a crowing hen supposedly brings bad luck (a common superstition; people tend or tended to kill such hens). On the other hand, crowing hens allegedly do not lay eggs, and this may be the reason behind the cruel practice (IV/12: 39). But a man from Cheshire stated (IV/12: 482) that crowing hens lay eggs quite well! Often *wife* occurs instead of *woman*. OED: 1850.

W22. *White horses*
NQ 1895 VIII/7: 46, 117, 173; VIII/8: 233.

'Foam on the top of the billow'. Some people thought that the phrase is derived from school slang, but this idea was refuted, and poetic texts were quoted. [The metaphor *white horses* for "waves" did not exist in Greek, and yet it has a Classical ring. Poseidon was associated with horses, and his obscure consort Amphitrite, when she appeared on the surface of the sea, was said to be riding her horses.] OED: 1805.

W23. *White stocking day*
NQ 1923, XIII/1: 352, 415, 516.

'Pay day' (a sailors' phrase). Two tentative explanations have been offered: wearing a showy article of clothing to mark the event? A lucky stocking for safe keeping the money? *

W24. *Who stole the donkey*
NQ 1872, IV/9: 463; 1898 IX/1: 267, 395, 495; 1898 IX/2: 211.

"A joke on the material supposed to be used for white hats, at the time that Orator Hunt and other leading Radicals wore them as badges of the party" (p. 463). A more detailed explanation appeared in 1898: "'Who stole the donkey? The man in the white hat', was once a popular street cry, but is now seldom or never heard. It appears to have been applied in derision to Radicals, who were supposed to affect white hats as head-gear. In the obituary notice of Edmund Tattersall, in the *Times* newspaper, it is mentioned that: 'Lord Wharncliffe was the first Tory who wore a white hat after Henry (Orator) Hunt had made it a distinguishing mark of a Radical'" (p. 267). Cf. also: "At the time of the agitation concerning the great Reform Bill, and for some years both before and after it became law, white hats were worn by the Whigs as political symbols, and 'He's a Whig that wears a white hat' became a common street cry. These hats were especially affected by those persons who devoted their energies to party organization. When the Reform excitement cooled down and other questions became prominent, the white hat ceased to have much of its old significance" (p. 395). White hats were also worn by other radicals (p. 495). *

W25. *Winchester Goose*
NQ 1871 IV/8: 419.

'A venereal disease causing a swelling in the groin'. To the question about the meaning of the phrase, the editor answers: "'Winchester goose', the name for a discreditable malady, is thought to have originated from the circumstance of the public stews at Bankside in Southwark being under the jurisdiction of the Bishop of Winchester. Hence Ben Jonson calls it 'The Wincestrian goose, Bred on the Bank in time of popery, When Venus there maintain'd her mystery. *Execr. of Vulcan,* vi. 410. Consult Nare's *Glossary.'*" OED: 1609.

W26. *Wind a horn, to*
NQ 1881 VI/4: 293, 416; 1885 VI/11: 163.

'To blow a blast on a horn'; (figuratively) 'to make merry'. The short discussion concerned itself with the meaning and the pronunciation of *wind* [since in nineteenth-century poetry the noun *wind* rhymed with *kind,* the discussion is rather confusing]. The verb *wind* in *wind a horn* has a short vowel. OED: 1872.

W27. *Wise after the event*
NQ 1874 V/1: 409, 514; V/2: 218, 354.

The saying is international. [Perhaps French *esprit de l'escalier* is especially well-known.] On p. 218, a 1591 version is cited in Latin *(sapere post facta)*. But it is older than that (p. 218). Examples from the Roman period and from Greece are given on p. 354. OED: 1582 *(Afterwise)*.

W28. *Wise men of Gotham*
ANQ 4, 1890: 109.

'Foolish people'. The phrase, known from the nursery rhyme ("Three wise men of Gotham/ Went to sea in a bowl,/ If the bowl had been stronger, / My story would have been longer"), has numerous analogs, but the main question (why Gotham, a village of this name in Nottinghamshire) remains unanswered. OED: 1526. See also *He that would eat a buttered faggot, let him go to Northamton.*

W29. *With a wet finger*
NQ 1885 VI/11: 223, 331; 1897, VIII/12: 147, 236, 338.

'Easily, directly'. Numerous quotations from 1472 on are given, the *OED* and Brewer have also been referred to, as well as *wetfinger* in Nares. The following hypotheses were cited in VIII/12: 236 "Some think *this saying arises from the practices of wetting the finger to turn over more readily the leaves of books*; others from wetting the finger to rub out wrong figures on slates, as boys when doing their sums; yet others think it alludes to carousing gallants writing the names of their ladies with wine spilt on the tables." It was also suggested (p. 236) that *with a washt hand* in the 1652 translation of *Don Quixote* might have the same meaning. Curiously, in Dutch (VIII/12: 338) *met een natten vinger* is used with *belopen* (one is said to be able to walk the distance *met een natten vinger,* because the distance is so short). The *OED* (1542) favors the hypothesis given above in italics. OED: 1542.

W30. *Within sound of Bow bells*
NQ 1914 XI/9: 167, 237.

'A native of London'. "As Cheapside was for many centuries pre-eminently the centre of the commerce and social life of London, and St. Mary-le-Bow in that thoroughfare enjoyed priority above all other parochial churches of the metropolis as the mother-church of the thirteen peculiars of the Archbishop of Canterbury, and in consequence became in ancient times the place of sitting of the Court of Arches, to be born or to live 'within sound of Bow bells' became a proverbial expression to denote a citizen of London—a Cockney *par excellence*" (p. 237). *

W31. *With the hook*
MM 3, 1913: 57.

This is a slang expression, as in "are you going to do so and so?" "Yes, with the hook," meaning "I have no intention of doing so." Possibly a variant of the phrase *Go ashore with the sheet anchor, to.* *

W32. *Wooden shoes*
NQ 1886 VII/2:169, 273, 331.

The phrase was not uncommon in eighteenth-century books and referred to France. According to William Sykes (p. 331), it "does not refer to French democracy, as suggested, but to the tyranny of James II, who was a vassal of France, and might be supposed to wish either to force English people to adopt French customs or to desire to coerce them by means of French troops. The old Orange toast used to stand something like this: 'The pious, glorious, and immortal memory of King William III., who saved us from brass money, *wooden shoes,* the Pope, the Devil, and the Pretender'." OED: 1607.

W33. *Worth a Jew's eye*
NQ 1869 IV/3: 265, 348–9; 1884 VI/9: 209, 298; 1910 XI/2: 208; 1921 XII/9: 169.

'Worth a great value'. The distinguished philologist A. L. Mayhew overheard a merchant saying to another merchant: "Ah, if I could only get that it would be *worth a Jew's eye.*" Mayhew quoted Halliwell who called the phrase very common and wondered whether is was used in old dramatists. The reference to *The Merchant of Venice* II, 5: 43 appears in all sources: "There will come a Christian by/ Will be worth a Jewess' eye." On p. 298, Brewer is quoted to the effect that "as a matter of serious philology the word *Jew's-eye* is simply a corruption of the Italian *gióia (a jewel)."* [An improbable etymology!]. On p. 208, the statement from *The Jewish Year-Book* 1899–1900 is quoted: "It is difficult to understand how the idea of things being 'as precious as a Jew's eye' arose," and three uninspiring explanations are offered. [The explanations are indeed uninspiring: "Due to the brilliance of that organ with most Jewesses. Their dealing in precious stones may have in some way suggested a simile between these and the Jew's eyes. It has also been suggested that the expression . . . means 'worth being looked at even by such judges of values as Jew is" (p. 283).] As far as English is concerned, the phrase undoubtedly goes back to *The Merchant of Venice.*" It is unclear where Nares and Hotten got their information, quoted in IV/3: 265: "That worth was the price which persecuted Jews paid for the immunity from mutilation and death. When our rapacious King John extorted an enormous sum from the Jew of Bristol by drawing his teeth, the threat of putting out an eye would have the like effect upon other Jews." IV/3: 349 contains similar information. Though there is little doubt that the phrase was popularized, rather than coined, by Shakespeare, there is a chronological problem. King John reigned between 1199 and 1216. His and other kings' ill treatment of the Jews has been fully documented, but the Jews were expelled from England in 1290, while the idiom goes back to the reign of Queen Elizabeth. There must have been some provocation for the sudden emergence of the phrase. A popular show? A ballad? In Yorkshire, one can hear the expression: "'You are worth a Jew's eye full of buttermilk'. It is usually said to children who have rendered some trifling service" (p. 169). OED: 1593.

W34. *Wrong end of the stick*
NQ 1895 VIII/7: 486; VIII/8: 33, 71.

The saying is *to get hold of the wrong end of the stick (staff),* that is, to make a mistake, with reference to the end that is soiled with mud or something less savory. OED: ?1793 (originally North American).

Y

Y1. *Ye gods and little fishes*
NQ 1902 IX/9: 369; 1902 IX/10: 77, 114; SNQ 1901-2 II/3: 175.

'A burlesque invocation'. It is addressed to the highest and the lowest. Nothing is said about its origin. The first note called the phrase a familiar exclamation. The earlier communications add little to its history. According to the *OED*, it expresses indignation, disbelief, or amazement, especially in a consciously archaic or grandiose way. OED: ?1534 (*O ye goddes immortall*) and the full phrase in 1820.

Y2. *Yorkshire warehouse*
NQ 1894 VIII/6: 328, 437; 1895 VIII/7: 76.

'A shop with a questionable reputation'. Although the citations are from eighteenth-century books, *Yorkshire* remained a slang word for "cheating, trickers" for a long time. Cf. *Look as vild (= worthless) as a pair of Yorkshire sleeves in a goldsmith's shop, to.* *

Y3. *You are the white hen that never lays astray*
NQ 1909 X/11: 448; 1909 X/12: 16.

The phrase probably goes back to Juvenal's *filius albæ gallinæ* ['the son of a white hen']. It is said to children who make great professions of innocence when some fault has been committed by persons unknown (p. 448); ". . . a white hen would not have much chance of laying eggs and hatching them in a hedgerow without being detected." The *OED* confirms Juvenal as the source and quotes *the son of a white hen* 'a fortunate person or thing': 1540.

Y4. *You may go look*
NQ 1912 XI/5: 226.

'Hard to tell, who knows?' The note offers a 1634 example of this phrase which in 1912 was still current in Lancashire. *

Y5. *Yours to a cinder*
NQ 1918 XII/4: 189, 228, 257; 1925, 148: 187, 265, 413, 464.

An emphatic variant of *yours ever*. Perhaps a humorous rendering of Latin *usque ad cineres* [the same meaning], once a common subscription and valediction. In vol. 148, it is related that around 1700, young men at British universities used other fanciful phrases of the same type: *yours to the antipodes* and *yours to the center of the earth*. The following note by Edward Bensley (vol. 148: 265) is especially informative: "These extravagant expressions are well illustrated by the story told of Isaac Barrow. I am sorry that at the moment the only source from which I can take it is Hone's 'Every-day Book', under May 4, the date of Barrow's death in 1677: 'He was a great wit: he met Rochester at court, who said to him, 'Doctor, I am yours to my shoe-tie'; Barrow bowed obsequiously with 'my lord, I am yours to the ground'; Rochester returned this by 'Doctor, I am yours to the centre'; Barrow rejoined 'my lord, I am yours to the antipodes'; Rochester, not to be foiled by 'a musty old piece of divinity', as he was accustomed to call him, exclaimed, 'Doctor, I am yours to the lowest pit of hell'; whereupon Barrow turned from him with 'there, my lord, I leave you'." Many people exercised their wit in inventing ever new variants of this formula. *Yours till hell freezes* is mentioned on p. 413. *

Z

Z1. *Zoot suit*

ANQ 3 1943: 54; NY June 19, 1943: 14.

'A man's suit of extreme cut.' The periodicals cited here do not antedate 1943 and make it obvious that zoot suits were a great novelty at that time and that such suits were first made in the US, most probably in New York. Even if they go back to 1937, as has been suggested, the phrase is hardly earlier than 1942. The discussion touched only on the question about the inventor of the fashion. The word *zoot* seems to have been coined more than once *(OED)*, but it is the origin of the phrase that matters. Allegedly, *zoot* is a variant of *suit,* but no one has explained who pronounced *suit* with a voiced consonant (or whose accent was parodied), and where this voicing was common. Yet such a type of reduplication is not improbable, with *zoot* being an emphatic, facetious variant of *suit* (*zoot suit* = a great, fashionable suit?). Green writes: "?New Orleans patois." However, the home of the phrase seems to be New York. OED: 1942.

Indexes

A quotation without a reference is like a geological specimen of unknown locality.

—Walter W. Skeat, *Notes and Queries,* 1884

"An eminent book collector, noted for his good nature, declared that a man who published a book without an index ought to be put into the thistles beyond hell, where the devil could not get him."

—*Temple Bar,* quoted in *Notes and Queries,* 1884

Word Index

An asterisk indicates that the word occurs in a variant of the idiom.

Abraham: ~'s bosom; to sham ~.
Abroad: Schoolmaster is ~.
Absence: conspicuous by one's ~.
Account: to pipe-clay one's weekly ~s.
Ackytoashy: That beats ~, and ~ beats the Devil.
Acquaintance: to scrape an ~.
Acre: God's ~.
Act: to ~ upon the square.
Adam: ~'s ale.
Add: ~ insult to injury.
Adder: as deaf as the ~.
Admiral: to broach the ~.
Admiration: mutual ~ society.
After: ~ meat—mustard; Fegges ~ peace; to send Jack ~ yes; wise ~ the event.
Against: not ~; over ~.
Age: ~ of Roden's colt; of a certain ~.
Aim: to draw the long bow.
Akebo: That beats ~.
Alderman: the parson's nose; the ~'s walk.
Ale: Adam's ~.
Alive: Man ~.
All: ~ holiday at Peckham; ~ Lombart street to a China orange; ~ my eye and Betty Martin;
~ on one side, like Rooden Lane; ~ on one side, like Takeley Street; ~ on one side, like the
Bridgnorth election; ~ on one side, like the lock of a gun; ~ over, like the fair of Athy; ~ right;
~ round Robin Hood's barn; ~ Sir Garnet; ~ talk and no cider; ~ the go; ~ the world and
Bingham will be there.
Allowance: give one monkey's ~.
Amuck: run ~.
Anchor: like the Dutchman's ~ at home; to swallow the ~; to weigh ~.
Andrew: ~Martin; ~ Millar's lugger; Merry ~.
Angel: ~s on horseback.
Annie: ~ Oakley.
Anthony: an ~ pig; Burying has gone by, and the child's called ~.

Ape: An ~ is an ~, be she clothed in purple; Old maids lead ~s in hell.

Apple: ~-pie order; ~pie bed; as sure as God made little ~s.

April: ~ fool.

Archer: *to draw the long bow.

Arm: make a long ~.

Armenian: to feed the ~s.

Arrow: to draw the long bow.

Ashore: to go ~ with the sheet anchor.

Asleep: to catch a weasel ~.

Astray: You are the white hen that never lays ~.

Athlone: as the Devil walking through ~.

Athy: all over, like the fair of ~.

Audley: John ~.

Aunt: How's your ~ie at Tiverton?

Away: cut ~; once and ~; right ~.

B: not to know a ~ from a bull's foot.

Baby: God's ~.

Back: *Caw me, caw thee; to have got Charley on one's ~.

Bacon: to pull ~; to save one's ~.

Bag: as dark as a swep's sut ~; to let the cat out of the ~.

Baggage: bags and ~.

Bail: Leg~.

Bait: as mad as the ~ing bull of Stamford.

Baker: Pull Devil, pull ~.

Baldheaded: Go it [or out] ~.

Ballad: hole in the ~.

Ballyhack: Go to ~.

Bank: to get down the ~s.

Bar: Katie, ~ the door.

Barn: all round Robin Hood's ~.

Barrel: Never a ~ the better herring; Neither ~, better herring.

Basing: That's ~.

Basket: to smile like a ~ of chips.

Bastard: to bear away the bell ~.

Bat: as warm as a ~.

Bath: to go to ~.

Battalion: to club the ~.

Battledore: to cry bee to a ~; to say bee to a ~.

Batty: as busy as ~.

Bay: at ~.

Bead: to draw a ~.

Bloom: from ~ till ~.
Blow: ~ing a raspberry.
Blue: a bolt out of the ~; true ~.
Boat: in the same ~.
Bob: ~by dagger; Kick up ~'s a-dying.
Bobtail: tag, rag, and ~.
Bodkin: to ride ~.
Bog: first in the wood and last in the ~.
Bolt: to draw the long bow; to make a shaft or ~ of it; to shoot one's ~.
Bone: funny ~; to make no ~s; never make old ~s.
Bonnet: bee in one's ~; to throw a ~ (cap) over the windmill (mill).
Book: green ~; man of one ~.
Boot: to hang the clean ~ (or shoe).
Borak: to poke ~.
Bore: to find a pin for every ~.
Born: bred and ~.
Bosom: Abraham's ~.
Boss: Ossing comes to ~ing.
Bottle: Bring another mayor and another ~; to crush a ~; man in a quart ~; stand like a Stoughton ~.
Bottom: Foggy ~.
Bow: to draw the long ~.
Bow bells: within sound of ~.
Box (noun): in the wrong ~.
Box (verb): to ~ Harry; to ~ the compass; to ~ the fox.
Boy: broth of a ~.
Brain: as bad as a cock's ~s.
Brass: to get down to ~ tacks; hungry enough to eat ~ tacks.
Brass-rags: to part ~.
Brass tacks: to get down to ~; hungry enough to eat ~.
Bread: to quarrel with one's ~ and butter; A sole is the ~ and butter of fish.
Breakfast: to give one ~.
Breeches: in one's buttons; to wear the ~.
Breed: Familiarity ~s contempt.
Breeze: to ride the ~.
Bridge: Don't cross the ~ until you come to it; Moulden's ~.
Bridgnorth: All on one side, like the ~ election.
Bridport: stabbed by a ~ dagger.
Bright: as ~ as a bullhus.
Bristol: shipshape and ~ fashion.
Broach: to ~ the admiral.
Broad: on the ~ level.
Broad gates: Send farthingales to ~ in Oxford.

Broom: to hang out the ~.

Brother: a man and a ~.

Brute: to feed the ~.

Bubble: ~ and squeak.

Buck (verb): to put to ~.

Bucket: to kick the ~.

Buff: to stand ~.

Bug: as ~ as a lop.

Builder: Jerry ~s.

Bull: as mad as the baiting ~ of Stamford; cock and ~ story; not to know a B from a ~'s foot.

Bullet: Every ~ has its billet.

Bullhus: as bright as a ~.

Bundle: to smile like a ~ of chips.

Bung: Go ~.

Burn: bishop that ~eth; Sing old Rose and ~ the bellows.

Bush: Go by the beggar's ~ or the game of trey-trip; Good wine needs no ~; Rag upon every ~; like an owl in an ivy ~.

Busy: as ~ as Throp's wife.

But: It stands stiff, and ~'s a mountain.

Butter: He that would eat a ~ed faggot, let him go to Northampton; to quarrel with one's bread and ~; A sole is the bread and ~ of fish.

Buttermilk: worth a Jew's eye.

Button: have a soul above ~s; in one's ~s; to make ~s.

Buy: not worth an old song; Toss or ~ for (kidney ones).

Cackle: Cut the ~ and get to the horses.

Cain: to raise ~.

Cake: to take the ~.

Calf: as wise as Waltham's ~.

Call (noun): ~ of the sea.

Call (verb): ~ a spade a spade.

Candle*: as straight as a die; Tace is Latin for ~.

Canvas: to receive the ~.

Cap: a feather in your ~; to set the ~; to throw a bonnet (~) over the windmill (mill).

Captain: Spring ~.

Card: on the ~s.

Care: not to ~ a fig; not to ~ a twopenny damn.

Carpet: on the ~.

Carter: more than ~ had oats.

Case: ground-hog ~.

Castle: Barney ~.

Cat: as dark as a stack of black ~s; as sick as a ~; to cast the ~ in the kirn; to grin like a Cheshire

~; It rains ~s and dogs; I wish I had our ~ by the tail; to let the ~ out of the bag; not enough room to swing a ~; to roast a ~; She's the ~'s mother; to turn the ~ in the pan; to watch how the ~ jumps; to whip the ~.

Catch: to lie at the ~.

Catholic: The Greeks have turned Roman ~s.

Cerberus: to give a sop to ~.

Certain: of a certain ~.

Chalk: as different as ~ from cheese; walk your ~.

Change*: Do the dancers; to ring the ~s.

Chap: That's the ~ as married Hannah.

Charity: as cold as ~.

Charley: to have got ~ on one's back; to play the ~ (wag).

Cheer: Bronx ~; What ~?

Cheese: as different as chalk from ~; just the ~; That's the ~.

Chelsea (Reach): as deep as ~.

Chelsey: as dead as ~.

Cheshire: to grin like a ~ cat.

Chest: Down ~s, up hammocks.

Chicken: Mother Carey's ~s.

Child: Burying has gone by, and the ~'s called Anthony; to make ~ren's shoes; Wheedled as ~ren with a penny in the forehead.

Chime: as slow as old Jon Walker's ~s.

Chimney: monkey on the ~.

China: all Lombart street to a ~ orange.

Chip: like ~s in porridge, neither good nor harm; to smile like a basket of ~s.

Chloe: as drunk as ~.

Choice: Hobson's ~.

Chuck: nip and tuck.

Church: to pick up the ~ lights; thrown out of the desk in ~.

Cider: all talk and no ~.

Cinder: yours to a ~.

Clean: as ~ as a clock; as ~ as a pink; as ~ as a whistle; to hunt the ~ boot (or shoe).

Clergy: benefit of ~.

Climb: The higher the monkey ~s, the more he shows his tail.

Clock: as clean as a ~; as cool as a ~; as false as Louth~.

Clothe: An ape is an ape, be she ~d in purple.

Coal: to carry ~s to Newcastle; to haul over the ~s.

Coarse: as ~ as bean-straw; as ~ as Garasse; as ~ as heather; as ~ as hemp.

Coat: Job Johnson's ~.

Coat-tail: to tread on one's ~s.

Cobbler: as proud as old Cole's (or the ~'s) dog.

Cock (noun): as bad as a ~'s brains; ~ and bull story; ~ of the walk; ~'s span; ~shut time; to be cried by the ~ and cryer; Every ~ is proud on his own dunghill; to know how to carry the dead ~ home.

Cock (verb): to ~ one's fud; knocked into a ~ed hat.

Cocker: according to ~.

Cockles: to warm the ~ of one's heart.

Coffee: No fore royal, no morning ~.

Coggeshall: ~ job.

Cold: as ~ as a maid's knee; as ~ as charity; ~ as a dog; a dog's nose ~; Feed a ~ and starve a fever; out in the ~; touch ~ iron.

Cold-floor: to lie ~.

Cole: as proud as old ~'s dog; Old ~'s dog.

Colly Weston: It's all along o' ~.

Colonel Chesterton*: to do the dancers.

Color/Colour: to fear no ~s; to nail the ~s to the mast; penny plain, twopence ~ed.

Come: ~ in if you are fat; Don't cross the bridge until you ~ to it; Lightly ~, lightly go; seldom ~s a better; till the cows ~ home; when my ship ~s home.

Compass: to box the ~; to fetch a ~.

Condition: in an interesting ~.

Constable: ~ of Oppenshaw sets beggars in the stocks at Manchester; ~ with a back on his bill; to outrun the ~.

Contempt: Familiarity breeds ~.

Contrairy: as ~ as Wood's dog.

Cool: as ~ as a clock; as ~ as a cucumber; as ~ as Dilworth's.

Coot: as mad as a ~.

Coote: son of a sea ~.

Cork: It is nothing but ~.

Corn: Down ~, down hops; Up ~, down horn.

Corner: hole and ~ with another.

Corporal: a fly on the ~.

Corsica: It is not every lady of Genoa that is a queen of ~.

Cotton: King ~.

Countenance: a copy of your ~.

Courage: Dutch ~.

Cousin: to call ~ with.

Coventry: to send one to ~.

Cow: to a ~'s thumb; Do as the ~ o' Forfar did, take a stannin' drink; Eat the mad ~; sacred ~; till the ~s come home; to a ~ before Tun; the tune the old ~ died of.

Cox: as fess as ~'s pig.

Crab: as sour as a ~; to catch a ~; ~ harvest.

Crack: to paper over the ~s.

Craw: to have sand in one's ~.

Crawley: as crooked as ~.

Cream: The cat is in the ~ pot.

Credit: to cry down ~.

Creditor: Pay off ~s with the foretopsail sheet.

Creel: to coup the ~s.

Cress: not worth a ~.

Cricket: It's not the ~.

Crook: by hook or by ~.

Crooked: as ~ as Crawley.

Cross: Don't ~ the bridge until you come to it; make a crutch of one's ~.

Crossroads: dirty work at the ~.

Crow: eat ~; to pluck a ~ with somebody; whistling woman and a ~ing hen.

Crowborough: as poor as a ~.

Crowder: as cunning as ~.

Crutch: as funny as a ~; Layers for meddlers, and ~es for wild ducks; Make a ~ of one's cross; *Rare-overs for meddlers.

Cry: Hue and ~; It's a long ~ to Loch Awe.

Cryer: to be cried by the cock and ~.

Cucumber: as cool as a ~.

Cunning: as ~ as crowder.

Cup: not my ~ of tea; St. Boniface's ~.

Cupar: He that will to ~, maun to ~.

Cupboard: a skeleton in the ~.

Curate: Like the ~'s egg, good in parts.

Curse: not worth a ~; not worth a tinker's ~; ~ of Scotland.

Curtain: ~ lecture; Iron ~.

Cushion: beside the ~.

Custard: Cowardly, cowardly, ~.

Cut (noun): ~ of one's jib; *tag, rag, and bobtail.

Cut (verb): to ~ and run; to ~ away; to ~ off one's nose to spite one's face; to ~ one off with a shilling; to ~ one's stick; to ~ the cackle and get to the 'osses [horses]; to ~ the loss; to ~ the mustard; to ~ the painter.

Dag: I'll have a ~ if I lose my spike.

Dagger: stabbed by a Bridport ~.

Daisy: to do gooseberry.

Damn: not to care a twopenny ~.

Damnable: old mother ~.

Dance: ~ in a pig-trough.

Dancer: to do the ~s.

Danes: to have the ~.

Daniels: Hook it.

Darg: to do one's ~.

Dark (adjective): as ~ as a swep's sut bag.

Dark (noun): Leap in the ~.

Davy: as drunk as ~'s sow.

Day: The better the ~, the better the deed; Ember ~; forty ~s of wet weather; furry ~; nine ~s wonder; to pass the time of ~; A pin a ~ is a groat a year; Sabbath ~'s journey; this ~ eight ~s; white stocking ~.

Day-nettles: to sing whillelujah (or willalew) to the ~.

Dazzler: Bobby ~.

Dead: as ~ as a doornail; as ~ as a herring; as ~ as Chelsey; as ~ as mutton; as ~ as Queen Anne; as ~ as a rat; mother of ~ dogs.

Deaf: as ~ as a beetle; as ~ as the adder.

Dear: Ask near, sell ~; O ~ me; ~ knows.

Death: *After meat—mustard; to cry out ~ before you are past Durham; like ~ on a mop-stick; a new terror to ~; to rhyme rats to ~.

Deceiver: Gay ~.

Deep: as ~ as Chelsea (Reach); as ~ as Garrick; between the Devil and the ~ sea.

Degree: third ~.

Delicate: *In an interesting condition.

Desk: thrown out of the ~ in church.

Derby: ~ ram.

Devil: as black as the ~'s nutting bag; as the ~ walking through Athlone; as true as the ~'s in Dublin city; between the ~ and the deep sea; blue ~s; clever ~s; ~ among the tailors; ~ overlooks Lincoln; ~ to pay (and no pitch hot); drag the ~ by the tail; Fight dog, fight bear (the ~ part you); Pull ~, pull baker; That beats Ackytoashy, and Ackytoashy beats the ~.

Diamond: nine of ~.

Dice: out of the ~; very well ~.

Dick: as queer as ~'s hat-band, that went nine times round his hat and was fastened by a rush at last; as tight as ~'s hatband; like ~'s hatband.

Die (noun): as straight as a ~; Kick up before Tun.

Die (verb): Bob's a-dying; the tune the old cow ~d of; We shall live until we ~, like Tantrabobus; Kick up Bob's a-dying.

Different: as ~ as chalk from cheese.

Dig: as fierce as a ~.

Dilworth: as cool as ~'s.

Dim: Darnall for ~ sight.

Dirty: a clean sword and a ~ Bible.

Dispose: Man proposes, but God ~s.

Diversion: Meg's ~s.

Do: to ~ as the cow o' Forfar did, take a stannin' drink; to ~ Gooseberry; to ~ the dancers; Let George ~ it; How ~ you ~.

Dock: Nettle in, ~ out.

Doctor: after meat—mustard.

Dog: as contrairy as Wood's ~; as lazy as a ~; as lazy as Laurence's ~; as lazy as Ludlum's ~; as lazy as Lumley's ~; as proud as a ~ with side-pockets; as proud as Old Cole's ~; to beat a (the) ~ before the lion; between the ~ and the wolf; butter out of a ~'s mouth; Fight ~, fight bear (the Devil part you); to go to the ~s; to have no more use (for something) than a ~ (or monkey) has for side-pockets; a hair of the ~ that bit you; It rains cats and ~s; Let sleeping ~s lie; matter of dead ~s; Old Cole's ~.

Dollar: Almighty ~; as sound as a ~; sixty-four ~ question.

Donkey: Hit the hay; Twopence more and up goes the ~; Who stole the ~?

Door: a chalk on the ~; Katie, bar the ~; to keep the wolf from the ~; to shut the stable ~ when the steed is stolen.

Doornail: as dead as a ~.

Down: Derry ~.

Dozen: baker's ~; to know how many beans make five; to play the ~; a rump and ~; thirteen to the ~.

Draff: As the sow fills, the ~sours; It is the still (= quiet) sow that eats up the ~.

Drake: ducks and ~s.

Drawer: out of the top ~.

Drift: to get Rorke's ~.

Drink: Do as the cow o' Forfar did, take a stannin' ~.

Drive: Bad money ~s out good.

Drop: not leaving the Devil a ~.

Drunk: as ~ as Blaizers; as ~ as Chloe; as ~ as Davy's sow; as ~ as mice; ~ as a dog.

Dublin city: as true as the Devil's in ~.

Duck: crutches for lame ~s; to hear the ~s; Layers for meddlers, and crutches for wild ~s; *Rare-overs for meddlers; Truff the ~s.

Duke Humphrey: to dine with ~.

Dulcarnon: at ~.

Dule: Friday's hair and Sunday's horn goes to the ~ on Monday morn.

Dull: as ~ as a fro.

Dunghill: Every cock is proud on his own ~.

Dunstable: as big as a ~ lark; downright ~.

Durham: to cry out death before you are past ~.

Dutch: to talk like a ~ uncle.

Dutchman: I'm a ~; like the ~'s anchor at home; to put a ~ in; to stoke the ~.

Ear: a flea in one's ~; to nail one's ~s to the pump.

Earnest: in good ~.

Earwig: to look like a throttled ~.

Eat: to have a feast and ~ it; He that would ~ a buttered faggot, let him go to Northampton; hungry enough to ~ brass tacks; It is the still (= quiet) sow that ~s up the draff.

Egg: as sure as ~s is ~s; curate's ~; Like the curate's ~, good in parts.

Eight: This day ~ days.

Elbow: neither my eye nor my ~; Never touch your eye but with your ~.

Election: All on one side, like the Bridgnorth ~; like the Bridgnorth ~.

Eleven: as long as the ~th of June; Forbes-Mackenzie hour of ~; by the ~s.

Emerald: ~ Isle.

End: to come out of the little ~ of the horn; mend or ~; to the bitter ~; the wrong ~ of the stick.

Englander: Little ~.

Enough: ~ to make a man strike his own father; hungry ~ to eat brass tacks; not ~ room to swing a cat.

Errand: a sleeveless ~.

Eve: Tib's ~.

Event: wise after the ~.

Everlasting: to do the dancers; to be hanged in an ~ jacket.

Exeter: How's your auntie at Tiverton?

Eye: All my ~ and Betty Martin; babies in the ~s; to catch the speaker's ~; my ~ and Tommy; Needle's ~; neither my ~ nor my elbow; Never touch your ~ but with your elbow; the parson's nose; to take the pearl from a piper's ~; worth a Jew's ~.

Face (noun): to cut off one's nose to spite one's ~; lose ~; save ~.

Face (verb): to ~ the music.

Faggot: He that would eat a buttered ~, let him go to Northampton.

Fain: ~s it; ~ it.

Fair (adjective): It ~ sheds.

Fair (noun): All over, like the ~ of Athy.

Faith: not to pin one's ~ upon somebody else's sleeve.

False: as ~ as Louth Clock.

Family: to have all one's ~ under one's hat.

Family way: in an interesting condition.

Farmer: an afternoon ~.

Fashion: shipshape and Bristol ~.

Fast: always a feast or a ~ in Scilly.

Fasten: as queer as Dick's hat-band, that went nine times round his hat and was ~ed by a rush at last.

Fat: Come in if you're ~.

Father: enough to make a man strike his own ~; spit of his ~.

Favor: a fair field and no ~.

Feast: always a ~ or a fast in Scilly; to have a ~ and eat it; like Madame Hassel's ~.

Feather: to show the white ~.

Feed: ~ a cold and starve a fever; to ~ the Armenians; to ~ the brute.

Fellow: damned literary ~s.

Fess: as ~ as Cox's pig.

Fever: buck ~; Feed a cold and starve a ~.

Fiddle: as fit as a ~.

Gosling: U P K spells ~s.

Goss: to give one ~.

Gotham: wise men of ~.

Gray: ~'s Inn pieces.

Grease: stew in one's own ~.

Great: ~ Scot.

Grey: The ~ mare is the better horse.

Grief: to come to ~.

Grig: as merry as a ~; as sour as a ~.

Grin: to ~ like a Cheshire cat; to ~ like a weasel in a trap.

Grind: an axe to ~.

Groat: Ninepence, Nanny! Two ~s and a penny; A pin a day is a ~ a year.

Ground: Tom Tiddler's ~.

Ground-toad: as awkward as a ~.

Grudge: a chalk on the door.

Guam: to clear out for ~.

Guest: Aldelphi ~.

Gun: All on one side, like the lock of a ~; as sure as a ~; What you but see when you haven't a ~.

Guy: to shoot the ~.

Hair: Friday's ~ and Sunday's horn goes to the dule on Monday morn; Keep your ~ on; to take a ~ of the dog that bit you.

Hairdresser: as jealous as a couple of ~s.

Hal: to play ~ and Tommy.

Halfpenny: the egg and the ~; not to have a ~ to bless oneself with.

Halgaver Court: present in ~.

Halifax: to go to ~.

Hamlet: to play ~; to raise ~ on one.

Hammock: Down chests, up ~.

Hand: The eye of the master (is worth both his ~s); to make a ~ of.

Hang: as queer as Tim's wife looked when she ~ed herself; He has hung up his hat; Let every herring ~ by its own tail; *to set the cap.

Hangman: married by the ~.

Hannah: That's the chap as married ~.

Hap'orth: to spoil the ship for a ~ of tar.

Hard: between a rock and a ~ place.

Hare: as mad as a March ~; First catch your ~.

Harm: Like chips in porridge, neither good nor ~.

Harness: hell in ~.

Harrow: harp and ~; a toad under a ~.

Harry: to box ~.

Harvest: Crab ~.

Hook (verb): ~ it.

Hops: Down corn, down ~.

Horn: as crooked as a ram's ~s; come out of the little end of the ~; Either make a spoon or spoil a ~; Friday's hair and Sunday's ~ goes to the dule on Monday morn; Got sends the shrewd cow short ~s; in a ~; Up corn, down ~.

Horse: as sick as a ~; Charley ~; Cut the cackle and get to the ~s; to get upon one's high ~; The grey mare is the better ~; Horse and ~; Like Hicks's ~s, all of a snarl; out of the ~'s mouth.

Horseback: angels on ~.

Horselock: Tace is Latin for ~.

Hose: to smother in the lode and worry in the ~.

Hot: Devil to pay and no pitch ~; ~ as a dog; in ~ water.

House: a skeleton in every ~.

Hour: Forbes-Mackenzie ~ of eleven.

Humble: to eat ~ pie.

Ice: as independent as a hog on ~.

Increment: unearned ~.

Independent: as ~ as a hog on ice.

Inheritance: God's providence is mine ~; Service is no ~.

Injun: Honest ~.

Injury: to add insult to ~.

Inkle-maker: as thick as ~s.

Inn: Gray's ~ pieces; Paltock's ~.

Innocent: as ~ as a bird.

Insult: to add ~ to injury.

Intellect: march of ~.

Intention: Hell is paved with good ~s.

Interest: Dog's ~.

Interesting: in an ~ condition.

Iron: Touch cold ~.

Isle: Emerald ~.

Itchul: as black as ~.

Ivy: like an owl in an ~ bush.

Jack: ~ Pudding; Poor ~.

Jacket: to be hanged in an everlasting ~.

Jack: before one can say ~ Robinson; to send ~ after yes.

Jackson: jammed like ~.

Jam: ~ed like Jackson.

Jealous: as ~ as a couple of hairdressers.

Jericho: Go to ~.

Jew: worth a ~'s eye.

Jewel: Fair play is a ~.
Jib: the cut of one's ~.
Jingo: By ~.
Job: a Coggeshall ~.
Joe the Marine: *as lazy as Ludlum's dog.
Jog: the Minnesota ~.
John: Hopping ~.
John Noble: I know it, my lord, I know it, as said ~.
John Toy: Like lucky ~, he has lost a shilling and found a two-penny loaf.
Johnny: ~ Crapaud.
Johny Pyot's: ~ term day.
Join: to ~ giblets; to ~ the majority; ~ your flats.
Jolly: as ~ as sandboys.
Jon Walker: as slow as old ~'s chimes.
Journey: Sabbath day's ~.
Jump: to watch how the cat ~s.
June: as long as the eleventh of ~.
Just: to sleep the sleep of the ~.

Kettle: a pretty ~ of fish.
Kettle crook: to put a sneck in the ~.
Kibber: Jibber the ~.
Kibosh: to put the ~ on.
Kidney: rump and ~ man.
King: A cat may look at a ~; God save the ~; ~ cotton; the ~'s highway.
King John's man: ~ —four feet nothing.
Kingswear boys: *All on one side, like the Bridgnorth election.
Kirn: Cast the cat in the ~.
Kiss: as easy as a ~.
Kite: to fly a ~; higher than Gil(de)roy's ~.
Knee: as big as a bee's ~; as cold as a maid's ~.
Knocker: as black as Newgate ~.
Know: Dear ~s; He ~s how many go to the dozen; He ~s nothing about diss; I ~ it, my lord, I ~ it,
    as said John Noble; Not to ~ a B from a bull's foot.
Knowsley: Lathom and ~.

Lady: It is not every ~ of Genoa that is a queen of Corsica; little old ladies in tennis shoes; old ~
    of Threadneedle street.
Lame: crutches for ~ ducks; *Rare-overs for meddlers. *See also* Rooden Lane
Land: to swallow a yard of ~.
Lantern: to go to the ~.
Large: by and ~.

Lark: as big as a Dunstable ~; as queer as a ~.

Last: First in the wood and ~ in the bog.

Late: tToo little and too ~.

Latin: Tace is ~ for candle; Tace is ~ for horselock.

Laurence: as lazy as ~'s dog.

Law: Halifax ~; Lynch ~; Possession is nine points of the ~; Tiler's ~.

Lawrence: Lazy ~.

Lawyer: It would puzzle a Philadelphia ~.

Layer: ~s for meddlers.

Lazy: as ~ as a dog; as ~ as Laurence's dog; as ~ as Ludlum's dog; as ~ as Lumley's dog.

Lead (v): Old maids ~ apes in hell.

Lean: as ~ as MacFarlan's geese.

Leather: hell for ~; There's nothing like ~.

Leave: to take French ~.

Lecture: curtain ~.

Left: over the ~.

Leg: ~ bail; to make a ~; to pull one's ~.

Level: ~ best; on the broad ~.

Lie: Let sleeping dogs ~; ~ at the catch.

Life: * to do the dancers.

Light (adjective): Leave is ~.

Light (noun): in your own ~, like the mayor of Market-Jew; to pick up the church ~s; rising of the ~s; sweetness of ~.

Lightly: ~ come, ~ go.

Like: All on one side, ~ Rooden Lane; All on one side, ~ Takeley Street; All on one side, ~ the Bridgnorth election; All on one side, ~ the lock of a gun; All over, ~ the fair of Athy; as ~ as two patterns; to drink ~ a fish; to grin ~ a Cheshire cat; to grin ~ a weasel in a trap; In your own light, ~ the mayor of Market-Jew; It shines ~ Holmby mud walls; jammed ~ Jackson; to look (stare) ~ a throttled earwig; to run ~ a skeiner; to sleep ~ a top; to smile ~ a basket of chips; stand ~ a Stoughton bottle; to talk ~ a Dutch uncle; There's nothing ~ leather; We shall live till we die, ~ Tantrabobus.

Limb: to tear ~ (or Lymm) from Warburton.

Lincoln: the Devil overlooks ~.

Lincoln Heath: From ~, God help me.

Line: hard ~s; thin red ~.

Lion: to beat a (the) dog before the ~; to paint the ~; to see the ~s.

Lip: Button your ~.

Literary: damned ~ fellows.

Little: ~ Billing; to come out of the ~ end of the horn; ~ Englander; far-fetched and ~ worth; too ~ and too late.

Live: We shall ~ till we die, like Tantrabobus.

Loaf: Like lucky John Toy, he has lost a shilling and found a two-penny ~.

Loch Awe: It's a long cry to ~.

Lock: All on one side, like the ~ of a gun.

Lode: to smother in the ~ and worry in the hose.

Loitch: as straight as a ~.

Lombart Street: All ~ to a China orange.

Long: It's a ~ cry to Loch Awe; to make a ~ arm.

Look: as queer as Tim's wife ~ed when she hanged herself; A cat may ~ at a king; Devil over~s Lincoln; It ~s dark over Rivington; to ~ like a throttled earwig; to ~ nine ways for Sunday; You may go ~.

Lop: as bug as a ~.

Lord: *as sore as a pup; I know it, my ~, I know it, as said John Noble.

Lord Harry: By the ~. *See also* My lord

Lose: I'll have a dag if I ~ my spike; Like lucky John Toy, he has lost a shilling and found a two-penny loaf; No love lost.

Loss: cut the ~.

Louth Clock: as false as ~.

Louse: as pert as a ~; as proud as a ~.

Love: Cold pudding settles one's ~; to make ~; no ~ lost.

Lucky: Like ~ John Toy, he lost a shilling and found a two-penny loaf.

Ludlum: as lazy as ~'s dog.

Lugger: Andrew Millar's ~.

Lumley: as lazy as ~'s dog.

Luncheon: Blue plate ~.

Lymm: to tear limb (or ~) from Warburton.

MacFarlan: as lean as ~'s geese.

Mad: as ~ as a coot; as ~ as a hatter; as ~ as a March hare; as ~ as a tup; as ~ as the baiting bull of Stamford.

Madame Hassel: like ~'s feast.

Maggot: as fierce as a ~; *as wick as a scopril; when the ~ bites.

Maid: as cold as a ~'s knee; old ~s' day; Old ~s lead apes in hell.

Majority: to join the ~.

Make: ale that would ~ a cat talk; Either ~ a spoon or spoil a horn; Money ~s the mare go; Nine tailors ~ a man.

Man: Dead ~'s chest; Enough to make a ~ strike his own father; Every ~ has his price; Every ~ is a fool or a physician at forty (thirty); Grand old ~; John Thomson's ~; King John's ~ —four feet nothing; ~ proposes, but God disposes; a ~ and a brother; ~ in a quart bottle; ~ in the street; ~ of one book; ~ of straw; ~ of wax; Nine tailors make a ~; one ~; rump and kidney ~; wise men of Gotham.

Manchester: Constable of Oppenshaw sets beggars in the stocks at ~.

Manners: twopence for ~.

Mantle: ~ -maker's twist.

Many: to know how ~ beans makes five; ~ a mickle makes a muckle.

Mapstick: to cry ~s.

March: as mad as a ~ hare.

Mare: The grey ~ is the better horse; Money makes the ~ go; Tamson's ~.

Marine: Tell that to the ~s.

Mark: *to draw the long bow; God bless the ~; Save the ~.

Market: drug in the ~.

Market-Jew: In your own light, like the mayor of ~.

Maria: Black ~.

Marrow-bone: Ride in the ~ stage.

Mary Palmer: as hot as ~.

Mast: to nail the colors to the ~.

Master: The eye of the ~ (is worth both his hands).

Masthead: champagne to the ~.

Match: to cry ~es; three on a ~.

Mayor: Bring another ~ and another bottle; Here's to the ~ of Wigan; In your own light, like the ~ of Market-Jew.

Meat: After ~ —mustard; to carry ~ in one's mouth; to cry roast ~.

Meddler: lay-o'ers for ~s; Layers for ~s, and crutches for wild ducks; rare-overs for ~s.

Melder: dusty ~.

Mense: meat and ~.

Merry: in a ~ pin.

Mess: tidy ~.

Mickle: Many a ~ makes a muckle.

Milk: to run ~.

Milestone: to answer by ~s.

Miller: to drown the ~.

Million: for the ~.

Mind (noun): month's ~.

Mind (verb): ~ one's P's and Q's.

Mint: ~ state.

Mistake: and no ~.

Mitten: to give the ~.

Moment: psychological ~.

Monday: Friday's hair and Sunday's horn goes to the dule on ~ morn.

Money: Bad ~ drives out good; fiddler's ~; hard ~; pin ~; short-day ~.

Monkey: to broach the admiral; give one ~'s allowance; to have no more use (for something) than a dog (or ~) has for side-pockets; The higher the ~ climbs, the more he shows his tail; ~ on the chimney; ~'s parade; to pay in ~'s coin; to put one's ~ up.

Monster: green-eyed ~.

Month: Dutch ~.

Moon: man in the ~; once in a blue ~; Shoot the ~.

Mop-stick: like death on a ~.

Morn: Friday's hair and Sunday's horn goes to the dule on Monday ~.

Morning: cry of the ~; a dog in the ~; to give one the seal of the ~; No fore royal, no ~ coffee; pride of the ~.

Mother: ~ of dead dogs; Old ~ Damnable; She's the cat's ~.

Motto: to put in one's ~.

Mountain: It stands stiff, and but's a ~.

Mouse: as drunk as mice.

Mouth: born with a silver spoon in one's ~; butter out of a dog's ~; to carry meat in one's ~; drink by word of ~; to make up one's ~; out of the horse's ~.

Muckle: Many a mickle makes a ~.

Mud: It shines like Holmby ~ walls.

Mug: ugly ~.

Mull: a regular ~.

Mummy: to beat to a ~.

Mungret: as wise as the women of ~.

Music: to face the ~.

Musket: as lazy as Joe the Marine, who laid down his ~ to sneeze.

Mustard: after meat— ~; to cut the ~; * to send Jack after yes.

Mutton: as dead as ~.

Mutual: ~ admiration society; Our ~ friend.

Nail: cash on the ~; drawing the ~; paid down upon the ~.

Nap: caught ~ping.

Narrow: as ~ in the nose as a pig at nine-pence.

Nasty: cheap and ~.

Near: Ask ~, sell dear.

Neck: hair in one's ~.

Ned: to raise ~.

Neighbo(u)r: Have the French for friends, but not for ~s.

Newcastle: to carry coals to ~.

Newgate: As black as a ~ Knocker.

News: duck's ~; Piper's ~; Roper's ~.

Niagara: to dam up ~ with a pitchfork.

Nice: as ~ as a nun's hen.

Nick: in the ~ of time.

Nine: as queer as Dick's hatband, that went ~ times round his hat and was fastened by a rush at last; cloud ~; to look ~ ways for Sunday; ~ days wonder; ~ of diamonds and the curse of Scotland; ~ tailors make a man; Possession is ~ points of the law; seven and ~; seven by ~ politician.

Nine-pence: as narrow in the nose as a pig at ~; to bring a noble to ~ and ~ to nothing; to give the old woman her ~; His noble has come down to ~; A nimble ~ is better than a slow shilling; ~, Nanny! Two groats and a penny.

Nip: ~ and tuck.

No: whether or ~.

Noble: to bring a ~ to nine-pence and nine-pence to nothing.

North: to go ~ about.

Northampton: He that would eat a buttered faggot, let him go to ~.

Norton: Hog's ~ where pigs play on the organ.

Nose: as narrow in the ~ as a pig at nine-pence; blue ~; Cut off one's ~ to spite one's face; a dog's ~ cold; the Parson's ~; to pay through the ~.

Nosebag: out of the ~.

No(s)ey: ~ Parker.

Notchel: to cry one's wife ~.

Nothing: to bring a noble to nine-pence and nine-pence to ~; It is ~ but cork; King John's man—four feet ~; Say ~ and saw wood; There's ~ like leather.

Nun: as nice as a ~'s hen.

Nutting bag: as black as the Devil's ~.

Oat: more than Carter had ~s; sow one's wild ~s.

Object: Distance no ~.

Office: carry one's ~ in one's hat.

Oil: Pour ~ upon the troubled waters.

Old: as slow as ~ Jon Walker's chimes; to give the ~ woman her ninepence; grand ~ man; little ~ ladies in tennis shoes; Never make ~ bones; not worth an ~ song; same ~ two-and-sixpence; the tune the ~ cow died of.

Old Gooseberry: Play (up) ~.

Old Rose: Sing ~ and burn the bellows.

Old Weston: to go to ~.

Oliver: to give a Roland for an ~.

One: All on ~ side, like Rooden Lane; All on ~ side, like Takeley Street; All on ~ side, like the Bridgnorth election; All on ~ side, like the lock of a gun; like ~ o'clock.

Only: ~ too thankful.

Oppenshaw: Constable of ~ sets beggars in the stocks at Manchester.

Order: Apple-pie ~.

Organ: Hog's Norton where pigs play on the ~.

Out: at ~s.

Outshoot: *to draw the long bow.

Owl: as stupid as an ~; like an ~ in an ivy bush; ~ in ivy bush.

Own: enough ~.

Oxford: Send farthingales to Broad Gates in ~.

Painter ("rope"): to cut the ~.

Pan: to turn the cat in the ~.

Pancake: hands full of ~s.

Parade: monkey's ~.

Parish: *in a merry pin; to make one's ~.

Parker: nos(e)y ~.

Parsnip: Soft words butter no ~s.

Patch: Not a ~ on it.

Paternoster: No penny, no ~.

Pattern: as like as two ~s.

Paul: pigeons of ~'s; to rob Peter to pay ~.

Pave: Hell is ~d with good intentions; London ~d with gold.

Pay: Devil to ~ and no pitch hot; ~ through the nose.

Pea: Every ~ hath its vease.

Peanut: *seven by nine politician.

Pearl: to take the ~ from a piper's eye.

Pearmonger: as pert as a ~.

Pecker: Keep your ~ up.

Peckham: All holiday at ~.

Peg: a round ~ and square hole.

Pence: *See* Penny

Pencil: blue ~.

Penny: Brown and Thompson's ~ hotels; Ninepence, Nanny! Two groats and a ~; No ~, no paternoster; A ~ saved is a penny got; Victor ~; Wheedled as children with a ~ in the forehead.

Pennyworth: Robin Hood's ~s.

Perfection: counsels of ~.

Persimmon: to pass one's ~.

Pert: as ~ as a louse; as ~ as a pearmonger; *as proud as a louse.

Peter: to rob ~ to pay Paul.

Phibbie: dance the ~.

Philadelphia: It would puzzle a ~ lawyer.

Physician: Every man is a fool or a ~ at forty (thirty); fool or a ~.

Pickle: a rod in ~.

Pie: to eat humble ~.

Piece: Gray's Inn ~s; pence a ~.

Pig: an Anthony ~; as dark as black ~; as fess as Cox's ~; as narrow in the nose as a ~ at nine-
pence; to buy a ~ in a poke; cold ~; Hog's Norton where ~s play on the organ; *to let the cat
out of the bag; to please the ~s; *to send one to Putney.

Pigeon: blue ~; not my ~.

Pig-trough: to dance in a ~.

Pikestaff: as plain as a ~.

Pimlico: I am in ~ with my feet; to keep in ~.

Pin: to find a ~ for every bore; in a merry ~; Jack silver ~; nick the ~.

Pink: as clean as a ~.

Pinprick: the policy of ~s.

Piper: pay the ~; to take the pearl from a ~'s eye.

Pismire: as merry as a ~.

Pitch: Devil to pay and no ~ hot.

Pitchfork: to dam up Niagara with a ~.

Place: between a rock and a hard ~.

Plain: as ~ as a pikestaff.

Plate: blue ~ luncheon.

Play (noun): as good as a ~; dresser of ~s.

Play (verb): Fair ~ is jewel; Hog's Norton where pigs ~ on the organ; *It's not the cricket; *Lie doggo; to ~ all sharps; to ~ Hal (or hell) and Tommy; to ~ the goat; to ~ the dozen; ~ up Old Gooseberry; to ~ possum; to ~ the bear; to ~ the charley (wag); *to raise Hamlet on one.

Pleased: *See* As sore as a pup

Pocket: *See* Side-pocket

Point: Possession is nine ~s of the law; potato and ~.

Pokey: hokey ~.

Politician: seven by nine ~.

Pontypool waiter: as round as a ~.

Poor: as ~ as Crowborough; as ~ as Job's turkey.

Pop: ~ goes the weasel; *monkey on the chimney.

Pope: to know no more than the ~ of Rome; *the parson's nose; the ~'s nose; the ~'s eye.

Porch: infants in the ~.

Porcus: Latins call me ~.

Porridge: a chip in ~; Like chips in ~, neither good nor harm.

Posset: Give one sneck ~.

Possum: to play ~.

Post: from pillar to ~.

Pot: The cat is in the cream ~; to go to ~.

Potato: ~ and point; quite the (clean) ~.

Pour: to ~ oil upon the troubled waters

Previous: to move the ~ question.

Price: Every man has his ~; rock-bottom ~s.

Print: in ~.

Prime: to pull ~.

Priscian: to break ~'s head.

Propose: Man ~s, but God disposes.

Proud: as ~ as a dog with side-pockets; as ~ as a louse; as ~ as old Cole's dog; Every cock is ~ on his own dunghill; He was as ~ as a toad with a side-pocket.

Pudding: Cold ~ settles one's love; Jack ~.

Pump: to nail one's ears to the ~.

Punch: *as sore as a pup.

Pup: as sore as a ~.

Purple: *An ape is an ape, be she clothed in ~.

Put: to ~ a Dutchman in; to ~ a sneck in the kettle crook; to ~ a sponke in one's wheel; to ~ in
   one's motto; to ~ one's foot into it; to ~ one's monkey up; to ~ out the Besom; to ~ side on; to
   ~ the kibosh on; to ~ to Buck; to ~ to the horn; ~ up with.
Putney: to send one to ~.
Putty: on the ~.
Puzzle: It would ~ a Philadelphia lawyer.

Quaker: It always rains ~ week.
Quality: defects of his qualities.
Quart: man in a ~ bottle.
Quarter: Bolton ~; to give ~.
Queen: as dead as ~ Anne; It is not every lady of Genoa that is a ~ of Corsica.
Queer: as ~ as Dick's hat-band, that went nine times round his hat and was fastened by a rush
   at last.
Question: to move the previous ~; Sixty-four dollar ~.

Racket: to stand the ~.
Rag: chew the ~; *get (a person's) shirt out; tag, ~, and bobtail.
Rain: as right as ~; It always ~s Quaker week; It ~s cats and dogs.
Ram: Derby ~.
Rannal-Bawk: thrown over the ~.
Rap: not worth a ~.
Raspberry: blowing a ~.
Rat: as dead as a ~; as weak as a ~; *half ~ and half weasel; to smell a ~; to rhyme ~s to death.
Red: thin ~ line.
Regard: kind ~s.
Respectability: oppresive ~.
Rest: to set up one's ~.
Return: to ~ thanks.
Ride: to ~ bodkin; to ~ hell-for-leather; ~ in the marrow-bone stage; to ~ the breeze; ~ the high
   horse.
Rig: run a ~.
Right: all ~; as ~ as a trivet.
Riley: the life of ~.
Ring: to do the dancers; to rule the ~.
Rise: take a ~.
River: sold down the ~.
Roach: as sound as a ~.
Roast (noun): to cry ~ meat.
Roast (verb): to rule the ~.
Robin: round ~.
Robin Hood: all round ~'s barn.

Rock: between a ~ and a hard place.

Roland: to give a ~ for an Oliver.

Roman: Greeks have turned ~ Catholics.

Rome: know no more than the Pope of ~.

Rooden Lane: All on one side, like ~.

Roofer: Hutton ~s.

Rope: dance the ~s.

Rorke: to get ~'s drift.

Rose: bed of ~s.

Round (adjective): as ~ as a Pontypool waiter.

Round (noun): to go the ~(s).

Rube: Hey, ~.

Rug: to pull the ~ (from under).

Rule (noun): The exception proves the ~; ~ of thumb; There must be ~s.

Rule (verb): to ~ the ring; to ~ the roast.

Run: to cut and ~; ~ amuck; to ~ a rig; to ~ like a skeiner; to ~ milk; ~ of his teeth.

Rush: as queer as Dick's hat-band, that went nine times round his hat and was fastened by a ~ at last.

Rust: It is better to wear out than ~ out.

Sack: *Fine words butter no parsnips; to give the ~.

Saddle: boot and ~.

Saint: Banbury ~; to braid ~ Catharine's tresses; to get (~) Lawrence on the shoulder; little summer of ~ Luke; ~ Boniface's cup; ~ Pawsle's e'ens; ~ Peter's fingers.

Salad: lamb and ~; to take a ~.

Salt: as ~ as fire.

Sanctity: odor of ~.

Sand: to have ~ in one's craw.

Sandboys: as jolly as ~.

Save: A penny ~d is a penny got.

Saw: Say nothing and ~ wood.

Sawder: soft ~.

Say: before you can ~ Jack Robinson; ~ nothing and saw wood.

School: tell tales out of ~.

Science: Scotch ~.

Scilly: always a feast or a fast in ~.

Scopril: as wick as a ~.

Scot: Great ~; kindly ~.

Scotland: curse of ~.

Scrape: to get into a ~.

Scratch: *Caw me, caw thee; up to ~.

Scrub: Hightem, tightem, and ~.

Swim: in the ~.

Swing: not enough room to ~ a cat.

Sword: a clean ~ and a dirty Bible.

T: to fit to a ~; suits to a ~.

Table: to knock under the ~; to turn the ~s.

Tack: to hold ~; to get down to brass ~s; hungry enough to eat brass ~s; *nip and tuck.

Tail: as proud as a dog with two ~s; drag the Devil by the ~; The higher the monkey climbs, the more he shows his ~; However far a bird flies it carries its ~ with it; I wish I had our cat by the ~; Let every herring hang by its own ~.

Tailor: the Devil among the ~s; Nine ~s make a man.

Takeley Street: All on one side, like ~.

Tale: tell ~s out of school.

Talk: ale that would make a cat ~; all ~ and no cider; ~ through one's heat.

Tall: as ~ as the Devil's nutting bag.

Tandem: like the Dutchman's anchor at home.

Tantrabobus: We shall live till we die, like ~.

Tap: to broach the admiral.

Tape: red ~.

Tar: to spoil the ship for a ha'porth of ~.

Tea: dish of ~; not my cup of ~; ~ and turn-out.

Teacup: storm in a ~.

Teapot: storm in a teacup.

Tear: crocodile's ~s.

Teem: lading and ~ing.

Tell: a little bird told me; ~ tales out of school; ~ that to the marines.

Temper: God ~s the wind.

Tennis: little old ladies in ~ shoes.

Terror: a new ~ to death.

Thames: to set the ~ on fire.

Thankful: only too ~.

Thanks: to return ~.

Thatch: *as wet as thatck.

Thatck: as wet as ~.

Thick: as ~ as butter; as ~ as inkle-makers.

Think: I don't ~.

Thirteen: not worth a ~; to throw the ~s about one.

Thompson: Brown and ~'s penny hotels; John Thomson's man.

Threadneedle Street: old lady of ~.

Thresher: like a ~.

Throp: as busy as ~'s wife; as throng as ~'s wife.

Throng: as ~ as Throp's wife.

Throttle: to look like a ~d earwig.

Thumb: to a cow's ~; rule of ~.

Thunder: to steal one's ~.

Thursdays: when three ~ meet.

Tick: as fierce as a dig; as full as a ~.

Ticket: give somebody the ~ for soup; That's the ~.

Tide: to go out with the ~.

Tight: as ~ as Dick's hatband.

Tightem: Heightem, ~, and scrub.

Tim: as queer as ~'s wife looked when she hanged herself.

Time: as queer as Dick's hatband, that went nine ~s round his hat and was fastened by a rush at last; to have a good ~; to pass the ~ of day.

Tinker: not worth a ~'s curse.

Tip: to give the straight ~.

Tiverton: How's your auntie at ~?

Toad: He was as proud as a ~ with a side-pocket; a side-pocket to a ~.

Tod: Remember ~.

Toil: horny-handed sons of ~.

Tom Coxe: a ~'s traverse.

Tommy: to give one hell and ~; my eye and ~; to play Hal and ~; to play hell and ~.

Tom Tiddler: ~'s ground.

Tongs: as mean as ~.

Tooth: from the teeth outward; the run of his teeth.

Top (noun): to sleep like a ~.

Top (adjective): out of the ~ drawer.

Topsham: to come from ~.

Touch: in ~ with.

Track: inside ~.

Trap: grin like a weasel in a ~.

Traverse: a Tom Coxe's ~.

Tress: to braid St. Catharine's ~es.

Trey-trip: Go by the beggar's bush or the game of ~.

Trivet: as right as a ~.

Trouble: Pour oil upon the ~d waters.

Trout: as sound as a ~.

True: as ~ as the devil's in Dublin city.

Tuck: nip and ~.

Tune: the ~ the old cow died of.

Tup: as mad as a ~.

Turkey: as poor as Job's ~.

Turn: The Greeks have ~ed to Roman Catholics; Tea and ~-out; to ~ the cat in the pan; to ~ the tables.

Turn out: Tea and ~.

Turnip: to give ~s.

Turvey: It's time to be off to ~.

Tut: stick to one's ~.

Twelvemonth: month's mind.

Twig: to hop the ~.

Twist: mantle-maker's ~.

Two: as like as ~ patterns; to sit between ~ stools.

Two-and-sixpence: same old ~.

Twopence: Penny plain, ~ colored.

Two-penny: Like lucky Jon Toy, he has lost a shilling and found a ~ loaf; not to care a ~ damn.

Two-shoes: Goody ~.

Uncle: to talk like a Dutch ~.

Upstairs: to kick ~.

Vease: Every pea hath its ~.

Verdict: a Scotch ~.

Verse: chapter and ~.

Vocative: found in the ~.

Wag: to hop the ~; to play the Charley (~).

Waggon: to hitch one's ~ to a star.

Walk: as the Devil ~ing through Athlone; cock of the ~; to fetch a compass; the Parson's nose.

Wall: It shines like Holmby mud ~s; to lay a ship by the ~s; to lie by the ~; three holes in the ~;
   The weakest goes to the ~.

Waltham: as wise as ~'s calf.

War: point of ~.

Warburton: to tear limb (or Lymm) from ~.

Warehouse: Yorkshire ~.

Warm: as ~ as a bat; out of God's blessing into a ~ sun.

Warning: Scarborough ~; Skyreburn ~.

Water: Blood is thicker than ~; in hot ~; It won't hold ~; Pour oil upon the troubled ~s.

Wax: man of ~; nose of ~.

Way: the American ~; to go the ~ of all flesh; to look nine ~s for Sunday.

Weak: as ~ as a rat.

Wear out: It is better to ~ than rust out.

Weasel: to catch a ~ asleep; grin like a ~ in a trap; half rat and half ~; pop goes the ~.

Weather: forty days of wet ~; under the ~.

Week: It always rains Quaker ~; month's mind.

Weigh: under ~.

Wet: as ~ as thatch; forty days of ~ weather; with a ~ finger. *See also* As sore as a pup

Wheel: to do the dancers; to put a spoke in one's ~.

Whillelujah: to sing ~ (or wollalew) to the day-nettles.

Whistle: as clean as a ~; pig and ~.

White: to show the ~ feather.

Who: ~ stole the donkey.

Whole: to go the ~ hog.

Wick: as ~ as a scopril.

Widow: grass ~.

Width: Walk ~ and stride sidth.

Wife: All the world and Bingham will be there; as busy as Beck's ~; as busy as Throp's ~; as queer as Tim's ~ looked when she hanged herself; to cry one's ~ notchel; a whistling woman and a crowing hen.

Wig: as sour as a ~.

Wigan. *See* Mayor

Wiggle: Get a ~ on!

Wild: Layers for meddlers, and crutches for ~ ducks; sow one's ~ oats.

Wind: to get the ~ up; God tempers the ~; Pigs can see ~; to raise the ~; a Robin Hood ~; to whistle for the ~.

Windlass: to fetch a compass.

Windmill: to throw a bonnet over the ~.

Wine: Good ~ needs no bush.

Wings: if they had ~.

Wise: as ~ as the women of Mungret; as ~ as Waltham's calf to preach (talk).

Wit: One's ~s are gone wool-gathering.

Wolf: between the dog and the ~; to keep the ~ from the door.

Woman: as wise as the women of Mungret; Berm ~; to give the old ~ her ninepence; a whistling ~ and a crowing hen.

Wonder: nine days ~.

Wood (name): as contrairy as ~'s dog.

Wood: first in the ~ and last in the bog; Say nothing and saw ~.

Wool-gathering: One's wits are gone ~.

Word: drink by ~ of mouth.

Work: dirty ~ at the crossroads; gin ~; ~ like a dog.

World: All the ~ and Bingham will be there.

Worry: to smother in the lode and ~ in the hose.

Worth: The eye of the master (is ~ both his hands); far-fetched and little ~; not ~ a cress; not ~ an old song; not ~ a rap; not ~ a tinker's curse.

Yam: Toko for ~.

Yard: to swallow a ~ of land.

Year: donkey's ~s; month's mind; A pin a day is a groat a ~.

Yes: to send Jack after ~.

Name Index

An asterisk indicates this name is mentioned in "An Annotated List of Dictionaries and Reference Works" in the "Sources and Abbreviations" section of this book.

Abraham, biblical character: **A1, G51, S32**.

Adam, biblical character: **A5**.

Adams, F.: **A71, L17, N36, R14, S28**.

Addy, S.O.*, 1848–1933: **B49, H12, L5**.

Adelphi Theatre, theatre in Westminster, London: **A7**.

Adolphus, Gustavus, 1594–1632. King of Sweden. Reigned 1611–1632: **B28**.

Adventures of B.M. Carew*: **C69**.

Alexander and Campaspe, 1584: **M27**. *See* Lily, John.

Alice in Wonderland, 1865. **A110**. *See* Carroll, Lewis.

Ambrose, Isaac, 1604–1664. English author: **B46, C77**. See also *Media; Or Middle Things*.

American Preceptor, 1794: **M32**. *See* Bingham, Caleb.

Amphitrite, goddess of the sea and wife of Poseidon: **W22**.

An Antidote against Idolatry, 1669: **A55**. *See* More, Henry.

Andrew Martin: **A14, A29**.

Andrew Millar (Miller): **A30**.

Anna Matilda, **A32**. *See* Cowley, Hannah.

Anne, 1665–1714, Queen of England, Scotland, and Ireland, 1702–1707. Queen of Great Britain and Ireland, 1707–1714: **A75, D49**.

Annie Oakley, 1860–1926. American sharpshooter: **A33**.

The Annotated Bible, 1879–1880: **A1**. *See* Blunt, J.H.

Anonymiana, 1818: **L5**. *See* Pegge, Samuel.

Antoinette, Marie, 1755–1794, Queen of France, 1774–1792: **B20**.

Apley Estate, commonly referred to as Apley Hall, near Bridgnorth, England: **A17**.

Apperson, G.L.*, 1857–1937: **A8, A11, A13, A16, A17, A25, A27, A45, A48, A52, A59, A73, A84, A85, A89, A95, A103, A104, A114, A126, A146, A157, A164, A167, B13, B25, B32, B65, B68, B69, C15, C16, C21, C40, C44, C50, C59, C73, D29, D35, G67, H12, H36, H44, I30, K2, K20, K21, L3, L5, L8, L9, L33, N5, N20, R25, R28, S22, T2, T14, U10**.

The Apprentice, 1756: **A3**. *See* Murphy, Arthur.

Arber, Edward, 1835–1912. English scholar, writer, and editor: **B7**.

Arnold, Matthew, 1822–1888. English poet and critic: **S87**.

Assembly of Divines, 1643–1653. Appointed to reconstruct the Church of England; referred to as Westminster Divines, or *Divinities*: **C22**. *See* Selden, John.

At Last: A Christmas in the West Indies, 1871: **D8**. *See* Kingsley, Charles.

Bow Bells, the church bells of St. Mary-le-Bow in London, England: **W30**.

Bowes, Sir George, 1527–1580. English military commander: **B10**.

Bradford, John, 1510–1555. English reformer and martyr: **P38**.

Bradley, Henry, 1845–1923. British philologist and senior editor of *The Oxford English Dictionary*: **C77, G34**.

Brady, John, ?–1841. English author and clerk. See also *Varieties of Literature*: **U10**.

Brainless Blessing of the Bull, The, 1571?: **A167**. *See* Huth, Henry.

Braithwait, Richard, 1588–1673. English poet: **B8**. See also *Drunken Barnaby's Four Journeys*.

Brand, John*, 1744–1806: **I10**.

Brewer, E. Cobham*, 1810–1897: **B76, G9, G29, U12**.

Bridgnorth, town in Shropshire, England: **A17**.

Bristol, city and county in Southwest England: **C9, S34, W33**.

Brougham, Lord Henry, 1778–1868. British politician and one-time Lord High Chancellor: **F33, N9, S14**.

Browning, Robert, 1812–1889. English poet and playwright: **P13**. See also *The Pied Piper of Hamelin*.

Bruce, Robert, known as Robert the Bruce, 1274–1329, King of Scots, 1306–1329: **C9, N14**.

Bulwer-Lytton, Edward George Earle, 1803–1873. English author: **J9**. See also *Pelham. Mabinogion**, **S54**.

Bunyan, John, 1628–1688. English writer and Puritan preacher: **L21, M2**. See also *The Pilgrim's Progress*.

Burke, Edmund, 1729–1797. British statesman and political writer: **F33**.

Burns, Robert, 1759–1796. Scottish poet: **B76, N14, U2**.

Butler, Samuel, 1612–1680. English satirical poet: **A152, N21, O1, O35, P22**. See also *Hudibras*.

Byron, George G., 1788–1824. English poet: **C18, O5**. See also *Don Juan*.

Cairn, river in Dumfries and Galloway, Scotland: **N14**.

Cambray, Philip G*, **L40**.

Camden, William, 1551–1623. English historian and topographer: **T1**.

Campbell, Daniel, 1671–1753. Scottish merchant and politician: **N14**.

Camperdown, Battle of. Naval engagement on October 11, 1797, between the British and the Batavian Navies: **N2**.

Canterbury, city in Kent, England: **C4, W30**.

Carew, Bampfylde-Moore*, 1693–1759: **C69**.

Carlyle, Thomas, 1795–1881. Scottish historian and writer: **F3, M22, M39, U5**.

Carroll, Lewis, 1832–1898. Pen name of the English writer Charles Lutwidge Dodgson: **A110**. See also *Alice in Wonderland*.

Catriona, 1893: **T11**. *See* Stevenson, Robert L.

Chambers, Robert*, 1802–1871: **C60, G6**. See also *Book of Days*.

Chance, Frank, 1826–1897. Medical doctor and philologist: **A168, B45, B76, C12, G57, H71, H73, I7, R29, T5, T47, W6**

La Chanson de Roland*, **G17**.

Crawley, town in West Sussex, England: A68, B30, C59, F37, T35.

Cromichan, former British town in the Midlands: S24.

Cromwell, Oliver, 1599–1658. Lord Protector of England: B28, G17.

Cromwell, Thomas, Earl of Essex, 1485?–1540. The chief minister to King Henry VIII of England: G23, P30.

Crowborough, town in East Sussex, England: A122.

Cruikshank, George, 1792–1878. British caricaturist: H58.

The Cryes of the City of London, Drawne after the Life, 1711. A series of seventy-four portraits drawn by Marcellus Laroon the elder and published by Pierce Tempest: C70.

Culloden, Battle of, 1746. The final battle of the Jacobite Rising of 1745: N14.

Cupar, town in Fife, Scotland: H37.

Cursor Mundi*, A143.

Curtaine Lecture, 1637: C78. *See* Heywood, Thomas.

Crystal, David. G28. See also *That's the Ticket for Soup!*

Dana, Richard Henry Jr., 1815–1882. American lawyer and politician: D1. See also *Two Years before the Mast.*

Daudet, Alphonse, 1840–1897. French novelist: P42. See also *Tartarin de Tarascon.*

De Morgan, Augustus. 1806–1871. British mathematician and logician: A3, A151.

De Quincey, Thomas, 1785–1859. English essayist: P9.

Della Crusca, pen name used by a group of European poets founded by Robert Merry (1755–1798): A32.

Derbyshire, county in the East Midlands, England: A45, D12, I40, K19, N5, N15.

Devonshire, county along the English Channel, England. A17, A18, A52, B75, C43, H70, I1, K2, K17, M10, P60, R29, W11.

Dickens, Charles, 1812–1870. English writer: A100, D19, G1, O23, O26, T50, W13. See also *Martin Chuzzlewit, Nicholas Nickleby,* and *The Pickwick Papers.*

Dictionary of the Noted Names in Fiction, a. 1923: A26, M25. *See* Wheeler, William Adolphus.

Don Juan, 1824: C18. *See* Byron, George G.

Donnybrook Fair, fair held in Donnybrook, Dublin, from 1204 to 1866: T54.

Dorsetshire, county in Southwest England: D3, S71.

The Double Dealer, 1693: O4. *See* Congreve, William.

Drayton, Michael, 1563–1631. English poet and playwright: A66. See also *Poly-Olbion.*

Drunken Barnaby's Four Journeys, 1716: B8. *See* Brathwait, Richard.

Dublin, capital of Ireland: A160, B52, N1.

Ducrow, Andrew, 1793–1842. British equestrian performer: C85.

Dunstable, town in Bedfordshire, England: A44, D36.

Dunton, John, 1659–1733. English author and bookseller: P18.

Dysart, Lord. The reference is to Lionel Tollemache, the third Earl of Dysart, 1649–1727: I3.

Ebrietatis Encomium, 1812: S4. *See* Oinophilus, Boniface.

Edward IV, King of England, 1442–1483. Reigned 1461–1470 and 1471–1483: S15.

Edwards, Eliezer*, 1824–1891: **A39, B12, B36, C14, C29, D15, S10.**

Egan, Pierce, 1772–1849. British sportswriter and author: **T45.** See also *Life in London*.

Egypt, warfare in 1880s. The reference is to the British Conquest of Egypt in 1882, specifically the Battle of Tell El Kebir: **A22.**

Emerson, Ralph W., 1803–1882. American essayist, philosopher, and poet: **F30, H45, M15.**

Englische Philologie, 1881: **D25.** *See* Storm, Johan.

Essex, county in Southeast England: **A16, A167, C40, I7, P30, S9, U7.**

Estienne, Henri, 1528–1598. French printer and classical scholar: **G43.**

Evans, Arthur B.*, **H48.**

Exeter, Devonshire, city in England: **A17, H70.**

Expedition with Mackay's Regiment, 1637: **B28.** *See* Munro, Robert.

Felton, Cornelius Conway (C.C.), 1807-1862. English professor and President of Harvard University, a member of the Five of Clubs: **M44.**

Ferrar, James: **A166.** See also *The History of Limerick*.

Fielding, Henry, 1707–1754. English writer: **S23, T1.** See also *Tom Thumb*.

Five of Clubs. *See* **M44.**

Folk Etymology. See Palmer, Abram Smythe.

Forby, Robert*, 1759–1825: **K7.**

Forfar, town in Angus, Scotland: **D23.**

Frischlin, Philipp Nicodemus, 1547–1590. German poet, playwright, astronomer, and philologist: **B55.** See also *Priscianus Vapulans*.

Froude, James Anthony, 1818–1894. English historian and author: **M27.** See also *Life and Letters of Erasmus*.

Fuller, Thomas*, 1608–1661. English churchman and historian: **O29.** See also *Good Thoughts in Bad Times*.

Funk, Charles Earle*, 1881–1957: **A5, A21, A78, A97, A172, A173, B28, F1, F38, G5, G12, G59, G73, H4, I45, K5, L24, L25, R2.**

Furnivall, Frederick James, 1825–1910. English philologist and editor of the *OED*: **A143, M35, O11.**

Gardiner, Samuel Rawson, 1829-1902. English historian and author: **B8.** See also *History of England from the Accession of James I to the Outbreak of the Civil War*.

Garnet, Sir Wolseley, 1833–1913. Anglo-Irish officer in the British Army: **A22.**

Garrick, David, 1717–1779. English actor and playwright: **A80.**

Gentleman's Recreation, 1721: **B9.** *See* Cox, Nicholas.

Geoffrey the Grammarian*, fl.1440: **F36.**

George of (a) Greene, fictional character: **A95.**

Gerarde, John, 1545–1612: **A80, S15.** See also *Herball, or Generall Historie of Plantes*.

Gifford, William, 1756–1826. English editor and poet: **A32, R8.** See also *The Baviad*.

Gilbert, W.S., 1836–1911. English dramatist and poet: **O38.** See also *H.M.S. Pinafore*.

A Girl's Cross Roads, 1903: **D20.** *See* Melville, Walter.

Gladstone, William E., 1809–1898. English statesman and a four-time prime minister: **F11, G65.**

Glasgow, city in Scotland: **C84, N14.**

Glasse, Hannah: **F20.** *See* Mrs. Glasse.

Glencoe, Massacre of February 13 of the MacDonald clan by Archibald Campbell's Soldiers. 1692: **N14.**

Gloucestershire, county in Southwest England: **A152, B75, D19, K4, S43.**

Goebbels, P. Joseph, 1897-1945. Minister of Propaganda of Nazi Germany: **I27.**

Goldsmith, Oliver, 1728-1774. English poet, novelist, and playwright: **B76, B77, G47.** See also *The Good Natur'd Man* and *The History of Little Goody Two-Shoes.*

Good Thoughts in Bad Times, 1645: **O29.** *See* Fuller, Thomas.

The Good-Natur'd Man, 1768: **B77.** *See* Goldsmith, Oliver.

Goranson, Stephen*, **C87, H47, K1, K7, P66.**

Gotham, village in Nottinghamshire, England: **H38, W28.**

Gray, Albert, 1850-1928. British lawyer and civil servant: **K10.** See also *The Voyages of François Pyrard.*

Great Fire of London, fire in London from September 2-6, 1660: **B75.**

Greene, Robert, 1558-1592: **N21.** See also *Menaphon.*

Gresham, Sir Thomas, 1519-1579. English merchant and financier: **B4.**

Grimm, Jacob*, 1785-1863: **F36, S61.**

Grose, Francis*, 1731?-1791: **A14.**

Guam, island territory of the United States in the Pacific Ocean: **C31.**

Guevara, Antonio de, 1481?-1545. Spanish novelist and Franciscan bishop: **H34.**

Gulliver's Travels, 1726: **A44.** *See* Swift, Jonathan.

H.M.S Pinafore, 1878: **O38.** *See* Gilbert, W.S. and Sullivan, Arthur.

Halgavor Moor, Cornwall, England: **P48.**

Halifax, town in West Yorkshire, England: **A2, G55, H5, J5, K9, S13.**

Halliwell, James Orchard*, 1820-1889: **B8, B75, B76, C82, D36, G37, I30, P35, W33.**

Hampson, R. T., 1793-1858. British author: **R22.** See also *Medii Ævi Kalendarium.*

Hamlet, 1603: **F30, G6, N31, P31, R2, R3, S64.** *See* Shakespeare, William.

Handel, George F., 1685-1759. German composer who moved to England in 1712: **G65.**

Hartshorne, Charles Henry*, 1802-1865: **A17.**

Harvey, Gabriel, 1553?-1631. English writer: **I39.** See also *Pierce's Super.*

Harvey, John H., 1911-1997. English historian: **A14.** See also *The Heritage of Britain.*

Hatton, Sir Christopher, 1540-1591. English politician and Lord Chancellor of England (1587-1591): **I40.**

Have With You to Saffron-Walden, 1596: **R23.** *See* Nashe, Thomas.

Hazlitt, William Carew*, 1834-1913: **F33, I39, N11, P23.**

Hearne, Thomas*, 1678-1735: **M28.**

Hedda Gabler, 1891: **D18.** *See* Ibsen, Henrik.

Henry V, 1600: **B13.** *See* Shakespeare, William.

Henry VIII, 1491-1547. King of England. Reigned 1509-1547: **G23, G57, P30.**

Herball, or Generall Historie of Plantes, 1597: **S15.** *See* Gerarde, John.

Herbert, George*, 1593–1633: **G43**. See also *Jacula Prudentum* and *Wits Recreation*.

The Heritage of Britain, 1941 and 1943: **A14**. *See* Harvey, John.

The Hero in America, 1941: **B41**. *See* Wecter, Dixon.

Heywood, John*, 1497–1580: **C16, C78, N13, N21, T40**.

Heywood, Thomas, early 1570s–1641. English playwright: **C78, N21**. See also *Curtaine* Lecture.

Hillard, George S., 1808–1879. American lawyer and author; a member of the Five of Clubs: **M44**.

Hislop, Alexander*, 1807–1865: **A157, D23, H2, H37, L17, M19**.

History of England from the Accession of James I to the Outbreak of the Civil War, 1896: **B8**. *See* Gardiner, Samuel Rawson.

The History of England, 1848: **H28**. *See* Macaulay, Thomas Babington.

History of Limerick, 1787: **A166**. *See* Ferrar, James.

The History of Little Goody Two-Shoes, 1765: **G47**. *See* Goldsmith, Oliver.

Hoffman, W. Frederick, Royal Navy Captain: **H9, K13, T46**. See also *A Sailor of King George*.

Hog's Norton, village in Leistershire, England: **H48**.

Holdenby House, historic house in Northamptonshire, England, also known as Holmby: **I40**.

Holt, Alfred H.*, **A71, A173, B20, B75, C27, D7, H47, K6, S54**.

Hood, Thomas, 1799–1845. English poet: **F20**.

Hook, Theodore, 1788–1841. English composer: **D25**. See also *Parson's Daughter*.

Horæ Hebraicæ et Talmudicæ. Five books published between 1658 and 1674: **A1**. *See* Lightfoot, John.

Hotten, John Camden*, 1832–1873: **F40, I22, O23, T18, T58, W4, W33**. See also *The True Story of Lord and Lady Byron*.

Hudibras, 1663: **A153, G30, N21, O1, O35, P22**. *See* Butler, Samuel.

Hulme, Frederick Edward*, 1841–1909: **M1**.

Humphrey, Duke of Gloucester, 1390–1447: **D19**.

Hunt, Henry, 1773–1835. British politician: **W24**.

Huntingdonshire, county in east central England: **A62, G58**.

Huth, Henry, 1815–1878. English book collector: **A167**. See also *Brainless Blessing of the Bull*.

Hyamson, Albert M.*, 1875–1954: **A14, A37, A103, A121, A158, B5, B20, B34, B75, C10, D19, G7, H4, I20, M35, N13, O11, P39, S14, S55, S63, S66, T59, W19**.

Ibsen, Henrik, 1828-1906. Norwegian playwright: **D18**. See also *Hedda Gabler*.

Ireland, **A19, A29, A156, B75, C45, C84, D37, E7, F21, G4, G31, G47, G60, H2, H15, N34, R19, S10, S45, T18, T33, T34, T58, T61, U2**.

Irvin, Washington, 1783–1859. American author: **A26, S53**.

Isle of Man, Great Britian: **H43**.

Isle of Wright. Perhaps the reference is to the Isle of Wight, an island in the English channel: **G7**.

Ivanhoe, 1819: **M5**. *See* Scott, Sir Walter.

Jackson, Mason, 1819-1903. British wood-engraver: **R35**. See also *The Pictorial Press: Its Origins and Progress*.

Jacobites, supporters of James II after the Revolution of 1688: **N14, W8**.

Jacquerie, peasant revolt in France, 1358: **B76.**

Jacula Prudentum, 1652: **G43.** *See* Herbert, George.

James II, 1430–1460. King of Scotland, 1437–1460: **W32.**

James VI, 1566–1625. King of Scotland, 1567–1625. King of England and Ireland, 1603–1625: **A106, B44.**

Jamieson, John*, 1759–1838: **A110, D46, D52, H17, H55, S80.**

The Jests of Scogin, 1626: **S15.** *See* Boorde, Andrew.

Jim Crow, state and local laws that enforced racial segregation in the United States: **J8.**

Joan, Pope, woman who was supposedly pope during the Middle Ages: **N14.**

Johnson, Samuel*, 1709–1784: **C68.**

Johnson, Trench H.*, **C48, G6.**

Jonson, Ben, 1572–1637. English playwright and poet: **D42.** See also *Poetaster.*

Joseph Chamberlain: An Honest Biography, 1914: **L40.** *See* Mackintosh, Alexander.

Junius, Francis*, 1591–1677: **S65.**

Kearney, Denis, 1847-1907. California labor leader: **H62.**

Kent, county in Southeast England: **F4, G7, I6, I9, R36, S63.**

King Lear, 1606: **F19, H38, S32.** *See* Shakespeare, William.

Kingsley, Charles, 1819–1875. English novelist and social reformer: **C25, D8.** See also *At Last: A Christmas in the West Indies.*

Kingswear, village in the county of Devon, England: **A17.**

Kipling, Rudyard, 1865–1936, English poet and novelist: **A34, C3, H32, O7, R15, W8.** See also *Shillin' a Day.*

The Knight's Tale, **A85.** *See* Chaucer, Geoffrey.

Knowles, Elizabeth*, **B4, F20, S14, T25, T26.**

Knowsley, village in the county of Merseyside, England: **L3.**

Lancashire, county in Northwest England: **A15, A89, B23, B60, B68, C73, D25, H23, I29, J6, L1, L3, L46, M2, P38, S86, Y4.**

Languedoc, former province of France; its territory is now within the region of Occitainie in Southern France: **G43.**

Leicestershire, county in central England: **A89, H48.**

Leland, Charles Godfrey, 1824–1903. American humorist and folklorist: **A37, G36, P65.**

Lexicon Balatronicum et Macaronicum, **A12, H56.** *See* Bee, John.

Liber Albus, a compilation of laws, ordinances, and regulations, related to the city of London, 1859: **B7.**

Lichfield, city in the West Midlands, England: **S24.**

Life and Letters of Erasmus, 1894: **M27.** *See* Froude, James Anthony.

Life in London, 1821: **T45.** *See* Egan, Pierce.

Life of P.T Barnum, The, 1855: **A110.** *See* Barnum, Phineas.T.

The Life of Richard Brinsley Sheridan, 1909: **O10.** *See* Sichel, Walter.

Life of Samuel Johnson, 1791: **H34.** *See* Boswell, James.

Lightfoot, John, 1602–1675. English rabbinical scholar and Vice-Chancellor of the University of Cambridge: **A1**. See also *Horæ Hebraicæ et Talmudicæ* (1658–1674). 1602–1675.

Lily, John*, 1553–1606: **M27**.

Lincoln, city in Lincolnshire, England: **B30, C59, D15, F37, M26, S3, T35**.

Lincolnshire, county in the East Midlands, England: **A58, A113, A125, C27, J13, L23, L27, S57**.

Littré, Émile*, 1801–1881: **P5, S9**.

Lombard Street, street in London, England: **A13**.

Long Island, the Battle of, August 27, 1776. Battle fought during the American Revolutionary War: **S16**.

Louis I, Prince, 1786–1868. Also known as Ludwig I. King of Bavaria. Reigned 1825–1848: **C25**.

Louis XIV, 1638–1715. King of France. Reigned 1643–1715: **M29**.

Love's Labour's Lost, 1598: **G65, S68**. *See* Shakespeare, William.

The Love of the World Reproved, 1782: **G51**. *See* Cowper, William.

Luther, Martin, 1483–1546. German reformer: **M27**.

Lye, Edward*, 1694–1767: **G6**.

Lymm, village in Cheshire, England: **T14**.

Macaulay, Thomas Babington, Lord, 1800-1859. British historian and politician: **G72, H28, K9**. See also *The History of England*.

Mackay, Charles*, 1814–1889: **A85, A110, G9, P66, W8**.

Mackintosh, Alexander, 1858–1948. Scottish political journalist: **L40**. See also *Joseph Chamberlain: An Honest Biography*.

Macklin, Charles, 1697–1797. English actor and dramatist: **G34**.

Macpherson, James, 1736–1796. Scottish poet: **B18**. See also *Ossian*.

Manchester, city in England: **C50**.

Mansfield, First Earl of; the reference is to William Murray, 1705–1793, British politician and judge: **G34**.

March from Birmingham to Shrewsbury: Military march in 1642 during the Civil War in England: **S24**. See also Civil War in England.

The Mark o' the Deil, and other Northumbrian Tales, 1894: **G23**. *See* Pease, Howard.

Markham, Christopher A.*, **H38, I30**.

Marlborough, First Duke of, John Churchill, 1650–1722. English soldier and statesman: **S24**.

Marryat, Frederick, 1792–1848. British novelist. See also *Peter Simple*.

Martin Chuzzlewit, 1842: **D19**. *See* Dickens, Charles.

Martini, Johann, 1440?–1498?. French composer: **C56**. See also *Microcosmos*.

Martin Mar-Prelate, name used between 1588 and 1589 by an anonymous author whose primary focus was an attack on the episcopacy of the Anglican Church: **B7**.

Mayhew, Anthony Lawson, English philologist: **B63, B76, C9, D11, H50, I15, N29, O4, W33**.

Mayne Reid, Thomas, 1818–1883. Irish-born American novelist.

Media; Or Middle Things, 1650: **G22**. *See* Ambrose, Isaac.

Medii Ævi Kalendarium, 1841: **R22**. *See* Hampson, R.T.

Melville, Walter, 1875–1937. English theater manager: **D20**. See also *A Girl's Cross Roads*.

Queen Victoria Coronation, June 28, 1838: **P44, T33.**

Rabelais, François, 1483?-1553. French writer: **F23.**

Reay, Lord, or Donald Mackay, 1591-1649. Lord of Reay County in Scotland: **B28.**

Recollections and Reflections, 1872: **J15.** *See* Planché, James Robinson.

Reform Act of 1832, British law that reformed the electoral system: **W24.**

Remaines of Gentilisme and Judaisme, 1881: **I1.** *See* Aubrey, John.

Ricardo, David, 1772-1823. British political economist: **C86, U4.**

Richardson, Charles*, 1775-1865: **D12, R32.**

Richardson, Samuel, 1689-1761. English writer: **H35, P15.** See also *Clarissa.*

Riley, Henry Thomas, 1816-1878. English translator, lexicographer, and autiquary.

Riley, James Whitcomb, 1849-1916. American author: **L25.**

The Rime of the Ancient Mariner, 1798: **S39.** *See also* Coleridge, Samuel Taylor.

Robert the Bruce. *See* Bruce, Robert.

Robertson, Canon, 1813-1882. James Craigie Robertson, Scottish Anglican churchman: **R23.**

Robin Hood, legendary outlaw: **A21, A95, F41, R24, R25.**

Rogers, Charles, 1825-1890. Scottish minister and author: **R17.** *See also Social Life in Scotland.*

Romeo and Juliet, 1597: **M18, W6.** *See* Shakespeare, William.

Rooden Lane, hamlet in Greater Manchester, England: **A15.**

Rorke's Drift, Battle of, 22-23 January 1879. Battle in the Anglo-Zulu war: **G10.**

Saffron Walden, town in Essex, England: **B30, C59, F37, M26, R23, S3, T35.**

A Sailor of King George, 1901: **R23.** *See* Hoffman, W.F.

The Sailor's Word Book, 1867: **N19.** *See* Smyth, William Henry, Frederick, W.

Saint Andrew, 5?-60. The patron saint of Scotland: **N14.**

Saint Anthony, 1195-1231: **A36, P21.**

Saint Anthony Hospital: **P21.**

Saint Boniface, 675?-754. English bishop. The patron saint of England and Germany: **S4.**

Saint Catherine of Alexandria, 287?-305? Fourth century martyr, patron saint of unmarried girls: **B53.**

Saint Peter, 1?- 65 AD?. First Bishop of Rome and Antioch: **S6.**

Saint Muireadach O'Heney: **T19.**

Salopia Antiqua, 1841: **A17.** *See* Hartshorn, Charles Henry.

Sam Weller, character in Charles Dickens's *The Pickwick Papers*: **I2.**

Scarborough Castle, medieval fortress located over Scarborough, England: **S13.**

Scarborough, town on the North Sea Coast in England: **S13, S24, S50.**

Scotland: **A59, A60, A61, A62, A112, A157, A162, B17, C19, C37, D10, D23, D27, D31, D46, D5, D51, D52, E5, F21, F24, F29, G6, G9, G25, G31, G68, H2, H37, H55, I37, J12, M24, N14, P28, P59, R17, T58, U2, W6, W13.**

Scott, Sir Walter, 1771-1832. British novelist and poet: **G21, H1, M27, O31.** See also *Ivanhoe, The Pirates,* and *Waverly.*

Seaford, town in East Sussex, England: **A41.**

Selden, John, 1584–1654. English lawyer and scholar who participated in the 1643 Westminster Assembly of Divines: **C22**.

Selmeston, village in East Sussex, England: **A64**.

Shakespeare, William, 1564–1616. English playwright and poet: **A30, A71, B13, B14, B77, C39, D21, G6, G64, G71, L44, O7, R13, S10, S15, S64, S67, S80, T58, W6, W18**. See also *Hamlet, Henry V, King Lear, Love's Labour's Lost, The Merchant of Venice,* and *Romeo and Juliet.*

Shapiro, Norman R., 1930–2020. Romance scholar and translator. **S67**.

Shaw, George B., 1856–1950. British playwright: **I36**.

Sheridan, Richard B., 1751–1816. British playwright and poet: **B20, O10, S68**.

Shillin' a Day, 1890. Poem from the series *Barrack-Room Ballads:* **W8**. *See* Kipling, Rudyard.

Shrewsbury, town in England east of the Welsh border: **S24**.

Shropshire, county in England bordering Wales: **A17, L32, M11**.

Sichel, Walter, 1855–1933. English biographer and lawyer: **O10**. See also *The Life of Richard Brinsley Sheridan.*

Skeat, Walter W.*, 1835–1912: **A45, A57, A71, A85, A92, A115, A118, A158, A172, B7, B14, B71, B73, B75, B76, C1, C18, C39, C68, C77, C80, D41, E14, F23, F41, G46, G57, G71, H8, H11, H50, H57, J6, O2, O4, S5, S29, S54, S87, T27, T40, U7, W1**.

Skelton, John, 1463?–1529. English poet and tutor to King Henry VIII of England: **A109**. See also *The Book of Philip Sparowe.*

Skinner, Stephen*, 1623–1667: **T41**.

Smith, Adam, 1723–1790. Scottish economist: **U4**.

Smith, John Thomas, 1766–1833. English painter, engraver, and antiquarian: **A93**. See also *The Streets of London.*

Smyth, William Henry, Frederick. See also *A Sailor's Word Book.** 1788–1865: **N19**.

Social Life in Scotland, 1886: **R17**. *See* Rogers, Charles.

Somersetshire, county in Southwest England: **A144, A145, B75, G53, L31, P19**.

Southey, Robert, 1774–1843. English poet: **A104, M22**. See also *Collection on Progress of Society.*

Spain: **C10**.

Sportsman's Slang, 1825: **B50**. *See* Bee, Jon.

Stafford, Thomas, 1533?–1557. English aristocrat executed for treason: **S13**.

Staffordshire, county in the West Midlands of England: **A17, B41**.

Stair, John Dalrymple, First Earl of, 1648–1707. Scottish politician and Secretary of State. In office, 1691–1695: **N14**.

Stamford, town in Lincolnshire, England: **A113**.

Sterne, Laurence, 1713–1768. Anglo-Irish novelist: **A34, G43**.

Stevenson, Robert Louis, 1850–1894. British novelist and poet: **D8, P17, T11** See also *Catriona* and *Treasure Island.*

Storm, Johan*, 1836–1920: **D25**. See also *Englische Philologie.*

Stormonth, James*, 1824–1882: **P41**.

Stoughton, village in West Sussex, England: **S74**.

Stowe, Harriet Beecher, 1811–1896. American abolitionist and author: **S60**. See also *Uncle Tom's Cabin.*

Strachan, Lionel Richard Mortimer, b. 2876. Social and religious historian: M27, W19.

The Streets of London, 1815: D53. *See* Smith, John Thomas.

Stuart, Charles E., 1720-1788. Leader of the Jacobite uprising: N14.

Stuckey, Vincent, 1771-1845. English merchant and banker: S13.

Suffolk, county in England: A105, C30, D34, I3, L22, S3, U7.

Sullivan, Sir Arthur, 1842-1900. English composer: O38. See also *H.M.S. Pinafore.*

Sumner, Charles, 1811-1874. American politician, member of the 'Five of Clubs' and Massachusetts Senator. In office, 1851-1874: M44.

Sunday, William Ashley, 1862-1935. American athlete and an influential evangelist: C24.

Sussex, county in Southeast England: A41, A48, A50, A64, A122.

Swalwell, a village in Gateshead, Tyne and Wear, England: P35.

Swift, Johnathan, 1667-1745. English author: A75, D44, N9, S87, T1, T38, T57. See also *Gulliver's Travels* and *Polite Conversations.*

Svartengren, Torsten Hilding*, 1879-1964: A43, A45, A47, A48, A49, A52, A53, A54, A55, A56, A57, A58, A59, A60, A61, A62, A63, A64, A65, A66, A69, A71, A72, A73, A74, A75, A76, A77, A78, A79, A80, A81, A82, A83, A84, A85, A88, A89, A91, A94, A95, A96, A99, A100, A103, A104, A105, A109, A110, A111, A112, A113, A114, A115, A117, A118, A120, A121, A123, A124, A125, A127, A128, A129, A130, A131, A132, A133, A134, A136, A137, A139, A142, A145, A147, A148, A149, A150, A151, A152, A153, A158, A159, A163, A164, A167, D36, D45, I40, L27, L28, L35.

Tacitus, Cornelius, 56 - 120 Roman historian and politician: C49, E12.

Tailors Riot, 1805, riot in London by tailors; it inspired the play *The Tailors; a Tragedy for Warm Weather*: D14.

Takeley, parish in Essex, England: A16.

Tartarin de Tarascon, 1872: P42. *See* Daudet, Alphonse.

The Task, 1785: F6. *See* Cowper, William.

Tatian*, I15.

Tattersall, Edmund, one of the many Edmund Tattersalls. The British Tattersall family was a prominent horse auctioneer: W24.

Taylor, Archer, 1890-1973. American folklorist: A98.

Tempest, Pierce, 1653-1717. English printseller: C70. See also *Cryes of the City of London, Drawn after the Life.*

Thames, river in England: B75, C12, M39, S28.

That's the Ticket for Soup! Victorian Views on Vocabulary as Told in the Pages of Punch. G28. *See* Crystal, David.

Theodore I of Corsica, 1694-1756. German adventurer who was the King of Corsica. Reigned 1736: I33.

Thomas à Kempis*, 1380-1471: M19.

Thomas Aquinas, 1225-1274. Italian philosopher, priest, and patron saint of Academics: M16.

Tiverton, town in Devon, England: H70.

Tom Thumb, 1730: S23. *See* Fielding, Henry.

Tooke, John Horne*, 1736-1812: S54.

Topsham, town in Devon, England: A41, C43.

Theme Index

Numbers in parentheses indicate a tangential correspondence to the subject.

Alliteration (phrases with alliterating words): A8, A27, A43, A49, A50, A52, A53, A55, A65, A66, A68, A69, A71, A81, A91, A95, A103, A104, A105, A111, A117, A118, A120, A121, A132, A140, A152, A159, A160, A167, A172, B5, B27, B28, B33, B45, B58, B63, B71, C52, C55, C56, C67, C72, D2, D6, D31, D32, D36, D37, D48, E11, F3, G1, G5, G56, H6, H16, H33, H62, (I40), J4, J9, K12, M32, N4, N7, N21, P38, P56, R18, R23, R31, R32, S11, S12, S25, S66, S67, T8, T13, T19, T40, T48, T49, T54, W8.

Americanisms: A4, A20, A23, A26, A28, A33, A43, A93, A97, (A123), A171, A173, B21, (B26), B27, (B36), B38, B41, B42, B62, B67, C 10, C25, (C71), D38, E1, E13, F1, (F11), F40, G3, G5, G9, G16, G29, G51, (G52), (G55), G75, H4, H30 H39, H45, (H46), H54, (H62), H65, I8, I28, I45, K16, (L16), (L19), L36, L41, L48, M36, M44, N17, O17, O19, (O28), (O37), P36, (P58), P60, (P66, end), Q1, R4, (R19), R26, (R39), S2, S7, S12, S16, S18, S30, S31, S41, S47, S53, S60, (T7), (T9), (T10), (T42), T49, T53, U3, (W12), (W14), W34, Z1. (The American provenance of some idioms is uncertain, and in some cases American usage is different from British usage: references to these idioms are in parentheses.)

Animals: A10, A31, A36, A 39, A62, A76, A78, A85, A88, A97, A102, A103, A104, A105, A117, A124, A135, A137, A140, A 153, A157, A163, A166, B14, B52, B69, B71, C12, C13, C15, C16, C24, C35, C41, C61, C76, C85, D3, D24, D26, D27, D28, F16, F20, G73, H6, H23, H41, H48, H63, H64, H65, I17, I39, I137, I146, K3, L17, L18, L31, L32, M33, M34, M39, N25, O8, O11, O32, P11, P20, P23, P33, P34, P37, P38, P64, R13, R18, R22, S2, S33, S43, S55, T11, T38, T41, T42, T57, T58, T59, T62, W19, W22, W24.

Appliances, Tools, Utensils: A10, A57, A71, A77(?), A86, A114, A121, A131, A139, A147, B12, B27, B39, B51, B54, B75, C1, C9, C15, C66, D40, E5, F14, F18, G5, K7, L9, M1, N11, O13, P20, P60, T43, U11.

Army life: A150, B16, B43, B47, C34, F1, H15, H32, K15, P2, P40, R6, S24, T25, T29.

Beverages: A5, A11, A23, C20, H58, I11, N26.

Biblical allusions: A1, A5, A39, A63, A78, B70, B73, C21, C22, C23, C33, C77, D35, G50, G57, H12, H14, H57, I3, I44, J6, L13, L39, N3, P38, P62, R2, R23, S1, S5, S6, S32, T51.

Birds and Fowl: A44, A89, A98, A106, A109, A123, A149, A155, B40, C35, C38, C39, C60, C63, C65, C68, D48, D49, D50, E1, E10, H30, H68, K15, L27, L39, M37, N27, P15, P39, S35, T56, W21, W25, Y3.

Body parts and Organs: A1, A14, A43, A62, B32, B69, B70, C14, C81, E15, F39, F40, K4, K5, M45, N5, N8, N11, N22, P14.

Church and Clergy: A29, A54, A77, B22, B32, B33, C76, F25, G42, L37, M35, N21, O3, O12, O30, P7, P19.

Circus. *See* Theater, Circus, Music Hall

Clothes: B47, G8, C41, H42, K15, N24, T3, Z1.

Color: A47, A48, B37, B38, B39, B40, B45, B64, B65, C64, C71, G70, G71, G72, O15, R9, S42, T55, W22, W23.

Customs. *See* Idioms and Customs (Folklore)

ANATOLY LIBERMAN is a professor at the University of Minnesota. He is a Guggenheim and a Fulbright fellow and has published more than twenty books, including *An Analytic Dictionary of English Etymology: An Introduction* and *A Bibliography of English Etymology: Sources and Word List,* both from the University of Minnesota Press.